DING HAO
America's Air War in China, 1937–1945

DING HAO

America's Air War in China
1937-1945

By WANDA CORNELIUS
and THAYNE SHORT

PELICAN PUBLISHING COMPANY

GRETNA

Manufactured in the United States of America

Published by Pelican Publishing Company, Inc.
1101 Monroe Street, Gretna, Louisiana 70053

Contents

Contents

Introduction

The first time I met Charlie Olsen, I was in veterinary practice on Baronne Street in New Orleans, and he was the contractor who had been hired to remodel the building.

He immediately reminded me of the comic-strip character Smiling Jack, but I had no idea that he had actually been a fighter pilot during World War II until one night when he, his wife, Lucille, and I wound up in the hospital room of my recuperating senior partner, Dr. Homer Watts. Homer introduced the subject of the private airplane I flew, and referred to Charlie's own wartime flying career. When I found out that Charlie had flown P-40s for Claire Chennault, a man I had admired since childhood, I don't think we discussed poor Homer's back injury again.

During the continuing course of the Baronne Street remodeling, I took frequent breaks to visit Charlie, sitting either on top of the hospital or under it, depending on whether he was repairing shingles or shoring up the floor. I kept trying to steer the conversation toward his adventures with P-40s and China, and he would talk about it some, but invariably changed the subject to horseracing. As the years passed, I became a bit more persistent, and Charlie a bit more talkative about air combat.

I made a couple of trips to Switzerland to study orthopedics, moved to Baton Rouge to open a small-animal hospital, and more years passed—but I still had a secret desire to gather Charlie's stories in writing. I had managed to extract a few near-complete tales from him and had discussed those exciting days of aerial combat with a few other people, but had done no hard-core research. I simply lacked the training to proceed systematically. For one thing, I wanted desperately to interview the legendary Tex Hill of Flying Tiger fame, and I didn't know anything about interviewing. For another, writing is always laborious and time-consuming.

This book would probably still be in preparation if a raven-haired lady named Wanda Cornelius and her son Kent had not come to my office with their newly acquired "It-followed-me-home-from-school-and-can-I-keep-it?" dog for a rabies shot. Wanda, it developed, was a free-lance writer, and before she left, we had a hand-shake contract to collaborate on a book: she would provide the professionalism, and I would furnish the aviation expertise.

While we were getting query-letter responses from members of Charlie's old Seventy-fifth Fighter Squadron, we even managed to publish a few magazine articles.

Everett O. White offered every assistance, including a photograph and newspaper clippings.

Lt. "Flash" Segura (now Brig. Gen. Wiltz P. Segura, retired in New Iberia, Louisiana) came to Baton Rouge to reminisce in person, with invaluable materials and his wife Joy, who is said at one time or another to have fed the entire U.S. Air Force. It was he who arranged a meeting with his old squadron commander Tex Hill.

The next thing I knew, Wanda and I were flying to San Antonio, where we and my legendary hero examined his staggeringly extensive collection of memorabilia for hours that were punctuated by telephone calls from his squadron buddies, with whom he keeps in touch. We photographed some of the materials and borrowed some. We were also especially appreciative of the warm hospitality of his wife, Mazie.

Back in Baton Rouge, Wanda and I encountered Charles T. Wang, a local businessman, who in conjunction with the Republic of China on Taiwan was planning to build a memorial in Baton Rouge to Lt. Gen. Claire Lee Chennault. Wanda and I had the unprecedented chance to submit a guest list—and we included every character in *Ding Hao*.

Tom Cotton and his wife, Jinx, flew in from California. We met for the first time James and Gladys Anning who live in Lake Charles (from whom we learned that "Hill's Harry Raiders" had the reputation of being so mean that they didn't even brush their teeth). By the end of the day, many memories had been stirred, which later prompted the resurrection of aging documents and many letters and phone calls.

Next, Wiltz arranged an interview with one of the Seventy-fifth doctors, Dr. Jones Laughlin, currently practicing in Eagle Lake, Texas, who offered us his large photographic collection and two rolls of recording tape with fascinating accounts of the men of the Seventy-fifth.

We regret that space doesn't allow us to list the countless other men and women who have contributed in some tangible way to this book.

William S. Chennault, the general's younger brother who lives in Sweetwater, Texas, produced considerable valuable material, as did the general's youngest son David, of Monroe, Louisiana. Dan Chase, the general's nephew, and his wife, Lillie, in Baton Rouge shared photographs, and Dan was especially helpful in reading the chapter involving the immediate Chennault family.

The American Volunteer Group in China was immensely helpful with this important chapter, and we particularly want to thank Albert E. "Red" Probst of Baton Rouge, as well as Loy R. "Sy" Seamster and Melvin W. "Woody" Woodward whom we interviewed in New Orleans. Special appreciation is also due AVG member and later Medal of Honor recipient Brig. Gen. James H. Howard (ret.) for lending us the name of his famous P-51 Mustang, "Ding Hao," for our title—as well as for reviewing the AVG chapter.

In addition, there were AVG pilot John R. "Dick" Rossi of the Flying Tiger Line, Inc., and pilot Tom Cotton, who tried in vain to locate the lady in *The Lady and the Tigers,* by Olga Greenlaw; Robert T. Smith, who provided insight into the AVG involvement and furnished photographs; John M. Williams, official historian of the American Volunteer Group; and other AVG members.

Of dramatic importance was Henry I. Wood, who chose Wanda and me to reveal his 36-year-old secret by walking into the 1978 reunion of the Seventy-fifth in Nashville, Tennessee, when everybody had thought him dead in flames over war-torn China in 1944. An entire chapter tells his story.

Not directly connected with the narrative itself, but of great value, were Baton Rouge businessman Damuth V. Bogan, who helped with the photographs, and William Bryan French, a young veterinary student at Louisiana State University, who provided the cover maps and helped in the research of Japanese aircraft.

Finally, there were the three principal manuscript editors: Dr. R. K. Baker, our close personal friend and fellow author, who spent considerable time reading every single draft; John Easterly, a young Ph.D. whose masterful job of final editing didn't infringe on our intent or purpose; and Grindle, the Olsens' 130-pound, eight-month-old Great Dane puppy, who ate two of the final manuscript chapters. Charlie and Lucille spent the better part of the next four days putting them back together and retyping them. Those were the two chapters in which Charlie appears.

Wanda and I are truly grateful for all the help and encouragement we received. That can never be repaid.

THAYNE R. SHORT

DING HAO
America's Air War in China, 1937–1945

Prologue

Until the death of Ch'ien-lung, the last powerful emperor of the Manchu dynasty, in 1799, China had been ruled by "Heavenly Mandate" through a series of consecutive family dynasties extending back for more than two thousand five hundred years. Emperor Ch'ien, like all those before him, had ruled with an iron hand, enjoying absolute obedience to his Confucian system of government-religion, according to which the past was sacred and any change corrupt. But Ch'ien-lung was the last emperor to successfully keep foreign powers at bay. When he died, as all mortals must, dynastic control over China's sovereignty began to weaken.

The first attempt by Ch'ien-lung's heirs to deal with foreign influence was a complete failure. It involved the Opium War of 1839–1842 between China and Britain, in which the grandson of Emperor Ch'ien attempted to stem the opium traffic the British had introduced into China. This first clash with foreign powers resulted in the "Unequal Treaty" that China was forced to sign in Nanking in 1842. This treaty opened the door for the various foreign powers that by now were circling China like vultures ready to pick the spoils. The British gained admission to major coastal ports such as Shanghai and Hong Kong and continued privileges for their missionary work in China. The "most favored nation" clause in the Nanking treaty also opened the door for the other major Western powers to follow suit.

Weakened and disorganized, China now lay prostrate before the encroaching influence of foreign powers which were content to profit while feeling no responsibility to help govern or otherwise contribute to the country's internal stability. As a matter of fact, the feeling that prevailed among the Western residents and "Old China hands" was that China's inability to govern herself actually assured her continued exploitation.

In 1860 China fought a second "Opium War" against Britain and France, culminating with the fall of the northern capital of Peking itself. She had to grant new privileges to the Western powers, and her sovereignty over her far-flung masses diminished to such a point that Russia annexed vast unpopulated areas of Chinese territory in Siberia and central Asia in 1860 and 1871. The French then took all of Vietnam from China in 1885, and the British took Burma in the same year. Not to be left out, Japan marched into Chinese Korea in 1895 in the first step of the Sino-Japanese War. After digesting their first Chinese territorial meal, Russia decided to take a large bite out of Chinese Manchuria right under Japan's nose. Thus, like dogs fighting over a juicy bone, Japan and Russia fought over the southern half in 1905, with Japan emerging as the winner.

Seeds of discontent began to surface as China fought to retain some degree of sovereignty over her remaining territories. Conservative and liberal factions began to emerge within China's different geographical, historical, and cultural areas, and each faction felt that its solution was the only cure for the country's ills. In 1900 there was the bloody Boxer Rebellion in which the treacherous Empress Dowager encouraged an antichristian and antiforeign movement that erupted in northern China. The Boxers murdered countless Christian missionaries, and then, abetted by the Empress Dowager, besieged Peking's foreign residents and assassinated in the streets the German minister and the counselor of the Japanese Legation.

One can imagine the rage of the foreign powers, who rushed an international military relief force to the coastal city of Tientsin. These soldiers soon pushed inland to Peking to suppress the "Society of the Harmonious Fists" (approximate translation of the Chinese word Boxer). The atrocities perpetrated by these "civilized" Western powers upon the Chinese residents at Peking would have made Genghis Khan blush. They were bent upon teaching them a lesson they would not soon forget.

With this "loss of face," the Empress Dowager and her court became completely incompetent and ineffective for the remainder of her life, which ended in 1908. So contemptuous were her subjects near the time of her death, that Chinese husbands referred to their overbearing mothers-in-law as "Mother Dowagers." The Western world watched with morbid curiosity as the seeds of discontent, internal corruption, and finally foreign intervention brought Chinese dynastic rule to its eventual demise.

The beginning of the end came when an explosion ripped through a house in Hankow in central China. It was the premature emergence of Dr. Sun Yat-sen's eleventh revolutionary attempt against the ruling dynasty in Peking. The house was later revealed to have been a grenade factory used by the supporters of Dr. Sun, who was in the United States at the time soliciting funds. This eleventh attempt ended successfully one year later, in 1912, when the Manchu dynasty in Peking abdicated. The Western world was amazed that China would choose the republic of Sun Yat-sen rather than a new dynasty, and it looked on with contempt while the new republic failed to establish lasting stability in China.

Lack of adequate central control resulted in the localization of various military and political powers within the different provinces of China, with a continued struggle for power centering around the old dynastic capital of Peking. Thus the great "Warlord Era" erupted during this time of instability. It lasted for over ten years and was a period of great confusion in China's history which would leave a lasting impression on the world at large and upon the Chinese people who endured it.

With the aid of Soviet advisors, the republic of Sun Yat-sen again rose to prominence around 1925 under control of the Kuomintang or National People's Party, whose army was soon to be led by a thirty-six-year-old Shanghai stockbroker by the name of Chiang Kai-shek. Chiang had attended a military academy in Japan prior to the revolution and was now sent to Russia to learn the latest military tactics. Upon his return he successfully overthrew the last of the warlords in 1926–1927 and transferred the capital of China to Nanking, while renaming the former capital city Peiping.

At first the world had colored Chiang "red" due to his prior associations with some members of the Kuomintang government who were also active members of the Chinese Communist Party. Dr. Sun had found it expedient to allow the Communists to join his early movement when he failed to obtain support from either the United States or Britain in his return to power following the warlord disruption. Yet Chiang, like many other members of the new government, viewed the Soviet involvement with contempt and increasing distrust. Furthermore, any doubt regarding his true political color was dispelled when on April 12, 1927, he carried out a sudden and bloody purge against the Chinese Communists who controlled the labor forces in Shanghai. Many thousands were killed or executed. Another swift stroke in the southern city of Canton, the old Communist stronghold, and Chiang was in complete power. A few days later he announced the formation of a new Nationalist government at Nanking, free of any Communist control.

By July 1927, the Chinese Communist Party was made illegal in China. From this time forward, Chiang was to pursue relentlessly the Chinese Communists, led by Mao Tse-tung, in a war of extermination that was interrupted only by Japanese imperialism in Manchuria.

Chiang's dogged pursuit of the Chinese Communists during the Japanese occupation of Manchuria in 1931-1932 and his resulting appeasement policy toward them while he waited for American intervention, led to great internal pressure on him and a near-revolt by his dispossessed Manchurian army commanders. Finally he was literally forced to call off his extermination campaign and deal with Japan. In 1936 Chiang negotiated an unstable truce with the Chinese Communists. The ban on the Chinese Communist Party was lifted, and the Communists acknowledged Chiang Kai-shek as the head of state and supreme commander of all Chinese forces—the Generalissimo. Japanese aggression had to be dealt with.

This unexpected turn of events left the Japanese very unhappy. They had previously offered to aid Chiang in his war against the Communists, but he had flatly refused. Before the new, unified China could solidify, Japanese reactionaries, despite some opposition at home, perpetrated an attack on the Chinese garrison near the world-famous Marco Polo Bridge outside Peiping on July 7, 1937, which some historians claim was the real beginning of World War II.

It was a foregone conclusion of credible American military minds cognizant of activities in the Middle East and Far East during World War II that the Axis powers (Germany, Italy, and Japan) showed repeated intentions of expanding their territorial conquests in a converging direction from Germany to Japan, from the Mediterranean Sea and North Africa across Saudi Arabia, India, Burma, and coastal China. Such control of vital land and waterways rich in raw materials would have assured the Axis powers of the necessary ingredients to sustain their war machines and appetites of conquest. The successful execution of such an ambitious scheme would have led to the prolongation of World War II and even possibly altered its final result.

The tenacity, resourcefulness, and tactical genius displayed in China by Claire Lee Chennault as expressed first, through his adventuresome American Volunteer Group (AVG) and later, through his leadership of America's smallest Air Force (the fourteenth), helped immeasurably to thwart the Axis powers' ambitious plan. With a minimum of supplies and manpower, this relative handful of Americans remained steadfast in their remote mountain bastion in Kunming, China, as an offensive deterrent to Japanese aggression.

This book is written about that struggle, about a near-forgotten band of gallant American airmen who found themselves, like visitors from another planet, in the midst of a strange land at a time of great turmoil. They came not as conquerors, as had those before them, but as co-defenders. They were appreciated by the most humble and grateful Chinese as evidenced by their encounters with the pitifully dispossessed and hungry peasants on back roads and in small villages. These people would smile to them in recognition, nod approval, and in many cases utter the only mutually recognizable words of communication: "Ding hao," meaning "It is good."

CHAPTER 1

The Burma Road:
Back Door to China

Tan Pei-ying cautiously walked to the edge of the cliff and peered into the depth of the gorge below. The sight and sound was disturbing to him and he was scarcely able to resist the impulse to hurl himself to destruction. It was high noon and only at this brief period of the day could the sun's rays penetrate deep into the gorge, which at any other time was shrouded in perpetual twilight, hidden from direct sunlight by the sheer cliffs on either side.

He was tired, very tired. It had been a monumental task. For a moment his eyes surveyed the angry Salween River far below, which reflected the rare sunlight in a bright gleaming blue as it bent and turned along its turbulent path. He listened to the changing tempo and intensity as the water traversed the narrow riverbed, and the sound grated upon his nerves. Because of some strange acoustical quality of the gorge, he could hear the faintest sound far away, the chirp of a bird or the snap of a twig. But by the time these sounds reached his ears, they were magnified all out of proportion into an unnatural echo and were no longer pleasant or comforting. They cast an eerie spell over his spirit too intangible to allow analysis.

The sound of the river was not the soothing monotone of a waterfall, he thought, but more like the sound of a demented beast. In such surroundings, whether a man believed in God or not, he could not help fully realizing the overpowering mystery and magnificence of nature, which laid bare the soul of a human being, making him seem in comparison as small as a grain of rice.

At any other time the predominant color of the Salween gorge was black, jet black from the limestone rock of the exposed cliffs on either side that rose nearly straight up from the jungle floor. The black face of the rugged cliffs was broken by small patches of grotesque trees growing horizontally out into space, tortured and disfigured by the cruelty of nature as they struggled to survive. These trees seemed analogous to some of the people who inhabited the region—descendants of the Tibetans. It was easy for one to understand, Tan reasoned, why they were so deeply religious or superstitious, having been exposed to this awesome sight for countless generations.

The Salween River was only one of the many obstacles conquered by Tan Pei-ying as director of the Yunnan-Burma Highway Engineering Administration, whose job it was to build a road from Kunming, China, to the seaport in Rangoon, Burma, thus opening a back door to China. Since 1931 Japan had occupied the northeast province of Manchuria, formerly part of China, establishing a puppet state of Manchukuo there. As a result, antagonism toward Japan had been growing in China for six years. By 1937 the anti-Japanese movement was so strong that Chinese Communists and Nationalists agreed to stop battling among themselves and form a united front against the Japanese threat.

On July 7, 1937, a small force of Japanese crossed China's Great Wall demanding entry into the tiny walled town of Wanping near the Marco Polo Bridge on the pretense of searching for one of their missing soldiers. But the Chinese soldiers refused and both sides began exchanging fire. Although neither side relished involvement in an all-out war, the fighting proceeded to spread to central China where Japan slowly began to score successive victories. Thus, like it or not, China was involved in World War II. She was bounded on the north by the formidable Gobi Desert, Mongolia, and the Soviet Union and to the east by the China Sea and beyond it, Japan. To the west were the treacherous Himalayas and other mountains which made anything except air traffic to western and southern China almost impossible. To the south a long land route to the seaport of Rangoon, Burma, was at the time the only way out of China and, more important, a way in for war supplies.

Fear of Japan's obviously aggressive intentions in the northern provinces prompted the Chinese to attempt the building of a road which would be accessible by truck for the purpose of bringing in the needed supplies to the defending armies. To any Western man, even with modern equipment, this task would have seemed impossible; but the Chinese coolie without so much as a second thought proceeded to claw out the Burma Road through that awesome terrain, using mostly bare fingernails and crude tools.

In 1937, when the central government authorized the building of the "back door," China was still in control of most of the seaports and Shanghai had not yet been taken. The Canton-Hankow railway was still transporting goods and the French Indochina railway moved supplies to Kunming. Thus arteries within China were still fairly good. Yet it quickly became evident that a route outside China into Burma would become strategically necessary should Japan close the ports around the China Sea. The government decided to build the Burma Road from Kunming to Lashio in Burma where it could connect with the railway system at Rangoon.

The only passable road to Burma at the time was the old Silk Road which was not a road at all, but a winding trail to be negotiated only by sure-footed horses and mules with experienced drivers. The trail twisted around mountains and jungles, the only bridges being suspension-type with handwrought iron chains.

The beasts of burden, trained by the Mongols, were so sure-footed they could traverse narrow ridges and slippery boulders, a feat almost impossible even for most humans. They traveled in caravans of up to three hundred, the lead animal being a mule decorated with a bright red feather on a stick attached to his headgear and numerous glass bells around his neck. This was done so that other animals could either see or hear the lead animal no matter how many curves they encountered. The men who accompanied the animals also walked, guarding the precious cargo of silk, tea, and other commodities. Some people wondered why the builders of the Burma Road did not simply expand the old Silk Trail, but it was too crooked and narrow.

In November 1937, General Lung-yun, governor of Yunnan, received orders to begin building the Burma Road immediately, for on October 21, the Japanese had landed troops near Hong Kong and captured the important coastal town of Canton. The straight-line distance between Kunming and Lashio is 320 miles, but the new road would measure 717 miles, winding around natural obstacles such as mountains and obstacles created by man as well, such as the tiny, precious rice fields, national monuments, temples, and cemeteries. Most of the road was in China, all except 117 miles of it. Chinese were to build the road as far as Wanting on the Burma-China border. The remainder was to be built by the British.

The first objective was to get the road open. The next was to gravel and surface it, and to straighten the hairpin curves. Then they would replace the makeshift bridges with those of a minimum capacity of ten tons.

Builders of the Burma Road had countless obstacles to face besides the terrain. First, the province of Yunnan, where most of the workers were recruited at the outset of the project, was sparsely populated. Furthermore, these workers were not trained and could only be obtained through ruling magistrates. In addition, skilled engineers were even harder to find than the laborers. China was just initiating its highway system before the war broke out and engineers were generally employed elsewhere. Others had moved from their northern homes after they were attacked and could not be located.

Then there was the problem of getting tools for the workers and a sufficient amount of rice to feed them. The road gangs required medical doctors and supplies, machine shops and garages, and even a training school for the truck drivers. Besides that, many workers were reluctant to come to work on the road, fearing the poisonous gases of the border provinces. A miasmic mist hangs over the jungles and swamps of the Shan country and many Chinese believe that the gas is the cause of malaria.

In the beginning none of the tools necessary to modern road building were available—no dynamite to carve out the steep mountains, no pneumatic rock drills, no heavy rollers. Perhaps it was just as well because the native laborers worked better with their own old trusted tools, using methods that were centuries old. Men, women, and children moved dirt and rock with bamboo baskets, carried by some with a thong across the forehead and by others suspended by cords from a yoke across the shoulders. The plentiful bamboo also came in handy for a comfortable, well-ventilated shoe, which even the engineers finally adopted as their own footgear.

To transfer water out of swampy areas to work sites for making slurry, which held the rock base together, the workers used another ancient Chinese implement. It was the old wooden water pump, which consisted of a series of buckets attached to an endless wooden chain powered by foot treadle. Ten of these pumps finally made it to the building site from Kunming. This feat was accomplished by using two mules, one on each end of the fragile machinery.

Workers refused to use hammers with long elastic handles or good chisels recommended by the engineers, opting instead for their own style of hammers made to order by the village blacksmith. As a result, they wasted about half of the rock by breaking it into chips instead of into pieces of regulation size. Using the largest stones on the base and the smaller ones on top, the rocks were held together by the earth-and-water slurry called water-bound macadam.

Packing the freshly-built road was also a problem, since no heavy diesel-powered rollers were available at the beginning. So once again the local magistrates were called upon, this time to produce primitive rollers that would be pulled by hand. The rollers were cut by hand with a hammer and chisel from limestone found to be solid and free from fractures. It was not easy because the harder the limestone, the more likely it is to contain fractures. Yet these workmen amazed the engineers by producing remarkably smooth and uniform rollers.

The size of the rollers was consistently in proportion with the amount of rice available to the people in a given community through which the road would pass. When the people were well nourished they could pull heavy weights and took pride in pulling the heaviest roller possible. Generally the rollers were as tall as six feet and weighed from three to five tons each.

Transferring the roller to the building site was not an easy task. It necessitated travel through jungles as well as up the sides of treacherous mountains. Anything in the roller's path had to be removed, whether it be trees or rocks. Sometimes it took a hundred men to pull the heaviest rollers up a hill.

There were accidents when a roller would break loose on an upgrade, but these were minimized when a simple brake was constructed. It consisted of a log of wood attached to the axle by ropes. Two men moving alongside would drop the log in its path and thus slow its forward movement. These huge boulders resulted in the untimely demise of many workers until this simple system of control was developed. Yet some accidents continued to happen and workers, including women and children, continued to fall before the oncoming rollers. Thus an untold number literally contributed their blood, sweat, and tears to the making of the road before diesel rollers arrived from England through Rangoon. Not only were lives spared but precious time was gained as well with the arrival of this modern machinery. But there were few imported tools to serve as earth-moving equipment. Anyway the farmer-laborers preferred to pull the earth along in their crude scoops, which consisted of baskets on a long handle.

Among the most difficult of all problems for the engineers was getting enough rice to feed the throngs of workers which numbered at least twenty thousand at all times. At first the central government approved the payment of ten cents for a sixteen-ounce caddy. This amount supplied food for one laborer for a day. But inflation soon plagued the administrators who were responsible for the feeding of the masses, with the price of rice fluctuating wildly and sometimes multiplying hundreds of times. The price of rice also varied in districts, contingent on how bountiful the supply was in the area. Whenever workers did not live close enough to the road, makeshift housing had to be established, and officials attempted to see that they got adequate rice, vegetables, meat, clothing, and a little smoking tobacco, as well as a little money.

In addition to rice, staff members and engineers required a few more luxuries, such as vegetable oil, Chinese sauce, vinegar, salt, tea, and fuel. Nobody was paid a decent living wage, not even the staff members. In 1938 engineers averaged the equivalent of fifty dollars per month in United States currency.

Yet the people continued to work with enthusiasm. Surveying the road, a task which would have ordinarily taken two years to accomplish, was completed within seven months by thirty men. No modern surveying instruments were available. They used an ordinary spirit level, often forming judgments with the naked eye and common sense, basing decisions upon such sound precepts as the feel of the ground under their feet. Through unmapped jungles and sides of steep mountains these brave men charted their course. When they could not negotiate the mountain trails, the native Yunnan country people, who were accustomed to such precarious footing, carried them on sedan chairs.

The finished road would consist of a series of hairpin turns, thus more than doubling the straight-line route. A major reason was an order from the governor to bypass precious rice paddies and avoid disturbing monuments, temples, and cemeteries. Ancestor worship was important in China and therefore the preservation of graves was a sacred duty. In fact, a special spring festival was customarily held every year for repairing and reconditioning graves. Occasionally a cemetery had to be moved and engineers were careful to select the best possible location and to restore the monuments when the task was completed.

Crushed stones formed the surface of the Burma Road, which was twenty-three feet wide and from seven to ten inches deep on the China side. A total of 3,860,000 yards of rock was cut from boulders or from the hillsides in graduated sizes. The largest ones formed the base, followed by smaller stones. The top layer was composed of one-inch stones held together by the slurry of mud and water.

Every stone was set in place one at a time and by hand. But before the stones could be laid, the ground had to be leveled for the roadbed. It was dug out with picks and mattocks and carried away in bamboo baskets. Next the ground was tamped down with a primitive instrument called a "hang." It consisted of a rounded top and bottom made of timber, joined with four strips and operated by two men.

While laborers used the crude hammer—with thong to protect fingers—to cut the stone down to size, the stonemasons created retaining walls using a century-old method without cement. They had no problem cutting stones into precise rectangles and squares with their special concave hammers and chisels. Using his own tool, each artisan brought his own little brazier to heat his chisel and to keep its cutting edge sharp. Instead of cement, the masons used the Chinese mortar of limestone, sand, and mud for the dry places, and red soil burned at a high temperature in a charcoal kiln along with the limestone and sand for the wet areas.

Their work was not unlike that which created the Great Wall, which roughly follows the border between Inner Mongolia and China proper. It was a costly monument to Shih Huang-ti (reigned 221–206 B.C.), founder of the Ch'in dynasty. The wall was built of different materials, varying from the large granite blocks over the base of earth in the east, to earth tamped with wooden tools in the west. Its height ranged from fifteen to twenty feet and its width at the base from fifteen to thirty feet. The top was approximately twelve feet wide. Along its length, the wall was marked by towers reaching several stories in height. Although it was begun more than two hundred years before Christ, the last segment of the Great Wall was only completed during the Ming dynasty, A.D. 1368-1644.

While stonemasons working along the Burma Road were experts at cutting stones, getting the natives to do the same job was not that easy. They could not understand measurements in terms of inches and centimeters. Engineers tried standardized stones in different colors as a pattern, but this tactic failed. Workers spent too much time comparing the pattern with their own work and soon the colored stones disappeared. Finally engineer Tan Pei-ying told them to make a circle of the thumb and forefinger, explaining that any stone which could go through the circle would be acceptable, and this worked for the smallest size.

Besides the ordinary natural obstacles along the road, the rainy season brought yet another danger—landslides. And with the mud came boulders rolling down the mountainsides burying not only the road but anything and anybody in their way.

Rock excavation was accomplished without dynamite or powerful pneumatic drills. Instead, workers used black Chinese gunpowder, the type used for their firecrackers. The powder was inserted in holes drilled by many workers, each using only a crude hammer and steel rod.

Only a small blast could be accomplished with each charge since the hand-drilled holes were no more than one and a half to two feet deep. The deeper the holes were dug into the rock, the more difficult it became for the worker to remove the fine rock dust at the bottom of the hole. So the Chinese workman devised a method of using a Chinese coin with a hole in the center, through which he tied a long string. He would peer intently while lowering the coin into the hole, then carefully fish it around the bottom until it had scraped up a sufficient amount of rock dust. He would then withdraw the string, clean off the coin, and methodically place it back into the hole for another thimble full of dust. It was very time-consuming but effective and thus typical of many of the procedures used during the building of the road. Only the sheer number of workmen on the project made it possible or this type of slow progress by an individual workman to be tolerated and still maintain hope for completion of the road on time.

Those men who had the job of cutting turns into the road around the sides of steep gorges had the most excitement and the best view.

Hanging high above the valley, these men would balance on a beam suspended by a rope at each end, held by fellow workmen on the top of the cliff. Dangling in midair they performed a marvelous feat of balance which would make a circus performer eat his heart out. Not only did they walk the beam back and forth, without benefit of safety rope, but they would hold a steel rod against the face of the cliff to chisel a hole for blasting. Swinging a five-pound hammer, using both hands, it was a breathtaking feat when observed by spectators, who marveled at their ability to keep balance on the swinging perch. Of course these were the survivors. Others who were not up to the task simply fell from the beam only to be replaced by new workers who scurried down the ropes to continue the job.

Blasting was another exciting adventure for the workmen. Many holes had to be made, all in a geometric pattern. Gunpowder was tamped in and homemade Chinese fuses set into place. These fuses were short but generally predictable in their burning times. Perched on the suspended beam, several workmen would sometimes light their fuses simultaneously. In some cases one man would light several fuses as he ran along the beam and then signaled for the workers above the cliff to pull him up, hopefully before the blast went off. Usually the blast would gravitate downward as planned, and the procedure would be successful. But occasionally an unpredictable fissure in the rock would cause the blast to go upward, thus relieving the men on the cliff top of their suspended burden, and they would be left standing there in amazement with only two lengths of frayed rope in their hands.

Bridge building was another task, for besides the numerous small streams, there were three great rivers to cross—the Salween, the Mekong, and the Yangpi. Every river was swift. Setting piles was out of the question because there was no pile-driving equipment, and even had it been possible, the debris sent down the river during the rainy season would have quickly destroyed the piles. Thus engineers were forced to build single span bridges, the longest of which was 410 feet.

Building foundations for the suspension bridges posed nothing but problems. In order to dig holes in the river bed for the foundations, cofferdams first had to be built around the places in which the holes were dug. Then water had to be pumped out with hand-operated bamboo plunger-type pumps used formerly in the rice fields. As soon as foundations were completed the building of masonry bridge towers was begun. They were capped by grooved saddles at the top over which cables would be passed. But getting cables across the river was the most difficult problem of all.

Since the bridges were built at the narrowest part of the river, they were thus built over the swiftest part. Getting across the river in a ferry in the treacherous current was impossible, so workmen would volunteer to attempt to swim across, pulling a small rope with them. Many were lost in the current and others were smashed to death on the rocks before one finally made it across. After the men stretched the cord across the river, they tied it to a slightly larger rope and pulled it across. They repeated this procedure several times with ropes of increasingly larger diameter until the cable itself could be pulled across.

Once the precious bridges were constructed, engineers were anxious that they would not be destroyed by vandals. Therefore they followed an ancient tradition. Whenever a former governor built a bridge which he did not want to be destroyed, he simply made the bridge a part of the religion of the people, creating a bridge god for its protection. It was not unusual for a little bell to be placed at each end of the bridge so that the traveler could pause and ring it in respect for the god. Sometimes monuments were also placed nearby. This way the people protected their bridges and the builders never had to worry about them being defaced or misused.

The Burma Road was built and made passable in one year's time, an incredible feat. But it took several more years before the refinements made it passable in all kinds of weather.

So the heavily overloaded trucks carrying their precious cargos traveled the winding, narrow gravel road through the Salween gorge. Tan Pei-ying watched and listened. By now the engineer was accustomed to hearing the sounds made by the approaching trucks as they descended or ascended the steep grades on either side of the river. "I noticed that coming upgrade," he wrote later, "the trucks that were heavily overloaded always made a curious whining noise as though the engine was crying out, 'I can't make it anymore. I can't do it anymore.'"

Oddly enough the Chevrolets cried like a woman, the Dodges deep like a man, and the Internationals gave a distinct cry of agony that would be recognized far away. Between three and four hundred vehicles a day would cross the Salween bridge, driven by young men from all provinces, drivers who were as reckless and carefree and colorful a breed as any of the American Volunteer Group fliers who were later to come to China. Most were clever, many dishonest, and all took many chances with their lives. Of course a man had to have nerves of steel to be able to drive the Burma Road. More than one fell prey to the spell of the Salween when suddenly confronted with the awesome sight of the gorge, losing control and plunging into its depths.

All day long the trucks and cars poured along the road, across the bridge, their drivers oblivious to the blood, sweat, and tears that the engineers and workmen had shed during its construction. But Tan knew, oh, how he knew, and his thoughts returned to the time a few months before, when he first knew he was saddled with the responsibility of building the road.

Tan's eyes fell back to the floor of the gorge. He watched as the last rays of sunshine disappeared from the gleaming, bright blue waters of the Salween River and up the face of the cliffs on the eastern side, chased by darkness, leaving behind only a moist, cloudy vapor of tropical heat hovering above the patches of luxuriant jungle far below.

Suddenly out of nowhere came a cold wind and he shivered.

CHAPTER 2

Claire Chennault:
From Louisiana Swamps
to China Skies, 1890–1938

Halfway through a man's life there inevitably comes a time when he must weigh his accomplishments against his failures. This personal reassessment generally comes on the heels of some profound disappointment.

Fear and bitterness can easily permeate one's thoughts when he is forced, at a time of mental and physical fatigue, to contemplate for the first time the full meaning of the word *compromise*. Fear of being forced to alter principles at a time in life when change is so difficult can be compounded by bitterness towards real or imagined adversaries who appear to be responsible for the dilemma in the first place.

Such were the thoughts of "Acting Major" Claire Lee Chennault as he lay in his hospital bed in Hot Springs, Arkansas, during the winter months of 1936. He found little comfort in this new title, a gratuitous rank given him merely because of his age and seniority, after having been passed over for attendance at the Command and General Staff School at Fort Leavenworth until he had exceeded the maximum allowable age for acceptance. He was now forty-six years old.

Channault had fought the good fight as an Army pursuit pilot for twenty years, and now he was exhausted and in ill health. He had been permanently grounded by the Army for reasons of low blood pressure, chronic bronchitis, and encroaching deafness. Because of these infirmities, his age, and his unyielding stand throughout his military career on the importance of the pursuit plane in times of war, Chennault had begun to see the handwriting on the wall. He knew that he was destined for an early retirement from the Army.

From early in his life Claire had sought a military career. He was a descendant of French Huguenots who came to America from France in 1700 and settled in Virginia. His ancestors had fought in every American war since that time. These ancestors included several generations of pioneering families who had pushed steadily westward, and it finally became Claire Lee Chennault's lot to be born in Commerce, Texas, in 1890.

Claire's earliest recollections, however, were not of the Texas plains but rather of the cypress swamps near the Mississippi River flood plains in northeast Louisiana where his grandfather had settled in 1842. The Chennault home was about two miles west of Bayou Macon, a small river which originated near McGhee, Arkansas, and flowed perhaps a hundred miles in a winding course into the Tensas River. The surrounding land's deep black soil had the distinction of being perhaps the finest farmland in the world. There was an abundance of big timber, with cypress only in a few brakes along the streams. Mostly it was hardwood of very fine quality. It was there that Claire and his younger brother Bill did their hunting, and since there were a lot of small lakes in the area, there was also fine fishing. Claire and Billy caught crappie or white perch eighteen inches long and something like six inches around.

The boys were related to the founder of Texas, Sam Houston, on the Chennault side of the family, and to Robert E. Lee on their mother's side. This rich heritage, in combination with the unusual freedom that Claire enjoyed during the development of his character, molded a man somewhat different from his later associates; a man not entirely suited for the society in which he entered as a young adult.

When he was only eight, Claire's mother died, leaving him and his brother Bill in the care of a kindly father who provided well for the needs of his young sons and allowed them the freedom to roam through the pastoral beauty of the Louisiana wilderness. Throughout his adult life, Claire frequently referred with great fondness to his Louisiana swamps and rivers with their abundance of fish and game.

In December 1902 Claire's father married Miss Lottie Barnes. She was a schoolteacher who taught both Claire and Bill, and Claire had already learned to love her. For the next five years, until her untimely death in 1908, Miss Lottie became his best and generally his only companion. She not only encouraged his natural tendency to want to be the best in every endeavor, but taught him the importance of scholastic achievement as well. After her death, he was once again often alone, and the experience of losing the two most influential women in his formative years was deeply traumatic to Claire.

Years later his brother Bill recalled:

Dad married Miss "Dill" Martha Young in December 1910, the mother of our younger brothers, Nelson and Joe. Our early life seemed in no substantial way different than one would expect, given the stated set of circumstances. Claire and I were much closer in the early days when we were younger boys. He being older, Claire naturally took the lead in our boyhood exploits and in many cases was associated with boys nearer his own age than with me.

I do recall one occasion when Vernon Ellerbe and I, pals as we were, heard great shouting and commotion from our favorite swimming hole in Deer Creek where it flowed through the woods a few hundred yards from the schoolhouse ('twas summer after school was out), and supposing the place to have been invaded by youth of the darker hue (we having no educated conception of civil rights) we cautiously approached the west bank after first arming our pockets, shirt fronts, etc. with green walnuts from a convenient tree. Arriving at the higher bank and discovering that the noise emanated from Claire and several of his fellows who had come horseback to the lower east side of the stream, we took counsel of ourselves and decided the walnuts should not be wasted, particularly in view of our tactical advantage of higher ground, coupled with the fact that the horses, clothes, and other effects of the enemy were on the other side of the creek. Hence, we launched simultaneous attack upon all and sundry. Some resistance was offered, chiefly by divers who sought shelter in their approach, but our fire was rather devastating until our ammunition was exhausted, whereupon we effected a strategic withdrawal and selected our ranges with unusual care for several days. I remember that one of my missiles hit my brother above the left eye, inducing a right respectable goose egg. So much for early warfare.

Claire was a very strong, active boy, very fond of the outdoor sports of hunting, fishing, and the like. There's been a lot of baloney written about him going forth, age ten, or maybe nine and a half, into the dark recesses of Tensas swamps and being out of pocket for days. We did go fishing and hunting and by the time I was somewhat twelve or thirteen, I did my share of that part of it, but we were scarcely classed as lone rangers.

One writing had it that Claire worked around various farms for scant pittances in times when he wasn't catching bears or wildcats. Not so. Gosh knows, there was plenty of work to do on our own farms, of which the family owned several, all small that's true, but pretty good dirt and about a half section of it. Our dad was always, I think, rather too kind with his tenants and frequently they didn't even pay out what he had advanced them for making crops, so the financial aspect wasn't too rosy.

Claire and some of the other boys in his general age group organized the Alligator Society on the occasion when a local citizen killed a gator not far from our little village. The purpose was ostensibly friendly, cooperative, and peaceful, but soon met competition from the Gilbert Military Club, composed mostly of "town boys" with some resultant friction and a few pretty good fights. I was permitted to align myself with the Alligators after a bit of time and initiation and bore my honors proudly.

When Claire and I were quite young, we used to trap birds both red and black. Some of the Negroes on the place taught us how to build pyramid traps, using narrow strips of wood, beginning at something like eighteen inches long, for the bottom four, then reducing length as we progressed upward, until we had a four-cornered structure about eighteen inches square at the bottom and ten to twelve inches to the top. That was completed with a green wood stick each end of which was tied with a string to the bottom stick of the trap on opposite sides of course and the tension on the stick held the whole thing pretty firmly together. No nails. No glue. Using a figure four trigger, baited with a few oat or corn grains, when a bird came inside to peck the grain, the trigger flew apart, letting the trap fall. We caught a bird or two. Someone in the house would fry them and we would feast. I can't recall that they were very good, but think of the enterprise we showed! And we split up a lot of good cypress boards to get those sticks. It was less odoriferous than catching polecats. Claire did become quite a trapper in later years and realized some profits from sale of furs, mostly skunk and coon. This was going on when he was circa fourteen.

Although Claire Chennault did not become exactly antisocial, he was nonetheless inclined to be shy and sensitive to ridicule and rarely related his true feelings to anyone older than himself. This trait he carried over into his military career, for he always found it difficult to convey his thoughts to his superiors. Chennault never felt compelled to explain his actions and became defensive if asked to do so. He felt he produced his best results when left to his own initiative.

Because of his innate shyness or perhaps his will to do as he pleased, he avoided following the leadership of older boys, preferring instead to lead all activities himself, instilling in others who were younger and less proficient an incessant urge to win. Yet when they did win, he himself seldom felt elated.

While in grade school, he developed an attraction to history and read with an all-consuming passion every history book in his grandfather's well-stocked library. He was particularly interested in the exploits of the great military leaders such as Genghis Khan, Napoleon, Lee, Houston, and Jackson, and took very seriously the lesson to be learned from them—that the battle is won by superior force at the point of contact. He was also intrigued by the tactics and armor employed during the Peloponnesian and Punic wars. This quest for historical knowledge prompted an interest in religion and the Bible. He was baptized into the Baptist Church at the age of eleven.

But as a young man, he was equally interested in geography and mathematics, as any young aspiring general should be, and he studied in seclusion and diligence. Before he was thirteen, he had completed ten grades of his local school. Too young to enter college, he continued to study on his own until the spring of 1908 when he entered Louisiana State University in Baton Rouge.

While at LSU, Claire lived in room 7-B of the Pentagon buildings, built in 1822, grayed from age, with wide porches at front and rear. Bill, who lived in room 9-B of the same building, recalls that a very dark Lafayette Street terminated in the space between "A building" and an overgrown area toward the Mississippi River. Cadets requiring nocturnal refreshment, a time-honored practice, would take a bucket and walk down Lafayette about three blocks, duck through an alley to a rear door of a boozery adjacent to the Worsham Hotel, knock on the door and be attended by a person within who took the bucket, filled it with beer, and took the cadets' two bits. Then the cadets went their happy way back to the barracks, exercising extreme care against observation by duty officer, senior officer, or other person of official status. One got fifty demerits for being off limits at night, or rather "50–30," the fifty being demerits and the latter being "tours," each tour consisting of one hour of walking in a circular path around the flagpole in the center of the Pentagon. Daytime, it was only "25–15," but with some cadets even twenty-five demerits were enough to result in their departure for the term or even longer. Bill Chennault later recalled:

A cadet had to stand guard duty on the ground floor, walking the post between the stairways at meal times for an hour until others returned to quarters. When a bugle signaling "call to quarters" was sounded, it was imperative to be in the quarters afterward or you got "7–7" for it, unless under the honor system practiced at that remote period, you could satisfactorily explain your non-presence at inspection. Cadets in that unenlightened period did not object to or question the merit of the honor system. In fact, I believe, we were rather proud of it. Allowing for a few exceptions, of course, the honor system didn't last too long.

While at LSU, Chennault applied for admission to both West Point and the U.S. Naval Academy. One day during the summer of 1910, he set out for Annapolis to take the entrance exam. After viewing those grim gray walls and learning of the compulsory two-year restriction to campus which would accompany acceptance, he quickly decided he did not want to be an admiral after all, not if it meant confinement for two whole years. His Louisiana adventures in the cypress swamps had left him intensely unsuited for such a confined life. He handed in his incomplete examination papers, notified his father that he had failed, and headed back to Louisiana.

As Claire wet his hook in the Tensas River that summer he contemplated what his future was likely to be and how things seemed to be moving so slowly. Like all young, impetuous men, he was sorry that he had been born so late—all the glamorous frontiers of the west had already been conquered. His future seemed destined to be dull and uneventful indeed. But at the 1910 Louisiana State Fair in Shreveport, Chennault's eyes were turned toward a new horizon. He looked upward and saw for the first time a rickety old Curtiss pusher biplane wobble through the hot, sticky Louisiana sky, bobbing up and down in the thermals just above the heads of the onlooking crowd. That was it, he thought. That was his new frontier.

Through the intervening seven years between the sight of the old Curtiss and his entrance into the U.S. Army Air Corps, Chennault struggled as most young men do to feed a growing family. He went from job to job, first teaching grade school in rural Louisiana, where overgrown farm boys made life miserable for timid teachers. Chennault, himself still a minor, mixed reading, writing, and arithmetic with a goodly portion of knuckle sandwiches in those early one-room schoolhouse days. This went on until he was able to channel the superfluous energy of these robust country lads into baseball. When the teacher pitched, the opposing team could not distinguish the teacher from the students. Within a year of his arrival, his small rural team at the Athens school was undefeated in north Louisiana.

After that first teaching experience during the spring of 1912, Claire went back to school at Louisiana State Normal College at Natchitoches. The following fall, he accepted a job as principal of a new four-room school about ten miles northeast of Athens, which was consolidated. It took in two or three one-room schoolhouses and was logically called Central School. Here he quickly developed an undefeated baseball team. This was beginning to be a Chennault trait—taking the side of the underdog, whipping them into an organized unit, and setting an impressive record without regard to insurmountable odds.

After a couple of terms there, Claire went forth again and wound up in New Orleans, working as athletic director in a YMCA. Tiring of that venture, he struck northward to work for Goodyear in Cleveland, and later, in 1916, he worked in Akron in a war plant making automobile tires for the Allies.

By the time the United States declared war on Germany in April 1917, Chennault had passed his twenty-seventh birthday and was the sole support and breadwinner for a wife and three children. His prompt request for duty in the Air Corps was flatly rejected on the grounds that "applicant does not possess necessary qualifications for a successful aviator." It was signed by a Capt. H. H. Salmon, Jr., a name that Chennault never forgot. His rejection would have been easier to accept had they simply stated that he exceeded the age limit for flight school.

Chennault pondered the situation and calculated that his best bet to get into the Air Corps would be through the "back door" while the "Captain Salmons" were not looking. He had been accepted for regular army officers' training school at Fort Benjamin Harrison in Indianapolis and figured that this would be his back door. So in ninety days, he emerged as one of the world's finest ninety-day wonders, complete with shiny silver first lieutenant's bars, a commissioned infantry officer in the United States Army.

His first duty station was Camp Travis in San Antonio with the Thirty-sixth Texas Division. Camp Travis was just across the city from a recently cleared cotton patch called Kelly Field, a rather humorous heritage for what would later become one of the most famous pilot training centers in the world. The year was 1917.

While serving as the athletic director at Camp Travis, Claire maintained a watchful eye on the "cotton patch" where the Signal Corps was training army pilots in that magnificent flying machine, the Curtiss JN-4, affectionately nicknamed the "Jenny." When Kelly Field sent out a request for officer volunteers in December, Claire was quick to respond. He could just see those coveted silver pilot's wings pinned to his tunic. But Chennault was not to hear the exhilarating sound of an aircraft engine coming to life in preparation for his long-awaited first flight. Instead he heard the "Hup two, hup two, . . ." of his own voice as he found himself bellowing infantry drill orders to a bunch of green aviator cadets. The Air Corps was oblivious to his aspirations.

But he stayed at Kelly Field for almost a year, and he saw to it that all was not the familiar "hup two." While the Salmons of the Air Corps were busy turning down his three consecutive requests for flight training on the grounds of "lack of inherent flying ability," Chennault was already in the air. As it is so common in the military, "birds of a feather . . ." and Chennault found a friend in a young pilot, Lieutenant Ralph, who would taxi out a Jenny to the flight line and exchange places with Claire, who would then take it up solo. Lieutenant Ralph knew, of course, that Chennalt had "prior instructions on the fundamentals of flying" from a couple of conspiring instructors and felt assured no harm would come to him. But he could have had no idea that this flying aspirant would one day become the commanding general of the Fourteenth Air Force during World War II.

In order to make these unofficial solo flights easier, Chennault managed to wrangle a transfer to an outlying staging field where he was placed in charge of the training planes. His job, as far as the

Army was concerned, was to maintain a maximum amount of flying time for the field. Naturally, to Chennault that meant that whenever a cadet was not prompt in taking up a freshly-fueled plane, he was to take it up himself and bootleg another hour of flying time. Chennault was not, however, the only frustrated would-be pilot in the Army. One soldier, who had joined the Army specifically to be a pilot only to find himself a mechanic, used less cunning than Chennault and stole a Jenny for his first flight. Having not carefully mastered the fundamentals of flying as Claire had done, he proceeded to fly it directly into a water tank while trying to land at nearby Brooks Field. Imagine the embarrassment when the military brass tried to prosecute the surviving mechanic/would-be pilot when they found that there were no Army regulations covering such an incident. The confusion surrounding early aviation at Kelly Field was such that Chennault once went AWOL for an entire week in a Jenny on a trip to Dallas and neither he nor the plane were missed.

As the war in Europe wound down, Chennault found himself at Langley Field, Virginia. He was stationed there when the great influenza epidemic struck. Planes were removed from the hangars, which were converted into hospital space as a steady flow of stricken soldiers began to pour in. Claire was locked in a hangar under quarantine and in charge of more than a hundred patients. Stretcher-bearers carried the sick into one end of the hangar and the dead out the other end. Later Chennault was stricken himself while aboard a transport in Hampton Roads. He was removed for treatment and promptly recovered.

At long last Chennault received his flying orders and soon found himself on his way back to Kelly Field when the Armistice was declared on November 11, 1918. World War I was officially over. He arrived at Kelly Field as an official flying cadet at the age of twenty-eight, and since he already had eighty hours of boot-legged flying time, he was confident that he would do well. This was just prior to meeting his first instructor, the fiery-tempered and bullheaded "Pop" Liken.

Operating on the premise that every king has his kingdom, Pop demanded absolute control while instructing students. At the slightest provocation he would wrench the control stick from a student's hand while flying as instructor in the rear cockpit. He never bothered to explain what "pilot error" prompted his reaction. Claire had learned a few bad habits while flying solo under his own tutorage, and, being just as recalcitrant and hot-tempered as Pop, the stage was set for a clash of personalities as Chennault climbed aboard for his first official flight instructions.

After a taste of Pop's instructional techniques, Chennault told him in no uncertain terms that the next time Pop grabbed the stick he would refuse to take it back and fly. But during a practice forced landing, while gliding with the engine off, Pop grabbed it again and Chennault calmly folded his arms, took his foot off the rudder pedals, and assumed a whistling-Dixie attitude. The wind reverberated through the wing-strut wires in a prelude to death as Pop waited for Chennault to recover. When Pop became convinced of Chennault's unyielding stubbornness and was faced with an impending crash in the cornfield, at the last split-second he applied full power and pulled out just in time.

Pop had the washout form filled out for Cadet Chennault before the ground crew had time to refuel the plane for the next student. But the washout board viewed the case with a little less emotion than Pop and decided to give Chennault another chance. He was given to Ernest M. Allison, a superb instructor with an even better understanding of human nature.

As Cadet Chennault and instructor Allison climbed into the "washing machine," so-called because it "washed out" so many cadets, Claire told Allison his story. In the hour which followed, Allison took Claire through conventional flight and then right into the world of aerobatics, which young Chennault had never experienced. Allison did so with the precision and fidelity that could come only from years of harmony between man and machine. Coordinating stick and rudder, power and mind, "Allie" progressed through an aerial sequence that could have been set to classical music. Loops, rolls, Immelmanns, and then straight up into a power climb easing man and machine into a sensation of weightlessness. . . . The sequence was epitomized by a gentle wingover, and then back down through a screaming power dive and high-speed pullout.

For a moment, then, the serenity of level flight, soon followed by a violent snap roll, then a half snap into inverted flight . . . oh, that inverted flight. For the first time Chennault just hung there by his seat belt waiting for his mind to become reoriented, so he could savor the view of an upside-down world with a new-found delight.

Suddenly the engine quit from inverted flight fuel starvation, and they glided along for a while as Chennault surveyed this new inverted world from wing tip to wing tip. Fluffy clouds where the earth should be and the earth in the sky . . . all dramatized by the sound of the wind singing through the wing struts. Chennault looked up, and thus down, at the earth below and then came a gentle stall and inverted flat spin until the earth had begun to turn into an intoxicating whirl, leaving Claire's mouth wide open in awe like a big Tensas River bass. He knew he was hooked on flying for life.

Until the spring of 1919 when he graduated from flying school and received the wings of a fighter pilot, Chennault continued to learn all that Allie could teach him about aerobatics. But as fate would have it, after enjoying his hard-earned fighter pilot rating for only a year, he was discharged from the wartime Army in the spring of 1920. Claire went back to Louisiana, bought a small tract of very good farmland, and waited for word on his application for a regular commission. It was granted in late summer, and in the fall he became one of the first thousand Air Corps regulars whose ranks were destined to swell to over three million during World War II.

Back into military harness at Ellington Field, Texas, during the summer of 1921, Chennault became associated with several World War I aces like Carl Spaatz of the First Fighter Group stationed there. They were still flying the French Spads and the British SE-5s, for at this time the United States did not have any pursuit planes of its own that could equal the performance of the French and British fighters. Spaatz's planes were painted with the stars and spangles war paint which they had made famous over the battlefields of France.

Chennault graduated with top honors from the first fighter tactical course given by this group and was assigned to "Monk" Hunter's famous "Hat in the Ring" Ninety-fourth Fighter Squadron. The peaceful Texas sky was not the same after Chennault graduated. He and the other new graduates would participate with the veterans in long formation flights starting at dawn. Sometimes they would suddenly peel off and scatter into mad dogfights all over the sky in typical World War I fashion. It was fun for Chennault, but even then he realized that it was all wrong. He felt that one-on-one fighting was no more than medieval jousting. It violated sound military precepts and failed to exploit the full potential of the pursuit plane. Besides, he always came out second-best against the war-hardened veterans.

In keeping with his nature, Chennault wanted to be best. So he naturally set out to improve on the tactics employed by the aces. One evasive tactic they used—the "split S"—consisted of a sudden maneuver in which the aces would snap to an inverted position and dive away when being attacked from the rear. Chennault felt that an Immelmann—a quick half loop straight up with a half snap roll on top—would be a more difficult maneuver for the attacker to follow. It might even put the would-be victim, if he was lucky, into a position to take the offensive and turn the tables on the attacker. After all, that was the name of the game—to him.

Working with two other classmates from the fighter tactical course, Joe Cannon and Don Stace, Chennault set out to prove his point. However, he wisely suggested that they practice the Immelmann in simulated combat among the three of them before trying it on the veterans.

Joe Cannon got in the SE-5, and Don Stace and Claire in the poorly-climbing Spads. Don had never even done an Immelmann before. Claire and Don climbed to five thousand feet and Joe quickly came on in his SE-5 diving after both of them in hot pursuit. With this, the two Spad "victims" crammed full throttle for their upward climb into the Immelmann. As Claire half-snapped on top of his half loop he noticed that his cohort Don was falling off into a tight inverted spin, actually falling back into the path of Joe in the pursuing SE-5. A midair crash was inevitable and bits and pieces of both planes blew all over the sky. Don managed to limp back and land without sustaining any injury, but Joe's SE-5 was cut into shreds and he fell to the ground with his stricken ship from five thousand feet.

Claire watched in horror as pieces separated from the fuselage before the plane plunged into the ground. Though parachutes were known at the time, the men had never seen one. As Chennault flew low over the wreck he was convinced there was no way for a man to survive such a crash. But Joe did survive, although he sustained injuries to his face and chest and had his nose slightly rearranged. It was two years before anyone would talk to Chennault about any new fighter tactics again. Claire's brother Bill recalled:

After Ellington Field, near Houston, Claire was assigned to Biggs Field, Fort Bliss, near El Paso. In the two years at Biggs, his duty consisted mostly of flying border patrol along the Rio Grande during a period of rather hostile relations with the Mexicans. Although their planes were unarmed, they occasionally received a rifle bullet through a wing or fuselage when they flew over Mexican terrain. Therefore, they adopted a tactic of loading their planes with good throwing rocks at some intermediate point (they were observation planes and carried an observer in the rear seat), and of using such stones to bomb the areas proven hostile. The rocks were said to have produced quite a dust when they struck houses and paved streets below and naturally no plane carried a single rock back to base.

In 1923 Chennault was assigned to Luke Field on the island of Oahu, where he received his first command. "It was like a boy's first love," he later wrote in his memoirs about his Hawaiian duty from 1923 to 1926. Here were his happiest memories of the U.S. Army Air Corps. He was physically at his peak, tan and robust, and had grown a huge black mustache waxed at the tips—a fighter pilot tradition. He was now the commanding officer of the Eighteenth Fighter Squadron at Luke Field at Pearl Harbor, which later was to bear the brunt of the Japanese sneak attack on December 7, 1941.

The "Fighting Cock" squadron flew the Thomas-Morse Aircraft Company's MB-3 biplanes, the first American single-seat fighter to be used by the services. In the best spirit of their emblem, Chennault and his men made life miserable for both the Navy and the Army artillery personnel stationed there. At that particular time, artillery gunners were enjoying a heightened reputation due to the widely-accepted hypothesis that artillery fire was capable of rendering aircraft completely obsolete because it could employ antiaircraft fire to destroy any attacking force before it could reach its target. This, of course, irked Chennault and his men, and they were prompted to prove otherwise even though the odds were against them. The long-established Army artillery officers outranked the newly-formed Army Corps officers and were able to exercise their power to impose their own rules during war games. For example, during artillery gunnery practice, artillery officers instructed bombers to tow targets over the coastal firing range at a fixed course, speed, and altitude, thus assuring a good target for their antiaircraft gunners.

Chennault spent long, boring hours as a bomber copilot on such monotonous excursions. On more than one occasion the bomber containing copilot Chennault would initiate a sudden maneuver sufficient to snap the target tow-cable and then fly home, leaving credit for a direct hit to the gunners. One day, while leading his squadron of Fighting Cocks, however, Chennault just happened to be flying high over the coastal gunnery range. He noticed a lone bomber droning back and forth towing a target for the artillery gunners, which were lined up neatly in a row along the beach, all firing away. Sitting in his cockpit leading his pursuit squadron, Chennault decided to inject a bit of reality into this one-sided game. Motioning his squadron to follow him down, he proceeded to dive-bomb and strafe in a simulated attack upon the unsuspecting gunners. Not once, but several times, the entire squadron made strafing passes so low as to send the gunners scurrying for cover in complete panic. On one pass Claire recognized the gunnery commander by his shiny, bald, sunburned head. He received great personal satisfaction in chasing him up and down the sandy beach, even leaning out of his cockpit to render an audible laugh as the commander waddled into the deep sand.

When the squadron landed back at their field on Ford Island, headquarters had been burning up the CO's telephone in indignation over the attack. Chennault listened innocently as his commanding officer attempted to justify his squadron's action. After he hung up the phone, Chennault asked, "Any ideas who did it?"

"No," replied his CO, "but the artillery colonel in charge of the firing range said it was that damn Frenchman with the big black mustache." Though his experience was bought and paid for by a week of confinement to the base, Chennault had added another page to his repertoire of fighter tactics which he was later to employ very successfully in China.

Claire continued to work hard on developing his new pursuit tactics. He availed himself of every opportunity of testing these theories with his men. He believed that pursuit planes should fight as a team, concentrating their combined firepower by flying in close formation while pressing an attack.

After the near-fatal adventure in Texas involving two green pilots, Chennault was very careful about the manner in which he brought up the idea again with fellow pilots. He was also particular in that, when he decided to experiment once again, he selected the two oldest and most experienced pilots in his squadron. Even his approach was different. He began with an innocent discussion about the "possibility" of three seasoned pilots flying in formation during aerobatics, which previously had always been a solo performance. This idea started a general conversation, into which Chennault injected challenging remarks whenever it began to lag, until it became increasingly heated and moved on to the main point of air pursuit tactics involving flying in formation. Then someone suggested that three of them should actually try it. Chennault was quick to agree and volunteered. They practiced in secret until they worked out the bugs and then demonstrated the maneuver over the field for all to see. The effect was so astounding to their fellow pilots that they had ample recruits after that, lest one should lose face in the squadron.

During joint maneuvers with the Navy in 1925, the squadron had an opportunity to try their fighting tactics on a group of Navy dive bombers which were approaching Pearl Harbor in a simulated bombing run. Though the interception by Chennault and his men was detected by the Navy pilots, who were flying at a high vantage point, the fighters were considered to be too low to be any threat to the bomber formation. This was exactly what Chennault had hoped for. He led his entire squadron up in a formation Immelmann and came out in perfect position for a tail-end attack upon the Navy bombers. They pressed the attack diving right through the bomber formation and so startled the Navy pilots that one bomber actually stalled and spun out of formation. Chennault felt that his faith in the effectiveness of the formation maneuver had been confirmed.

In those early days in Hawaii there was no warning communication net to alert defending fighter pilots of approaching enemy planes. With the Army's existing tongue-in-cheek attitude toward the pursuit plane, Chennault looked to an effective warning net as a much-needed aid in tipping the scales to the advantage of the defense. His first early warning system consisted of two enlisted men with binoculars standing back to back on a water tower, each searching 180 degrees of the horizon. On the last day of the Army-Navy maneuvers, a Saturday, one of the enlisted men spotted a lone Navy observation plane approaching from the sea about six miles out. Chennault felt he should answer the alert. So he scrambled his plane, took off, and intercepted the Navy invader in a diving rear surprise attack that brought him so close that he almost chewed the guy's tail off. Chennault never forgot the expression of horror on the pilot's face when he turned and saw the huge whirling prop about to tear into the plane's rear. The Navy pilot pushed over into a vertical dive hoping to put a little more space between his tailfeathers and Chennault's prop but the black-mustached pursuer did not give him an inch, continuing to follow him into the dive. "When he failed to pull out at two thousand feet I pulled up alongside to wave assurance," Chennault said. "He was staring straight ahead, frozen to the controls."

Chennault pulled out of his dive but the Navy plane plunged into the sea. Though injured, the pilot survived to receive the wrath of the carrier admiral in charge of Naval operations during the war game. It seems that the admiral had prematurely prepared a statement for the newspapers, which the pilot was carrying. It announced the complete triumph of the carrier-based Navy planes over the land-based planes of the Army Air Corps. Unfortunately for the admiral, the document was found by the Army rescue team when they fished the Navy carrier pilot out of the drink. The admiral had written the news release thirty-six hours before the end of the maneuvers.

The Navy pilot was supposed to fly in to the Army base undetected, close enough to enable him to land before being challenged. He was then to surrender himself to the neutral observer on the base as a prisoner of war. At this point, so the admiral's strategy went, the Navy pilot was to sneak the observer the premature message for release to the Sunday newspapers, thus achieving a big splash of Navy propaganda—all this while the poor Army was still preparing its news release. Such practices were frequently employed by both branches of the service in an effort to maintain favorable public opinion during those lean years of the 1920s when both branches were forced to compete for the meager military appropriations.

The Navy considered Chennault's tactics of sufficient importance to swallow their pride long enough to send a yeoman over to Ford Island to take notes. Chennault also wrote a new manual of fighter tactics for the Air Corps based upon his experiences up to that time. The latter received an official commendation and then began to gather dust. Chennault's resourcefulness in developing an effective early warning net from the simplest of resources was characteristic of his ingenuity at times of need. The extensive Chinese warning net which he so effectively employed in the vast underdeveloped region of remote China in World War II was simply an extension of his embryonic two-man water tower system.

After bidding aloha in 1926 to beautiful Hawaii and the fondest, most enjoyable time in his Army career, Chennault headed back to Brooks Field in San Antonio. Here he became flying instructor and later director of primary training. Things soon became boring again, and after a while he became involved with a couple of parachute experts. Together they proceeded to develop some paratroop techniques which were originally advocated by Billy Mitchell. Claire's brother Bill later recalled:

> Claire became convinced that airborne infantry, delivered by chute, could be used with extreme effectiveness; that is to say adjacent to industrial plants, power dams, or a wide variety of locations where even a platoon-sized contingent could seriously impair the enemy's war-making capability. He did not suppose that an entire army could be so disposed, but that only specially-trained and equipped personnel could be so employed.

Chennault and his assistants worked out a maneuver where Claire, flying a Ford Trimotor transport, led a "V" formation of DeHavilland two-seaters, each carrying one parachutist. The transport carried the ammunition and supplies, and on Chennault's command the "kickers" would dump all the transport's equipment as the paratroopers jumped from the DeHavillands. The result was that everything hit the ground about the same time with the supplies landing in the central area. Within a minute, all the men were armed and firing. When word reached Chennault's old Hawaii commander, Gen. Charles P. Summerall, now Army chief of staff, he decided to visit Brooks Field for a demonstration. Chennault and his men practiced beforehand to a point of precision and were immensely proud of their maneuver. However, during the demonstration, as soon as the chutes blossomed, General Summerall turned and left abruptly, muttering something about "more of his damn aviation nonsense." The true purpose of the exercise escaped him.

Summerall was typical of the Army leadership under which the Air Corps struggled to develop during the late 1920s. He was of the opinion that a fighter squadron could be formed if and when needed during war, in a couple of days' time. This was the degree of importance he placed upon the role of the pursuit plane. He so testified to the Air Corps' detriment during Billy Mitchell's trial in 1925. As a ground general, he did not wish even to investigate the possible merits of air power other than as a tool for support of his ground forces. He was completely satisfied with World War I army tactics. As chief of staff of the Army, Summerall had absolute power over the Army Air Corps and chose to remain uninformed and unimpressed about aerial combat effectiveness.

Just when Chennault had decided that his latest inspiration for aviation had gone unnoticed, a caravan of black limousines poured onto his field one day shortly after the paratroop demonstration. It was led by General Baranoff of the Russian military mission. He was armed with U.S. War Department orders for the base commander to show him and his party everything he wanted to see. The paratroopers jumped and the limousines then roared away, leaving behind only one Russian who stayed for several rounds of vodka, chocolate, and caviar with Lieutenant Chennault. He soon got to the point, however. Would Chennault go to Russia to train paratroopers for the Russian Army? Chennault tactfully passed the paratrooping act off as "show business" and quickly reiterated that he personally was only a fighter pilot.

The Russian did not buy it and told him so. "Write and let me know your terms," he said. Not often is one afforded the opportunity to write his own terms, and the matter weighed heavily upon Chennault's mind for the next few weeks. He had been in the U.S. Army for nine years and was still a first lieutenant, making a meager salary with a large family to support. He had met with frustrations in the past, but he felt that none were insurmountable. He still dreamed of being a part of the building of a mighty American Air Force. He toyed with a reply in which he felt his terms were actually ridiculous —a thousand dollars per month salary plus expenses, the rank of colonel, a five-year contract, and permission to fly any plane in the Red Air Force. It was probably the first time Chennault ever had his bluff called. The Russian promptly wired back: "When can you leave?"

Now the fat was in the fire. Obviously the Russians were enjoying some favor with the U.S. War Department at the moment, and what Chennault had thought to be a diplomatic evasion with a little fantasy had turned out to be a sticky situation. He stalled, saying it would take some time to settle his family and conclude his affairs, but the Russians kept after him. They kept after him for several months, in fact, until in desperation Chennault simply began to return the Russian's letters unopened. His reward for resisting the temptation of higher rank and salary and the freedom to develop his fighter tactics soon came in the form of an official communiqué from the U.S. War Department to "stop that parachute nonsense before somebody gets hurt."

The year 1931 found Chennault a student again, now in tactical school at Langley Field, Virginia, where World War I fighter ace Clayton Bissell was teaching U.S. Army Air Corps fighter tactics of the 1918 vintage. Like Bissell, many of the Western aces were beginning to gravitate towards Billy Mitchell's concept of stragetic bombardment. They were all older and higher in rank now and had outgrown fighters, moving towards bigger and better things. As the lumbering bombers became larger and faster through technological advances, it was easy for some to become caught up in the excitement. But not Chennault, the belligerent crusader for fighter development, not even after publication of the book *The War of 194-* by the Italian General Giulio Douhet. Douhet portrayed great hordes of heavily armed bombers defending themselves easily as they flew to and from their targets without hindrance from fighters or flak. The theory became plausible with the appearance of the heavily armed five-gun, fast-flying (235 mph) Martin B-10 bomber. When this relative giant was compared to the best Army and Navy fighter of the day, the 225-mph two-gun Boeing P-26, bomber stock naturally went up. Many who were not already convinced began to feel that fighters were perhaps obsolete and that the next war would be won by the heavy bombers. This was not unlike the fallacy of the push-button war theory which followed World War II, according to which the foot soldier would be obsolete.

With the rapid exodus of the fighter pilots to the bomber pilot ranks, the fighter development program began to suffer drastically. In addition, the peacetime Army Air Corps did not have sufficient funds to support both bomber and fighter development programs simultaneously. Consequently, there was a constant and bitter battle waged between the two factions at social affairs, bars, nightclubs, in the hangars, in the air, and even in the classrooms between instructor and student.

One can see Chennault sitting day after day in Clayton Bissell's class listening to him talk about dawn patrols and other antiquated fighter tactics as he virtually abandoned the idea that fighters might be able to shoot down bombers. Bissell occasionally threw the fighter pilots a bone, most likely in Chennault's direction, by recommending, quite seriously, that a future role for the pursuit pilot might be to drop a ball and chain device from above an enemy bomber formation in hopes of fouling up their propellers. It is doubtful that Chennault contained himself on such occasions, for Bissell later emerged in World War II as a thorn in Chennault's side.

As the Douhet theory rapidly gained popularity with the bomber generals, they ruthlessly began to suppress any opposition to their bomber program within their own ranks just as the ground generals had suppressed the development of the Air Corps itself a few years earlier. The bomber generals had a short memory.

Upon graduating from the Air Corps Tactical School, Chennault was assigned to Maxwell Field in Alabama as a senior instructor in fighter tactics. Here, in the sanctity of his own classroom, Chennault enjoyed a much more favorable medium for expressing his personal views. He continued to work hard on developing his fighter concepts and studied everything he could get his hands on regarding pursuit plane tactics.

He was still firmly convinced that pursuit planes should fight as a team, concentrating their combined firepower for maximum effect instead of breaking off into individual dogfights all over the sky. While studying World War I documents, he learned that many strategies he had developed in Hawaii had in fact first been employed by Manfred von Richtofen's instructor, Oswald von Boelcke. A German ace, he had advocated that two planes could maneuver and fight together through all kinds of intricate combat maneuvers while pressing an attack on a lone enemy plane. This strategy had devastating effects when tried against hapless Western pilots by Richtofen's Flying Circus, proving Boelcke's theory. Chennault calculated that two such planes fighting as a team increased the odds in their favor not to merely two to one, but actually to four to one. He based this calculation upon the old military axiom that the difference between the firepower of two opposing forces—all other factors being equal—is not the difference in number of fire units, but rather the square of the difference of the number of fire units. Richtofen's Flying Circus was never defeated until after his death when it was led by Hermann Goering, who reverted to the one-to-one dogfight tactics.

Chennault could not understand why the Air Corps would not accept the inevitable role of the pursuit plane in combat. He felt that the greatest single factor affecting fighter efficiency was the unnecessary blind man's bluff approach to bomber interception. Long on tenacity and short on patience with the status quo, he set about to correct this discrepancy with the vigor and enthusiasm he had displayed so often in the past. What fighter planes needed, he surmised, was a steady flow of accurate information on approaching bomber formations so they could be properly intercepted before they reached their target. What they had under the current system, however, was a loose patchwork of aircraft spotters who reported in by telephone with general information directed more to warning the civilian population of an impending air raid than to supplying accurate information to the defending fighters. During the 1931 Air Corps maneuvers, one fighter group commander did not even so much as see the attacking bombers in two weeks of simulated warfare. At the end of the maneuver, the official umpire concluded, "Due to increased speeds and limitless space, it is impossible for fighters to intercept bombers and therefore it is inconsistent with the employment of air force to develop fighters."

The fighters were getting a bad reputation which proceeded to worsen when Lt. Col. "Hap" Arnold conducted additional maneuvers on the Pacific coast concerning the same problem a year later. He sent squadrons of Martin B-10 bombers to attack March Field in California, where the defending fighters took off according to the military protocol of the day. There was no vulgar scramble for takeoff when the alarm was sounded. One by one the fighters took off and formed over the field with spectacular military precision, merging into squadrons which then circled the field as the group commander took off and found his way to the head of the formation to lead them in pursuit of the bombers. The only problem was that by then the bombers had already bombed their target and were returning home. The only fighters which intercepted the bombers had been a few from an outlying base which had "scrambled" into the air without benefit of protocol as soon as they heard the alert.

Arnold's conclusion from the Pacific coast maneuvers was that fighters would be ineffective in wartime. When this report reached the tactical fighter school for comment, there was a reply forthwith from Chennault in the form of an eight-page rebuttal. It prompted an inquiry from Arnold to the school—"Who is this damn fellow Chennault?"

Claire's insistence on the necessity of an effective warning net for fighter interception prompted additional Air Corps maneuvers at Fort Knox, Kentucky, in 1933. Yet the plans for the maneuvers were drafted by a board of Air Corps officers, none of whom were fighter pilots. This time, however, the defending fighter forces were allowed to set up their own observation posts with communications directly to a central fighter control station. Day or night, high or low altitude, it did not matter, the fighters intercepted every approach made by the bombers. The warning net was so effective in allowing the fighters to intercept the bombers before they reached their target that the ruling bomber advocates began to limit the freedom of action of the fighters even before the maneuvers were half completed.

Chennault later divulged that he had been studying warning net systems developed by the English and Germans in his spare time back at fighter tactical school. Yet all that he had added to the existing warning net had been three mobile cavalry field radios which he had manned with trained observers. Following these maneuvers, Chennault wrote a new textbook for the Air Corps which he called *The Role of Defensive Pursuit,* which he later used in teaching air combat tactics to a most unlikely gathering at Toungoo, Burma, in the summer of 1941.

In the early 1930s, the tactical school where Chennault taught had become the focal point where Air Corps policy was being developed. However, the fighter-bomber gap continued to widen with each heated debate. Thus, with the increasing reduction of Air Corps appropriations, it finally came down to a question not of how many or what kind of fighters the Air Corps would have, but of whether there should be any fighters at all. It became a regular part of the agenda at each annual meeting of the tactical school faculty to entertain a motion to drop the fighter courses completely from the curriculum. This occurred each year for three years until finally the motion passed. Chennault was assigned elsewhere, but there must have been some second thoughts. At the last moment he was recalled to teach a part-time course on fighter tactics.

In his defense of the fighter development program and air power in general, Chennault stepped out of ranks on several occasions during his early military career. He was ofttimes so outspoken as to blight this career. In 1934 Claire literally tightened the noose around his own neck when he and four other officers from the tactical school at Maxwell Field, Alabama, volunteered to testify before the Clark Howell Federal Aviation Commission committee, which was investigating the military's handling of air power development during peacetime.

That same year, just prior to the Howell committee hearings, there had been a series of maneuvers conducted under the auspices of Gen. C. E. Kilbourne of the War Department general staff. These maneuvers had resulted in bitterness and controversy between the Air Corps and the Army's ground commanders. The controversy developed from a situation involving an amphibious landing in the face of hostile forces similar to those to be so commonly carried out during World War II—except in this case the general's defending blue army was entrenched thirty miles from the beach.

The red invading forces landed without opposition and proceeded to march inland unmolested for thirty miles before encountering resistance from the blue defenders, whereupon they too dug in and a World War I–type trench-warfare stalemate resulted in which nobody moved. The Air Corps then quickly prepared to strike at the red army's vulnerable thirty-mile-long supply lines and support vessels far to their rear. Kilbourne stopped the effort cold by restricting the entire air force to bombing the red trench positions only. The tactic was completely ineffective as the red forces continued to receive reinforcements from their uninterrupted supply lines. The Air Corps' participation in the maneuver was so ridiculous that their commanders became completely frustrated with their role.

When the Howell committee hearings got under way, General Kilbourne himself was in attendance along with his two secretaries, who were to record testimony. Kilbourne listened silently as Chennault's four fellow officers discussed the theory and practice of strategic air power with the members of the committee. Chennault's time came, and he proceeded to dissect the general's tactics during the recent maneuvers. When he had finished, the general jumped to his feet and insisted upon making a rebuttal even though he was not scheduled to appear before the committee. He was visibly upset as he defended his tactic against Chennault's criticism. When he finished and all the dust had settled, Claire added one small footnote, remarking, "General, if that is the best you can do in the way of planning for future wars, perhaps it is time for the Air Corps to take over."

After the hearings, it is doubtful that any officer in the U.S. Air Corps had to ask "Who is this damn fellow Chennault?" A few weeks later, Chennault's name was permanently removed from the list of officers scheduled to attend the Command and General Staff School at Fort Leavenworth, Kansas. Nobody, but nobody could hope for a command or significant promotion in the peacetime U.S. Army without having the blessings of this school in his service record.

Yet Chennault remained a staunch advocate of teamwork and formation fighting as the fundamentals of all fighter tactics. When his commander at the tactical school saw a performance of Navy Helldivers, an aerobatic team, in 1932, he commissioned Chennault to form an Air Corps team of Boeing P-12 fighters to steal their thunder. Chennault was quick to respond, for this was an excuse to perfect his fighter tactics with official sanction. Drawing upon his earlier experiences at Luke Field in Hawaii, he began to select his team. It was a simple procedure. He invited all comers to stick on his wing during violent aerobatics. Many tried but only three could handle it—a second lieutenant named Haywood "Possum" Hansell and two flying sergeants, John H. "Luke" Williamson and Billy Mac-Donald. After a year Possum moved on, and he later became General Hansell.

For the next three years Claire, Luke, and Billy performed all over the country from the cotton patches of Louisiana to the Cleveland Air Show in 1935, where the newspapers of that city named the group "The Three Men on the Flying Trapeze." They would do all aerobatic maneuvers in perfect formation including one producing a squirrel-cage effect in which each plane rolled around the other while doing an individual barrel roll. They also performed three-turn tailslides in formation and came out in formation even though all three planes were out of control during the spin.

Bill Chennault later described the performance:

> The demonstration consisted of taking off, flying, looping, spinning, and landing in formation and included a bit of a stunt where they tied the wing tips of the three planes, abreast, with thirty-foot cotton ropes, took off, looped a few times, and landed with the three

planes still tied together. That was a real thriller for the crowds although Claire always said it was the easiest of all and far less dangerous than spinning in formation. The crowds were pleased, the
media was thrilled, but probably not one of the spectators ever suspected they were witnessing a basic concept of warfare which would
later thrill the world in the exploits of the "Flying Tigers."

Because of the Great Depression, Air Corps funds were finally cut
so drastically that it was increasingly difficult to obtain enough gas to
fly the four hours a month necessary to collect flight pay. Consequently, the running battle between fighter and bomber advocates
grew even more bitter in competition for the little money available.
One disappointment led to another for Chennault in these years.
In 1936 Williamson's and MacDonald's enlistments came to an end.
Claire felt that Luke and Billy had been discriminated against by the
Army when they were passed over for a regular commission in 1935.
They were allowed to fly the air shows as lieutenants but after returning to their home base, they were required to put their sergeant's
uniforms back on and assume flying jobs the officers didn't care to
handle. They were the type of men Chennault felt the Air Corps
needed. Bitter with disappointment, he gave a statement to an important newspaper in the area, the *Montgomery Advertiser*. "Williamson
and MacDonald are outstanding pilots in any type of airplane," he
said. "If we were to go to war and I was ordered to the front, I
would choose these two men to accompany me into combat, and that
is the highest compliment a combat formation leader can pay."
They decided to fly one more performance as the "Flying Trapeze." Among the spectators of the Pan-American Air Show in
Miami, Florida, in 1936, was Gen. Mow Pang Tsu of the Chinese
Air Force. "The Three Men on the Flying Trapeze" were destined to
fly together again.
Earlier Chennault had received a letter from Roy Holbrook, a
former Air Corps pilot who had gone to China as a flight instructor.
Roy requested Chennault to recommend twelve good pilots to in-
struct at the Chinese Flying Aviation School at Hangchow, south of
Shanghai, China. Claire recommended Luke and Billy and a number
of technicians. Both of his former partners sailed for China that
summer.
By this time Chennault's health was failing. His frantic pace of the

past five years on the tactical school staff and the increased responsibilities and disappointments associated with his membership in the pursuit development board, led to frequent bouts with the sickbed. He was soon transferred to Barksdale Field in Louisiana as executive officer of the Twentieth Fighter Group, where his health became so bad that he was restricted to a two-seater training plane with a safety pilot in the front seat. In the fall of 1936 he was permanently grounded by the flight surgeon and transferred to a hospital at Hot Springs, Arkansas.

His main interest now lay in the letters bearing Chinese postage stamps which began to come in to his hospital room. They brought news about his old friends Billy, Luke, and Roy. It was good to hear of their accomplishments in their new jobs in faraway China. Some of the news was disturbing, however, such as the growing tension over Japanese aggression in northern China, which Chennault felt might eventually have dire ramifications for the United States. Then one day a letter came from Roy Holbrook saying that Madame Chiang Kai-shek was inquiring if Chennault would consider a three-month assignment in China. His task would be to provide her with a confidential evaluation of the combat readiness of the Chinese Air Force. Madame Chiang, as newly-appointed head of the Chinese Aeronautical Commission, was in the process of reorganizing and cleaning out corruption in the Chinese Air Force in preparation for the forthcoming conflict with the Japanese.

Thus, having accepted an attractive offer providing both a good salary and expenses, and including the right to fly any aircraft in the Chinese Air Force, Chennault knew that he had found a way to keep flying and put into practice his theories on fighter tactics. He accepted retirement from the Army as a captain on April 30, 1937, and on the following day, back on the comfortable Chennault farm in Waterproof, Louisiana, Claire said good-bye to Nell and their seven children. It was a solemn moment as first Jack, the oldest son, came forward and shook hands with his father. Jack would later command a fighter group in the Aleutians and then would join his father in China. Then Max came forward. He became an air-traffic controller in the Air Transport Command. Next it was Pat, who would serve as a Mustang P-51 pilot in England, followed by Charles, who would become an Army Air Corps radio mechanic. Then came Bobby, later an aviation cadet, and finally David, who stood just tall enough for his father to ruffle his hair. David was later to join the Navy and fight in the Solomons aboard the *U.S.S. Helena*. Then there was a special moment as Claire picked up Rosemary, his daughter, and pressed her to his chest. He then departed on his long journey to China and into the pages of history.

On May 31, 1937, after a month at sea, the *President Garfield* settled against the wharf in Kobe, Japan. Chennault stood inconspicuously near the rails of the ship as his eyes searched the crowd on the dock below. While waiting to meet Chennault, Billy MacDonald had been traveling incognito in Japan on a Chinese passport as an assistant manager for a group of touring acrobats. Had the Japanese secret service known the true identity of either man, they would surely have been under scrutiny.

Claire and Billy chuckled to themselves about their hidden motives as they rented a car and set out to see not only Kobe, but Kyoto and Osaka as well. Chennault had decided to avail himself of this opportunity to visit Japan as a military observer disguised as an American tourist. Just as hundreds of Japanese citizens were touring the United States, photographing themselves in front of military and shipping installations, so now here they were, complete with camera and notebook pads which soon began to swell with military information as they made their way to Kyoto and Osaka, south of beautiful snowcapped Mount Fuji. In Osaka they boarded a ship and sailed down the inter-island coast, continuing to photograph and make notes of the beehive of military and shipping activities. They felt the ominous pulse of a nation secretly preparing for war. After brief stops at Mojii and Shimonoseki, they sailed out into the mystical Yellow Sea.

Chennault was later amazed to learn that the volume of military information he and Billy collected on their little trip was far greater than all the data on Japan compiled by the entire U.S. War Department as of early 1942. When in early 1942 Jimmy Doolittle planned a B-25 bombing raid on Tokyo, he found nothing in the U.S. government's files regarding possible strategic targets for his military bombers.

It was early June 1937, when Chennault watched his long awaited destination, Shanghai, China, slowly rise along the western horizon of the Yellow Sea. It was China's largest city, equal in size to New

York or London, and its huge harbors were crowded with ships flying flags of all nations. Built upon the delta deposits near the mouth of the great Yangtze River, Shanghai was home to a swarming populace of diverse masses unlike the populace of any other city in the world. To the adventuresome Chennault, it represented the gateway to a new beginning, but to the "old China hands" who resided there, it meant a grand way of life superior to any they knew of at home. Unknown to them, they were living in the twilight of extraterritoriality, and theirs was a way of life doomed to extinction. Each nation was represented by a legation smugly ensconced within the area of its own four walls, which was called its "settlement." Each legation was bent upon pursuit of its own separate national interests, while China footed the bill.

Beyond Shanghai and across the rich farmland of the Yellow-Yangtze delta plain stretched the vastness of inland China, with a teeming population of human souls that staggered the imagination. From deep in the heart of Mother China came the sweating coolie shouldering an extraordinarily heavy burden of riches and raw materials. Down from the mountains he carried this burden, along rough, mountainous trails and across steep gorges to the navigable waterways of the Yellow and Yangtze rivers. Here his cargo was transferred to waiting sampans and poled along the muddy rivers, eventually making its way to the factories and docks of the city of Shanghai.

The Yangtze itself served not only as the most important navigable thoroughfare for the masses to and from the interior of China, but acted as a geographical division between northern and southern China much as did the hypothetical Mason-Dixon line in the United States. In Shanghai the Chinese coolie lived in marked contrast to the foreigners whom they hosted. Their dwellings were crowded in clusters along the lower river beds adjacent to the industrial complexes, which in turn occupied the higher ground free from the danger of floods. These shanty towns, built from the frailest of materials, afforded poor protection from the elements and bred poverty beyond the power of the Western mind to conceive. Beggars, thieves, and prostitutes were plentiful in these areas of despair. Such was the extreme contrast between the highest and lowest classes in the Shanghai of 1937.

Scars of the Sino-Japanese fighting in 1931 were still evident in

Shanghai as Claire and Billy disembarked. In the north, Japanese armored infantry, on the pretense of holding maneuvers, continued to make steady advances. Reports of border violations vibrated back and forth through an alarmed Chinese community. What was actually saber rattling by the Japanese was misinterpreted by the "old China hands" as simply being random outbreaks of no significance. Chennault was quick to surmise that in general they actually had hopes that Japan would teach the Chinese a lesson so that they could settle down and go back to business as usual. China's indignation over Japan's maneuvers was affecting their profits. The poor Chinese fighting a meaningful war with powerful Japan? Nonsense!

Our aging traveler from Waterproof, Louisiana, was soon to meet two very important people in Shanghai who would help shape his destiny. Little did he realize when he began his career as an airman that time and circumstances would, years later, entwine his life with the gallant struggle of a great nation twice the size of his own country. Never in his wildest dreams could he have imagined that through his deeds in the years to come, his name would live on in the hearts of countless millions of grateful Chinese long after his passing. This was the destiny of Claire Chennault as he stood on the threshold of historical prominence upon arriving in China in 1937, nearing the age of fifty.

W. H. Donald and Madame Chiang Kai-shek were the two people who enlisted Chennault permanently and irretrievably into China's cause. Donald was an adventurous Australian newspaperman who had been wandering around the interior of China lending his expertise to various warlords as a foreign consultant. Though he had been involved in the exotic and sometimes dangerous game of Chinese politics, he had risen as few foreigners had to a place of prominence and respect among the Chinese leaders. He had done so with typical Australian individualism, even to the point of refusing to speak Chinese or to eat Chinese food. Yet Donald managed to attain a position of considerable influence with Chiang Kai-shek, at least until the 1940s.

This rugged, sandy-haired Australian pursued his task of routing corruption out of the Chinese government until he stepped on so many toes that it finally led to his banishment from China. He wound up in the Philippines, was captured by the invading Japanese, and spent the war in a concentration camp, his true identity never being known by his captors. It is fortunate that Donald befriended Chennault in those early days soon after his arrival, which formed a period of adjustment. Astute in the ways of Chinese politics, he cautiously advised and tutored Chennault in the customs of the Chinese and acted as intermediary for Chennault to the Generalissimo and also to Madame Chiang on many occasions. From the beginning he was a staunch supporter of the necessity for air power. This quickly endeared him to Chennault. Without Donald's tireless support and friendship, Chennault later related, he would surely have failed in his early efforts in China.

Chennault spent some time his first few days in Shanghai analyzing the climate, both political and meteorological, until on one sultry afternoon, Roy Holbrook showed up to escort him to the French settlement to be introduced to his new employer, Madame Chiang Kaishek. Upon entering the concession, they were told officially that Madame Chiang was not in, but were then ushered into a waiting room in a nearby cool corridor. In a moment a young girl appeared clad in a modest French frock. Chennault assumed it was one of Roy's young friends and so remained seated, a position he quickly altered as Roy said, "Madame Chiang, may I present Colonel Chennault?" Chennault was so captivated by her youthful, warm, sincere manner and rich southern drawl that he later wrote in his diary, "She will always be a princess to me."

Despite her youth, charm, and sincere friendliness, she was all business. She got right to the point. She wanted to know the exact condition of the Chinese Air Force, she wanted the absolute truth, and she wanted it in a hurry. Such was the confusion of the times that all sorts of conflicting reports regarding the air force and its combat readiness were reaching the Generalissimo. This vexed him greatly, so much that he placed his young and trusted wife in charge. Chennault promised her a complete report in three months, a promise that he was unable to keep due to the persistent aggression of the invading Japanese in the north. Chennault's role began as an advisor, but gradually shifted due to the various circumstances to a more active personal role until he found himself completely engulfed in China's struggle for survival. He was not to see Waterproof and his family for some time.

Chennault's orders from Madame Chiang were to begin his inspection at Nanking, capital of China, situated west of Shanghai up the

Yangtze River and across the rich Yangtze delta near the base of the mountains. At the Hangchow Flying School southwest of Shanghai he gathered his entourage. It consisted of Billy MacDonald; C. B. Smith, a mechanic; and a Chinese, Col. P. Y. Hsu, a former YMCA secretary who served as Chennault's interpreter throughout his China years. This was an inauspicious beginning for the man who was to become Commanding General of the Fourteenth Air Force in China.

They piled into two Douglas biplanes, Billy piloting one plane and of course Chennault the other. He later wrote, "Flying to Nanking, I had my hand on a throttle again for the first time since the Air Corps grounded me the previous autumn. It felt good to be in the air again with Billy on my wing and a broad muddy river below that could easily have passed for the Mississippi."

Yet the Yangtze below and the brilliant green carpet of growing rice and the web of canals and black slate-roofed villages reminded him it was really China. Since the noise of the engine and whistling wing struts of the open cockpit prevented any possible conversation with Smith in the rear, Chennault had ample time during the 180-mile journey to Nanking to study the countryside and reflect upon his meeting with Madame Chiang. He also contemplated strategy for carrying out his new job. And these thoughts were punctuated by an occasional gesture and smile to Billy MacDonald, flying close by his side.

Upon landing, Chennault noticed a marked contrast between the complacency of Shanghai and the political turmoil and tension of Nanking. Here he felt the reason for Madame Chiang's urgency. The countryside was gripped with tension. From the north came rumors of continued Japanese atrocities and demands that they be permitted to train Japanese troops on Chinese soil. Anti-Japanese feelings were intense. Students were demonstrating in the streets.

At Nanking Chennault also got his first whiff of Chinese corruption involving the Chinese Air Force. It was only after the Japanese occupation of Manchuria and the first attack on Shanghai in 1931 that the Chinese government gave serious thought to an effective air force. It quickly became obvious that China, with its weak navy, would surely lose access to the outside world should they be blockaded by the superior Japanese Navy. This consideration, coupled with the continued aggression by the Japanese motorized infantry in the northern province of Manchuria, shed a light on the importance of a strong Chinese Air Force. Since air power was actually a Western import to China, its significance was little understood or appreciated by the Chinese even at this late date of 1937. After the 1931 attack on Shanghai, T. V. Soong, an older brother of Madame Chiang, successfully organized the first significant Chinese military air power. Before this, almost every warlord of any consequence possessed foreign-made flying machines in his arsenal and had foreign pilots to engage them in combat against his enemies, but these could hardly be said to constitute organized air power.

It was through Soong's perseverance that the United States finally sent an unofficial American mission to China in 1932 to establish the flying school in Hangchow, which was based upon sound American military precepts of pilot training. It was this mission led by Col. Jack Jouett that laid the foundation for the modern Chinese Air Force. Roy Holbrook and some twenty other U.S. Air Corps reserve officers turned out some excellent Chinese pilots during the next two years. But the Americans lost face when they refused to help the central government in putting down a coastal rebellion in the mountainous province of Fukien across the straits from the island of Formosa (Taiwan). The rebels were well fortified in an ancient, thick-walled town, leaving air bombardment the most efficient method to breach their fortifications. When Jouett refused aid, Gen. Mow Pang Tsu of the Chinese Air Force took up six rickety crates and successfully bombed a hole in the thick walls of the town, thus allowing the government ground forces to enter and root out the rebels. The success of these air and ground tactics gave the Generalissimo his first real interest in aerial warfare.

Jouett's refusal to participate in China's internal affairs coincided with an event taking place many miles to the west, in Italy, where Mussolini was experiencing financial difficulties in expanding his air force for war. Mussolini successfully managed to ingratiate himself to some adversaries of T. V. Soong. Soong had temporarily fallen from grace because of the Jouett refusal. The meeting concluded with Mussolini sending a General Scaroni and one hundred engineers and mechanics to establish an Italian aircraft factory at Nanchang, China, to assemble Italian planes. After the arrival of the Italians, with no continued official support from the United States for the Jouett mission, the influence of the American aviators faded. Jouett was soon to return home, but several Americans remained at the Hangchow school now run by the Chinese. It was this group that Billy MacDonald and Luke Williamson had joined after the Stateside disbandment of the "Flying Trapeze" in the summer of 1936.

By the time Chennault arrived in Nanking, the Italians had a firm grip not only on the Chinese Air Force but the Chinese aviation market as well. Chinese orders for Italian military planes and supplies totaled millions of dollars, which helped finance Mussolini's expanding aircraft industry. But unlike the German mission to China, which trained crack Chinese ground troops, the Italians did all they could to aid their own cause at the expense of China and the Chinese Air Force. Yet the Italians delighted the Chinese with their flowery courtesy and colorful uniforms, which they displayed everywhere. Even General Scaroni, bedecked with medals and shiny gold braid, would tour the city in his open black limousine. This pompous ceremony impressed the Chinese more than had the businesslike conduct of the American predecessors. But other than their flamboyant entertainment, the Italians did little to benefit the Chinese Air Force. Under their direction a flying school at Loyang on the Yellow River graduated every single Chinese cadet who managed to survive the training program. It was a direct contrast to the American system of weeding out incompetents early in the training program and graduating only those who possessed leadership and genuine flying ability. Since most cadets were drawn from the affluent families of Chinese society, it was frequently a source of embarrassment to the Generalissimo when he received protests from the parents and relatives of a cadet who had washed out at the Jouett school.

The Generalissimo therefore was relieved of this social awkwardness by the Italian 100 percent graduation method and ill-advisedly allowed it to persist. It solved his social problems but almost wrecked the Chinese Air Force. To make matters worse, the Italian aircraft factory at Nanchang turned out inferior fighters and bombers. The Fiat fighters were a firetrap and the Savoia-Marchetti bombers were obsolete at the time of their manufacture. The Italians also initiated the unheard-of practice of carrying on the roster all planes regardless of their condition of airworthiness or even their continuing existence. No plane was ever dropped from the official roster for any reason. It made for an impressive air force on paper, but no one knew the true status of its combat readiness.

Chennault ascertained that the official Chinese Air Force roster listed five hundred planes, but he found only ninety-one fit for combat. It was no accident that just before war between China and Japan began in earnest, the Italians tried to influence the Chinese to buy no more combat planes but to confine their purchases to trainers instead. Later Mussolini became the first person officially to suggest that China accept Japan's peace terms. It was all part of his game plan.

It was while Chennault was inspecting the Italian flying school at Loyang on July 7, 1937, that the Marco Polo Bridge Incident occurred on the outskirts of Peiping. China would now be unavoidably and totally committed to war with Japan. Chennault wired the Generalissimo immediately to offer his services in any capacity. Two days later he received this reply: "Your voluntary offer of services gratefully accepted. Proceed to Nanchang. Direct final combat training fighter groups there."

Combat training at Nanchang was a nightmare for Chennault. The only pleasant memories he later related were those few moments that he spent each evening with Gen. Mow Pang Tsu drinking cold beer and eating iced watermelon to wash down the choking dust churned up on the airfields during the day's hectic training activities. General Mow had been in charge of the air force in Nanchang prior to Chennault's arrival and though they disagreed on many things, they became good friends. General Mow had been trained in Russia and was a most capable pilot. There were three fighter groups supposedly ready for combat stationed at Nanchang. The first group was equipped with Curtiss Hawk-3 biplane dive bombers and the second with Hawk-2 biplanes. The third group consisted of two squadrons of Fiats and one squadron of Boeing P-26s.

The latter proved to be excellent combat planes. The Chinese pilots consisted of several American-born Cantonese pilots and some graduates of Colonel Jouett's Hangchow school. All these were excellent masters of their machines. The rest were mostly Italian-trained on the 100 percent graduation principle at Loyang and were an absolute menace to aviation. As Chennault pushed for combat readiness, some of the latter group would spin in doing basic maneuvers in trainers and kill themselves. There were as many as five crack-ups a day in taxi accidents alone.

As General Mow, Billy MacDonald, and Chennault struggled to train combat pilots, the Generalissimo sat silently in his summer capital high in the mountains off the western shore of Po Yang Lake. Here he pondered the fate of China. The tempo of war was beginning to quicken. Like a good poker player, he was examining his hand. China was still divided. He lacked the complete support of dissident warlords and other representatives of China's far-flung masses. Should China attempt to make a stand against the invading Japanese? If so, he must unite all China for this supreme effort. And since China had never been united before, one can appreciate the gravity of Chiang's situation. Though China possessed the highest ranking admiral in the world, who took precedence at all world naval gatherings, it actually had no navy with the exception of a few gunboats, which was scarcely a force to contend with the mighty Japanese armada. Here China could only expect complete and rapid annihilation. His German-trained army of about eighty thousand was well-equipped, complete with goose-step, and while ample for maintaining order among ambitious warlords, it was no match for the vast mechanized Japanese Army with its inexhaustible supply of men and materials. This left him with an air force not yet five years old and of dubious strength.

General Mow and Chennault were summoned to the Generalissimo's summer quarters for a conference with him and Madame Chiang. They flew to Chiuchiang at the foot of the mountains and then hired sedan chairs for the long trip up the rocky slopes to Kuling. This was to be Chennault's first meeting with the Generalissimo. As Claire observed the seriousness of Mow's expression and the steady flow of sweat from his brow, he felt that the general must have some inkling of what lay ahead.

The Generalissimo spoke no English, so as Madame Chiang introduced them he smiled and shook hands with Chennault, Western fashion. He then turned to General Mow and in crisp staccato Chinese began to question him regarding the Chinese Air Force. Remember, the Generalissimo had paid dearly for his Italian-trained air force, having practically financed the recent expansion of the Italian Air Force as a result. He now asked General Mow had many planes in the Chinese Air Force were ready for combat. Madame Chiang translated for Chennault. "Ninety-one, Your Excellency," Mow replied, as he stood at rigid attention, eyes staring straight ahead. Chennault later recalled, "Chiang turned turkey red, and I thought he was going to explode. The Generalissimo strode up and down the terrace loosing long strides of sibilant Chinese that seemed to hiss, coil, and strike like a snake."

Suddenly Madame Chiang stopped translating and the color drained from Mow's face. "He has threatened to execute him," she whispered to Chennault.

After a while the Generalissimo's anger subsided somewhat, and he turned to Chennault and asked in Chinese, "What does your survey show?"

Madame Chiang interpreted as Chennault replied, "General Mow's figures are correct." Upon Madame Chiang's urging him to tell the whole truth, Chennault continued for the next twenty minutes to enlighten the Generalissimo concerning the true condition of his air force. The meeting ended with three results: Best of all, Mow retained his head. Madame Chiang obtained the necessary authority to oppose remaining dissidents within the government's Aero Commission. Finally, Chennault earned for himself a reputation for frankness and honesty. From then on, the Generalissimo always let Chennault have his way once he was convinced that it would help the war effort. Later he even allowed Chennault to deal directly with his archenemies the Chinese Communists when Chennault felt it was necessary to rescue downed American pilots and obtain information on targets.

The Generalissimo returned to Nanking, having concluded that he should continue his policy of minimum compromises with the threatening Japanese. He felt he should stall for time as long as possible to build up his air defenses and wait for United States intervention, which he felt would surely come. It was not a very popular policy.

Upon returning to Nanking, the Generalissimo again summoned Chennault for a meeting. Upon arriving there, Chennault noticed the acute quickening in the pulse of the city. Vendors were hawking gas masks in the streets. Public buildings and buses were being camouflaged. Students were demonstrating and newspaper headlines heralded the message, "Stand and fight. An end to compromise." But most important of all, the leaders and warlords of every Chinese province were arriving in Nanking to seek audiences with the Generalissimo. One at a time, these powerful and often dissident leaders approached the Generalissimo and spoke their minds. W. H. Donald and Chennault were the only foreigners at a historic conference of Chinese leaders held at the Nanking Military Academy, ironically the same building where the Japanese would sign the formal surrender eight years later. The Chinese leaders' decision was unanimous. They called on Chiang to "Lead us against the Japanese and we pledge our troops and loyalty for the duration of the war." For the first time in modern history, China stood united. The conference lasted until August 6, 1937, and at its conclusion the Generalissimo spoke briefly, promising that China would compromise no more. The die was cast. They would fight to the death.

The Chinese Air Force was ordered north to Kaifeng near a key railroad junction on the Yellow River where heavy fighting was expected when the Japanese pushed south. The broad Yellow River was the only natural barrier across the open flat country between the invading Japanese to the north in Manchuria and the Chinese capital of Nanking to the south.

Chennault was preparing for this move when he received word from Madame Chiang to meet her in Chiuchiang, where she would stop briefly on her way from Kuling to Nanking. All his clothing had already been sent to Kaifeng, and when he met her he was clad in a polo shirt and shorts. She informed him that she had been advised that the Japanese attack would occur at Shanghai instead of on the Yellow River at Kaifeng as expected. The Generalissimo's crack German-trained troops were already marching to Shanghai to intercept the invaders. Her instructions to Chennault were to hasten to Shanghai to warn American officials that an attack on Shanghai was imminent. The Generalissimo's personal plane and pilot were made available and Chennault was flown to Nanking where he continued via train on to Shanghai. As he left Nanking, Chennault noticed a flood of Japanese civilians fleeing for Shanghai all along the Yangtze River to get under the protection of the Japanese guns before the fighting started.

Arriving at Shanghai, Chennault quickly purchased suitable attire for his visit to the embassy with money given him by Madame Chiang during their Chiuchiang meeting. It consisted of the standard foreigner's uniform, a white suit and shoes. He then hurried to the American Consulate and after having been kept waiting an hour, he was finally permitted to see some minor functionary who was not impressed at all with Chennault's urgent message. He assured him that there would be no war. Didn't he know that all skirmishes heretofore had been in the north? he asked Chennault.

In dismay, Chennault wandered down to the China National Aviation Corps offices and tried again. There he spoke to his old aerobatic instructor from Texas, Ernie Allison and another fellow by the name of H. M. Bixby. They were both highly amused but did offer permission for Chennault to recruit from their pilots should war erupt. But of course it wouldn't, they thought. By now, Chennault was wondering if Madame Chiang could be wrong. Still, he continued on to the Fourth U.S. Marine barracks to warn the commandant. Colonel Buck was polite but firm—there would be no war, he said. By now Chennault had lost his sense of urgency since only one foreigner had taken heed to his warnings. This was the Swedish minister, Baron Beck-fries, who did warn his Swedish legation.

By Wednesday Chennault was watching Japanese warships arrive in the harbor and noted that still no one seemed excited. That night Chennault took the eighty-mile trip back to Nanking by train, wondering if the trip had really been necessary. His doubts vanished, however, when about halfway to Nanking, his train was stopped and all civilians evicted. He watched as the train was quickly loaded with Chinese soldiers and sent back to Shanghai. Several more trains were likewise commandeered before Chennault could find one that was allowed to continue to Nanking.

His delay in returning caused Madame Chiang such concern for his safety that she sent Billy MacDonald to Shanghai in a two-seater Douglas to find her new air advisor and bring him back. Billy had landed on the outskirts of Shanghai the morning after Chennault had departed by train. Before his plane had completed its roll-out, the field manager ran up to Billy waving his arms. "Get out of here with that plane!" he yelled. "We killed a Jap officer and a soldier on the field last night. Fighting has begun in the city."

Instead of taking off, however, Billy borrowed the field manager's car and drove towards Shanghai. Along the way he noticed the city's Chinese quarters were deserted. He drove around the center of the city looking for Chennault and saw throngs of Chinese storming the international and foreign concessions seeking safety. Failing to find Chennault in all the turmoil, he returned to the field and flew back to Nanking only to report him missing just before Chennault walked into Madame Chiang's office.

On Friday night, August 13, there was an important war council meeting at Nanking Military Academy. Chennault and Donald were again present, off to one side with Madame Chiang interpreting. The Japanese threat to the city of Shanghai forced the war council to consider the fighting in the north to be of secondary importance. Shanghai was the key city of all China and the doorway to the rich Yellow and Yangtze river delta and to the industrial shipping thoroughfares into and out of inland China. The Chinese had fought the Japanese to a stalemate in Shanghai in 1931, and the Chinese leaders now felt that they actually had a better chance against the Japanese there in the city rather than on the northern plains where the foot soldiers of the Chinese infantry would be up against the highly mobile tanks and armored cars of the Japanese. Their only hope against the rapidly advancing Japanese motorized army in the north would be to hold the south bank of the wide Yellow River. To accomplish this, they had only their relatively small army of poorly equipped foot soldiers. Should they be defeated in this effort, and most probably they would be, all of China would be left virtually unprotected. So the Chinese leaders preferred the attack to occur at Shanghai.

A messenger came in and handed the Generalissimo a note which he read silently. He then handed it to Madame Chiang and began to speak to the council. Madame Chiang read the note in English to Chennault and Donald. Then she burst into tears. "They are shelling the Shanghai Civic Center. They are killing our people . . . They are killing our people," she said.

"What will you do now?" Chennault asked her.

She brushed away her tears, threw back her head and replied, "We will fight."

When Chiang finished his speech, the meeting broke up, and they all hurried away to make final preparations for war. The air force, which had previously been ordered to the Yellow River, was hastily returning to Nanking. The next day would be Saturday, August 14, 1937, a date destined to be known around the world as Shanghai's "Black Saturday." Madame Chiang asked Chennault how they should deploy the air force in the defense of Shanghai. Without hesitation he recommended that they coordinate high and low dive-bombing attacks upon the Japanese warships in the harbor which were providing their infantry with heavy artillery support.

Madame Chiang was suddenly confronted with the stark reality that she had no one, not a single person in the Chinese Air Force, with the experience necessary to plan and organize a military mission of this magnitude. She asked Chennault to take over, a decision she never regretted. He was the man. Now was the time and here was the opportunity. After twenty years of practicing war, after all the classroom debates and clashes with his superiors over how an aerial war should be waged, Chennault now found himself in control of an air force and planning his first combat mission against a real, fire-breathing enemy.

At the Chinese Air Force headquarters, the midnight oil burned until 4 A.M. as Billy and Claire prepared for their first real combat engagement. They had only the vaguest knowledge of the two opposing forces. Poring over the maps of the area, they discussed tactics, and Chennault concluded that he should deploy the dive bombers against the Japanese cruisers and the light bombers against the Japanese naval headquarters on board the heavy cruiser *Idzumo*. He knew that the *Idzumo* was anchored near the Japanese consulate next to the International Settlement because he had personally seen it.

Chinese pilots, prior to coming under Chennault's command, had been trained by the book in a specific method of bombing. They were taught to fly at a fixed airspeed and a specific altitude before releasing their bombs. Under such controlled circumstances, they performed rather well, but Chennault remembered the fiasco on the beaches of Hawaii many years before when he had introduced a note of realism to coastal artillery gunners who were firing under controlled conditions. When his pursuit planes appeared unexpectedly, the coordinated activity of the gunners completely fell apart. It was the possibility of encounters with the unexpected that worried Chennault regarding his combat-green Chinese Air Force. He specifically instructed them not even to fly over the International Settlement in approaching the *Idzumo* on their bomb run.

Unfortunately, there was a low cloud cover over Shanghai the morning of the attack. Confronted with this problem, the flight leader chose to make a shallow dive through the overcast rather than abort this important mission. The shallow dive increased the forward speed of the advancing bombers, and the low ceiling forced them to fly at fifteen hundred feet, rather than their accustomed bomb-run altitude of 7,500 feet. With the increase in speed and the unaccustomed low altitude, things began to go wrong fast. The spotting of the prized *Idzumo* after descending through the low overcast distracted the attention of the young crew members from such matters as adjusting their bomb sights for the new speed and altitude. In addition, they were flying directly over the International Settlement. The released bombs fell short of the *Idzumo* and smack dab into the middle of the International Settlement. Two eleven hundred-pound bombs landed on the main thoroughfare, which was crowded with people, but only one exploded. That single bomb blast killed almost a thousand people and injured many more. The extent of destruction caused by a single bomb in the center of a crowded city should have been a warning to the world. But it made only brief headlines and was quickly forgotten by all but the survivors. There was no damage to the *Idzumo* that day—only to the United States cruiser *Augusta,* which sustained some shattered glass.

That same morning Chennault had risen early after only a few hours of sleep and had decided to fly from Nanking as a "neutral observer" in an unarmed fighter plane to watch the aerial attack on Shanghai. Flying down the Yangtze River, he too had encountered lowering ceilings and rainstorms and had just about decided to turn back when he spotted six Chinese dive bombers regrouping after a bomb run over an unidentified warship. Noting that the ship was under full steam, white waves breaking off her bow, he could see the tiny flashes of machine-gun fire winking along her gray decks, still being fired at the passing planes. By the time Chennault could descend in an effort to identify the vessel, it began to belch a protective smoke screen, so he flew low and approached from below the smoke screen, astern of the ship. To his surprise he got an even closer look at the flashing machine guns, which were now trained on him, and also saw a huge Union Jack painted on her afterdeck. On his return flight he counted the bullet holes in his wings. Those limeys were mad. Back at Nanking he showed the bullet holes to C. B. Smith and his armament specialist, Rolfe Watson, and said, "Get some guns on this ship and get 'em in a hurry." His neutral observer days were over. The next time someone shot at him, he was going to shoot back.

On Saturday, August 14, 1937, Japanese bombers from northern Formosa annihilated the Hangchow Flying School just south of Shanghai. They beat their chests in victory and then boasted to the world that the capital city of Nanking would be next. They warned foreign diplomats in Nanking to evacuate. A typhoon swept the skies clear of enemy planes over Shanghai on Sunday, August 15, so that city was spared the ravages of war at least for one day.

The American State Department wanted to make sure that there were no American citizens involved in what might become an international incident since the United States was technically at peace with Japan. Consequently, they ordered all American citizens in China to evacuate the combat zones, and by the time the first air alert sounded over Nanking, U.S. Navy gunboats were waiting at the city's waterfront to evacuate the Americans.

Like hounds about to bay, American newspapermen from Shanghai converged on Chennault's "headquarters" at Nanking to witness the Japanese bombing of the city. After lunch, Chennault led the gathering to his observation post atop the Metropolitan Hotel. From this high point the observers were afforded a panoramic view of the ancient city. Nanking stretched out below them as a homogeneous pattern of gray structures punctuated by a green turf airfield just beyond the city walls. Near the foot of the nearby purple mountains was the gleaming white tomb of Dr. Sun Yat-sen. It was a hot stale summer day with thin clouds hanging over the city at five thousand feet. Hidden from the view of the spectators, at about ten thousand feet, was a circling ambush patrol of Chinese fighters buzzing like angry bees, waiting for the approach of enemy bombers.

Presently, they spotted eighteen Japanese twin-engine single-tail bombers approaching the city from the north but well below the five-thousand-foot overcast. The drone of the thirty-six heavy engines grew louder and louder as the bomber formation came nearer the city. There was little evidence of any of the city's residents taking cover. Most simply stared upwards in curiosity or amazement as the bombers appeared overhead. The bombers broke formation and in single file descended to an altitude below two thousand feet and machine-gunned and strafed the defenseless city below. It was an awesome sight, seeing the tracers arch in all directions as one by one each bomber paraded across the city and then turned to bomb the empty airfield. The bombers passed so close to Chennault and his rooftop observers that they could plainly see the blood-red meatballs painted on the wings, an insignia which appeared so immense when first encountered, as many American airmen would soon find out.

After the last plane had released its bombs over the empty

airfield, they all climbed through the overcast and disappeared from view completely unmolested. Not a single Japanese fighter had escorted the bombers. This suggested to Chennault that the Japanese also subscribed to General Douhet's theory about the invincibility of the modern bomber. He took careful note.

The newspapermen were visibly disappointed. This was it? This was what they had traveled all the way from Shanghai to witness? While Chennault was trying to explain how the low ceiling over the city had hidden the bombers' approach from the circling Chinese fighters, he was interrupted by the sound of machine-gun fire overhead. Ding hao! Contact had been made.

By the time the party had descended to the lobby of the hotel, all the telephones were ringing. The Chinese Air Force was claiming seven Japanese bombers shot down. The newsmen were skeptical, so they followed Chennault to the airfield beyond the city where they all saw, in the distance, three separate columns of black smoke rising from the crashed wreckage of Japanese bombers. With this tangible bit of evidence, all the newsmen hurried back to Shanghai to file their stories.

Chennault continued in the direction of the smoke columns. He wanted to ascertain the complete effectiveness of his Chinese fighter defense. Delightfully, he counted . . . four, five, six . . . eight smouldering wrecks for a verified total of eight enemy bombers shot down that day by the Chinese fighter pilots.

This convinced Chennault of the vulnerability of bomber formations devoid of fighter protection and of the decisive role he had conceived for the pursuit plane in air combat. As he surveyed the wrecked bombers, he was also convinced of the effectiveness of his warning net. The warning net, which was put into effect in late July with the help of an Australian communications engineer named Austin Malley, was simply the same type of net used by Chennault back at Maxwell Field, Alabama. It consisted of trained spotters who utilized a system of telephone and telegraph facilities in the Shanghai-Hangchow-Nanking triangle. It proved to be invaluable, providing ample warning of approaching enemy aircraft to allow time for the Chinese pilots to warm up their fighters and climb to the altitude necessary for interception. The greatest predicament imaginable for a pursuit pilot is being caught on the ground, where he is totally useless in defense of his territory.

Though inflicting some damage to the unprotected city by machine-gun fire, the Japanese bombers for the most part had only served to drop their bombs on an empty airfield whose forewarned fighters were already lurking in ambush. Caught with their pants down in overconfidence, the Japanese had made the costly mistake of underestimating their enemy, a mistake never attributed to Chennault. He knew his foe, having closely studied their tactical moves as well as their implements of war. He had taught his students about the vulnerability of Japanese bombers and how to fire their guns in such a way as to strike the engines, gas tanks, and wing roots at close range, thus making every precious round of ammunition count. He taught them the "Flying Trapeze" principle of three fighters concentrating on a single bomber, one attacking from above, one from below, and the third holding back in reserve to press home for the final coup de grâce.

After their first air defeat over Nanking, it took a few days for the Japanese to figure out what was happening. Old habits are hard to break, so they sent their bombers back on three occasions within the next few days. As a result there were forty more wrecked Japanese bombers left smouldering in China while an unknown number of others crashed in the Formosa Straits trying to return to their base.

It was no doubt about this time that the Japanese strategists gathering around the conference tables in Formosa attempted the pronunciation of the French name Chennault. At any rate it was the last of their unescorted daylight bombing raids in China. If the American Eighth Air Force in Europe had heeded this lesson, the air war over Germany later would have been a different story. For when Hermann Goering looked up over embattled Berlin and saw American bombers being escorted by fighters all the way to their targets and back, he knew the war was over in Germany.

After the Japanese collected their thoughts for three days and contemplated their recent losses of fifty-four bombers, they decided to try night bombing. Quickly Chennault countered by relocating all the antiaircraft artillery and the huge Sperry searchlights around the capital. He arranged the searchlights in a grid pattern covering all approaches to the city. As a bomber approached the periphery of the city at night, a searchlight would pick it up and simply pass it along to the next light, which in turn would hand it off to the next. And so it would continue all along the path of the bomber. Bombers were poorly equipped for night flying, and even more so for night bombing. Japanese pilots were often blinded by the searchlights and unable to see downward. This was what Chennault had anticipated, so he taught his fighter pilots to attack from below, from which direction the bombers were defenseless.

In a way, this was a reverse corollary of the attack-out-of-the-sun (or the World War I "Hun in the sun") principle, which was utilized during the day. Bombers were thus vulnerable to both the calculated attacks of the Chinese fighter pilots in the air and the antiaircraft fire of the artillery on the ground. It is very likely that Chennault himself actively participated in the perfecting of this technique, and it is almost certain that he personally tested the effectiveness of his entire system before teaching it to his Chinese pilots through an interpreter. (Chennault spoke little Chinese at this early date.) Some pilots managed to pick it up quickly. Using these tactics, one young man shot down three bombers on his first and second nights of combat.

Like a child upset at the loss of his marbles in a game of "keeps," the Japanese resorted to making official demands to the United States that all American airmen leave China. When word reached Chennault of action being taken by the State Department to comply, Chennault wrote in his diary, "I guess I am Chinese."

Subsequent requests from the consul general in Shanghai for his departure were met with little response by Chennault, and as a result he was ultimately threatened with arrest and deportation. He responded by saying that he would be happy to leave China when the last "Jap" had departed. In this matter the Chinese bureaucracy and red tape for once actually came to his aid. All attempts by United States officials in Shanghai to reach Chennault simply never made it through Chinese channels.

For example, on his way to the airfield one day, Chennault was stopped abruptly by a Chinese armed guard and asked for his papers, which the guard very carefully scrutinized. This was unusual, since by this time Chennault was well known by the local Chinese authorities in Nanking. What was even more unusual was that this same procedure was repeated every hundred yards until he finally reached his office. Thoroughly vexed and bewildered, Chennault dispatched his interpreter to the Chinese authorities to find out what was going on. Late that afternoon the exhausted interpreter returned stating that he had had to go all the way to the Generalissimo before he could find anyone with an answer. It seems that the troops were stationed along his path to prevent him from being "molested by foreigners." He later learned it was his omnipresent friend, H. W. Donald, who had contrived this bit of Oriental red tape when he learned of the intentions of the United States officials in Shanghai to deport him. Donald just wanted to make sure the United States sheriff in Shanghai would have difficulty getting to him to serve him with the warrant, and it worked.

Though some of the local American officials in Nanking, such as Ambassador Nelson Johnson, knew Chennault's true identity and whereabouts, they managed to look the other way officially. When a delicate situation did arise, however, it was handled very gently. It was a rather small world around Nanking for the local foreign contingents. They naturally frequented similar places such as the hotels and country clubs that catered to foreign guests.

Chennault and his entourage lived at the Nanking Country Club where Ambassador Johnson frequently dined with other foreign dignitaries. On one such occasion Nelson was dining with the Russian and Italian ambassadors when Chennault, Billy MacDonald, Rolfe Watson, C. B. Smith, and Harry Sutter (Chennault's Swiss radio expert) strolled through the lobby on the way to their quarters after a day at the airfield. There is little doubt that these adventuresome five would have gone unnoticed.

"Who are those men?" asked the Italian ambassador.

"They look like Russians to me," replied Johnson, whereupon the Russian dropped his fork.

"They are *not* Russians. I know all the Russians in Nanking. They are definitely not Russians."

Chennault dined with Johnson and the other members of the embassy staff on many occasions, but officially he was always "somewhere in the interior."

Word reached Chennault that in America it was rumored that his official disappearance in China was due to his having assumed an alias. This infuriated him, so in September 1937 he wrote an open letter to his "Maxwell Field Friends" through the medium of the *Montgomery Advertiser* to let them know where he stood. He assured them he could always be addressed by his real name and proceeded to give vent to his feelings regarding American indifference towards China in her hour of need. He also stated that the war would soon come home to the United States and that China's fight would surely become "our own."

In October, the city of Nanking once again heard the unsettling sound of approaching Japanese bombers, and Chennault was quick to note that they were now being escorted by no less than twenty-seven of their finest Type 96 (Nate) fighters, which proceeded to shoot down eleven of the sixteen defending Chinese fighters. The Japanese' abrupt about-face from the Douhet theory allowed their bombers to do their job and return home without sustaining any losses. This willingness to change tactics as the result of the lessons of war, plus their superior numbers and better weapons, turned the tide of air victories in favor of the Japanese. Chennault watched as his "Three Men on a Flying Trapeze" tactic was reduced to only two and then finally one, and thus back to the World War I one-to-one tactic as the Chinese fighters began to disappear from the sky over the Yangtze Valley. With the continued presence of fighter escorts on all subsequent bomber raids, Chennault knew that Nanking's days were numbered and possibly even those of the Kuomintang government as well.

By now the Japanese had a firm grip upon China's coast as far south as Hong Kong. The naval blockade finally squeezed the life out of any hopes for continued supplies or help from the outside world. Within a few weeks, the last Chinese fighter and bomber squadrons would be eliminated from the Chinese skies. With inferior planes and training, and now without any hope of replacements, the Chinese Air Force was doomed. The Japanese sent a hundred planes a day back and forth to Nanking while down below their foot soldiers continued their steady march toward the capital.

During the twilight period of the Chinese air defense, Madame Chiang Kai-shek repeatedly went to the airfield at Nanking to help bolster the confidence of her young pilots. She knew every plane and pilot. She served hot tea and talked with them. She watched them fly off to fight against the ever increasing odds, stayed through the long wait for their return, and felt the shock and sorrow at the inevitably diminished numbers. She saw the sadness in the faces of the survivors and listened intently and with compassion to their stories.

Not all casualties were inflicted by the enemy, however. For example, on one occasion following a night dive-bombing mission, she waited at the airfield in the early morning, delighted to see the return of all eleven planes and pilots previously dispatched. But to her horror, she witnessed the proficiency of the students from the Italian 100 percent graduation school at Loyang. The weather was perfect, but the first plane overshot the runway and crashed, followed by the second, which ground-looped and burned. The third plane landed safely, but the fourth crashed into the fire truck that was racing towards the second burning plane. A total of five of the planes wrecked on landing and four pilots were killed. Madame Chiang wept bitterly.

Just before the outbreak of fighting in Shanghai, the Curtiss-Wright people exhibited their latest model at Nanking. The "Hawk Special" was a fast, trim monoplane export version of the later Air Corps P-36. "I fell in love with the Hawk Special the first time I flew it and asked Madame Chiang to buy it for my personal plane. She paid Curtiss-Wright fifty-five thousand dollars for the plane," Chennault said.

In this plane he applied his first air combat fighter tactics and learned lessons which would later save the lives of many American fighter pilots. One such lesson was that a Chinese pilot should not try to turn inside a Japanese lightweight maneuverable monoplane fighter. The Japanese sacrificed everything for maneuverability. They considered combat aircraft to be expendable and expected a short combat life. They depended on total replacement of aircraft from home production rather than trying to repair major combat damage in the field. In air combat over the Yangtze, Chennault was able to compare Chinese and Japanese aircraft effectively and also compare his own fighter tactics with those of the enemy. The Hawk Special sacrificed maneuverability for firepower, durability, and diving speed. This distinction between the fighter planes of the two countries persisted throughout the war.

To close the gap in maneuverability, Chennault removed all the nonessential hardware from his Hawk Special. There were no air-to-ground communications in China in 1937, so he removed the heavy radio equipment from the compartment behind the pilot's headrest. The void left was used by Chennault for his personal things such as his bedroll. Stripped down, the Hawk became the fastest plane in China. It was used extensively for reconnaissance not only by Chennault but also by Billy MacDonald, and General Mow. The Hawk provided the means for such excellent reconnaissance on enemy activity that a Japanese fighter group based near Shanghai became dedicated to its destruction. They spotted it many times, but the Hawk remained elusive and always returned to base, though this was frequently not true in the case of its pursuer.

The Hawk Special was finally damaged beyond repair. It did not happen in combat, but through an accident on the runway at Nanking. An American test pilot was taxiing it out to a strip for a test flight after repairing holes in the cowling that had been caused by machine-gun fire. The Hawk did a ground loop, and the resulting damage was too extensive to repair, much to Chennault's disappointment.

As enemy ground troops neared Nanking, Japanese planes bombed and strafed the city relentlessly. Every morning at the hotel breakfast room, conversation would begin with, "I wonder when they'll come in today?" The city's merchants tried to anticipate the times of the air strikes so that they could plan on doing business before and after them.

Early on one such morning in October 1937, merchants were as usual trying to conduct their business before the morning air raid. Nanking streets and businesses were crowded. From all appearances it was a normal day. Then came the sound of the German-made air raid siren. Frightened residents rushed into the crowded streets which quickly swelled with the surge of humanity as people searched frantically for bomb shelters throughout the city. The mass of people subsequently overflowed into the countryside. Some would never return. A deadly quiet then fell over the deserted city streets. The people turned their attention upward, awaiting the sound of the approaching enemy bombers.

In the stillness from his hotel rooftop, Chennault knew it was time. He summoned his crew, and they raced through the deserted streets of Nanking towards the airfield beyond the city walls—walls that would offer them no protection in the air war today.

The warning net had given the city time to prepare. They passed through streets normally filled with bustling activity but which now seemed eerie due to the absence of the clanging ricksha bells, shouting coolies, and countless bicycles zig-zagging through crowded pedestrian traffic. Only the rich blend of aromas from the curbside restaurants, the vendors' steaming noodles, and the sweetshops' sticky candy remained as evidence of the recent inhabitants. They sped by silken banners fluttering in the breeze, announcing bargain sales to empty streets. Chennault briefly heard in passing, the cacophonous blare of Chinese music as it filtered into the street through the closed shutters of a shop, the wound-up phonograph nearing its last revolution.

Arriving at the airfield, he was greeted by the staccato sound of aircraft engines, one by one, coughing to full throttle. The few remaining Chinese fighters skeltered for takeoff. Chennault sped directly to his Hawk Special, engine held at idle by a solemn-faced Chinese mechanic anxiously watching for his arrival.

Just then the second ching pao air raid alarm warning of the approaching bombers was sounded by bugles, bells, gongs, and sirens —anything handy that could be used to relate the urgency of the situation. Chinese civilians strained to hear the faint drone of the approaching bombers, which steadily increased its volume as the city quivered in anticipation, all eyes searching the sky. Each minute passed slowly for the people below.

Flak bursts pinpointed the location of the distant bombers in the sky, divulging the route of their approach to the city. The sound of battle built to a crescendo. Outnumbered Chinese fighters engaged the Japanese armada as dogfights broke out to the sound of flak bursts all over the sky.

A Japanese fighter plane, its pilot shot through the head, his dead body locking the controls of his doomed ship, looped over and over until it struck the ground. Chinese antiaircraft guns pumped flak into a string of bombers erasing two in puffs of smoke as fuel and bombs exploded, leaving a void in the formation which continued on course. A flak burst directly beneath the tail of another bomber flipped it over on its back, dislodging both engines as fire exploded along its wings. As the crewmen bailed out, two of their chutes were burning and, like falling comets, they streamed to the earth. American movie photographers on the ground recorded the events for American moviegoers.

Chennault and his stripped-down Hawk pressed attack after attack, proving more than a match for the aggressive and cocky Japanese fighter pilots. Vastly outnumbered, the Chinese pilots were simply swatted down like annoying flies one by one, falling to earth and leaving telltale streams of black smoke pointing to the place of impact. They were simply no match for the nimble Type 96 Japanese fighters.

Chennault watched the bombers turn and knew that their bombs had been dropped. He looked beneath them as bits of China exploded into the air, marking each bomb's deadly impact with the earth. Fires started in the stricken city and were quickly windswept into an inferno being fed by bamboo and wooden structures. More bombers released their bombs and turned in formation, and there was more death and destruction below as the burning city belched flame and smoke beneath the path of the bombers. As exploded bits and pieces of China slowly drifted back to earth through the choking clouds of rising smoke, the whine of a single siren sounded the all clear.

Back on the ground, Chennault removed his bedroll from the empty radio compartment of his Hawk Special. Wearily he returned to his quarters through the smouldering city. He found little encouragement in the fighting. On many occasions, such as the present one, he had been discouraged, disgusted, and ready to quit, but always he somehow managed to persevere.

He was personally well prepared for this kind of combat. For the most part it was the Oriental customs that vexed him. For example, pilots refused to bail out of stricken planes because of some greater fear of losing face. Military orders required two days to execute because they had to be meticulously hand-painted character by character. He was weary of such things as trying to teach men who had never fired a weapon how to use artillery; or having to intervene in an execution by firing squad to save the life of one of his pilots who had been sentenced to death because he had disobeyed some ridiculous order. Those were needless killings, those executions. To him it seemed that the war was killing his pilots fast enough. In addition, there was the matter of time. He thought in terms of minutes and hours while the Chinese appeared to think only in terms of dynasties.

Then there were those occasions when he was forced to come to grips with the full reality of his own personal participation in this air war. On more than one occasion, for example, before going to sleep at night he spread out his bedroll taken from the Hawk's empty radio compartment behind his head and spent Japanese bullets fell from its folds.

A few remaining Northrop light bombers flying out of Canton made a gallant but over the long run feeble attempt to loosen the stranglehold of the naval blockade on China. They repeatedly bombed as far as fifty miles off the coast of China and sank a few vessels, but were systematically shot down one by one by the Japanese until they were all gone.

The Chinese Air Force was rapidly declining. Of eighty fighters that had begun the war, less than twelve remained. Most of the Chinese pilots were dead, and for the rest it was only a matter of time.

In November 1937, Chiang Kai-shek engineered a final offensive to try to drive the Japanese out of Shanghai, the results of which astounded the world. Chennault was ordered to muster all available aircraft, which he did. Even so he was able to provide only five minutes of pre-dusk bombardment over their target before the German-trained Chinese ground troops moved out into a night of wild hand-to-hand fighting. The Chinese infantry managed to drive the Japanese all the way back to the Wangpo River but lacked the reserves in men and ammunition necessary to sustain that effort, and their brief offensive failed.

Madame Chiang, rushing to the front, was critically injured when her driver, distracted by a low-flying aircraft, crashed the car into an irrigation ditch. She never fully recovered from the accident. Her injuries were so severe that she was compelled to give up most of her official duties for a while.

With the collapse of the Shanghai thrust, the Chinese knew that at best they were in for a long and bitter struggle against the Japanese. As the front collapsed and the tattered and battle-weary survivors retreated, some of the "old China hands" in the treaty ports made bets that the Sino-Japanese war would be over in three months. What they failed to take into consideration was the tenacity and sheer determination of both the Chinese people and their Generalissimo, and their capacity to endure hardships.

With the fall of Shanghai, on November 8, 1937, Chiang knew that it would be only a matter of time until he lost the entire Yangtze Valley, including the capital at Nanking. Understanding the full implications of this eventuality, he planned a systematic retreat all the way up the Yangtze River to the Szechwan basin located high in the mountains of western China. There, no invader in four thousand years had been able to penetrate. Even the invading Mongols of the great Khans were forced to bypass this natural fortress in their conquest of east Asia.

When Chennault was apprised of Chiang's plan to retreat two

thousand miles up the twisting Yangtze River to Szechwan Province, he gained new admiration for the Chinese people. He witnessed one of the most spectacular mass migrations in human history. He watched as millions of uprooted Chinese peasants, laborers, factory workers, soldiers, scholars, merchants, women, and children merged into a human stream flowing into the mountainous interior of Mother China. They traveled by every mode of transportation conceivable in the circumstances—by sampan and junk, by railroad and ricksha, and on foot. Day after day, they continued their westward journey, carrying on their backs their meager possessions and in their hearts a will to survive inspired by tales of the bravery of their defending armies.

Up from the rich delta plains they came in untold numbers, in retreat and in fear of the atrocities perpetrated by the advancing Japanese armies—atrocities which shocked the civilized world. There is no way of knowing how many countless millions died from the hardships inflicted by disease and hunger during the retreat. Yet many endured, and these survivors were the very heart and spirit of the Chinese culture. Their determination, as well as the tales of bravery they related, served to inspire the eighteen to twenty thousand Chinese that came of age every day—such were the masses.

There were two types of Chinese soldiers who participated in the war against the Japanese. Those identifiable uniformed and conventional members of the Kuomintang Army of the Generalissimo would fight the Japanese in frontal confrontations typical of all previous wars. The other faction, the Chinese Communists, would for the most part remain behind in the territories occupied by the Japanese to fight the enemy from within. They used a new type of guerrilla warfare conceived and taught so effectively by their leader Mao Tsetung. During the bitter months of battle to come, there would be much internal conflict between the Nationalist army and the Chinese Communists.

During the last days before the fall of Nanking, Chennault concentrated on dawn and dusk missions in order to prevent the further loss of men and aircraft. He singled out one fighter group and taught them a newly-contrived scheme of night dive-bombing. One night he outlined the shape and dimensions of a Japanese destroyer using lanterns placed on the Nanking airfield. He then instructed his skeptical Chinese pilots on how they could dive at a low altitude, release their bombs and effectively hit their targets—even in the night. The interpreter had to work overtime, but Chennault finally convinced them that they could do it and pull out safely. Then they headed for the Yangtze River and the Japanese ships. This was probably the world's introduction to night dive-bombing, and it proved an effective tactic almost every night until the fall of Nanking.

During the organization of the retreat up the Yangtze River to Chungking, capital of Szechwan Province, via Hankow, the Hawk Special flew constant reconnaissance missions as the primary source of reliable information regarding the advancing enemy. By early December the sounds of the approaching Japanese artillery could be heard in Nanking. Mussolini personally urged the Generalissimo to surrender to the invading Japanese, whereupon Chiang promptly expelled the Italian Aviation Mission from Chinese soil.

On December 11, 1937, just two days before the fall of Nanking, the Generalissimo personally ordered Chennault to leave the city even while remaining there himself for one additional day with the quiet stubbornness for which he was known. Chennault gathered up what few personal belongings he could stuff into the empty radio compartment of the Hawk and arrived at the bomb-cratered airfield at midnight. As he fueled his plane, he heard the incoming Japanese artillery shells bursting around the field. He coaxed the 875 horsepower Wright Cyclone radial engine to life and cautiously taxied the Hawk in the darkness to the end of the runway. There, with the engine idling and his hand resting on the throttle, he waited for the first glint of dawn to break over the city wall and light the dark runway, and as he did so, he reflected upon the situation.

The protective warning net had crumbled before the advancing vanguard of the Japanese infantry. Overhead Japanese fighters were on the prowl. The stricken city was completely defenseless and lay prostrate for the enemy as the last remnants of the Chinese armies and air force were already in retreat up the Yangtze River to Hankow. Chennault watched as a pink glow began to appear in the eastern sky as a gentle prelude to the rising sun, and he thought thoughts known only to himself. Perhaps he felt the great distance between himself and his family in Waterproof and even wondered if he should remain in China. Although the war was going badly, he had learned valuable lessons from the recent combat.

In the opening days of the war, Chennault had learned that the Japanese pilots were able, experienced, well-trained, and aggressive.

They were veterans of earlier conflicts against the Russians and against the Chinese in Manchuria. Although they were good fliers, they lacked individual initiative when confronted with the loss of their leaders, a fault which Chennault quickly learned to exploit. These Japanese airmen who had survived the air combat over the Yangtze River would later sweep victoriously over the South Pacific during 1941 and 1942 until ultimately they would be confronted in Burma by Chennault's American Volunteer Group. Here, in large part because of the lessons Chennault had learned in his early days in China, the Japanese pilots would be outflown and outfought by the AVGs.

The Japanese pilots worked together well, using their confidence, precision, and experience to develop many tricks which Chennault was able to observe. Their favorite trick was one involving three planes. One plane would fly awkwardly through space or do sloppy aerobatics in an effort to attract the attention of an adversary while the other two would lag behind hiding in the blinding sun, awaiting an opportunity for an ambush. When the unsuspecting adversary took the bait and attacked the lead plane, the two lagging planes would pounce on him, diving from an altitude advantage and busting him in the rear with concentrated machine-gun fire. Hence the spent Japanese bullets in Chennault's bedroll.

Then Chennault saw the first ray of sunlight breaking over the city wall lighting the damaged runway stretched out before him. He applied full throttle and roared over the city wall as the rising sun began to cast a blood-red color over the stricken city, perhaps a foreshadowing of the "Rape of Nanking" that soon was to follow.

During the autumn of 1937, in the aftermath of the Japanese attack on Shanghai, the Chinese turned to the major Allied powers for help. It was a time when American businessmen were selling scrap iron and aviation fuel to the Japanese. Russia was the only country to respond to China's need. Japan had been a thorn in Russia's side for twenty years due to various skirmishes along their mutual Siberian border. The Russians felt that it was in their best national interest to give aid to the Generalissimo, whom they felt represented the only real hope for mounting effective opposition to the advancing Japanese. They did this in spite of the fact that there was at the time a communist movement in China that was itself greatly in need of support. But the total amount of Russian aid in China went to the government of the Generalissimo, which was ironic since he had in 1927 successfully purged the Russian-supported Chinese Communists from the Kuomintang government, having slaughtered them by the thousands. The Chinese Communists to this day remain bitter about the purge of 1927. The Russians had no love for the Generalissimo. It was simply that at this point in time aiding him was in their best interest.

Russia gave the Generalissimo twenty million dollars in credit and four hundred combat planes along with six Russian squadrons—four fighter and two bomber squadrons completely staffed and equipped. This included antiaircraft artillery. The Russians stayed for a year and a half, until they were called back to serve at the European front in late 1939.

A supply line was opened up from the railhead in Russian Turkestan over the ancient silk caravan route through Sinkiang Province to the city of Chungking. This supply line actually carried more materials to sustain China's war effort than did the famous Burma Road. Thus the bulk of China's aid from the outbreak of war in the summer of 1937 until American involvement in 1942 came from Russia.

The Russians set up flying and artillery schools and operated a string of hostels from Hami in Sinkiang Province to Nanking. They brought along almost everything they needed, including their own guards and supplies, even their own vodka. They partook of the Chinese prostitutes. No Chinese town that had quartered Russians during this time ever complained in later years about the rowdiness of American combat personnel.

The Russian aviation mission was under the command of General Asanov, who worked in good professional harmony with Chennault and Generals Mow Pang Tsu and C. J. Chow in planning China's military operations. But the Russians kept to themselves when not on duty. The average Russian pilot was older than the average American pilot, more mature, and had never heard of combat fatigue. They could drink all night and fight all day. General Asanov enforced iron discipline on his pilots when they were standing alert duty, as opposed to the American policy of allowing pilots on alert duty to lounge and play poker in the alert shack.

The Russian pilots, on the other hand, would sit stiffly all day long in the cockpits of their fighters, which were arranged around the field in a circle. When an air raid warning sounded, they took off in all directions in a mad Russian scramble in which Chennault never failed to see at least one collision. It was an exercise which he personally never felt obliged to participate in.

The Russian combat behavior was unpredictable. Some days they just decided not to fight at all, but when they did they fought with teamwork and tenacity. Similar to the Japanese, they were overly fond of rigid air discipline, which often backfired when their leader was lost. One day there was a Russian scramble to intercept Japanese fighters which were preceding a formation of bombers. The Russian flight leader's engine was hit, and he turned out of the fight and headed back to the base. Every member of the Russian flight followed him down and landed with him just as the bombers hit the field. That day the Russians suffered their worst defeat during their stay in China.

Due to the tenacity of the Russian air defense, the Japanese generally avoided bases known to be occupied by Russians. Consequently their visits were rather infrequent over the provincial capital of Hankow during the spring of 1938, so infrequent, in fact, that to encourage them to come, a little surprise party was planned for Emperor Hirohito's birthday on April 29, 1938.

On this day the Japanese were expected to attack the base at Hankow in an effort to claim some spectacular air victory, the news of which they could present to the Emperor on his birthday. A meeting of the Russian commanders, Generals Mow and Chow, Chennault, and some of the Generalissimo's aides led to a decision to strip Hankow airfield of its fighter protection in an ostentatious departure of all fighters just at dusk on the evening of April 28. Circling the city for all to see, they made a noisy departure in the direction of Nanchang, further away from the Japanese front. As anticipated, Japanese secret agents residing in Hankow reported their departure, unaware that just before dark all the planes had turned back to Hankow, slipped in at treetop level, and quietly landed back on the airfield in complete secrecy under the cloak of darkness. Atop the tallest building in Hankow, Billy MacDonald and Chennault failed to see or hear their return. So the trap was set.

The Japanese sent fifteen bombers from Nanking up the Yangtze River toward Hankow. Along the way they picked up a larger fighter escort from their forward staging field at Wuhu, thus conserving fighter fuel since the fighters did not have the same fuel capacity and range as the bombers. Even with this precaution it would be a tight squeeze for the fighters to conserve enough fuel for limited combat over the Hankow target and still return safely to their base at Wuhu.

On this day Chennault and his cohorts planned to make it even more difficult. Twenty Chinese pilots flying Russian planes were dispatched to the southern approach of the Hankow airfield to engage the Japanese fighters as long as possible for the sole purpose of making them use up some of their precious fuel. The main Chinese force of forty Russian fighters was stationed thirty miles east of Hankow on a direct Hankow-to-Wuhu course happily doing lazy eights and waiting in ambush for the returning Japanese when their gas would be so low that they could not stay and fight.

But the Japanese swung further to the south than anticipated and successfully bombed the airfield before the Chinese fighters could intercept them. The Chinese did manage to knock down a few bombers during a brief fight before a Japanese fighter commander wiggled his wings as a signal for his comrades to head for home. Chennault chuckled as he watched them re-form and fly a direct course for Wuhu, where the Russian fighters were circling in the sun, waiting like a pack of hungry vultures. The first Russian onslaught separated the Japanese bombers from their fighters, which were so low on gas that they could not fight without burning up their remaining fuel and thus not be able to make it home.

The Japanese fighters chose to run, and so while half of the Russian fighters picked them off one at a time, the others slaughtered the bombers. Three Japanese bombers managed to return to base, but not a single fighter. Either they were chewed up by the Russian onslaught, or they ran out of gas on the way. Yet that night the Japanese radio announced that fifty-two Chinese planes had been shot down at Hankow in celebration of Hirohito's birthday.

In reality they had lost thirty-six out of thirty-nine aircraft. The Chinese had lost four pilots and nine aircraft. The Russians lost two planes and no pilots. The Russians were using China as a proving ground for their equipment and combat tactics, just as they had done earlier in Spain fighting against the Germans and Italians. Squadrons were rotated every six months to spread experience throughout the Red Air Force.

Very early in the war Chennault was astounded by the fact that he could tear the aluminum skin of the incredibly lightly-constructed

Japanese fighters with his bare fingers. Japanese manufacturers placed the greatest emphasis upon maneuverability, which necessarily meant a sacrifice in armor protection and firepower. Without self-sealing fuel tanks, the Japanese fighters were easily destroyed once they received concentrated bursts of gunfire. They were unable to sustain much punishment without tearing apart. With this in mind, Chennault taught Chinese pilots the difference between Japanese fighters and their own aircraft, emphasizing the strength of the latter's heavy, braced wings. He believed that to lock wings with an enemy fighter and then apply full throttle would tear off the wing of the lighter aircraft. He no doubt tried this successfully himself before mentioning it to his students. Unfortunately, the first student to try this tactic used it on a Japanese bomber when he ran out of ammunition and tore off his own wing and sliced off his tail. This resulted in a spin from which he barely managed to recover before hitting the ground. The next morning he reported to Chennault with a big patch over one eye whereupon Chennault proceeded to explain that he must be careful in choosing his opponent for this tactic, avoiding heavy bombers, for example.

Several Chinese pilots used the ramming technique, successfully shearing off the wings of Japanese fighters with little damage to their own. The Russians took to it like ducks to water, particularly since their short-ranged machine guns made it necessary to get within fifty feet of a target anyway. They later became famous for the successful use of this technique against the Germans, yet the idea germinated during their tenure in China. With the development of the metal propeller, the Russians altered their procedure and used it to chew off the tail of enemy aircraft later in the war against Germany, employing the Bell P-39 Air Cobra.

Russian bombers made the first raid on Formosa in May 1938, shortly after Chinese pilots in Martin B-10 bombers earned the honor of being the first Allied pilots over Japan in February 1938.

The final battle over Hankow took its toll on Chinese pilots and aircraft to the point that Madame Chiang began to consider the flood of offers from foreign pilots to aid China's cause. The idea of a foreign air legion in China had been fermenting for a long time. It was first considered at the time of the first Japanese attack in 1931, but was opposed by Jouett on the grounds that it would hinder the development of a sound and independent Chinese Air Force. Now in the fall of 1938 Chennault opposed it in theory on the same grounds. But since he was desperate to maintain some semblance of a Chinese Air Force, and since a group of Vultee bombers had just been delivered by salesman Bill Pawley, he decided to give it a try. These new bombers had a range of over two thousand miles, and Chennault hoped to use them to extend his offensive to the Japanese ships off the coast of China.

So he began the difficult task of selecting good pilots for his new International Squadron from a motley array of would-be soldiers of fortune. The result was a collection of four Frenchmen, a Dutchman, three Americans, and a German, along with six of his best Chinese bomber pilots. The three Americans were Jim Allison, who had fought the Germans and Italians in Spain; a man named Gibson, who had completed U.S. Air Corps training in the States; and another named Weigel, a self-taught pilot from a Stateside cow-pasture flying school.

Trouble began immediately with Chennault's decision to use the foreigners as flight leaders in the new International Squadron. In response the Chinese pilots struck, refusing to fly on such missions lest they lose face following these foreigners. This situation was complicated by a sympathy strike on the part of the Chinese bombardiers, who were also officers but the Chinese gunners refused to strike for their own reasons. They had been recruited from the Chinese Army, where they were forced to march and carry weapons. They found air gunnery much to their liking since they no longer had to march and were provided with plenty of ammunition to fire.

But once the strike was resolved, Chennault faced a more serious problem with his foreign pilots. They proceeded to make their headquarters in an unsavory Hankow slum area called Dump Street, which was inhabited mostly by barkeepers, opium peddlers, and prostitutes. Sustaining themselves on high octane beverages, they repeatedly related anything they knew about Chinese air operations, adding a few things they did not know.

There were a few successful missions against some Japanese railheads in northern China, but Chennault had been right—for the most part the International Squadron was not worth the trouble. About the time Chennault was planning an important strike against a large Japanese troop movement near Tsinan in Shantung Province, the security leaks via Dump Street proved to be the demise of the International Squadron. It was to be an early morning mission, and to avoid any interruption of their nightly excursion into Dump Street, the International crew decided to load and service their planes the night before and thus avoid the necessity of having to arrive at the airfield too early on the day of the raid. But by the last rays of the setting sun, Japanese bombers came in and laid their bombs across the flight line of the parked planes. One Japanese bomb set off a chain of explosions that destroyed the entire row of planes. This event terminated the careers of the pilots of the International Squadron.

With the early demise of the squadron, Madame Chiang brought ever increasing pressure on Chennault to give up combat so that he could form a new Chinese Air Force by training Chinese cadets in the American tradition. Unknown to Chennault, the city of Kunming was soon to become home to him and remain so for the next seven years.

CHAPTER 3

Chennault and the American
Volunteer Group, 1938–1942

The cool, dry, invigorating climate of the mile-high Yunnan Plateau was a beautiful setting for the building of an all-new Chinese Air Force. Yet Chennault's heart was not in the task.

Madame Chiang Kai-shek had pressured him to give up his personal role in the air war over Hankow to travel to the green turf airstrip next to the city of Kunming. But he found himself feeling like an exile.

Chennault had accumulated a year of valuable combat experience and had recorded thirty-seven confirmed air-to-air kills while serving with the Chinese, but the thought of forging a new Chinese Air Force on the American concept left him less than optimistic. In fact he even applied for a return to active duty in the U.S. Air Corps, where he thought his services could be put to better use. Providence intervened once again, however, for during this summer of 1938 the official reply was that there were no funds available for the return of retired officers to active duty. It might as well have been written in Madame Chiang's hand. He flew his last fighter mission in October 1938.

Yunnan province was the most remote and underdeveloped, although not the most uncultured, province in southwestern China. It bordered upon Indochina, Burma, India, and the high Himalayan Mountains of Tibet. Kunming, its capital, appeared to Chennault as a sleepy, backwoods, Oriental town. But to the French of Indochina, it was a Shangri-La, a welcome respite from the sweltering heat of their colonial stations. They had forged a small-gauge railroad from the lowlands of Hanoi up through the treacherous Yuan gorge and onto the Kunming plain which grew forbidden poppies in its snowy white fields. Though opium production was forbidden by the central government, the "warlord" governor of Yunnan had never completely relented to the will of Chiang Kai-shek. Opium was still Yunnan's principal export. It was through the young governor's cunning "permission" that Chennault was allowed to set up the training camp near the capital city.

At the beginning of each summer, the little French train puffed and whistled through the poppy fields as it wound its way towards the ancient city carrying affluent French colonists. Some were bound for their elaborate servant-staffed French villas which appeared as unnatural appendages to this ancient landscape, while others gleefully anticipated the first glimpse of their personal houseboats floating fully stocked on the beautiful jade-green waters of Lake Kunming.

In this timeless land the hours passed slowly for Chennault as he set himself to the task of staffing the Kunming training school with American Air Corps reserve officers. Later he said of them, "They were a lusty crew, excellent airmen, vociferous gripers, and dangerous men around the poker table." They were by name: Johnny Preston, Frank Higgs (who was the model for the character Duke Hennick in the comic strip "Terry and the Pirates"), C. B. "Skip" Adair, Jim Bledsoe, William Heston, Emil Scott, Harold Johnson, Billy Cherymisin, Harold Mull, Boatner Carney, and last but not least, Billy MacDonald. (Luke Williamson had previously returned to the United States to join Delta Airlines.) For those wives who endured the hardship with them, Chennault had only praise.

Chennault's problems at the training school were not all technical. Not only did he have to deal with the problem of practical-minded Westerners trying to teach classically-educated Orientals, but there was also the ubiquitous problem of bribery whenever one dealt with the Chinese. Bribery and corruption were particularly rampant following the Chinese retreat to the interior and the resulting stalemate in the war. Graft and corruption within the central government were as grave a problem for Chiang Kai-shek as the invading Japanese. But Chennault had learned lessons about the Chinese, and with patience and perseverance he tactfully reduced his personal contact with this national practice. He never gave or accepted elaborate gifts. He presented only fountain pens and mechanical pencils as tokens of his appreciation. In later years he remarked, "I took it as a tribute to the success of this policy that after 1939, no Chinese ever bothered to offer me a bribe."

By now Chennault had completely given up on the old guard of the Chinese Air Force, which he considered incorrigible. Trained in the early days and in old techniques, they also usually pursued a course that would insure their personal safety and comfort. They were totally unprogressive.

On the other hand, Chennault found new hope in the young cadets who were now finding their way into his school. They were a new type of Chinese, eager to learn and eager to fight in defense of their homeland. For most of their lives they had been pointedly aware of the atrocities of the invading Japanese. Their responsiveness, so uncharacteristic of the Chinese pilots Chennault had known before them, inspired him to new optimism, and he soon became a staunch supporter of the training program. In addition, he saw their role in a postwar China as one of such importance that he sought to send them to the United States not only for additional military and technical training, but also for firsthand exposure to American democracy. He was not disappointed in the results and said of his new graduates, "Given equal training and equipment, I rate them well above the Japanese as airmen."

While Chennault and his fellow instructors labored to turn out new pilots for a Chinese Air Force which was at the moment nonexistent, great numbers of Chinese coolies intensified the airfield building program begun before the fall of Nanking. In some cases, over a hundred thousand men, women, and children could be seen building five-thousand-foot solid runways for huge bombers of a type not yet built in America. These fields were being built in places east of Kunming, places with strange-sounding names like Liuchow, Kweilin, Lingling, and Hengyang, names which would all too soon become quite familiar to hundreds of American airmen.

After the fall of the Chinese provisional capital of Hankow on October 25, 1938, the Japanese advance into the interior of China slowed to a standstill. Chinese armies, protected by their mountainous stronghold, were formidable foes, and the Japanese were unwilling to invest the men and materials necessary to root them out. It would require considerable effort and expense, and anyway their armies had fish to fry elsewhere. They elected to bomb them into submission. In early 1939, the Japanese began a sustained bombardment of every major city in Free China. Once again it was the Douhet theory—destroy the people's will and capacity to resist through air power. They struck Chungking its first blow in January, pounding the training school at Kunming and killing Chinese cadets in their barracks as well as helpless civilians in the city.

On one occasion in May 1939, when the dismal winter had lifted over Chungking, Chennault happened to be present when an air raid warning sounded. Having ample time, he located himself on a hillside with binoculars and movie cameras and later described the drama that unfolded:

There were twenty-seven bombers in a perfect "V" formation, like Canadian geese heading north from Louisiana in the spring. Approaching the bomb run, they swung into line abreast with a precision that aroused my admiration for their airmanship. Open bomb bays sprinkled the city with hundreds of silvery incendiaries that burned the heart out of the capital and left raging fires for three days. More than ten thousand persons were killed by smoke and flame.

The war continued to go badly for China, and the daily grind of teaching at the training school was scarcely relieved by evening social events such as viewing the very old movies at the local Nanping theater or playing cribbage or poker into the wee hours of the morning. Mail took six weeks to get to the United States via a most interesting route—down to Hanoi by the little French railroad, then by Air France to Marseilles, and finally by steamship to America. Save for an occasional bombing by the Japanese Air Force, these isolated centurions of the new Chinese Air Force were for a time little influenced by the outside world. But in September 1939, the little French train whistled its tune with an unusual sense of urgency and headed back down to Hanoi carrying all the French citizens of military age. Employees of the German Eurasia Airlines uprooted their families and headed for Hong Kong. Germany had invaded Poland and England and France had responded with a declaration of war on Germany.

That winter the new American military attaché to China visited Kunming and invited Chennault to dinner at the hotel there. As they dined they discussed the Chinese Air Force. Chennault's pleasant host was a scraggy, leather-faced West Point graduate by the name of Col. Joseph Warren Stilwell, who spoke fluent Chinese.

Christmas of 1939 found Chennault enjoying his family and friends in Louisiana. During this trip he again offered his service to the U.S. Army Air Corps and was again refused. However, he did avail himself of this opportunity to discuss the war in China and Japanese military tactics with anyone who would listen. At this time he turned over extensive information to the War Department on a captured Japanese Army "Nate" (Nakajima Ki 27) which he had personally test-flown and compared to Allied aircraft. It was the forerunner to the "Oscar" (Nakajima Ki 43 Hayabusa), which would later play a major role in the war. Chennault realized the potential of the Nate for aerial combat against the Allies. It was superior to the current Allied fighters—the Curtiss P-36, the British Gloster Gladiator, and the Russian I-16. He had meticulously noted its most detailed specifications and had taken many photographs, all of which he turned over to the military intelligence branch of the War Department. Months later, after his return to China, Chennault received a letter from the War Department thanking him for his trouble but stating, "We have been informed by aeronautical experts that it is impossible to build an aircraft of the performance stated with specifications submitted."

Chennault returned to China in early 1940 and spent the next year flying from city to city observing firsthand the awesome and pitiless destruction of a gentle people—their lives, their homes, and their businesses. He walked through the rubble of bombed-out cities and smelled the choking stench of death all around him. "Everywhere I went," he recalled later, "I took movies of the Japanese formations, filled my notebook with comments on their tactics, and added to the measure of my impotent rage at the sight of the unmolested forays."

On September 13, 1940, Chennault witnessed the final demise of the Chinese Air Force as led by the old guard pilots. He had recently voiced his disapproval of their defensive tactics, which he considered ineffective, but his advice had gone unheeded. He watched in disgust as the Japanese Navy's new combat prototype "Zero-Sen" decimated the Chinese defenders when twenty-seven I-15s, I-16s and Curtiss

Hawk IIIs plunged to earth. "Like hawks in a chicken yard they shot down the Chinese fighters before the defenders knew what hit them," Chennault said.

However, this was not the first appearance of the Zero over Chungking. They had appeared on two prior occasions, on August 19 and 20, but the Chinese fighters had remained safely out of sight. The two squadrons of crack Japanese fighter pilots to which this valuable allotment of fifteen pre-production, handmade Zeroes had been entrusted were so disappointed that they devised the scheme for the September 13 encounter. Japanese bombers made their run over Chungking unmolested by Chinese fighters. As they left the target for home, the accompanying Zero pilots pretended to leave with them but then returned in about a half hour after giving the Chinese defenders ample time to congregate over the city in a noisy display of defense. The Zeroes dove out of the sun and promptly went for the jugular vein. Not a single Chinese fighter returned to base; all the Zeroes returned safely. Japan now enjoyed absolute rule over China's skies as Japanese fighter pilots searched vainly for worthy opponents. Finding none they became convinced they were invincible.

Flushed with victory, Japanese bomber pilots were so contemptuous of the Chinese people that they flew their bomber formations unmolested over Chinese cities with open bomb bays, making three and four passes over their targets before releasing their bombs. Japanese fighter pilots, finding no aerial targets, showed their scorn for Chinese airmen on October 4 by actually landing four precious Zero fighters during a strafing attack on Chengtu airdrome in the heart of Free China. Then, while fellow airmen above them continued the strafing attack, they abandoned their planes in an effort to set fire to Chinese aircraft parked under nearby camouflage nets. Had just one of the four pilots been incapacitated by even one stray Chinese bullet, Chennault would have had himself a shiny new Zero.

The Japanese Navy Zero-Sen (Mitsubishi A6M Zero-Sen, official code name Zeke, but generally referred to by the Allies as simply the Zero), would rapidly become the most famous Japanese fighter. It was the first carrier-based aircraft ever to outperform land-based aircraft, and it appeared ubiquitous. It was a shock to the Allies when they later "discovered" the existence of the A6M-2 after the attack on Pearl Harbor, even though its prototype had appeared over Chungking as early as August 19, 1940.

Japanese pilots now so completely ruled Chinese skies that their student pilots flying out of captured Canton "practiced" bombing on cities of southeast China—Liuchow, Nanning, Kweilin, Kienow, Kanchow. Meanwhile navy planes from Hainan Island pounded day after day at the training base in Yunnan. They had no intentions of allowing China to hatch another air force.

The Douhet theory was working. There is a limit to what a nation can endure. In October 1940, Generalissimo Chiang Kai-shek sent for Chennault. As Chennault landed in his Beechcraft at Chungking, Japanese bombers were carrying out an air raid on the city. He hurriedly took off and flew to another strip where he waited out the bombing. When he returned, he found the Generalissimo unusually depressed and worried. Unless the bombing raids on Chungking were stopped, he was afraid that he would have to surrender. But he had a plan. His plan was, in essence, to buy the latest American fighters and hire American pilots to fly them. What did Chennault think? Chennault had not allowed himself to become unfamiliar with what was going on back home, and he knew that these goals would be difficult if not impossible to attain. His answer was pessimistic. The Generalissimo was unimpressed and continued, "You must go to the United States immediately. Work out the plans for whatever you think you need. Do what you can do to get American planes and pilots."

The next thing Chennault knew, he and General Mow Pang Tsu were island-hopping on a Pan-American clipper out of Hong Kong on their way to meet T. V. Soong, Madame Chiang's brother, in Washington. One after the other, Manila, Guam, Wake, Midway, and Oahu fell behind them as Chennault pondered his task.

Chungking was the capital of Free China and considered to be Japan's primary target in their bombing scheme. It had immense psychological importance. If the Japanese Air Force could destroy this remote city even though it was inaccessible to their ground armies, then who could question that China was theirs for the taking? The Japanese, therefore, were sending up to a hundred and fifty bombers a day to level Chungking, and they were succeeding. They also had enough reserve strength to double that number of bombers over their primary target, Chennault calculated, should they encounter sustained opposition. Chennault knew his enemy, but he also knew the American pilot and his capabilities in combat, given the latest American fighter plane. He figured that a group of seasoned American pilots could destroy enemy aircraft at the initial rate of five to one, with a higher ratio once the Japanese lost their confidence. No air force could sustain a five-to-one attrition rate and remain in business. If he could successfully defend Chungking, then the Japanese would be forced to seek targets less well-defended. Aided by his Yunnan net, Chennault would know in advance where the Japanese planned to strike next, and he could then intercept them with his highly mobile volunteer air force. They could take off from one of the newly-prepared airfields and intercept the enemy before he knew what hit him. They would then land at another field and be fueled, rearmed, and ready to fight again even before their engines cooled. Using this strategy would make it difficult for the enemy to retaliate since he would not know where to find them.

By the time Chennault and General Mow reached Washington in the latter part of October 1940, their enthusiasm for an American volunteer air force was at an all-time high. The longer they stayed there, however, the dimmer the prospects became. "It appeared that what few Americans did not have their head in the sand about the coming war, had their attention focused on Europe where England was fighting for survival. No one appeared to be interested in China," Chennault recalled in later years.

Chennault brought with him the data on the first Zero that had appeared over Chungking during the past August and September, and gave it to the Air Corps. He was appalled to learn that their technical manuals still contained nothing on the subject of Japanese aircraft despite the detailed information that he had given them on the Nate the year before.

With the help of a friend who was able to check the War Department files, Chennault learned that the appropriate file contained only a copy of their letter to him in China. The Nate dossier was missing. Even after Chennault provided the Air Corps with the data on this first model Zero, it was after Pearl Harbor before American pilots were supplied with this information and then only after firsthand confrontation with the aircraft in actual combat.

Chennault spent most of his time during the winter months of 1940–1941 at a desk at the China Defense Supplies headquarters in Washington as an employee of the Chinese government. Here he planned the strategy that he would later use in China when, officially, he would first be a Louisiana farmer employed as an "advisor" to the Bank of China, and then later a general in the United States Air Corps.

With the fall of France and their surrender to Germany on June 25, 1940, the Japanese troops began to occupy the seaports of French Indochina. As a salty tentacle of the Japanese military octopus tightened around the neck of frightened French colonists and confidence in their expansion program grew, Japan began to rattle its sword with increasing arrogance. On July 18, 1940, the British responded by closing the Burma Road, the only remaining link between Free China and the rest of the world. On September 22, Japanese soldiers entered northern French Indochina, and four days later the United States imposed a total embargo on steel and scrap iron shipments to Japan. Japan responded on September 24, signing the Tripartite Pact and joining Germany and Italy to form the Rome-Berlin-Tokyo Axis. The fat was in the fire now. On October 18 the British reopened the Burma Road. Things were beginning to happen very fast.

It did not take a soothsayer to predict what the Japanese were doing—they were preparing for further aggression. Chennault watched Japan's activities with a jaundiced eye as he made his plans. "My plan proposed to throw a small, but well-equipped air force into China," he wrote later. "Japan, like England, floated her lifeblood on the sea and could be defeated more easily by slashing her salty arteries than by stabbing for her heart. Air bases in Free China could put all of the vital Japanese supply lines and advanced staging areas under attack."

The hour was late and the midnight oil burned in Chennault's office at the China Defense Supplies headquarters. The first phase of operation, he surmised, would be to pound the staging fields on Formosa, on Hainan Island, and in occupied Canton, and in the occupied cities of Indochina, where Japan was steadily building up strength before launching her southern offensive. Sufficient success in this endeavor might force the Japanese to postpone or even cancel their offensive expansion program. Given success in the first phase, the second phase of Chennault's operation would be to burn out the heart of the industrial empire on the Japanese home islands with fire bombs and thus bring the aggressors to their knees.

All Chennault needed, he figured, was a force of 350 Curtiss P-40 fighters and 150 Hudson bombers to operate from China's various airfields to be reinforced the following year by seven hundred Republic P-43 fighters and three hundred Douglas A-24 dive bombers. Granted this "and a cadre of experienced American pilots to lead the Chinese," Chennault felt willing and able to take on the entire Japanese war machine, leaving Germany and Italy to the Allies. It seemed fair enough to Chennault, but American military planners of 1941, absorbed in Europe's problems, failed to share his strategic ideas about China. "It was not until the Trident Conference of 1943 that I found any appreciation of my strategy or any support for the plans to implement it," Chennault said later. "This support came from two civilians, President Franklin D. Roosevelt and Prime Minister Winston Churchill, and was offered against the strong advice of their military advisors."

Chennault submitted his carefully-laid plans to T. V. Soong. This is what he needed to defeat Japan, he said, down to the last round of ammunition and paper clip. What he actually got, however, was the First American Volunteer Group—three hundred adventuresome pilots and ground crewmen, a hundred early Curtiss B model P-40 Hawks or, as they were designated by the British, Tomahawks (with no spare parts) horse-traded from the British, and a whole bunch of headaches. One is reminded of Tan Pei-ying, builder of the Burma Road, who could have surely related to Chennault's plight.

By January 1941, China's most urgent needs were twofold: the defense of Chungking and the protection of the Burma Road with its trickling of supplies coming up from the Rangoon harbors. Obtaining planes proved to be as difficult a problem as recruiting American military personnel. In fact, both were impossible until it became evident to Chennault that China had a small but influential circle of friends close to the White House, including presidential advisor Thomas Corcoran, Secretary of the Navy Frank Knox, Secretary of the Treasury Henry Morgenthau, and Dr. Lauchlin Currie. All were close friends of Dr. Soong and men very capable of rushing projects through the Washington political maze prior to World War II. It was through their efforts that considerable red tape was cut, allowing Chennault to assemble his First American Volunteer Group.

None of the military commanders of the American Army or Navy wanted Chennault to touch their personnel. General Arnold was diametrically opposed, stating that he could not spare a single staff officer without endangering his own expansion program. It was the same with Rear Adm. Jack Towers, chief of the Bureau of Aeronautics, who also viewed Chennault's program as a direct threat to his expansion program. Chennault wrote later, "It took direct personal intervention from President Roosevelt to pry the pilots and ground crews from the Army and Navy. On April 15, 1941, an unpublicized executive order went out under his signature, authorizing reserve officers and enlisted men to resign from the Army Air Corps, Naval and Marine Air services for the purpose of joining the American Volunteer Group in China."

Richard Aldworth was hired to head the recruiting staff, which was to be directly supervised by Skip Adair and assisted by Rutledge Irvine, Harry Clairborne, and Senton L. Brown. They hit the Marine barracks at Quantico, then went on to Norfolk, San Diego, Pensacola, and Jacksonville looking for Navy pilots. Then it was on to Billing, Selfridge, McDill, March, Mitchell, Langley, Hamilton, Eglin, Craig, Maxwell, Barksdale, and finally Randolph in search of Army volunteers. Base commanders were not too receptive to Chennault's recruiting staff. Nevertheless it was from these forays that the nucleus of his AVG emerged.

Albert E. "Red" Probst was a graduate of the class of 1940 at Randolph Field, Texas, and a second lieutenant in the Air Corps. After graduation he was ordered to remain at Randolph Field as an instructor, which did not cater to his fancy. He disliked Randolph and considered it the worst duty in the world since during those pre-war days it was the Army's spit and polish showplace and was known as the "West Point of the Air." He later reminisced about how he joined the AVG:

I wrangled a transfer into a new organization in the Air Corps where we trained advanced flying students in gunnery and formation flying at Selma, Alabama. The field wasn't ready when I got there so they put us at Barksdale, Louisiana, for temporary duty until Selma was finished. While at Barksdale, we formed this new procedure for training advanced gunnery and tactical and formation flying under the direction of a very enterprising commanding officer who later became a four-star general in Korea. There was a fellow named Ajax Baumler who had been a wingman in Spain during the Spanish civil war and had actual combat experience. He was assigned to our outfit because he was the only man who had ever shot at another airplane.

He could spin us stories and would tell us about it when we could get him sober. He had violated his passport, having gone from Paris, France, to Spain.

One morning about two o'clock, we were all in bed and all of a sudden there was a big commotion. Ajax was drunk and he had brought back from Spain or England some tracer shotgun ammo and he had become aggravated with the streetlights shining through his window. So he just shot them all out.

After Red had transferred to Selma, one day a giant of a fellow came into his office. It was Skip Adair.

He wanted to know where Ajax was. I told him that Ajax was on a gunnery mission down at Eglund field, but that he would be back in a few days. Adair then started talking to me, and the first thing I knew, he had recruited me for his AVG group that same afternoon. He not only recruited me but also my buddies, Matthew W. Kuykendall and Robert W. Sandell, who were also instructors.

I didn't know anything about Chennault or anything about the AVGs until Skip Adair walked into my office. He talked to me a few hours. I was head over heels in debt, and he was going to pay me six hundred dollars a month. And, I said, "Let's see now, I am making two hundred ten dollars a month now, and you are going to pay me six hundred. I get a free trip to China, and if we go to war with somebody, I won't be on the first string, but the second string. I don't want to have anything to do with them Germans, so I'm going to get over there and help those Chinese." Kuykendall, Sandell, and I decided then and there that we would all go. We were buddies.

Skip gave us that afternoon and that night to prepare all the necessary paperwork for resignation from the U.S. Army. Skip even provided an envelope pre-addressed to the President of the United States and told us that our requests required the signature of the base commander. The base commander looked at the papers with surprise and then said to me, "I don't know who you think you are. War is imminent and it is with Germany! We're training fighter pilots and you're a fighter pilot and if you think you're going to resign you're out of your mind."

"Sir," I said, "I don't know anything except that I need for you to just endorse this request for resignation, approve or disapprove it—doesn't make any difference to me, sir!" So he disapproved it, but two days later he called me and said, "I don't know who you know, but I have a telegram that you have been resigned. You are to be processed off this base and separated from the Air Corps within twenty-four hours."

I said, "Yes, sir," and drove home to visit my mother who in the meantime got a scare when she made a routine call to the field to talk with me and one of the enlisted men told her, "No, ma'am, he's not here. He went to China."

Skip had given me a train ticket from my hometown of Thrall, Texas, to San Francisco, but I didn't take the train. Instead I flew from Dallas on the airlines. I was ready for a little adventure and the thought of being part of the air protection over the Burma Road from Rangoon, Burma, to Kunming, China, was exciting. Even the name Rangoon had an exciting sound.

One day out in San Diego at the Naval Air Station, Loy F. "Sy" Seamster was just getting out of the Navy. He had changed to his civilian clothes before departing and then remembered that a guy over at the hangar owed him five bucks. There was a depression on and that was a lot of money so he was not about to leave without collecting it. As he left the building and started walking towards the hangar, he met an old buddy named Mickey Mihalko, a tough, stocky Japanese-American.

"Hey Sy," Mickey said, "how would you like to go to Burma?"

"Burma?" Sy asked in disbelief.

"Yeah, Burma. Some damn fool is hiring people for five hundred bucks a month, going to pay all the expenses and all this good stuff to go there and have a ball. Come along and let's go see about it."

So Sy did a quick 180-degree turn, and together they walked to a hangar where some men were recruiting people for the AVGs. There was a captain in charge who told them, "Officially you are going to work for Central Aircraft Manufacturing Company in China." But off to the side he told them what they were really going to do. Sy decided to apply on the spot, but he needed an occupation to put down on his application form and his official job as a radio man would not do. So he put down his father's occupation back in Arkansas—lumberman. Sy joined the AVGs for something to do. He was a young man, single, and the world was his oyster. This was going to be some adventure, he felt. After taking thirty days' leave at home in Arkansas, he headed for San Francisco.

Meanwhile on the east coast at Norfolk Naval Air Station in Virginia, a young aviation machinist first class was sitting in his office during lunch. But Melvin H. Woodward was no longer skinning his knuckles, for he had just been talked into joining base security and was now leading petty officer for the security division. It had turned out to be pretty good shore duty. As he looked out the door he saw his good buddy of long standing, Wayne Ricks, coming in for a visit. Wayne was attached to the aircraft carrier *U.S.S. Wasp,* which was lying at anchor.

"You hear about some bastard in Hangar Four who's offering a chance to get out of the Navy, see the world, fight the Japs, and get good money?" he asked Woodward. Without waiting for an answer, he continued with a grin, "Shall we go talk with him?"

The AVG business was being conducted in a huge hangar which dwarfed the three tiny figures—one clerk and a couple of interviewers—sitting by a desk over in the far corner. Thirty-six hours later both Woodward and Ricks were out of the Navy and on their way to San Francisco. The date was June 25, 1941.

Chennault later wrote:

> Since we were still working in strict secrecy, William Pawley suggested to Dr. Soong that CAMCO be used as a blind to hire personnel. A confidential contract was drawn up between CAMCO and China Defense Supplies Inc., in which CAMCO agreed to handle all AVG financial matters at cost and provide complete maintenance and repair for our damaged aircraft at the Loi-Wing factory. In this contract, the AVG fighter squadrons were called advanced training units, the P-40s were advanced trainers and I was designated as supervisor.

To the volunteers, CAMCO (Central Aircraft Manufacturing Company) in turn offered a one-year contract to manufacture, repair, and operate aircraft. Their salaries ranged from $250 to $750 and included fringe benefits which were specified. There was no mention in the contract of a five-hundred-dollar bonus which would be given for every Japanese plane destroyed. This was originally intended to apply only to aircraft destroyed in the air but was later extended to include those destroyed on the ground as well. Of course, they had to be confirmed. The contract also specified that they would be subject to summary dismissal for insubordination, habitual use of drugs or alcohol, illnesses not incurred in the line of duty, malingering, or revealing confidential information. Chennault was to dismiss at least one man on every account, save revealing confidential information, before the contracts expired.

Before flying to San Francisco on United Air Lines to meet with the first contingent of the AVGs, Chennault made one final attempt to get six trained staff officers from General Arnold's Air Corps, but without success. He then pleaded for three and finally got one. Later the Air Corps would criticize Chennault for sloppy staff work, even though it was they who had left him in a situation in which he was obliged to use whatever American adventurer he could find knocking about loose in the Orient.

After a brief one-day meeting with his young recruits at the Mark Hopkins Hotel in San Francisco, Chennault boarded a Pan-American Airways clipper bound for Hong Kong. He had just received notice of confirmation of the President's approval for a second American Volunteer Group of bombers with one hundred pilots and 181 gunners and radiomen. They were scheduled to arrive in China by November 1941, with an equal number to follow in January 1942. Chennault was confident for the first time that he had the materials and men necessary to defeat the Japanese. The feeling was short-lived for troubles were to develop quickly.

Two days later, on July 10, 1941, the secretly assembled AVG personnel, listing their occupations on their passports as lumberman, musician, student, clerk, banker, etc., boarded the Dutch ship *Jaegersfontaine,* and they, too, stepped into the pages of history. No sooner did the ship weigh anchor than the Japanese radio announced that the first group of the American volunteer pilots planning to fight in China had left San Francisco by ship. They informed their listeners that the ship would never reach China. It would be sunk.

The Pan-American clipper landed at Hong Kong where a China National Aviation Corporation (CNAC) aircraft whisked Chennault on to Chungking, where Japanese bombers had resumed their massive air raids the month before. The Generalissimo was delighted to receive the news of Chennault's success and was impatient for the air battles to begin.

Chennault hastily made arrangements for the transfer of supplies from the old Russian flying school at Chengtu to Chungking for use by the AVGs. Then he immediately flew to Rangoon, where he found P-40s still sitting in their crates on the docks where they had been unloaded the month before. The repeated delays in Washington had scuttled his plans to train his AVGs at Kunming during the spring dry season and have them ready to meet the enemy over Chungking when the first clear summer days broke over the capital. In addition, the Japanese had beaten his timetable and started bombing the city on June 7. Now it was too late.

The monsoon rains had begun to turn the grass-covered airfields of Yunnan into quagmires. If he was to train his men now, it would have to be in Burma. This created a problem with the British. Under no circumstances would they permit actual combat training by the AVGs under the British flag, because they were afraid that such provocation might give the Japanese an excuse for further aggression in their direction. They were already heavily committed in desperate engagements in North Africa, the North Atlantic, and over their homeland. They might, however, permit the assembly and test-flying of planes in Burma.

Chennault now had three pressing priorities—where to assemble the planes, where to obtain the spare parts he so desperately needed to keep his planes in the air, and finally, where to find the time to train the volunteers in his unique concept of aerial warfare. General Mow, William Pawley and his brother Ed, and Chennault began a series of conferences with Sir Reginald Hugh Dorman-Smith, governor of Burma, and the British military commanders to discuss the legality of their situation. What developed was that the British gave the Chinese government a lease of the unmanned Kyedaw airdrome six miles from Toungoo and 170 miles north of Rangoon.

The Kyedaw field was in the middle of the monsoon belt, but it had a four-thousand-foot runway of asphalt. It became the home of the AVGs. The volunteers were soon to learn the reason why the field was available. During the monsoon season, the British RAF abandoned Kyedaw as being unfit for habitation by Europeans due to its foul, stinking climate and infuriating insects.

Consequently, there were no screen doors or windows or even electric lights provided. Chennault later recalled:

> The runway was surrounded by quagmire and pestilential jungle. Matted masses of rotting vegetation carpeted the jungle and filled the air with a sour, sickening smell. Torrential monsoon rains and thunderstorms alternated with torrid heat to give the atmosphere the tex-

ture of a turkish bath. Dampness and green mold penetrated everywhere. The food, provided by the Burmese mess contractor, was terrible and was one of the principal causes of group griping.

On July 28, 1941, the forward sea painter of the *Jaegersfontaine* arched its way down to the Rangoon docks as the finale to a most pleasant ocean voyage. Pilots and crewmen of the first contingent of the AVG gathered topside along the rails and surveyed the city before them. Suddenly an expletive was uttered as a sensitive nostril fell prey to the pungent Burmese air—air sauced with the aroma of decaying jackfruit, assorted garbage, and various fragrances of human filth. Sy Seamster felt a pang of reservation about his coming adventure, but for Mel Woodward, a born romanticist, Rangoon held possibilities; the road to Mandalay lay just beyond.

As the group trickled down the gangway to the waiting jeeps and flatbed trucks, they left behind the shipboard comfort and life of leisure which the spotless Dutch ship had provided. The excellent food, polished silverware, efficient servants, and first-class accommodations —all would now be given up for "those damn thatched roofs at Toungoo."

Chennault met with the men briefly on the docks, then dispatched them to the Rangoon train station for the "Up Mail" train ride to Toungoo, Burma, 170 miles into the interior. Seven miles north of Toungoo, at the Kyedaw airdrome, Boatner Carney was still setting up camp. "Captain" Carney had been recruited temporarily from the Kunming flying school and represented the sum total of Chennault's general staff. Obtaining staff members for the AVG had been a problem, since Chennault had to make his selection from what men he could find in the Orient. He had just recently recruited his chief of staff out of Hong Kong—one Harvey K. Greenlaw, who had not yet arrived. Harvey and his wife Olga were a story in themselves.

Harvey was a graduate of West Point and had resigned his commission to join the Jouett mission in China back in 1933. Shortly thereafter, he was joined by his new Stateside bride, and together they remained in China until late 1936 when they returned to the States.

In 1938 the Greenlaws went back to China and settled in the inland city of Hengyang, where Harvey, now a representative of North American Aviation Company, supervised the assembly and test flights of aircraft sold to China by North American. In this capacity they traveled extensively throughout China and mingled with the uppers and lowers of Chinese society, including one Claire Lee Chennault.

Things went pretty well for the Greenlaws until early 1939, when the approaching Japanese army overran the coastal area between Hengyang and Hong Kong and it became impossible for crated aircraft to be trucked overland to Hengyang for assembly.

With Hengyang beginning to come under increasing aerial attacks and with the retreating Chinese army making their withdrawal through the city, it seemed time for the Greenlaws to vacate. So they loaded up their 1928 DeSoto coupé and rattled off towards Indochina along a primitive road system to be endured only by the most stouthearted. Harvey continued to peddle his planes, or at least he attempted to, until June 1941. His business carried them from Hanoi to Haiphong to Hong Kong, then on to Chungking and Kunming and back to Hong Kong. Then it was down to Haiphong again and south to Siam and Singapore and then back to Rangoon. It was an endless cycle of packing and unpacking for Mrs. Greenlaw that was beginning to take the fun out of travel.

Finally, after British customs officials prevented the entry into Burma of fifty North American aircraft bound for the tattered Chinese Air Force, Harvey said to hell with it. He finally succumbed to the adamant insistence of his wife that they return to California. So June of 1941 found Mrs. Greenlaw frantically packing, vowing that at least *she* would be aboard the *President Coolidge* when it sailed. Harvey was stretched out on the bed suffering from an affliction frequently precipitated by such packing episodes, when the phone rang.

"Harvey, it's Mac on the telephone," she announced, a little vexed.

"Which Mac?" came a weak voice from the bedroom.

"Little Mac, the CNAC pilot!" she screamed. Whereupon a sleepy figure emerged from the bedroom and lumbered over to pick up the receiver left dangling by the cord.

Olga kept on packing, having little interest in the conversation until she heard the name Chennault. The "Old Man" is back, she thought. Only a few days before, she had heard that he was in the States. She then noticed a certain eagerness in her husband's voice. Suddenly he did not sound tired anymore. She began to get that old feeling again. It was the evasive eyes, that barely perceptible grin on his face when he came into the room that triggered the hysteria.

"Now babe, just keep your shirt on. I haven't the least idea what the Old Man wants to see me about," said her husband. Yet as he left to meet Chennault, she lost her enthusiasm in her packing. Though she would not admit it at the time, deep down she knew that the *President Coolidge* would sail without her.

With the exception of her raven black hair, Olga Greenlaw could have doubled for Barbara Stanwyck. She had the wit, the stamina, and the tenacious beauty, but any girl, no matter how resolute, had her breaking point. Olga wanted to go home, back to America to see her mother. For the time being, she had had it with the Orient. As she sat alone in her room and stared through the window at the harbor in the approaching darkness, she battled with her emotions.

One by one the tiny lights on the faraway hill twinkled into existence, and one by one Olga compiled points she would use in her rebuttal when Harvey walked through the door with some excuse for them not to go home. She certainly was not going to surrender easily. Through her head ran lines like, "Okay, Harvey, you run right along to wherever with your sour-faced little pal. Don't even give me a thought because I will be somewhere else." She wished Chennault would vanish or go back to Waterproof, Louisiana, or wherever he came from and quit giving her husband screwball ideas. She ordered tea and smoked several cigarettes, but it did not help. The night drifted on.

By the time Harvey Greenlaw, now executive officer and chief of staff of the new American Volunteer Group, opened the door, he was fully prepared to play out the drama that he knew was coming. He would, as he had so many times before, simply play on Olga's curiosity. Sure enough, it was not long until outright female indignation gave way to an inquisitive expression and finally she asked, "You mean this picked group of Americans are going to help the Chinese fight the Japs?"

Harvey knew he had her now because Olga Greenlaw was the kind of woman who would simply die if something exciting was going to happen and she was not in on it.

"It may be tremendously exciting, Olga," he injected just at the right moment and then added the coup de grâce. "I had a hell of a time getting the Old Man's permission for you to go along. He's dead set against women when . . ."

That did it. Olga was going to Burma with Harvey.

By the time the CNAC transport carrying the Greenlaws (and Olga's pet dog Lucy) arrived in Rangoon (via Hong Kong, Chungking, Kunming, and Lashio), the boys at Kyedaw were deeply involved in the usual military pastimes—bitching about the food, the accommodations, the mosquitoes and other bugs, and the absence of women and liquor. But the resourceful ones were making progress regarding the women, the liquor, and something to eat. The AVG had converged on Toungoo by jeep, by truck, by bicycle, and by thumb with all the enthusiasm and "can do" spirit that would see them through the difficult months ahead.

Toungoo, Burma—now there was a thriving metropolis for you. It was one of the many little whistle-stops along the British railway system that ran "Up Mail" and "Down Mail" all the way through the teeming bug-infested jungle, past Mandalay to its termination at the mountainous city of Lashio.

Toungoo had one main street which thundered continuously night and day under the heavily-laden trucks and vehicles traveling the length of the Burma Road all the way from Rangoon to Kunming, China. The road came north from the Rangoon docks to Toungoo and then went on through Mandalay to Lashio, a hundred miles from Wanting on the Chinese border. From Wanting it entered the treacherous Chinese mountain passes and went across the Salween and Mekong gorges to Tali, the highest city on the route, before descending along the Yunnan plateau to the Kunming plains.

Along the way, there were seven principal airdromes and airfields. The three British ones were Mingaladon (just outside of Rangoon), Kyedaw (seven miles north of Toungoo), and Magwe (250 miles north of Rangoon in a valley northwest of Toungoo). Just inside the Chinese border near Wanting was the aircraft factory at Loi-Wing, owned and operated by CAMCO. Another Chinese field, Paoshan, was situated on the mountainous ridge between the Salween and the Mekong rivers. Then there was the training field called Yunnanyi, located north of the road along the Yunnan plateau. Finally there was the main field at Kunming.

Toungoo had one restaurant, a few scrubby stores, and one little tailor working his fingers to the bone, making himself rich conjuring up unofficial uniforms for the AVG—khaki shorts, bush jackets, and jungle helmets. Toungoo also had an abundance of stray mongrel dogs of every description and heritage, lousy, flea-bitten, starving creatures that could elicit sympathy from the most calloused observer. And then there were the insects—the bugs, ones that bit and others that stung; big ones, little ones, colorful ones, and ugly ones; bugs that crawled up your leg, down your collar, into your food, across the floor, up the wall, and across the ceiling. They flew into your eyes, up your nose, and into your mouth. It was an entomologist's paradise. It seemed to the AVG that every conceivable insect that was ever known to man, that ever crawled or flew over the face of the earth, must have surely begun its journey at Toungoo, Burma. It did not take long for the novelty of being in a new place to wear off.

Basically, an AVG spending a night on the town in Toungoo had two ways to pass the time. He could participate in the activities going on at the Station Restaurant, or he could sit alone in the darkness and reminisce about things back home, possibly with the gentle refrain of "I'll be seeing you . . ." running through his mind, until jolted back to reality by the shrill whistle of an approaching train or the cry of a jungle beast. Sooner or later he would go to the Station Restaurant, which was always full to overflowing, mostly with all the same faces he had hoped to leave back at the airdrome. As time went by, a lot of griping and discontent from the airfield began to spill over into the social hour at the restaurant and on many occasions things got quite exciting. The AVG were a lusty, adventurous crew, and without wine, women, and song to dissipate their nervous energies, things would frequently get out of control.

Meanwhile, after meeting briefly with his troops at the Rangoon docks, Chennault had been summoned to Chungking, where during his stay he experienced the war's worst bombings to date. The Japanese were sending 150 planes a day over the city in a relentless effort to bomb the Chinese into submission. The bombings went on both day and night for seventy-two hours. Chennault found Chungking completely deserted—residents had sought shelter and were reluctant to return to their homes due to the frequency and intensity of the air raids. Communications and electrical lines were down and the city was without water.

As Chennault endeavored to conduct his urgent business with the various military attachés around Chungking, his progress was interrupted by repeated air raids. As he dodged their bombs, he found little satisfaction in the fact that in Burma he had the men and the equipment he felt were capable of reversing this trend.

It was two weeks before Chennault could return to Rangoon in his twin-engine Beechcraft to pick up his new chief of staff and go to Kyedaw to meet the assembled personnel. "The camp at Kyedaw was seething with griping when I arrived," Chennault recalled. "My first business was to accept the resignations of five pilots who were eager to return to the United States and airline jobs."

With the Old Man back on deck, organization began to improve and while the men did calisthenics and played volleyball to get themselves back in shape, Chennault sifted through the pilots' flying records. He was not impressed. He had wanted fighter pilots in their early and late twenties with at least five hundred hours of pursuit time. He recalled telling General Arnold this back in Washington. Arnold had replied, "If I were to give you a hundred pilots with that kind of experience, you would fold up my entire pursuit section." Chennault had shot back, "You're wrong. If you can't spare that many pilots with that kind of experience, you don't have a pursuit section to begin with." It was remarks such as this one that endeared him to Hap Arnold.

After going over all 110 flying records, Chennault tabulated the results. Twelve men met his qualifications and had at least seen a Curtiss P-40. Half of the remaining pilots had never flown a pursuit ship, and the age range was from a low of twenty-one to a high of forty-three. Planes with which the pilots were proficient varied from Army four-engine Flying Fortresses to Navy torpedo bombers, with a few pilots being current in multi-engine flying boats. It was going to be a long war.

Soon word got around that the Old Man was going to open a "kindergarten" to teach bomber pilots to fly P-40s. On hearing this some of the pilots were amused and appalled at the audacity of this beat-up old Army captain who had been buried in China for years thinking he could teach them anything. A lot of them felt that they were pretty hot stuff and were ready and willing to take on the "Japs" right then and there. They had been telling everyone this even during the ocean voyage. But Chennault had made himself a solemn promise, that none of these AVG pilots would be exposed to combat without first having mastered his technique of aerial warfare, a technique he had formulated from personal experience.

The crated Curtiss P-40s were at Mingaladon airdrome near Rangoon. They had to be assembled and flown to Kyedaw to be fitted with radios and armed for combat. But mechanics from the Loi-Wing factory were late in assembling the aircraft, causing a delay in Chennault's plans. On August 3, AVG pilots began ferrying the aircraft to Kyedaw. "We'd take the train down to Rangoon, party a couple or three days, and then fly them back," recalled Red Probst, who was one of the first pilots to undertake this mission. By the end of August, twenty-two P-40s had been flown to Kyedaw. As of November 28, all ninety-nine had been delivered.

While the Toungoo kindergarten matriculated pilots, Olga Greenlaw, who had remained in Rangoon until Harvey could get things set up for them in Toungoo, finally received word from him to catch the next "Up Mail." Harvey met her at the station in Toungoo with some of the boys, and it was obvious they had already become good friends. A couple of them she recognized, having seen them in the lobby of the Minto Mansion Hotel in Rangoon the night she and Harvey had arrived.

She recalled her amazement at how very young they had all looked when she first saw them in Rangoon. Harvey had replied that it was a young man's war. "At least they seem to be having fun," she had added, and Harvey agreed that they thought they were on a picnic but "Wait until the grind and boredom and homesickness set in," he had said.

Harvey introduced them one at a time to Olga, and it was instant admiration. "Olga, this is Jack Newkirk. And here's Bob Sandell—you can call him Sandy, and he'll call you Olga. This is John Armstrong and Pete Adkinson and this one's Bob Little. This is 'Ole' Olson, the terrible Swede, and here's Red Probst."

Olga remembered Red Probst all right. His fiery red hair was the first thing she nad noticed in the Minto Mansion lobby back in Rangoon. Red was obviously a Texan. To go with his red hair, he had a face full of freckles and wore a khaki shirt and shorts with cowboy boots.

After the introductions, there was a brief pause while seven quick minds gave Olga the "once-over" and calculated her vital statistics. Olga, for her part, was not idle either—she was looking them over, too. Then it seemed they all began to talk at once.

"Hmm, not bad."

"You're going to like it here, baby."

"Hey, Harvey, she's not bow-legged or cross-eyed. You lied to us."

"So you're the little mammy."

"What do you mean little?"

Olga blushed with all the attention and although she knew that she wasn't a bad looker, she was astute enough to keep everything in perspective. She was one of three American women out in the middle of nowhere with three hundred American men, all of voting age.

Harvey led the entourage to a house he had rented about three blocks out of Toungoo towards Kyedaw. This house, needless to say, became the "Greenlaw Hotel" to those Americans who cared to drop in, invited or uninvited, day or night, whether the Greenlaws were home or not. It was always open to any American stranger in the night in need of a little touch of home. Olga felt that it was just part of her job.

By early afternoon the following day Olga could not stand it any longer. The housecleaning would just have to wait. Her curiosity was killing her—she wanted to see the AVG airfield. So she drove out to Kyedaw. Though she was no newcomer to an airfield, she immediately felt something new and alive about this place. There was one runway in the center of a clearing which held the jungles at bay. Scattered here and there were a building or two and one hangar, with other buildings under construction. It really was not much to look at. The young kids scurrying here and there on bicycles and on foot gave it the impression of being a college campus, the atmosphere like the day before the big game. Olga would soon be able to match a name with each of the three hundred faces of the AVG, fifty of which she would learn to know quite well, with a dozen or so becoming permanently etched in her memory.

She continued her inspection. There were two mess halls, each with a spotless kitchen staffed with servants in immaculate white uniforms. One mess was for the "men," she noted, while the other one was for the "pilots." Olga thought for a moment. They were supposed to be civilians without any rank, according to Harvey. Then why the segregation? The powers that be were carrying over certain military traditions if only through habit, she surmised.

She wandered inquisitively around the airdrome for a time, with little escaping her attention. Finally she headed for Harvey's office, speaking pleasantly to everyone she encountered along the way. Harvey was glad to see her, for he was proud of Olga and rather enjoyed showing her off.

"Well, I've seen everything," she said, half-kidding him. But then she asked, "Where are all the airplanes and pilots?" This was a serious subject to the chief of staff, and Harvey responded with a rather formal military report. He was like that, thought Olga, so thorough when it came to military matters. He told her the number of men accounted for on that specific day and about the others due to arrive soon. He said that the planes were being assembled and flown up as quickly as possible and that at best there would be only ninety-nine of them and no spare parts.

"They're brand new airplanes, aren't they?" she asked, whereupon Harvey explained that while they were indeed fresh out of the wrappers, one less spark plug or one tire too few and a plane would be rendered out of service. It was the spare parts that kept them flying, he explained, and that was why without them, there would be such a grave problem. It was only a matter of time before they would have to cannibalize one ship to keep the rest in the air. Harvey continued and Olga listened, attentively at first and then less so after she had thought of her next question.

Waiting for a pause, she injected, "How much are these boys paid?" The question did not at all surprise Harvey, but he gave her a stern look anyway, the one reserved for her when he thought she was beginning to get a little out of hand. Yet he answered in detail concerning the CAMCO contracts and the range of salaries.

He then looked directly at her and said solemnly, "Look, Olga, I'm going to warn you. Don't become too attached to any of these kids. Some of them are going to get killed. We even have a part-time embalmer on the staff."

She was stunned, which Harvey had intended since he knew that she had not given it any thought. "One of these kids?" she asked. It did not seem possible to her. Harvey told her that the way things were going during training, it would almost certainly happen even before they got into combat.

The thought of death took the fun out of her inspection and perhaps prompted her sudden interest in the base hospital. She left Harvey to see what facilities were available and was met by Emma J. "Red" Foster. Red was a tall, pretty nurse who had everything in the right places except her heart, which she had given to a good-looking pilot by the name of John Petach. Their romance was probably the poorest kept secret on the field. Everyone knew about it including Chennault, who by now had the reputation of having eyes in the back of his head.

Red and Olga exchanged niceties and finally Red called out and introduced Miss Jo Buckner Steward, the chief nurse. She was slightly older, Olga noticed, and rather grey-haired. She had been a missionary to China before the coming of the AVG. During a casual conversation she remarked that they were not very busy since most of the boys were in good physical condition, so they were for the most part just unpacking their equipment. They discussed the doctors, who both nurses agreed were quite capable. There were Thomas C. Gentry, chief flight surgeon, and Samuel B. Prevo, Lewis J. Richards, and a Chinese doctor by the name of J. S. Lee. Both Gentry and Richards were also members of the AVG staff.

Rather mysteriously, Red Probst popped up just in time to volunteer to drive Olga back to Toungoo. As they crossed the field to pick up J. D. Armstrong to "do some shopping in town," it occurred to Olga that all this had been previously arranged by the two. They just wanted a little company, she thought with a smile. They think they are so clever. As Red began to pick up speed down the dusty road, Olga remembered what Harvey had told her, that some would die. Surely not one of these two kids, she thought. She liked them both. Armstrong, especially, was the kind of boy any mother would be proud of. Suddenly the thought occurred to her that they might all be listed as casualties before the day was over, the way Red was driving, recklessly dodging through the natives and canines in a death-defying assault on Toungoo.

A Dutch ship arrived with the second contingent of AVG pilots and crewmen during the last week in August. At the airdrome, the transition to the hot little P-40 was a breeze for a few men like David Lee "Tex" Hill, a long-legged, quiet Texan who had been born in Korea, the son of a Presbyterian missionary. Tex was a Navy pilot and had arrived on the second ship about a month after the first. He had been flying single-engine planes on aircraft carriers for the past two years, piloting a torpedo bomber called a TBD on the *Saratoga* and SB2U dive bombers on the *Ranger*. Yet Tex had only fifty-five hours of fighter time and that was in F4Bs back in Pensacola. Still he had more fighter time than most of the volunteers.

Other pilots like Bob Neale, George Burgard, and Charley Bond did equally well in their transition to the P-40. For others, it was a long, tedious, and in some cases an impossible task. As late as March 1942, Chennault still considered eighteen men not suited for combat.

Pilots having flown only multi-engine aircraft had difficulty "finding the ground" in a P-40, attempting to land it from fifty feet in the air. One morning Chennault witnessed six P-40 landing accidents, and before he could scratch the day's training, a crewman riding on a bicycle watching the last accident ran into the aileron of a parked P-40 and put it out of commission. "Christ from Vicksburg, seven P-40s!" he cursed. This was a heavier loss than they would later suffer in any single day of combat.

No matter how desperately he needed pilots in combat, Chennault never violated a promise that he made to himself—that no pilot would enter combat until Chennault was convinced he was suitably trained. Because of his dogmatic concern to conserve pilots and aircraft, both of which were absolutely irreplaceable, the Japanese would kill only four of his pilots and destroy only twelve AVG aircraft during six months of grueling air to air combat.

One cannot help but wonder how Claire Chennault and his men were able to accomplish such a feat. The group that some military experts predicted would not last three weeks in combat would not only prevail but would become an American legend.

In truth, the AVG was pushed toward glory by a combination of factors over which it had little or no control. It was a product of the times. Regardless of an individual pilot's motive for coming to China, all the future AVG members had one common characteristic that must not be overlooked. They were all Americans trained by the United States armed forces, which had done a good job of weeding out incompetents. In addition, the unpleasant environment surrounding the Kyedaw airdrome, the fact that these men were civilian volunteers not subject to military discipline, plus the demanding nature of Chennault's training program combined to insure that the inept, the incorrigibles, the misfits, and the malcontents were soon seeking passage back to the States at their own expense.

What distilled was a close-knit group with an uncommon amount of esprit de corps, something that did not come merely with the signing of the CAMCO contracts. The catalyst, without a shadow of a doubt, was one leathery-faced, clever, Louisiana ex-schoolteacher who was unusually adept at his trade. For Chennault, drawing upon his extensive personal knowledge of aerial warfare against the Japanese, taught his students as no other instructor could. He taught his men how to destroy the enemy and survive, and equally important, he taught them so thoroughly that they would be able to teach other pilots who followed them.

Tex Hill's first impression of Chennault was very favorable:

He was a rugged looking guy, the type you immediately felt a lot of confidence in. He exuded leadership. His own experience in combat was a matter of speculation, however. He made quite an impression during tactical lectures, and there just wasn't any doubt in our minds that he had some experience against the Japanese aircraft. During his tactical lectures he told us how to conduct ourselves, and we found, when we encountered the Japanese, that his tactics were right on. There were all kinds of rumors about him and he never denied or confirmed them. He wasn't the kind of man you would feel comfortable about asking personal questions. You felt that if he wanted you to know something about himself he would tell you. The Old Man had a lot of personal contact with us at Toungoo. Once we had learned the basic tactics, it was very easy to pass these things along. I got about fifty hours of doing mostly dogfighting and I learned to handle the P-40 at Toungoo. We had such few people. Everybody had to do what they could.

As the training progressed, one could feel the spirit developing. Pilots now coming back with new P-40s would really beat the place up, doing slow rolls over the field, each one trying to outdo the other. The Old Man did not care. The spirit was alive and well, and besides he knew the feeling. It may have been challenged later at Loi-Wing, after months of savage fighting under the most adverse conditions imaginable, but it nevertheless would prevail.

During the first week of September 1941, Olga Greenlaw was back at the field watching some of the planes landing when she witnessed her first landing accident. Sandy Sandell was not hurt but the same could not be said for his "pranged" P-40. With no spare parts available, the sun would not set on the nearby one hundredth P-40, which had been dropped into the Rangoon harbor during unloading, until it had been deprived of its propeller and one wing tip. This would become a pinch business transaction which crew chiefs and ground crews would conduct quite often in the months to come.

And so it went at the Toungoo kindergarten, Chennault holding technical classes in the teakwood classroom starting at six in the morning. He drew on his four years of combat experiences against the Japanese and taught lessons about geography, tactics, the enemy's equipment, and the enemy himself—what he was like and what to expect from him in combat. He told them about the Chinese warning net and how it functioned. Chennault was well-prepared with visual aids and drawings. Some, for example, detailed the specifications and performance data on the Model Zero-Sen.

"The Zero has a faster rate of climb, higher ceiling, and better maneuverability than your P-40," he told them. "They can turn on a dime and climb almost straight up. If they can get you into a turning combat they are deadly. With the P-40 you can count on a higher top speed, faster dive, and superior firepower." He told them over and over to fight in pairs and make every bullet count. "Use your speed and diving power to make a pass, shoot, and break away. God help the American pilot who tries to fight them according to their plans." He passed out mimeographed sheets of the Zero's specifications whereupon a few more pilots submitted their resignations.

Learning to pit the P-40 against such a nimble adversary required a little more than routine flying proficiency. Consequently, the actual learning process could become quite dangerous. Pilots were required to conduct dogfights with one another, for example. They were given fifty to sixty hours of combat training. This began each morning right after the theory classes while it was still cool and before the daily monsoon thunderstorms developed. A couple of pilots were sent up to dogfight under the watchful eye of their teacher perched high in the bamboo control tower with binoculars and microphone. He would watch, coach, and take notes which he would later refer to once the pilots were back on the ground. "I went over these notes with the pilot, giving him a detailed critique of his flying and tactics and prescribing specific practice methods to bolster his weak spots," Chennault recalled. As the pilots progressed, the coaching expanded to include formation flying and practice attacks on bombers and ground targets.

Then on September 18 what Harvey Greenlaw had predicted actually happened. There was a fiery crash in the blue Burmese sky as two P-40s collided in midair, then plunged unobserved into the jungle below. Once again Olga was at the field watching the return of the last of the morning training flights. She noticed that all planes landed but two. Harvey was summoned, since he was in command while the Old Man was in Chungking. A quick head count revealed that John D. Armstrong and Henry G. "Gil" Bright, Jr., were missing. None of the other pilots had seen anything. The atmosphere was tense as they all gathered in the mess hall to await the return of the two pilots. They were eating lunch when the telephone rang. It was the station master a little further up the line from Toungoo, and he reported that two airplanes had collided and both had gone down.

Harvey quickly dispatched two planes to the area and began to organize a rescue party. Presently one of the pilots radioed back that he had pinpointed the crash site and the rescue party sped away. While en route the rescue party sighted Gil Bright riding a bicycle which he had borrowed from a native, and he related the tragic incident. He and Armstrong had collided while dogfighting. He himself had been able to bail out, but he was sure that Armstrong had gone down with his plane. When the rescue party arrived at the scene, they found both aircraft buried deep in the mud. Armstrong's body was in one of them.

The airfield was no longer a college campus. Armstrong's death had a sobering effect on everyone. Chaplain "Padre" Frillman presided at the funeral, which was attended by almost everyone including the British. Johnnie Armstrong, a boy from Hutchinson, Kansas, was buried in a Christian cemetery in Toungoo, Burma. The American flag that draped his coffin was sent home to his mother for what precious little comfort it would give her.

After the funeral several of the men gathered at the Greenlaws. There were Jack Newkirk and Skip Adair, and somewhat later Sandy Sandell arrived. Harvey was fidgety and finally left to go back to the field. The rest of them sat on the veranda not talking much, mostly just trying to keep cool. They were not the same anymore, Olga noticed. The happiness and laughter, even the foolishness of prior visits were now replaced with an uncomfortable calm. Everyone was thinking about Armstrong. Sandy began to talk rather uneasily about how he and Matt Kuykendall and Red Probst had joined the AVG back in Alabama when Skip had come to their base. He talked about his desire to get in on the fighting for which he had been trained. It still seemed to him that joining the AVG had been the right decision for him to make. Then he started talking about the beautiful San Francisco Bay area where he had been raised and what he was going to do when he got back home. But Newkirk added sardonically, "How do you know we're even going back?"

But Sandy's reply was firm and confident. They were going back, at least he was. He did not want to be buried in this Godforsaken country. Olga wished that they would change the subject, which they promptly did.

Soon Skip left but Sandy and Jack remained quite late, obviously dreading to go back to the airfield. They spoke about the P-40 a little more respectfully than in the past, and finally Newkirk asked Sandy about Red Probst. Sandy replied that it seemed that someone had put a hex on Red. While at Selma, he had wrecked his car and stayed in the hospital recuperating for a long time. He had also lost an aircraft in bad weather. Maybe Red had figured his luck would change if he joined the AVG. They speculated about the motives for most of the volunteers' joining the AVG. These were mostly financial, they figured, or in some cases it was probably to get away from something they wanted to forget.

It took awhile for the pain of Armstrong's death to ease sufficiently for Olga to return to the field. When she did return, she was accompanied by Lucy. She had bought Lucy in 1940 from a British veterinarian in Burma who donated the proceeds from the sale of the litter to a Spitfire fund. Her papers listed her name as "Havoc," after the British destroyer, but Olga changed the name to Lucy which seemed more appropriate since she was female. Lucy resembled an old mop and was small enough to carry anywhere. Of all the monkeys, cats, birds, and dogs that Olga had befriended, Lucy was the only permanent member of the Greenlaw family.

It was her compassion for animals that prompted her "business" on the field on the day she returned or at least it was the excuse she used. She was selling tickets for a show, the proceeds of which would be used for the construction of a pound for all the stray Burmese dogs. But she met with considerable resistance. "Padre" Frillman responded to the request by saying that he did not believe in either euthanasia or dog hospitals. Doc Prevo was even more discouraging.

He said that it would be much cheaper to just run over the dogs. He got at least a couple a day himself, he said, and could increase it to four a day if she wished. Olga did not think it was funny but the boys surely did. The doc continued, "How would you like to have Lucy put away because she has fleas and ticks?" Olga was indignant and defied him to find a flea on Lucy. That was the end of the drive for the dog pound.

Everyone had barely recovered from Armstrong's death when on September 22 another pilot, Maax C. Hammer from Cairo, Illinois, was killed in a solo accident. He had "gone in" while trying to find the airfield, blinded by a heavy rainstorm. Maax had been a student at LSU. He had only been with the AVG for about a week.

Hammer's funeral was not as emotional as Armstrong's had been, in part because Armstrong's had been the first and had only recently occurred, and also because Hammer was not as well known as Armstrong. Maax was to be buried in the Christian cemetery next to Johnnie Armstrong. The night of the crash Harvey and the Old Man had discussed the difficulty of getting to the crash site at night due to the heavy rain. Harvey insisted that the morale of the men dictated that an effort be made. It proved impossible, but two fellow pilots stood guard over the crash site until morning when a crash party could retrieve Maax's body.

The telephone rang all day at the Greenlaw house, the British wives again offering their assistance and sending flowers. Once again the empty room of the Greenlaw house was used as a funeral parlor, Maax's coffin supported by two chairs. That afternoon at the funeral it rained and Olga, ill and depressed, did not attend.

A day or two after Armstrong's death a clerk dropped by and told Olga that a plane had gone down but the pilot had bailed out. Tension gnawed at her stomach until she found out that the pilot was safe. Frank Schiel and Eric Shilling had been practicing dogfighting, and Schiel had gotten into trouble and had bailed out. Thankfully, Frank was all right but there went another precious P-40.

An atmosphere of tension prevailed for the next few days, with everyone expecting something to happen. Olga continued to feel badly, and Harvey told her that she had worms. She was indignant but knew he was probably right. It was a common malady in the Orient.

On October 25, Peter W. Atkinson was diving a P-40 when the prop governor gave way allowing the propeller to "over-rev" and in a screaming power dive his plane disintegrated. Pete's death was both demoralizing and confusing to the men. He had been so well-liked. A devout Catholic, he never missed a mass.

Almost automatically, Olga arranged for the burial. The Catholic ceremony was most impressive—a high mass with the bishop and twenty priests and one hundred choir boys. A Gurkha soldier sounded taps over the graves of the three American boys who were buried side by side in that Christian cemetery in the shadow of the jungle. "Three of them gone already," Olga thought, "and our war hasn't even started yet."

After the funeral Olga returned home alone. As she passed the room used as the funeral parlor, she noticed a few remaining flowers and palm leaves and the two empty chairs, seemingly waiting for another coffin. In her mind she heard a final refrain of taps. That night she would tell Harvey that she felt like leaving, and he would be angry with her.

The third and final Dutch ship arrived, and among the pilots were Greg Boyington, Robert W. Prescott, Fred S. Hodges, and Robert C. Moss. Freddie Hodges soon acquired the name "Fearless Freddie" due to his paranoia over the Burma insects. Boyington was simply called "the Bulldog" because of his massive shoulders. Each had their various reasons for being there. Some were mysterious like Boyington, while others were as easy to read as an open book. Olga had their personalities and motives "filed and cataloged" in short order. Boyington was the toughest of the bunch. R. C. Moss was good-looking. Bob Prescott was a tall, rough-hewn Texan. After these fellows there would be no more men, no more aircraft, and above all no spare parts arriving for a long, long time.

Thomas A. Jones and Moss decided after a while that they would go on a tiger hunt in their spare time. Chennault thought this was something novel and gave his permission. They met at the Greenlaw home the night before where they made much to-do about all the equipment—heavy rifles, knives, flashlights. They had been advised where to hunt by natives, who guaranteed that the tigers would be as thick as Burmese flies. All they got when they arrived in the Chindwin Valley, however, was a case of malaria for Jones and the dengue fever for Moss. Jones became quite ill and suffered from the effects of malaria for several months.

Meanwhile the training continued, and no phase was neglected, including what to do if one was shot down—jungle survival. Word was out that the entire group would soon move to Kunming, China. It was a welcome thought that they might soon leave Toungoo. Suddenly things were happening again. Squadron leaders were posted—Ole Olson and Robert Sandell, ex-Army men, and Jack Newkirk, an ex-Navy man. The group was then divided into three eighteen-plane squadrons. The First Squadron called themselves the "First Pursuit" or "Adam and Eve" squadron. The Second Squadron named itself the "Panda Bears." Finally the Third selected the name "Hell's Angels." Dividing the men into squadrons promptly served to boost morale as each squadron began to smooth out its kinks and become a separate entity of the AVG. The emphasis was now on teamwork, and the Toungoo campus once again was just like the day before the big game.

Chennault's unorthodox manner of handling discipline varied somewhat from that of his military cohorts. So lax was the discipline on the ground that military observers regarded the AVG as an undisciplined mob. Rigid discipline was confined to the air, but in its enforcement Chennault was obstinate.

At first AVG activity was isolated from the rest of Burma and the world in general. During the five months of training at Kyedaw they were never in direct communication with the British in Rangoon or anyone else for that matter. Most military men who knew about the AVG simply figured that exposed to combat, these American volunteers would fall apart. But then all of a sudden the AVG started to get a lot of attention. Bigwigs started coming to Kyedaw.

Olga stood by the runway and watched as four large British Hudson bombers circled to land. Harvey had told her not to come to the airfield that day because they were expecting dignitaries, so there she was. Air Marshal Sir Robert Brooke Popham was the British Commander-in-Chief of the Far East. Harvey introduced Olga to Sir Robert whereupon seeing her camera he offered advice on how to take pictures of airplanes in formation. The AVG put on a show that left old "Popeye" much impressed.

Next the AVG was visited by the air officer commanding the Far East, Air Vice Marshal Pulford, and then in rapid succession by Field Marshal Sir Archibald Wavell and the American generals MacGruder and Brett. Olga got upset with Brett when his only comment about the organization was, "I never saw such a dirty kitchen in my life," figuring he had missed, intentionally or not, the combat potential of the group.

There also appeared a flood of newspapermen and correspondents, the most noted of which were men like Leland Stowe, Edgar Snow, and Vincent Sheean. The AVG did not have the time nor the manpower to give them a formal welcome, so they gave them the run of the base and the same accommodations that the men had. They were left to snoop around, and it did not take them long to discover the problems—the lack of spare parts, the fact that some of the AVG had quit due to fear or boredom, and the lack of discipline. A correspondent for one of the large American newspapers was not well appreciated by the men, who repulsed him with a shower of empty beer bottles when he approached their barracks for interviews. Olga liked Leland Stowe, however, and they talked at great length. She finally saw him off at the Toungoo station on the "Up Mail."

November 2 was called Soul's Day by the Burmese natives and the custom was to light up their temples, pagodas, and homes. Little oil lamps covered with colored paper could be seen everywhere, even in the trees and beside almost every grave in the cemetery. Toungoo looked like a huge Christmas tree. Olga thought about the three American youngsters buried in the Christian cemetery. She brought eighteen large candles and after dividing them equally between the three graves, she lit them. It was dark and she was all alone. Suddenly amidst the flickering little lights and shadows dancing around the graveyard, Olga became frightened and quickly left.

Boatner Carney was in Toungoo one day on AVG business and told Olga that his Chinese girlfriend, Rose Mok, would be coming through with one of her own convoys. He wanted to know if she could spend the night with her. Olga knew and liked Rose from days gone by. Rose was an enterprising young lady. She was setting up a restaurant in Kunming where she knew it would do good business when the AVGs arrived. She also used these passages to smuggle a few items, which was strictly against the law. The Burma Road traffic was restricted solely to necessary food and war supplies. She advised Olga to warn the boys about two very beautiful and notorious girls in Kunming who had been enjoying a large clientele until it was discovered that both had leprosy.

The AVG base was only sixty miles from the Thailand border. The Thais had been sandwiched between the French and British colonists for many years, and due to strained relations with them, they had been receptive to the Japanese propaganda with the message "Asia for the Asians." Consequently the Japanese were able to build many airstrips along the Thai border, starting as early as 1939. Chennault was well aware of their presence. He felt his group at Kyedaw was particularly vulnerable on this eastern flank since the British had only a single observer keeping an eye on the Thai border. He believed this to be seriously inadequate in spite of the two radar stations at Rangoon manned by the British, and he told them so. While they relied heavily on the radar stations for the protection of Rangoon, Chennault knew that both stations monitored only the southern approaches and left Toungoo to the north completely unguarded. For this reason he started dispatching daily patrols over the Thailand airfields in late October.

Intelligence reports disclosed that Japanese fighters were now being sighted on the French airfield around Saigon and further south in Indochina. In addition, there were reports that the total Japanese aircraft in all Indochina had risen from seventy-four to 245. It was obvious that things were coming to a head very rapidly. Ever since the United States had placed an oil embargo on Japan in the summer of 1941, Chennault knew that Japan would have to do something drastic or forfeit their ambitions for expansion. He saw ample evidence of their move toward further aggression to the south and west, as veteran troops were pulled out of China and replaced by puppet troops. Canton, Haiphong, Hainan Island, and Formosa were alive with activity, and Chinese intelligence informed him of significant Japanese naval movements down the coast of Japan. He personally spent the hours of dusk and dawn on the alert in the control tower, often accompanied in the evenings by Dr. Gentry. There was little conversation between the two as they watched in the direction of the Thailand border until it became too dark to see.

It was 11 A.M. on December 8, 1941. Chennault had just finished his morning vigil in the thatched roof tower and was climbing down. Across the date line to the east it was one day earlier, December 7, 1941, a date etched into the memory of every American. As Chennault walked towards his quarters he was met by a radioman frantically waving a message. It was the news of Pearl Harbor.

Practically every American alive at the time of the Japanese surprise attack on Pearl Harbor can relate to this day exactly what he or she was doing when the news came. The nation and all Americans around the world were stunned. Olga Greenlaw, even with all the wit and stamina and sheer resolution which she had mustered against the aches and bruises of an adventurous life, wept bitterly. Half the AVG were Navy men and some had friends at Pearl Harbor. Groups gathered around the radios and listened. Hong Kong, Batavia, Singapore, Manila—the Japanese appeared to have gone mad. As the radio poured out the news of December 7, Olga tried to refresh her memory. They were west of the date line. Therefore, in Burma today was yesterday—or was today tomorrow. She could not make up her mind.

There was a fever over the camp now. Every stride was quickened. Morning greeting among the men was punctuated by such sentiments as "those goddamn Japs, those monkey-faced little bastards." There was general agreement that they would "kick their little brown butts."

Harvey told Olga to pack a couple of bags and come to the field to stay at the hospital since Toungoo was not safe anymore. "We can expect to be bombed any moment," he reasoned. As she unpacked, she wondered how her mastermind husband figured that it would be safer there at the airfield, which he also expected to be bombed.

Kyedaw was now on war alert. Gas masks, World War I steel helmets, and sidearms were issued to the men. Olga was issued the gas mask and the helmet, but no sidearm. She definitely wanted a sidearm, so she went straight to Harvey. After all, she thought, what's the use in having an executive officer for a husband if it doesn't give one the inside track once in a while. Almost expressionless, Harvey looked at her for a moment, then told her to "scram." She barely got her mouth open again when he added, "Go to the tower and wait for orders."

Instead, she went directly to headquarters, to the Old Man's office. Inside she spoke to the clerk and inquired if "the Colonel" was in, then cautiously peeked through the crack in his door. He was sitting at his desk engrossed in paperwork. Suddenly without looking up, he startled her by saying, "Why aren't you working at the war diary? Take the empty desk in that room and get at it!" "Yes sir," she replied, almost saluting, and from that moment on she was the official AVG historian.

Chennault's foremost priority now was to make sure that the AVG did not get caught on the ground. They absolutely had to meet the attack in the air. As he recalled later, "Events of December 7 and 8 made it clear that the fighter group was the only salvage from all the elaborate plans that had been so painstakingly woven in Washington. Had I known then that for over a year this fighter group would be the only effective Allied air force to oppose the Japanese on the Asiatic mainland, I probably would not have entered the combat with such high hopes."

There was dissension among the Allies. The British were of the general opinion that the Japanese, in spite of what had already transpired, were incapable of dislodging them. They felt confident that they could defend Rangoon and the rest of Burma from attack and thus refused an offer from the Generalissimo to supply six divisions of the Chinese Army for the defense of Burma. The British were not interested. What they wanted was the AVG. Chennault came unwound. He had not "raised" the AVG to be taken over by the British. In such a situation he would lose his command over the group, and they would be under orders from Group Captain Manning, who was in charge of the British air defense over Rangoon. Manning used combat tactics that Chennault felt were suicidal, and he did not want the AVG to be subjected to such stupid orders. Needless to say, Chennault and Manning had not been getting along very well during the AVG's stay at Toungoo.

"We finally worked out an agreement satisfactory to both the Generalissimo and the British, whereby one squadron of the AVG would assist the RAF in the defense of Rangoon with the other two squadrons to be stationed at Kunming," Chennault wrote later. The squadron in Rangoon would remain under Chennault's direct command, subject only to operational control by the RAF. Thus AVG pilots in Burma would be free to follow their prior training and pursue their own operations.

Thailand capitulated to the Japanese on December 10, and Japanese troops and military equipment piled into Bangkok as the forward staging base for a planned assault on Burma and Malaya. Photographs returned by Eric Shilling, who had flown a reconnaissance mission over Bangkok accompanied by Ed Rector and Bert Christman, left Chennault aghast. The pictures showed the docks jammed with enemy transports disembarking troops and supplies. Don Maugg airdrome was packed with ninety aircraft parked wing tip to wing tip awaiting transport to the forward fighter bases along the western Thai border. Chennault literally ached for a few bombers. "This was one of the many times during the war when a kingdom was lost for want of a few planes," he remembered in later years. He would have given anything to have been able to dispatch twelve bombers to bomb the Don Maugg airdrome and thus save the city of Rangoon. Instead, he could only dispatch his fighters—the Third Squadron, the Hell's Angels—to Mingaladon airdrome ten miles north of Rangoon on December 12 to join the New Zealand and Australian pilots of the Sixty-seventh Squadron of the RAF. The First and Second squadrons flew to Kunming on December 18. At this time, only the planes of the Third Squadron were bore-sighted and ready for combat.

Ground forces were alerted, and three CNAC transports descended on Toungoo and quickly dispatched the AVG headquarters to Kunming before the morning of December 19. By sunrise, there were thirty-four Adam and Eve and Panda Bear P-40s gassed, armed, and ready to fight in Kunming, all this while the general staff, busy at paperwork, planned for the first engagement with the Japanese. Kunming had been bombed the morning before. This lightning-fast transfer of the entire AVG force was to be a vital characteristic frequently imposed by their wiry commander. Chennault breathed a sigh of relief. At least he had two of his squadrons under the protection of the Chinese net.

Until the fall of Rangoon AVG ground personnel were busy transferring all the supplies they could possibly get from the docks at Rangoon, trucking them up the Burma Road to Kunming. On December 19 all remained calm. There was no sighting of the enemy either in Kunming or at Mingaladon where Squadron Commander Arvid Olson was skillfully preparing his group for combat. They would have no warning of the approaching enemy, and he knew that he must be especially alert lest they get caught on the ground and wiped out.

On the morning of December 20, back at Kunming, Chennault's telephone rang, and he answered it quickly. The Chinese warning net reported that ten Japanese bombers had crossed the Yunnan border and were heading northwest. Quickly Chennault alerted the Second Squadron to make the interception and the First Squadron to remain in reserve at the standby area west of Kunming. Heavy engine noises were reported nearing station X-10. The net reports kept coming in—

"Unknowns overhead at station P-8," and finally, "Engine noises over the overcast at station C-23." The pilot on the fighter control board revealed the path of the approach of the Japanese bombers. They would soon appear about fifty miles east of Kunming.

But Chennault knew the Japanese airmen. They would begin a circling tactic to confuse the net, then dash for Kunming. He fired a red flare into the air and took off for the combat operations shelter on a small hill overlooking the field. Jack Newkirk led one four-plane element in search of the bombers while Jim Howard, son of a former medical missionary to China, led another element. He was to fly protective cover for the Kunming field. Robert Sandell, leading sixteen P-40s, took off and headed for the standby area.

Once inside the combat operation bunker Chennault and those with him found it too dark to see the duplicate plotting board, so Harvey struck matches as Colonel Hsu, Chennault's interpreter, manned the field telephone. As Colonel Hsu relayed the reports from the net, Harvey and the Old Man plotted the bombers' direction. They eagerly awaited the moment they had long dreamed of—experienced American pilots in American fighter aircraft aided by the extensive Yunnan net were heading to intercept the enemy before they could reach their target. It was a momentous occasion, especially for Chennault, because it was a dream of over four years come true. As Providence would have it, the fate of China now lay in the capable hands of those few American airmen, and Chennault yearned to be ten years younger and among them, "crouched in a cockpit instead of a dugout, tasting the stale rubber of an oxygen mask and peering ahead into limitless space through the cherry-red rings of a gunsight."

"There they are," a voice suddenly cracked over the field radio.

"No, no, they can't be Japs."

"Look at those red balls."

"Let's get 'em." Then there was a deafening silence.

Chennault made a quick calculation and then radioed Sandell to head for Iliang, thirty miles southeast of Kunming where he figured the Japanese bombers would approach. Just then the net reported that the bombers had turned and were heading back to Indochina, that there was the sound of gunfire and the heavy concussion of Japanese bombs near the mountains near Iliang.

That was it, Chennault noticed as he emerged from the dugout. The Chinese were already returning from their refuge among the grave mounds of the city, grateful there had been no bombing. He and the others returned to the field. Very soon Jim Howard and his element landed and reported that they had not seen anything. New-kirk returned and very sheepishly reported that they had suffered from buck fever when confronted with ten grey Ki-21 "Sally" twin-engine bombers, which puzzled them further when they quickly jet-tisoned their bomb loads and turned for home. Newkirk's bunch hesitated too long before organizing their pursuit and could not over-take them. Yet one pilot, Ed Rector, would not relinquish the chase because he "sure as hell wanted one." He threw all caution to the wind as he pressed his attack beyond the endurance of his aircraft. When the others turned for home, Rector was still in hot pursuit.

Suddenly sixteen shark-tooth P-40s broke low over the field. Chennault heard the wind whistling in their open gun barrels and knew they had been in a fight. They slow-rolled and buzzed and beat up the fields in general and appeared not to want to land at all. What a sight it was. Finally they landed and Sandy reported that they had intercepted the Japanese formation in full retreat over Iliang running along on top of a solid overcast with one lone P-40 in hot pursuit after the entire ten-plane formation. Sandy said that when they hit them it was not exactly with the lessons and teamwork learned at Toungoo. They "went a little crazy," and it was a wonder that they did not shoot one another as well as the Japanese. The tactics em-ployed in the ensuing 130-mile chase were not exactly ones to be repeated. After shooting down two bombers, Fritz Wolf got upset be-cause he thought his guns had jammed only to discover later in the excitement that he had simply fired all his ammunition. They were all talking at once, too excited to be completely coherent.

"Well boys," Chennault finally told his excited pilots, "it was a good job but not good enough. Next time get them all." He then held school on tactics and pointed out their mistakes in minute detail while the engagement was still fresh on their minds—before the next meal.

Years later Chennault was to learn from an escaped prisoner of war, AVG pilot Lewis Bishop, that only one Japanese bomber re-turned to base. Bishop obtained this information from a Japanese who had been on the flight. The other planes had been either shot down or so badly damaged in the fight that they soon crashed. Nine out of ten bombers were destroyed—not bad for the AVG's very first encounter. So completely had the AVG impressed the Japanese airmen that they never returned to bomb Kunming until the AVG had disbanded. The AVG lost only one aircraft when Ed Rector's plane force landed on its return due to fuel starvation.

However, it was the air combat over the city of Rangoon, soon to follow, that stamped the AVG for fame. At Rangoon, Arvid Olson and the Third Squadron were confronted with a somewhat different situation than at Kunming. They had to fight without proper warning of approaching enemy aircraft. Alerts would generally commence after a phone call from the RAF warning "bombers overhead," or after they had seen the dust boil up as the RAF's Buffaloes scrambled. Most interceptions would be made only after the Japanese bombers had bombed their targets and were returning home. The AVG was treated more or less like a stepchild by the RAF.

The first encounter for the Hell's Angels squadron was on December 23, when the first aerial spearhead of the Japanese invasion flew in from Thailand across the Gulf of Martaban to plaster Rangoon docks and the airfield at Mingaladon. There were forty-eight Sally bombers and twenty Nate and Oscar escort fighters. There was no warning for the AVG as the first unescorted wave of Sally bombers bombed the harbor. They were returning home by the time twelve P-40s and RAF Buffaloes could reach altitude to strike at the second wave of approaching bombers and fighter escorts which were heading for Mingaladon airdrome.

The Hell's Angels descended on this second Japanese formation like a pack of hungry wolves and shot down six planes. During the battle Ken Jernstedt and Charles Older each destroyed one Nate apiece just as Neil Martin's plane exploded. While Older shot down another Nate, two more P-40s were shot down. Henry Gilbert, the youngest AVG at twenty-one was caught by the top current of a Sally bomber and crashed, while two fighters converged on Paul Green's P-40 and sent him down. Fortunately he was able to bail out. Japanese fighters then strafed the crowds in Rangoon which had jammed into the streets to watch the raid. A total of seven Allied aircraft and six pilots were lost—three P-40s and two AVG pilots plus four Buffaloes and four RAF pilots. There were twelve confirmed enemy aircraft shot down with more probable ones being claimed.

The city panicked. The rich fled and the native Burmese rioted while those harboring hatred for the British started killing them in isolated ambushes. All the Burmese "hired help" abandoned the Mingaladon airdrome after the bombings, leaving the AVG personnel to cook and provide for themselves. The men ate what they could find, which consisted mostly of stale bread and hot beer which they drank in the 115-degree heat. The fun was beginning to go out of being an AVG.

On Christmas Day, December 25, 1941, a legend was born over the skies of Rangoon. On every front the Allied nations were taking a beating, and morale was low on the home front as the news of war filtered home. There was little cause for optimism. Americans were shocked and bewildered by the course of the war, for at this point they were clearly losing. The Japanese appeared invincible and the ubiquitous Zero had still not met its match. God was on the side of the Allies, the Allied nations knew. Or was He? To be right and lose was inconceivable. But where could they look for some encouragement? The name Rangoon might have a familiar ring to some, but few Americans could tell you exactly where it was, geographically speaking. Yet before the sun would set on this Christmas Day, the American people and the Allied nations would rejoice due to events near Rangoon.

Olson's squadron of twelve P-40s climbed to intercept the Japanese air armada of seventy-one Sally bombers and thirty to forty predominantly Oscar fighters. They would be joined later by sixteen Buffaloes of the RAF. The AVG intercepted the enemy formation for the first time before they reached their target whereupon they immediately knocked down fifteen bombers and nine fighters. Robert P. "Duke" Hedman destroyed two bombers in successive passes. Two AVGs lost their planes, one crash-landing then walking in, the other managing to land after colliding with a Nate. The RAF destroyed seven Japanese planes and lost nine of its Buffaloes with six of their own pilots being killed. The AVG was officially credited with twenty-eight kills. The good news swept to Allied nations around the world in a flash. Unknown to the AVG, their extraordinary feats of heroism against tremendous odds were making front-page headlines, not as the "AVG," which is what they called themselves, but as the "Flying Tigers." Journalists had what they needed now, a prescription for sagging morale, these colorful fighter pilots in their shark-tooth P-40s who were both American and winning. Their actions from now on would be front-page copy.

Radio communications between Olson and the Old Man in Kunming revealed that the Third Squadron was down to only eleven flyable aircraft. So on December 30, Chennault sent seventeen P-40s of the Second Squadron, the Panda Bears, to relieve the Hell's Angels. As the Japanese regrouped to organize a massive attack to finish off Rangoon, the AVG took the offensive. On January 3, 1942, Jack Newkirk and Tex Hill began to lead strafing attacks on the Japanese airfields in nearby Thailand to catch their planes on the ground. It was Tex Hill's first encounter in combat. He later reminisced about it:

> The first mission was run out of Mingaladon. Newkirk was leading it and I was flying wingman to Jim Howard. Christman was flying Newkirk's wing. Christman had to turn back because of engine trouble—planes were getting pretty worn by now. It got to where a plane was just as likely to go down from engine failure as from the Japs.
>
> The mission was to strafe an airfield at a place called Meshod in Thailand. We got over there at about ten thousand feet, and I got so preoccupied with seeing the enemy planes on the ground that I didn't think about looking up. The three of us bent 'em over and as we approached the field I looked up and there were three more planes in the traffic pattern with us. Like lightning, one Jap tacked on to Jim Howard's tail and was eating him up. I pulled around on him as quickly as I could and started firing as I did. I didn't even look through the gunsights, just watched the tracers like following a garden hose. With my diving speed built up I came right up on him and he blew up. I flew through the debris and pulled up to come around and meet another Jap coming straight at me. This was shortly before they learned that it could be painful to do that.
>
> The Japs soon learned that the P-40 had too much Allison engine and armor plating up front for their 7.9 mm rounds to get to the P-40 pilot and that his .50 caliber machine guns put them in reach long before they were in firing range. But for this Jap in my sights it was too late. Yet while I got him, he put a lot of lead in my prop. My plane started shaking real bad because it was now out of balance. Newkirk got two head on during the battle and then we started for home. We got five on the ground and three in the air.
>
> After we landed back at Mingaladon, we got to talking about what had happened and I didn't think Jim Howard was fully aware of all the activity that went on around him. So we went out to look

at the planes and counted eleven bullet holes in it that Jim was not aware of. I then noticed that mine had thirty-three from an overhead pass a guy made at me, and I didn't see why he didn't get me. I found out, too, why my plane vibrated so much—the 7.9 mm bullets that I had received during the head-on pass hadn't penetrated the prop, they just stuck in it.

The Panda Bears became such a nuisance to the Japanese activity developing in Thailand that the Japanese High Command mounted a sizable fighter sweep program in an effort to eliminate the remaining Allied air forces around Rangoon. The AVG's first contact with this effort came on January 4 when no less than thirty Japanese fighters pounced on six lonely patrolling Panda Bears. Three P-40s went down under fire from having been caught off guard. The others escaped from the ambush due to their superior diving speed. John "Gil" Bright belly-landed his burning P-40 in a rice paddy. He was nearly shot by his own guns as he hastily departed in front of his plane just as the intense heat of the fire began to cook off rounds in his machine guns.

The battle was the first in an all-out three-day Japanese aerial assault on Rangoon during which the AVG managed to plant thirty participating enemy aircraft permanently in the surrounding jungle and rice paddies. Just as many were thought to have crashed at sea on their return to their Thai bases.

Meshod was again strafed on January 8, and Charles D. Mott was forced down near the target and became, unfortunately, the first AVG prisoner of war. While Hill, Newkirk, Howard, and the other Panda Bears kept up the strafing activity through most of January, the Japanese were content to send solo bombers at night one at a time simply for purposes of harassment. All this while the ground crew and all nonflying personnel including Padre worked the Rangoon docks loading truck convoys with Lend-Lease equipment for shipment up the Burma Road to Kunming. When the Japanese bombers returned in force they had altered their tactics since their last encounter with the AVG. Now each bomber was protected by three fighters.

On January 12 Lt. Gen. Shojiro Iida's Imperial Japanese Fifteenth Army began its westward push into Burma from Thailand. By the end of the month his forces had driven Lt. Gen. Thomas Hutton's

British, Burmese, and Indian troops out of Moulmein, and the British retreat was on.

Between January 23 and 27, the Japanese made six major attacks on the AVG. Finally, by January 28 they were sending only fighter sweeps to concentrate on the American airmen. Newkirk wired the Old Man, "The more hardships, work, and fighting the men have to do the higher our morale goes. Squadron spirit really strong now." Yet they were down to only ten P-40s so Chennault replaced them with Sandy Sandell's Adam and Eve squadron. Things looked grim for Rangoon when Sandy and his men took over at Mingaladon. As they set up for business, the war-weary Panda Bears departed for Kunming. The Japanese Army had crossed the Thai border, and it was increasingly apparent that the British had neither the men, the equipment, nor the leadership to stop them. It was only a matter of time before Rangoon would fall.

Meanwhile back in Kunming, Chennault received newspaper clippings from friends back in Louisiana. He and the men were astonished to find themselves famous as the "Flying Tigers." Chennault later remarked, "How the term Flying Tigers was derived from the shark-nosed P-40 I will never know." He was quick to give credit for the shark's teeth to the British in North Africa and before them to the Germans during World War I. "The insignia we made famous was by no means original with the AVG. Our pilots copied the shark-tooth design on their P-40s' noses from a colored illustration in the *India Illustrated Weekly* depicting an RAF squadron in the Libyan desert with shark-nosed P-40s." Chennault also noted that the prolific imagination of some of the writers, though it made good copy, gave too much credit to some supposedly mystical power of the men and not enough to the solid facts on which their accomplishments were based. He also noted some writers had a little trouble with math, much to the amusement of the men. The old Curtiss-Wright P-40 was certainly proving to be an excellent fighter during the battles over Rangoon. At those lower altitudes he found the P-40 to be a superior plane to the Hurricane and at its best against the Japanese Army's Nates and Navy's Zeroes. In addition, Curtiss had built them to take punishment. The P-40 could be repaired after damage and back in the air while Japanese planes receiving similar damage would have been total losses.

January also found Claire Chennault prostrate with his annual attack of chronic bronchitis. He had a radio placed in his sickroom so that he could listen to the chatter of his pilots during combat over Rangoon. "It was over the radio that I heard of the Japanese attack on Toungoo, February 4. They struck at 6 A.M., there was no warning, and the men were asleep in their bunks. Six RAF Blenheims burned and three P-40s were lost," Chennault recalled later. "That might all too easily have been the fate of the entire AVG eight weeks earlier."

On February 7, squadron leader Robert J. Sandell was killed at Mingaladon while testing a P-40 after repairs. Sandy had been more military-oriented than the rest of the squadron leaders and objected to the social mixing of men and pilots. He was criticized for this by his fellow pilots, who at one point had made up a petition to have him relieved as flight leader. When the men in his squadron presented the petition to Sandell, he simply added his name to the bottom of the list. It was the best possible reaction, since seeing what a good sport he was, they tore up the petition and followed him into battle.

With the death of Sandell, it was Bob Neale who led the Adam and Eve squadron in the final phase of the air battle over Rangoon. Chennault ordered Neale to stop all strafing and bombing escort missions due to the deplorable condition of the squadron's aircraft. Their engines were much in need of major overhauls.

Neale radioed Kunming for instructions regarding final evacuation and received Chennault's often quoted reply—"Expend equipment, conserve personnel utmost, retire with last bottle oxygen."

On the night of February 27, a tired and hungry Bob Neale contemplated the Old Man's final message. Chennault had certainly left him enough latitude to act on his own judgment. The British had failed to hold the west bank of the Sittang River, which was the last natural barrier between the Japanese Army and Rangoon. The British were now beating a rapid retreat and the city's fate was certain.

Rangoon itself was in a shambles, with buildings burning out of control. The city had lost all of its services. Even the telephone operators had been flown out, the last organized force save for the British military, and even they were not too organized at the moment. The British authorities had released the undesirables, the criminals, the insane, and the lepers to fend for themselves. Looting was rampant. Uniformed British soldiers were shot or knifed from ambush by bitter Burmese. Tons of Lend-Lease supplies earmarked for China, piled high on the docks, were being bulldozed into the harbor, AVG trucks having already headed for Lashio. People driven crazy by fear overfilled harbor boats which capsized and sank. Finally, without initial direction and in complete disorder, refugees started to walk north towards India nine hundred miles away. Most were Indian civil servants endeavoring to carry with them some of the fruits of their toil. They began their exodus burdened with personal valuables, but swiftly became prey for the resentful Burmese, who had always despised them. The Burmese attacked them like wolf packs, raping and killing them, then carrying off their possessions. Some looters broke into jewelry stores, leaving with hats full of precious stones. Then after quarreling among themselves they would lose some of the valuables in the streets. These jewels would occasionally be found by AVG ground personnel.

Neale learned on February 27 that the British were withdrawing their radar station from Mingaladon to Magwe without warning him. This radar had been the only remaining semblance of an air warning net for the area. In addition, landline and radio communications between his squadron and the RAF, which had always been poor at best, was now almost nonexistent due to the confusion of the British retreat. Neale made his decision. He informed his element leader that they would depart Mingaladon the next morning and fly top cover for the "tailend Charlies" of the AVG truck convoy which was just a hop ahead of the Japanese. However, he and R. T. Smith would remain behind as long as possible for word of a missing AVG pilot, in hopes that he could be located before the Japanese secured the perimeter.

On February 28, Neale and Smith stripped out Neale's radio to enlarge the baggage compartment of his P-40 so if necessary it could be used to fly out the missing pilot. However, by early morning of the next day, there was still no word regarding Edward Liebolt.

The Japanese were traveling by night and attacking at dawn in a clever scheme of making a lot of noise in one place to attract attention, while they actually attacked at another place where they desired to move their main force. The scheme worked, allowing a rapid advance of twenty-five to thirty miles a day. In this manner, they quickly cut the Prome Road, the last roadway of retreat from Rangoon up the east bank of the Irrawaddy River towards the coveted Yenangyaung oil fields. Of the nine hundred thousand Indians who fled before this rapid advance, almost 90 percent perished as a result of pestilence and hunger. The pursuing Burmese who preyed on them did not fare much better. The Burmese were always more prone to violence than most other southeast Asians, their capital crime rate being the highest in the world.

The highland Burmese were generally more loyal to the British while the lowland Burmese used the Japanese "Asia for the Asians" policy as a means to their own goal of dislodging the British. They later showed no loyalty to the Japanese. They had been the major political force under the old Burmese monarchy of precolonial days and desired a return to power. Their agents frequently disguised themselves as "pongyis," orange-robed Buddhist monks, and carried out sabotage against the British so effectively that many Allied soldiers began to suspect all the Buddhist monks and shot them on sight. Consequently, the Japanese made rapid land gains in southern Burma with the aid of various dissident groups, leaving the Allies little time to regroup. The Burmese front simply fell into a rout.

Finally, Neale made the painful decision. They would have to leave without Liebolt, and he signaled to Smith to "wind 'em up" and shoved two cases of whiskey where he had hoped to shove Liebolt. The two sharks then whipped up the Mingaladon dust, skirted the bomb craters, and climbed out over the green jungle. They took up a heading of north-northeast for Magwe where the retreating British forces were hastily trying to organize a massive airlift to evacuate British civilians. As Neale and Smith climbed for altitude they left behind the burning city which had been under siege for seventy-five consecutive days.

Following a brief stay at Magwe the First Squadron flew on to Kunming after being relieved by Ole Olson and the Hell's Angels squadron. Neale and his guys were glad to be "back home" and were delighted with their forty-four air victories. William "Black Mack" McGarry had eight "Japs" to his credit, Bob Little had accumulated six. George T. Burgard had seven, and Neale had twelve. Most of the rest had more than two each.

With the fall of the important seaport of Rangoon on March 9, 1942, the Allies pondered the grave consequences of the loss of all of Burma. China, with the loss of the Burma Road, would certainly be in danger of final defeat and India would face the imminent threat of Japanese invasion. The Japanese had even trained an army of Indian dissidents they called the Indian National Army which they intended to use after the invasion to gain support of all Indians eager to overthrow British rule.

Consequently, Burma was the key to the defense of the China-Burma-India Theater. It was a rich prize sought by Japan for two purposes. First, its capture would sever the Allies' connection with China. Second, it was a country rich in natural resources, including oil, tungsten, and manganese, and most important, it was the world's largest exporter of rice. All these items were vitally needed by the Japanese people to sustain their aspirations for expansion.

During these turbulent times, Winston Churchill in an address to the House of Commons in April, expressed a similar conclusion. Concerning the Japanese, he said:

> Their best plan would be to push northwards from Burma into China and try to finish Chinese resistance and the great Chinese leader Chiang Kai-shek. We have not yet noticed any Jap movement lately which is inconsistent with this idea and there are several which support it.
>
> Certainly by driving China out of the war . . . Japan would be furthering her own interests. China is the only place where Japan can obtain a major decision in 1942.

Realizing the importance of holding northern Burma, the Allies, under the command of Lt. Gen. Sir Harold R. L. G. Alexander, decided to establish a defense line 150 miles north of Rangoon, running west to east from Prome to Toungoo, across the Pegu Yoma Mountains. Hopefully, this would enable the Allies to control the two major valleys in an effort to keep the advancing Japanese in southern Burma. Stilwell, with Chinese troops, would hold the east flank, which dominated the Sittang Valley and the Mandalay-Rangoon railway. The British Burma Corps under Lt. Gen. Williams J. Slim would hold the west flank at Prome near the Irrawaddy River. Thus the Allies hoped, with little optimism, to contain the advancing Japanese in southern Burma.

General Alexander, the British commander and Stilwell's boss, was a gallant soldier of World War I and a national hero after successfully commanding the British retreat and evacuation at Dunkirk. He was typically British, son of an earl complete with superb mustache and English drawl. Stilwell frequently vented his feelings rather colorfully in his diary, where he recorded his innermost thoughts. Following his first meeting with Alexander he wrote that the Englishman was "astonished to find ME, mere me, a goddamn American, in command of Chinese troops. 'Extrawdinary!' Looked me over as if I had just crawled out from under a rock." Stilwell frequently gave nicknames to those he did not respect and referred to the Generalissimo as "Peanut." So "Vinegar Joe," a gentleman long on guts and short on tact, arrived at Toungoo to command the 200th Division of the Chinese Fifth Army.

The Allied command—Alexander, Chennault, Chiang Kai-shek, and Stilwell—were never too cohesive because each seemed motivated primarily by his own interests. The Generalissimo wanted to retain actual control over his Chinese Army even though he had officially placed them, by agreement with the United States, under Stilwell's command. The British wanted to retain their colonial grip on Burma simply to secure India, the anchor of their Asian empire. Stilwell's goal was to keep the Chinese fighting by securing the Burma Road, and Chennault wanted to wage air war on Japanese staging ports and shipping lanes. The United States wanted China in the war ultimately as a springboard for an attack on the Japanese home islands.

General Stilwell thus had an impossible task from the outset. By the time he became established at Toungoo, he was already in danger of encirclement by the Japanese. The remaining Chinese Fifth Army still had not left China for various reasons given by the Generalissimo. There was much conflict also between Stilwell and the Chinese generals. When he gave them an order they first had to clear it with the Generalissimo six hundred miles away. Chiang persisted in giving instructions directly to his generals, which was very disturbing to Stilwell. Day after day the Chinese commanders procrastinated until Stilwell was to write of them in his diary, "The pusillanimous bastards. I can't shoot them, I can't relieve them, and just talking to them does no good."

Meanwhile in the valley west of the mountain range which separated the two Allied forces, Slim was being driven out of Prome and had begun a retreat along the Irrawaddy River towards Magwe. Captured British soldiers were stripped of their clothes and tied to trees and used for bayonet practice by the advancing Japanese. Captured

British ambulances filled with casualties were soaked with gasoline and set afire, burning men alive. When his defense completely collapsed on April 15, Slim destroyed the Yenangyaung oil fields, which consisted of over five thousand active oil wells.

Since February 24, AVG operations at Magwe had been difficult because the field was used extensively by the British to evacuate RAF personnel to India. Two DC-2s, four Hudsons, and twelve Blenheims were in the traffic pattern almost constantly. AVG pilots covered with dust slept near their planes on constant alert because the only radar warning system was pointed south, leaving their eastern flank unguarded.

On March 19, two AVG pilots, Bill Read and Ken Jernstedt, using Toungoo as a staging field, struck the Moulmein target in Thailand. Their successful raid netted them the highest individual score ever made by the AVG. The Japanese lost fifteen of twenty fighters lined up in a row at one outlying fighter base, and three bombers and one transport were destroyed at Moulmein. They never suspected that the AVG could strike so deep into Thailand. This, coupled with a successful bombing raid by the British on Japanese-held Mingaladon airdrome which netted the British twelve Zeroes shot down and sixteen aircraft destroyed on the ground, shocked the Japanese.

Determined now to destroy Magwe completely and put an end to the Allied air effort in Burma, the Japanese struck back on March 21. Two hundred sixty-six Japanese aircraft fighters and bombers pounded Magwe, killing crew chief J. E. Fauth and mortally wounding Frank Swartz, who died after being flown to a hospital in India. Meanwhile on March 22, George B. McMillan and three other pilots returned from India with four new P-40Es, a number which later swelled to six. To the AVG the six new planes seemed heaven-sent. By the middle of April AVG combat-worthy aircraft had risen to thirty-six.

On March 23 some of the best pilots of the First and Second squadrons left Kunming for Thailand to avenge Magwe. Bob Neale and Greg Boyington led six P-40s of the Adam and Eve squadron while Jack Newkirk led a four-plane formation of Panda Bears. It was a long flight which necessitated refueling at Loi-Wing and later at Heho and Namsang, two forward RAF fighter bases near the Thai border. From Namsang they took off on the morning of March 24 before dawn, and Neale's flight hit Chiengmai airfield just as the Japanese were assembling a striking force to return to Magwe. Forty fighters and bombers were lined up with engines turning, ready to take off. The six P-40s pressed a relentless attack and not a single Japanese aircraft got off the field. Meanwhile, Jack Newkirk, not finding targets at Lampang, began strafing the interconnecting road to Chiengmai, which contained a column of trucks and light armored cars. Diving on the column, Newkirk's plane took a direct hit, exploded, and crashed into the jungle and burned. William "Black Mack" McGarry was also hit and bailed out to survive in a Bangkok jail, returning to Chennault in early 1945.

The attack on Chiengmai put the Japanese on the defensive for a sufficient length of time for the British to resume the evacuation at Magwe. They were most appreciative of the AVG. On the same day Kyedaw airfield at Toungoo fell to the Japanese.

By April 8, the Japanese were on the offensive again and struck with a fighter sweep at Loi-Wing just before dawn. Then again on April 10, they struck just ahead of a formation of twenty-seven bombers which remained on top of a cloud cover and never found Loi-Wing. Shortly thereafter the Japanese fighters came back for a strafing attack, but the Chinese net had allowed a force of British spitfires and AVG P-40s time to scramble. They shot down eight Zeroes without loss to themselves.

On March 22 part of the AVG had withdrawn to Loi-Wing. By early April significant portions of the Second and Third squadrons were stationed there. The service of the AVG was nearing an end. Some of the war-weary pilots and aircraft had about reached their breaking point. Neither wanted to fly anymore. Several pilots began to look at the fine print of their CAMCO contracts. They detested the dangerous low-level "support missions" over the retreating and demoralized Chinese armies and were completely exasperated when they had to escort the slow British bombers, which more frequently than not missed the rendezvous point. In brief, they were physically exhausted and felt that to continue would be tantamount to throwing their lives away.

Air combat over Rangoon had previously consisted of clashes between two air groups at high altitude, but the war of the AVG had now deteriorated to repeated attempts by the few remaining P-40s at strafing ground targets in an effort to surprise the enemy on the ground. These missions were flown time and time again by small groups which sometimes stretched their missions as far as Thailand. They were able to continue these surprise attacks successfully until they lost their refueling airfields at Toungoo in central Burma to the Japanese. Now pilots were ordered to fly what were termed "morale" missions over the Chinese Army, which was dangerous if not impossible due to the seasonal smoke and haze that covered the area of retreat. These missions proved extremely hazardous and simply did not seem to be worth the risk.

The straw that broke the camel's back, however, came with the posting of orders for an escort mission with Blenheim bombers to Chiengmai. Not only did the British Blenheims fly so slow as to render the P-40 a sitting duck, but that airdrome in Thailand had a bad reputation since Newkirk and McGarry had been lost nearby. Pilots argued with Chennault angrily. The Old Man understood completely but argued that they should not disobey direct orders. Finally, an impasse developed, and a petition was drawn up stating that the undersigned pilots refused to fly the Chiengmai mission with the Blenheim bombers. One by one the pilots began to sign. The hottest signed first. Then, carried by the momentum, the others began to sign as well, until the petition reached Tex Hill.

The quiet Texan, dressed in a tattered and battle-worn flight suit, slowly rose to speak. He was obviously still very tired from the flight the day before. He was a tall man, yet not as tall as the day when he had posed with his fellow Panda Bear squadron members in front of a shiny new P-40 back at Toungoo, the day the squadrons were formed. That P-40 had not yet fired its guns in anger nor had his new flight suit begun to show the shoulder marks from the heavy parachute straps as it did today. Slumping slightly from the fatigue of battle, Tex surveyed the faces in the room. There were no smiles today—which was quite a contrast to the day they had posed for the picture in Toungoo, their faces showing feelings of comradeship and anxious anticipation. This seemed an entirely different group—unsmiling, battle-weary, their faces drawn with lines from too little rest. He understood their innermost feelings, especially the feeling of abandonment, being left to die one by one in a war the result of which nobody back home seemed to care about. Like himself, they were showing evidence of frayed nerves. It showed not only in their faces but in their speech, in their every movement. This was the problem, he knew, not

Statue of Gen. Claire L. Chennault in Taiwan. A similar statue donated by the Republic of China stands in Baton Rouge, Louisiana, near where Chennault lived while a student at Louisiana State University.

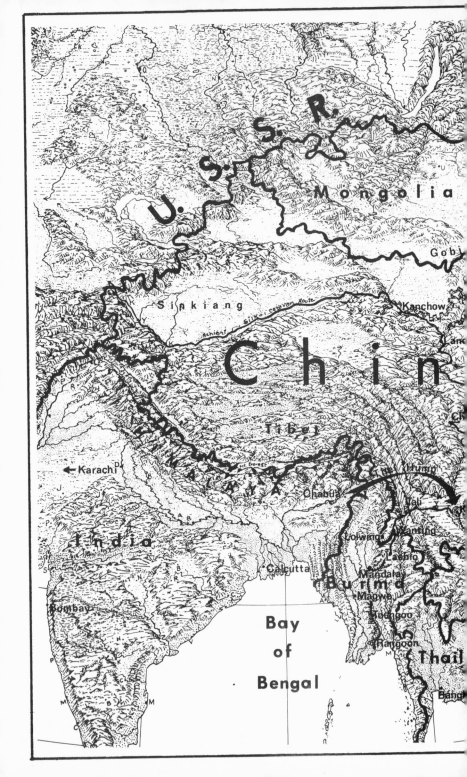

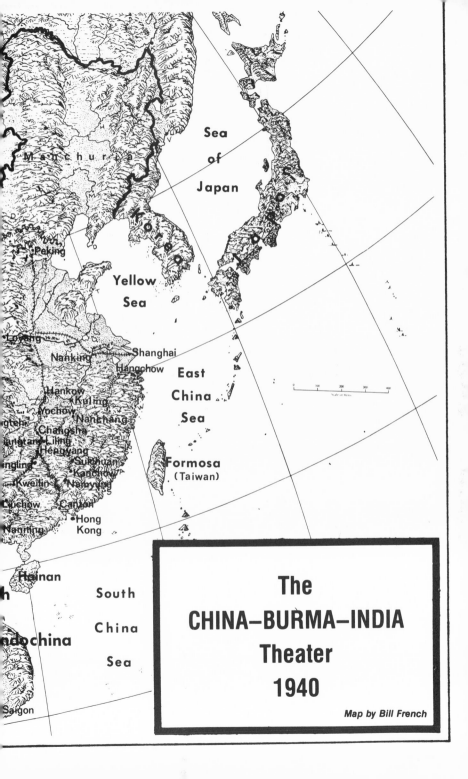

The
CHINA–BURMA–INDIA
Theater
1940

Map by Bill French

R. T. Smith and crew.

Human assembly line manufactures egg-sized stones to be used in building the Burma Road. (USAF photo)

Children use feet and primitive tools to mix slurry for an airfield in China. (USAF photo)

"Roller man" set cadence with a song. Similar tools were used in constructing the Burma Road. (USAF photo)

Huge limestone rollers made of native stone were used in building Chinese airfields. Large, heavy roller suggests the workers were reasonably well fed. (Wiltz Segura collection)

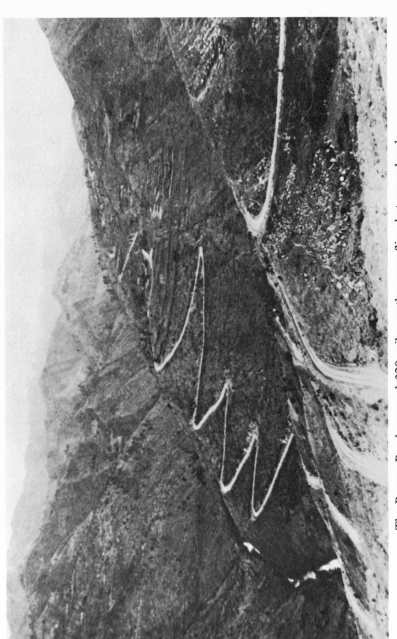

The Burma Road spanned 320 miles as the crow flies, but meandered 717 miles because of the many hairpin curves. (Tex Hill collection)

The path of the Burma Road wound around mountains, over rivers, and through rice fields. (Tex Hill collection)

lack of courage. Heaven knew that each man there had proved his "grit" time and time again. Yet Tex knew the solution was not in the signing of the petition. He addressed the men.

We came to China as mercenaries, there are no bones about that, but now we have a different situation. Our country is at war. And these are our orders. This is what the Old Man says we got to do. We ought to do it. They aren't going to send us out there to get killed on some useless deal. We aren't flying morale missions for the Chinese, we have specific targets. Our own guys are coming up that Burma Road just a step ahead of the Japs. Toungoo has fallen and they're trying to reach safety before they're captured. And here these Chinese armies are hanging on the ropes. It's an evacuation all the way, Burma has fallen.

Tex then told them that he would lead the mission in question, whereupon four men promptly agreed to accompany him—Ed Rector, an ex-Navy man with 6½ victories with the Panda Bears, later to be inducted into the Air Force, the man who had tried to chase the bombers out of Yunnan Province single-handedly on that first AVG flight; Robert P. Hedman, "the Duke," ex-Air Corps with 5½ victories with the Hell's Angels, who had once shot down five aircraft in one day over Rangoon; Frank Schiel, ex-Air Corps with seven victories with the Panda Bears, later inducted into the Air Force; and R. J. "Catfish" Raines, ex-Navy with three victories with the Hell's Angels. They left Loi-Wing before dawn, but the bombers did not show up so the flight returned.

When word of the pilots' revolt reached Kunming, Bob Neale, still resting from his ordeal in Rangoon, radioed the Old Man, "If those bastards won't fly for you, I'll bring my boys down to take over." Fortunately, Chennault had previously written Madame Chiang Kai-shek about the sagging morale and unproductiveness of the "morale missions" which the Generalissimo had ordered. While Chennault felt clearly compelled personally to carry out the Generalissimo's direct orders, he knew the effect it was having on his men and asked Madame Chiang to intervene. The night of the revolt he received the following timely reply: "Generalissimo consents use of the AVG for fighting Jap planes fighting our troops and not for low-altitude recon." So the matter of the revolt had resolved itself.

The Japanese Emperor's birthday was coming up again on April

29. Chennault felt certain that they would try to land a knockout punch at Loi-Wing, since some of his P-40s had shot down four Japanese reconnaissance planes the week before. He was ready for them on April 28. He dispatched five planes led by Tex Hill to fly top cover at fifteen thousand feet for ten P-40s led by Arvid Olson down at ten to twelve thousand feet. They were instructed to skirt the southern approach to Loi-Wing and look for any approaching Japanese bombers. As luck would have it, one hour after the fighters took off, no less than three U.S. Army C-47s landed at Loi-Wing with a much-needed cargo of fuel and ammunition. Chennault ran out to Col. Caleb V. Haynes, a double for Wallace Beery, and told him to get his transports off the runway because they were going to have an air raid at any moment. Haynes was hungry and wanted to eat first, but while they were arguing the first ching pao alert sounded and the C-47s hastily departed. Caleb remarked to his copilot, "That guy Chennault must be able to smell Japs."

Flying south-southwest, Tex Hill soon spotted twenty-seven Japanese bombers heading north about midway between Mandalay and Lashio. They were flying IFR ("I follow railroads") towards Loi-Wing. About this time Lashio radioed that they were under enemy aircraft attack. Olson dispatched half his flight to Lashio while the remainder of the Hill-Olson fighters continued towards the bombers. As they closed the distance, the AVG pilots spotted a Japanese fighter escort scattered above and behind the bombers. They had not expected company yet and hastily tried to assemble for the onslaught. The two fighter forces clashed as fights burst out all over the sky. Meanwhile the Japanese bombers flew north unmolested to bomb Loi-Wing and escaped without loss. Their fighters did not do so well, however, for the Hill-Olson group knocked down sixteen Zeroes while the other group over at Lashio got an additional six. There were no AVG losses, and while Loi-Wing sustained heavy damage from the bombers, the resulting 22-0 score was worth it.

On May 1 Loi-Wing and twenty-two burned P-40s fell to Japanese troops—two days after the last flyable P-40 had been withdrawn to Paoshan and Yunnanyi. The remaining Chinese territory east of Burma and west of the Salween River now lay in enemy hands.

By now Stilwell's position was gravely endangered, and he retreated sixty miles north of Toungoo and attempted a stand. The Chinese Fifty-fifth Division of the Sixth Army finally engaged the enemy, but was so strung out that the advancing Japanese Army swiftly cut its lines into several pieces. The Chinese took off for the hills. Stilwell was stunned, for the Fifty-fifth Division had vanished into thin air. In his diary Stilwell remarked, "There's not a trace of it. It's the goddamnedest thing I ever saw. Last night I had a division and today there isn't any." It vanished so completely during the chaos that it was removed from the rolls of the Chinese Army. Through this "hole" the Japanese raced towards Lashio. Stilwell tried to head them off but logistics and other insurmountable problems finally reduced his effectiveness to zero. The British were even worse off. They were now in retreat for their lives. Alexander confided to Stilwell that he no longer controlled his troops—they were too afraid of the Japanese.

The final days of the first Burma campaign witnessed scenes of horror and madness. The retreating Indians who had been brought to Burma to serve as colonial administrators and civil servants were more thrifty and industrious and hence more prosperous than the Burmese, who despised them. Consequently, the Burmese preyed upon the Indians throughout their entire retreat. When Indians were caught, the Burmese would behead them. The Burmese attacked the Chinese soldiers as well, since many Chinese had been successful merchants in Burma. In response the Chinese soldiers started shooting the Burmese on sight.

Faith in one's fellow man was at an all-time low in Burma when on April 25 Stilwell and Alexander met south of Mandalay. They agreed that a general retreat was the only hope of survival. During the meeting bombs blasted nearby, and all members of the meeting scurried for cover, that is, all except the two weary old soldiers. Though defeated, they were still comrades-in-arms, and they stood erect during the air raid, Stilwell chewing on an old black cigarette holder. The British would depart for India, it was decided, while Stilwell would endeavor to organize his scattered Chinese forces and retreat northward, hoping to establish a base of operations to be fed by an overland road from upper India. So began the famous walk out of Burma and the nightmare which had no parallel in military history. On May 16 the British Army's nine-hundred-mile retreat ended as the ragged and diseased soldiers emerged into India, still carrying their weapons.

Meanwhile, Stilwell had intended to start his retreat by train towards Myitkyino, but a Chinese general got to the train first and at gunpoint tried to escape north. But he soon collided with a southbound train which completely blocked Stilwell's route. The next day a C-47 landed to evacuate Stilwell and his staff. The pilots were a pair of crusty individuals by the names of Caleb V. Haynes and Robert L. Scott. They had barely managed to hedge-hop in from India through adverse weather. They were there under orders to evacuate Vinegar Joe. They found him sitting in his field headquarters wearing his old campaign hat and writing a letter. One of them said to him, "General Arnold sent us to rescue you, sir." It was the wrong choice of words. Stilwell told them in no uncertain terms where they could go. They were dumbfounded. As they returned to the transport Caleb is said to have told Scott, "Let's knock the old fool in the head and take him anyway." But they wisely left with only part of his staff.

Stilwell did not lead his party. He drove them, though he himself was nearly sixty years old. He was accompanied by about a hundred people, including twenty-six American officers, enlisted men, and civilians, sixteen Chinese soldiers, a seven-man British ambulance unit, a correspondent by the name of Belden, and an assorted lot of Malay, Burmese, and Indian helpers and cooks. Included also was a contingent of nineteen Burmese nurses and the "Burma Surgeon," Dr. Gordon S. Seagrave. The rest of the Chinese Fifth and Sixth armies had lost contact with Stilwell (and with each other) and were scattered in the Burmese jungle.

On May 2 one of the cars blew a tire and Stilwell shouted, "Burn the damned thing. Keep moving." Next an axle broke. "Burn the son of a bitch," came the order. Then a vehicle broke a crankcase. "Burn it," was the response. Finally a supply truck caught fire. "Turn 'em over. Get moving. Forward," Stilwell said. On and on he drove them.

Following the evacuation of Loi-Wing all AVG pilots returned to headquarters at Kunming. Soon Neale led four P-40s which flew to Paoshan field just north of the Salween River on the Paoshan plateau. On May 4 fifty Japanese bombers slipped in under the crumbling Chinese net and bombed Paoshan, which was gorged with Chinese refugees, killing thousands, including pilot Ben Foshee as he ran for his P-40. Only one AVG pilot got off the ground, and that was Charley Bond, who managed to shoot down two bombers as they were leaving the target. But Charley was jumped by three Japanese fighters and while in flames over the field he bailed out receiving severe burns.

The next day nine P-40s were dispatched out of Kunming, and after refueling at Yunnanyi, they hit the next Japanese attack party head-on over Paoshan. It was a clever bit of deduction on the part of Chennault, who with the aid of a decoded Japanese message learned of two bomber formations taking off from southern Burma. He calculated their speed, direction, and range and reasoned that they would pick up a fighter escort in time to arrive over Paoshan together. He therefore dispatched the nine P-40s at the correct time and direction for interception and told his men where to look for them. Not only did they find them, but they shot down eight of the first wave and then climbed back to altitude to meet the second wave. Upon seeing the shark teeth racing for their altitude, the second-wave pilots dropped their bombs and scurried for home without reaching their target.

On May 7 Maj. Frank Merrill, who would later lead Merrill's Marauders, collapsed from exhaustion trying to keep up with Stilwell, but Stilwell did not stop. No one would outmarch him. Finally on May 14 they crossed into India. The press had made him a hero, but the sober old army artillery officer, leading a ragtag column of emaciated men and women out of fallen Burma soberly addressed the reporters.

"I claim we got a hell of a beating," he said. "We got run out of Burma and it is humiliating as hell. I think we ought to find out what caused it, go back, and retake it."

By May 7, the spearhead of the Japanese motorized division had reached the west bank of the mile-deep Salween gorge about seventy-five miles inside the Chinese border. Chennault was fearful that Churchill's prophecy was about to be fulfilled. Now there was no obstacle between the Japanese and Kunming but a broken bridge and the AVG.

The Japanese Navy, following the fall of Rangoon, had sent a task force to expel the British Navy from the Bay of Bengal and had succeeded in doing so. They sank freighters steaming for Calcutta and harassed the British Navy in general until they rendered Calcutta useless as a major supply base. The Allies were thus forced to unload war supplies a thousand miles to the east at Bombay and at Karachi, where the British were preparing to receive Montgomery's defeated

Eighth Army should Rommel take the Nile delta. Also at this time Russia was battling for its survival on its western front, and the United States had almost lost the Philippines. The invasion of India by the Japanese seemed imminent since now all Japan had to do to knock China out of the war for good was simply cross the Salween River. It was one of the few times during the war that Chennault became really alarmed.

During the first part of May, pilots flying out of Paoshan conducted top cover flights protecting the last remaining AVG truck convoys coming up from Burma. The Salween suspension bridge had been destroyed during the evacuation, and now thousands of Chinese refugees were stranded on the west bank. In a short time the column of civilians and unarmed stragglers of the defeated Chinese Army had clogged the serpentine road coming down the west bank of the gorge to the floor of the Salween River bed.

From the cockpit of Bob Neale's P-40 it looked like a massive river of brown humanity, an awesome sight that he would never forget. Suddenly he spotted a motorized Japanese advance column up on the plateau racing down the center of the road through all the stragglers towards the west rim of the gorge. He radioed the Old Man in Kunming. The news was electrifying to Chennault, who in turn notified Madame Chiang in Chungking. His message said:

> Latest report says Japs on west bank of Salween River 1500 hours 5 May. Bridge destroyed. Japs meeting no opposition anywhere as soldiers, civilians panic-stricken fleeing east along road. Consider situation desperate and Japs may drive Kunming in trucks unless road and bridges destroyed and determined opposition developed. Due to fact many Chinese trucks west of Salween presumably in hands of enemy request authority His Excellency the Generalissimo to attack targets between Salween and Lungling city.

By the next day a long column of Japanese armored cars, trucks, artillery, and infantry were backed up for twenty miles behind the destroyed Salween bridge. There they waited to cross for the final dash to Kunming while engineers unloaded pontoons to build a bridge across the river. Following a quick affirmative reply from Madame Chiang, Chennault mustered his forces to stop the advance of the Japanese, something the British and Chinese armies had failed to do. In a sense, this was to be a unified effort by the armed forces of the United States—four sailors, three soldiers, and one marine. The Navy took the new P-40E aircraft, which were capable of deploying bombs, while the Army and Marine Corps flew the more "experienced" P-40s.

The eight-plane formation headed south. Tex Hill led the Navy dive-bombing experts (Tom Jones, Ed Rector, and Frank Lawlor), while the Army (Arvid Olson, R. T. Smith, and Eric Shilling) and the Marine Corps (Tom Haywood) flew top cover. The monsoon season had already started in central Burma, and as the flight crossed the Paoshan plateau, they were confronted by a gigantic and turbulent wall of cumulonimbus clouds sweeping up from Burma. It was a particularly dark and angry front, composed of many cells along the line, each identifiable by a flat base and rising warm air which sent billowing white clouds thousands of feet into the air. Tex studied the weather ahead. It would be suicidal to try to penetrate a cell with inner wind velocities easily capable of destroying every plane in the formation. If they chose to fly under the darkened bellies, rain and hail and hidden mountains would be a problem. In addition, it would be impossible to fly over the tops at those altitudes. There was only one solution, to thread the flight as nearly as possible between the cells, hoping to avoid the core of the buildup containing rime ice and hail. Tex picked his spot and the rest followed.

After thirty minutes of turbulent flying through severe up and down drafts the flight broke through into beautifully clear weather south of the front. The dust and smoke which usually obstructed one's vision had been cleared from the sky by the passing of the moist front. Visibility was excellent as the four dive bombers screamed towards their target. No longer hidden by the jungle of lower Burma, the Japanese column now lay exposed and trapped along the road. The column not only extended up the face of the western bank but ran for miles along the narrow road on the higher plateau, back towards Lungling. With a rock wall on one side and sheer bluffs on the other, the Japanese column could not disperse. Repeatedly, the dive bombers plastered the rock wall above the convoy, bringing down landslides to block their retreat. The dive bombers machine-gunned the column until all ammunition was spent, then signaled the top cover to come on down and join in.

When all ammunition was expended, all eight planes returned to Kunming.

For the next four days Chennault threw everything he had at the stranded Japanese, everything. He even used the antiquated SB-3 Russian twin-engine bombers borrowed from the Chinese Air Force, which were flown by Chinese pilots. Once these bombers returned to Kunming, they were so completely spent that they were left to rust where they had landed, such was their deplorable condition.

The Japanese dispatched a group of light tanks to effect a retreat but a flight of sharks led by Frank Schiel caught them on the road below Lungling. The AVG bombed and strafed every village and building where the Japanese might have stored supplies for their forward troops, even catching a truck column loaded with gas racing to the front. So effective was the onslaught that after May 11 only military traffic was seen moving south along the Burma Road back into Burma. Opposing forces entrenched in a stalemate with the Japanese dug in on the west bank and the Chinese dug in on the east bank. Since the Japanese had overstretched their supply lines and the monsoon season was beginning, they were unable to assemble enough men and materials to renew the offensive. The stalemate persisted for two years.

As early as December 30, 1941, the U.S. Army had authorized the induction of the AVG. However, they procrastinated until the following March 29 before doing anything about it. Now it appeared to have suddenly become an obsession with them to disband the group even at the risk of depriving the Chinese of an effective air army. Chennault did not want to lose control of the AVG because he wanted to remain in the fight. The Generalissimo did not want to disband the AVG because it was a bird in the hand instead of an empty promise from the Army. Finally, Chennault was called to Chungking to meet with the Generalissimo, Madame Chiang, Stilwell, and his old adversary from fighter school days, Clayton Bissell.

A man's past has a way of catching up with him. Bissell was now Stilwell's air officer. He had been sent to China initially to handle the western side of the Doolittle raid on Tokyo, about which he had been so secretive that he did not inform Chennault of it. When the bombers penetrated eastern China, they simply flew until they exhausted their fuel and then crashed. Had Chennault known of the raid beforehand he could have alerted the Chinese net so they could have guided the planes to friendly fields. As it turned out, all the bombers were lost and many of the pilots and crew members captured, some executed. Chennault could surely have used those bombers. The Doolittle raid was highly publicized in the United States for purposes of morale, but in reality it was of little effect militarily and resulted in severe retaliation by the Japanese. In a three-month campaign, the Japanese struck every village and town thought to have given aid to the Doolittle raiders, slaughtering every man, woman, and child and burning every building. They rampantly devastated twenty thousand square miles of China and plowed up landing fields so thoroughly that it was later easier to build new runways than to repair the old ones. Yet the Chinese continued to aid the Americans and at great personal risk continued to smuggle many downed pilots back to their home bases.

Chennault was made to feel by Stilwell and Bissell that his AVG would not receive any aid from the Army if he refused induction. He therefore accepted induction personally, but told them that his men would speak for themselves. Chennault received his orders on April 9 appointing him to temporary colonel, but nine days later he was promoted to temporary brigadier general. However, the Army promoted Bissell to brigadier general one day sooner than Chennault—thus effectively making Bissell senior to him. It was the old Army game again. Chennault was back in military politics, like it or not. Gen. Hap Arnold was now commanding the Army Air Force.

With this turn of events, the Generalissimo consented to part with the AVG upon receiving Stilwell's word that he would replace it with a complete American fighter group. Stilwell also promised that Chennault would remain as the senior American air commander in China for the duration of the war. Neither promise was kept. The Army insisted that the AVG be disbanded on April 30, but Chennault knew that it would take longer for the Army to replace them. He proposed to Madame Chiang that July 4 would be more appropriate, and finally all parties agreed.

The men of the AVG were not very enthusiastic about the idea of induction. When induction terms were posted in April, all but a few were fed up with the whole situation. Most of the men would have joined up in the field, Chennault felt, had they been offered a thirty-day furlough before returning to combat. But Bissell was desperate for them because he knew that he could not make the July 4 deadline. Under pressure he requested that Chennault "talk to his men" about foregoing the furlough. Chennault told him to go fly a kite, that the men needed and deserved the rest. Bissell next asked for permission to talk to the men himself, confident that he would succeed. He did talk to them, right after the Salween battle. As the men filed into the auditorium at Yunnan University, Chennault warned Bissell that he might get a rough reception. Bissell stated all the reasons why he thought the men should stay on in China without taking a furlough. He must have figured from all the stony faces that he was not getting anywhere, so in desperation he added, "And for any of you who don't join the Army, I can guarantee to have your draft boards waiting for you when you step down a gangplank onto United States soil." After that clincher, the induction board was able to find only five pilots and twenty-two ground men who were willing to stay out of the 250-man AVG.

Meanwhile, the AVG ran out their contracts by taking their bitterness out on the Japanese. On May 12 they struck Hanoi and lost John Donovan to flak. Then on June 5, Chennault moved the squadrons to a field near Chungking with a show of aircraft to convince the Japanese that they were ready to defend the city. But four days after, they left behind only four aircraft and several P-40 dummies and flew the rest of the squadrons to the eastern bases at Hengyang, Lingling, and Kweilin to take up the offensive again. Here the AVG ran up their score to 299 Japanese aircraft destroyed as fights broke out all over east China. The "Flying Tigers" celebrated their final day, July 4, 1942, by knocking down five enemy fighters over Hengyang.

It was not until just before the AVG was disbanded that the men had any kind of identifying group insignia to be worn on their makeshift uniforms. At the request of China Defense Supplies in Washington, Disney caricature specialist Roy Williams drew a winged tiger flying through a large "V" for victory as the AVG insignia. "General Chennault gave me credit for the 'Flying Tiger' insignia in his book *The Way of a Fighter,*" Williams said later. "But I must give credit where credit is due. I did the original idea and rough design but artist Hank Porter drew it up."

In his memoirs Chennault recalled with satisfaction the combat record of his AVG:

The group that the military experts predicted would not last three weeks in combat had fought for seven months over Burma, China, Thailand, and French Indochina, destroying 299 Japanese planes with another 153 probably destroyed. All of this with a loss of twelve P-40s in combat and sixty-one on the ground, including the twenty-two burned at Loi-Wing. Four pilots were killed in air combat; six were killed by antiaircraft fire; three by enemy bombs on the ground; and three were taken prisoner. Ten more died as a result of flying accidents.

He also reflected on what the experience had meant to him personally: "The AVG gave me the greatest opportunity an air officer ever had—to collect and train a group like that with complete freedom of action. It afforded me enormous satisfaction. Not only was I able to prove my methods sound, but in so doing I made a significant contribution to the common cause against the enemy I hated so bitterly."

At midnight on July 4, 1942, the American Volunteer Group, the legendary "Flying Tigers" who had whipped the Japanese Air Force in more than fifty air battles without a single defeat, passed into history. Churchill later said of them, "The victories of these Americans over the rice paddies of Burma are comparable in character if not in scope with those won by the RAF over the hop fields of Kent in the Battle of Britain."

CHAPTER 4

The Making of a China Pilot:
Charlie Olsen in Panama

It was a particularly humid Saturday morning, Emile Salles noted as he walked down from his family quarters over the general store to unlock the front door. Briefly he stepped outside onto Magazine Street to peer skyward from beneath the Salles' Grocery and Hardware sign. This morning, like yesterday and the day before, the sky was hazy and cloudless. He predicted no relief from the heat. Magazine was one of the main city arteries in old New Orleans. Already it was beginning to fill with traffic and pedestrians and fresh vegetable vendors who brought their produce directly to their customers from the market in the old French Quarter.

"Vegetables! fresh veg-etables!" they hawked as they slowly traveled the riverfront streets in the surrounding neighborhood. Already one was engaged in his curbside business with two early morning shoppers, weighing two golden cantaloupes as his first customer counted out her pennies in the palm of her hand with a probing finger. The day's pulse had begun.

"Good morning, Emile," came a familiar voice as Salles turned towards the store doorway from the porch.

"Morning. It's going to be a hot one," he replied to his next-door neighbor who was placing the last bit of merchandise on the sidewalk in front of his furniture store.

Straightening up the neighbor added, "Did you hear? The Japs are stirring up trouble in China. Heard it on the radio last night. What do you make of it?"

"I don't know. China is a long way off," Salles said. "Maybe business will be better today. This depression can't last forever." With a sigh he returned to the store. Once inside, he noticed that his son, Junior, had joined him and with a feeling of pride and a bit of humor, he watched him. Young Emile tarried through some menial chore in a token effort to help his father make ready for the day's business. It was the kind of morning filled with routine responsibility that is taken for granted by a breadwinner with a mature understanding of the realities of life, but for a boy of eleven, such a morning was actually painful. At that moment young Emile was more inclined to be building airplanes in his room, reading, or playing with the kids on the block, rather than working here in the store "building character," as his father would say.

His job was scarcely demanding. Rather it was designed by a thoughtful father to occupy idle hands. It was nonetheless a Saturday of drudgery and uninterrupted boredom that young Emile faced and must somehow endure.

Suddenly he felt a pang of excitement as he glanced across the street and recognized a slim figure dodging through traffic, heading straight for the store. It was Charlie Olsen, a sixteen-year-old boy whom young Emile idolized. Charlie, being older, possessed all of the qualities that teenage heroes were made of. As the door flew open the young figure of a man emerged carefully cradling the fuselage of a new model airplane.

"Can I use your scale, Mr. Salles?" Charlie asked.

"Sure Charlie. What kind is it this time?" Salles asked as he lifted the delicate balsa wood structure from Charlie's hands and placed it upon the meat scale. "Two and a half ounces, less than a good beefsteak," he grinned as he squinted at the scale.

"What are you building Charlie?" young Emile said, moving closer.

"It's my own design," Charlie replied without taking his eyes off the scale. Then, as if to be talking only to the elder Salles, he continued, "There's a big model contest next Saturday at the school, so I will be back when I finish the wings this afternoon if that's all right."

When Salles smiled and nodded his approval, Charlie turned and made a hasty exit. Young Emile knew that any more questions would just have to wait. Charlie was the kind of guy who made things happen, Emile thought, remembering the time he had stuffed a six-foot alligator and proceeded to scare the entire neighborhood.

Charlie never allowed his humble background to become a deterrent to his pursuit to adventure. Once he rebuilt an old Model T Ford and drove it up and down busy Magazine Street, teaching himself how to drive, much to his dear mother's chagrin. Charlie was so active and elusive that he was sometimes exasperating. One day while walking down Magazine she looked up to see her eldest son coming down the street in his Model T filled with kids, only to smack into the rear of another car which had brakes. Steam, water, and the usual clatter erupted, but Mrs. Olsen never broke her stride. With a quick side-glance, she shrugged her shoulders and continued ahead, hoping she had not been recognized by any of her neighbors.

Charlie was acknowledged by schoolteachers and friends as being an expert model aircraft designer and builder. His teachers had encouraged model airplane building and the school frequently sanctioned model aircraft competition. He learned to depend upon his cunning and resourcefulness by building an aircraft for one of the wealthy kids and making sure that sufficient materials remained to construct one for himself, so that he too might enter the competition.

Hence he frequently vied in competition against models he had built for others to enter. In one event, Charlie's designs took first, second, and third places, with his legal entry taking second. His pursuit of aviation was only occasionally interrupted in those early years by such diversions as alligators and Model T's.

Once it was a diving scheme. Charlie felt that if he could build a diving rig capable of sustained breathing at modest depths, he could, with the help of a support team of two trusted buddies, walk on the bottom of Lake Pontchartrain around the wharfs and fishing places and retrieve all sorts of valuable objects to be sold. In this way he hoped either to keep the gas tank of his Model T Ford full or to pay for flying lessons which he planned to begin. In this pursuit he designed a diving bell or hood from the top two feet of a discarded heavy metal hot water heater. He cut out places for his shoulders and attached two straps to buckle under his arms. To the front of the tank he cut out a rectangular area and attached a glass faceplate. At the very top he next welded an attachment to fit his mother's garden hose through which he could pump in breathing air and keep water out of the helmet. He then built a two-man pump to supply the compressed air.

Early one morning Charlie threw all the new equipment into the back seat of his Model T. He then recruited his two-man support team and took off to test his new equipment. Arriving at the New Basin Canal, the three boys piled out of the car and began to assemble the diving equipment under Charlie's supervision. Not waiting for volunteers (nor getting any) Charlie put on his diving gear, calmly and methodically, with all the pageantry of an astronaut. He was not completely oblivious to the expressions of awe on the faces of his companions, though he behaved as if he had made such dives before.

Charlie calculated that due to the excessive weight of the metal helmet, he would have no need for weighted shoes or belt to descend and remain on the bottom. He was absolutely correct. Fully attired, he noticed that it required a rather firm stance on his part to stand erect during the time his companions were fastening the garden hose from his helmet to the pump. Also, the metal ex-water tank was beginning to cut into his bare shoulders.

He motioned for one boy to begin pumping while the other fed out the hose. Upon hearing the reassuring hiss of the air coming into his helmet, Charlie waved a gesture of approval and then turned and walked to the water's edge. Here he paused for a brief moment, back turned to his companions, and then continued straight into the water and disappeared beneath the surface.

Problem number one—he slowly sank to his shins in the gooey, muddy bottom. He also noticed with some surprise that he could not see a thing beyond the faceplate he had so carefully installed in the helmet. In a moment a hand appeared before his eyes, a familiar hand even though it appeared distorted in the murky Mississippi water. He examined it very carefully, on both sides, before it suddenly shot up over the surface of the water as a prearranged signal to his crew. It was a clinched fist with an upturned thumb—all systems were go.

With considerable difficulty he traveled within the radius of his mother's garden hose, pulling first one foot out of the mud and then waiting for it to sink again before working on the other. Back on shore his support team pumped feverishly in the hot summer sun, supplying precious air to his helmet at the end of the fifteen-foot garden hose. Just a little too feverishly Charlie thought, as the compressed air cavalcaded from beneath the bottom of the helmet and bubbled past his faceplate further disturbing his vision. Each laborious step at this murky depth was punctuated by the interrupting hiss of the incoming air, the belching escaping bubbles, and the incredibly audible sound of his pounding heart. He was alone, completely engulfed by this strange new environment, and he loved it.

It was not long until his foot struck an object half buried in the mud. Was it a lost metal anchor or something else of value that might result in his first flight lesson in a real airplane? Being unable to see at that depth, he prodded the circumference with his bare foot in an effort to determine what it was. When this failed, he decided just to bend over and take a closer look. Unfortunately this led to the rapid exchange of all the air in his helmet with inrushing Mississippi River water, and Charlie gave up diving for good.

Yet somehow Charlie managed to save enough money to start his flying lessons. His first came in a Taylor Cub and his instructor was a lady named Mrs. Gardner. Later he recalled his transition from model-building to flying the real thing: "I became interested in flying mostly because there was an airport near the Huey P. Long Bridge, and I would watch Jimmy Wedell come in there with his famous No. 44 Racer. There were a couple of Jennys hangared there, too. I'd hang around thinking I might bum a ride. But I never got one."

Three years later, in the fall of 1939, when Charlie entered Louisiana State University in Baton Rouge to major in engineering, he had accumulated a student license and had already soloed. So when the Civilian Pilot Training Program first appeared on campus, he was ready to participate.

A couple of years elapsed while he was studying engineering and flying with the CPT. "I signed up for school that September, had bought my books and had come home to New Orleans to wait for school to begin when the Air Corps called me and told me to report to Jackson, Mississippi, for my physical. It was either turn them down and return to school or opt for the military. Things were pretty rough in 1941 so I headed for Jackson," he recalled. At Jackson, Charlie took his physical, was sworn in, and from there was transferred to nearby Maxwell Field for preflight ground school. From Maxwell Field it was back to St. Augustine Field at Jackson for primary training in the PT-17, a big, fabric-covered biplane.

Three-fourths of the guys washed out—for anything, physical, mental, or ability. The moment anyone goofed or got sick when they gave yellow fever shots or got airsick, he was gone. Fear was we weren't going to make it—until the war started. On December 7, 1941, when we got the news that night, then we weren't worried anymore. Nobody was. We figured they were going to push us through then, now that they needed everybody. As they expedited training, the men quit worrying so much about washing out and settled down to learning how to fly.

Forrest Dines, a civilian pilot too old for fighters and combat (he must have been in his early 30s) was my instructor and was a very nice man. He was real good. One day we were on a long cross-country flight and Dines had been doing a lot of instructing and was tired. He told me on the return leg of the trip that he was going to take a cat-nap and that when I had the field in sight to wake him up.

Charlie flew along for a while and suddenly ran smack into a snowstorm, since the month was November or December. Being from Louisiana he did not know what snow was, never having seen it before. The flakes, Charlie remembered, were as "big as potato chips." One of them must have hit the instructor in the face because something startled him into semiconsciousness. Seeing the huge snowflakes so suddenly, he immediately thought that the fabric plane was coming apart and he hollered to Charlie in the front seat, "Olsen, are we coming apart?"

"No," replied Charlie, "it's snowing . . . I guess." Dines remained awake the rest of the trip.

The life of an instructor in primary training has been described as hours upon hours of boredom punctuated by moments of stark terror. During early primary training one day, an instructor dropped something and it rolled out of his reach on the floor in his rear cockpit. He had to unbuckle his shoulder harness and seat belt to retrieve it. For some reason he failed to buckle back up while steadily giving instructions through the one-way voice tube to the student in the front cockpit.

"OK," he shouted, "now try to fly it upside down." When the student executed the maneuver, rather abruptly, the instructor fell from the plane.

Inverted and hanging by his seat belt, the cadet turned rather awkwardly to speak to the rear cockpit. "How is that, sir? Sir?" Then he saw the instructor's chute blossom far behind the plane.

After completing primary training, Charlie was assigned to the Greenville Army Air Base in January 1942. Here he made a transition to the Vultee BT-13 "Vibrator." It was smooth going—no accidents. "I don't think there was a single fatality," he recalled. The BT-13 Basic Trainer was a lot bigger than the PT-17 he had been flying. It had a lot more instruments and it was not covered with fabric nor was it a biplane. An all-metal job, it looked like a big heavy ship and Charlie liked that.

Actually they were still washing out cadets in basic training, but Charlie did not know it. There were enough pilots. It was the bombardiers and navigators they had a hard time getting. They were desperate for them. Most were washed-out pilots with flying experience who were familiar with the airplanes and had been through the engineering schools. They made perfect bombardiers and navigators. "Sometimes we thought they would wash us out just because they needed a thousand bombardiers," Olsen said later.

> Joke was if you washed out as a pilot, you had a choice of cutting your throat or becoming a bombardier. Not that it was that bad, except most of us wanted to be a pursuit pilot and that was what we were there for. If you didn't make it, you felt like a failure. You were washed out and sent home, waiting reassignment. It was embarrassing because all your friends and neighbors knew. Truth was, some wanted to be bomber pilots and a lot of the bombardiers were not washed-out pilots at all.
>
> I particularly liked the BT-13. It suited me to a "T" and was good for aerobatics. I loved to do aerobatics, but my instructor, Lieutenant Neffinger, was a poor fellow to teach aerobatics. So after we made the prescribed course, I used to go out and teach him aerobatics. In those days one never heard the words aerobatics or Air Force. It was rat-racing or acrobatics and Air Corps. We were rat-racing every day with other students in BT-13s. We went out on solo, six of us. We'd fly under wires and down the river, chase cows and a few of us even flew under bridges.

After basic training Charlie and company graduated to North American's high performance advanced trainer, the AT-6 "Texan." Arriving at Spence Field, Moultrie, Georgia, the group found the

"T-6" handled a little easier than the Vultee BT-13. They were heavier and along with the retractable landing gear, they were faster. "We picked up more formation flying, got some gunnery practice and took a course in armory. I don't remember much about the first time that I fired machine guns at a target; but it didn't particularly turn me on. It was a pain in the butt flying out for two hours at a time with fifteen guys shooting at the same target."

From March 18 to May 2, 1942, Charlie flew a total of 165 hours, the last few of which were nearly his last—his first night solo cross-country flight. The first few night flights had been with an instructor, and the whole group flew in formation, landed at some remote field, and then flew back. This particular night flight, however, began at the municipal airport at Atlanta, which was not a military base.

> We flew in that afternoon around 2:00 P.M. Some military accommodations were available as they gassed and serviced our aircraft for the evening flight. I am not sure about the actual number of aircraft involved in the exercise; but there were several, at least eighteen to twenty. I only knew a few of the cadets personally since the group consisted of cadets from other squadrons as well.
>
> After dark we were each assigned a takeoff time. One guy took off at 7:15, the next at 7:30, and the next at 7:45, and so forth, to allow for separation and safety. It was a clear night with the stars shining brightly since there was no moon at the time. The weather report was CAVU (Ceiling And Visibility Unlimited) along our route with no problems in sight. Just plot your own course and go. Destination was back at Spence Field with a couple of dogleg check points along the way to keep us honest.

Olsen was to take off at 8:30 after several planes had already departed. While he was going through his preflight, two brothers left just ahead of him, A. J. and R. J. Wilson. About ten to twelve minutes later, Charlie was given the wind-up signal by ground personnel and he energized the inertia starter on his AT-6. Charlie's pulse quickened as it began its high pitched wind-up. As the six-hundred-horsepower Pratt and Whitney cleared its throat, the lineman gave Charlie the signal to taxi onto the active runway. Charlie leaned out of the cockpit to the right and to the left, peering around the large radial engine which obstructed his view. A quick check to the rear—all was clear, and he noticed six or seven planes behind him waiting for their turn to take off. He taxied on to the runway and pushed the throttle all the way forward.

As the plane began to pick up speed, he quickly glanced from right to left, watching the edge of the runway speed by. He kept the plane properly aligned until the tail came up and he could see the center stripe down the middle of the runway. In a moment the main gear cleared the concrete, and he reached down on the left side of the cockpit, flipping the gear retract handle. He then eased up the flaps.

As the old Texan struck its blunt nose into the pitch black night and labored for altitude, Charlie could almost hear "the hiss of the incoming air, the belching of the escaping bubbles, and the incredibly audible sound of his pounding heart." Only by now he was becoming more accustomed to excitement and his heartbeat did not pound so loudly even though he was once again alone in a strange environment, and he loved it.

Charlie climbed to his assigned altitude of six thousand feet. They had assigned each cadet an altitude separation of a thousand feet. With each plane being a little higher or lower than the one in front in case one overtook the other en route, there would be less likelihood of a midair collision. Charlie knew that Cadet Wilson in front of him was supposed to be at five thousand feet during the entire flight.

After climbing through six thousand feet, Charlie pushed forward on the stick and lowered the nose of the Texan to pick up airspeed. By the time the airspeed indicator had wound up to 145 knots, he was exactly at six thousand feet, and he pulled off enough power to set his cruise speed. Relaxing for a moment, he moved around in his seat searching for a less lumpy encounter between his posterior and the uncomfortable parachute-seat, a discomfort which would be completely disregarded in the next few hours to come.

Once he had gone around in a quick circle over Atlanta to get his bearings, he picked up the little town of Elton, southwest about eight or so miles. He checked his map which was carefully positioned for ready reference during flight, crossed a small stream below, and was now coming up on course. Then the bridge, his first checkpoint, slid beneath him and he marked his time and settled back. He was on course. After forty minutes he would pick up his second checkpoint if his homework and weather predictions were correct.

Forty minutes came and passed with only the steady drone of the heavy radial engine. It was a dark night with few lights down below and the heavens were filled with billions of shining stars. Off to the left the moon had started to rise. Suddenly a small layer of fog flashed by his cockpit. Its unexpected appearance sent a cold chill down his spine. Then came another and another, in rapid succession they flashed by, and then there was complete fog all around. He was in the soup. Whether a warm front had backed in or what, he never knew, but it was certainly counter to weather predictions for the night. It was extensive, he later found out, covering the entire area involved in the student flights.

His first reaction was to descend, to get under the fog. But knowing that Wilson was at five thousand feet in front of him, he feared that they might collide. So he started to climb and as he did, he began calling Spence Field and then managed after a while to raise Augusta. He told them that the weather was socked in and added almost in protest, "It was supposed to be clear all the way. God, I've got fog up here and I'm climbing above it if I can so maybe I can at least see."

He broke out at about ten thousand feet above a downy layer of moonlit clouds that stretched for miles and miles as far as the eye could see. He had entered into that silver sanctity of space, "Where never lark, or even eagle flew." A place so serenely beautiful that he felt he could surely have "put out my hand and touched the face of God." For a brief moment, Charlie watched as a silver ray of moonlight danced along the leading edge of the aluminum wing beneath the full moon. Back and forth in concert with the slightest movement of the wing, Charlie breathed deeply and collected his thoughts. He was getting low on fuel.

"No time to fool around now. With ground fog there should be no wind, unless since I hit the fog bank head-on, a slight wind from the south has come up to contend with." He made a slight correction to the left in heading to offset a slight drift and flew the last leg of the flight solely on the basis of the prescribed period of time.

Then he began to hear voices in his headset. "One of 'em has crashed outside of Valdosta and a crash team is out . . . Another one is down in Mobile Bay. He pancaked in and I don't know the consequences."

A second voice came back, saying, "Somebody spun in north of Selma. Anybody got in yet?"

"Yeah, one guy got in at Montgomery, reported down and all

right," came the answer. "He was able to pick up some highway lights and he stayed right on the tree tops and was able to come in. He was lucky to get in over the power lines."

Charlie called them and told them that he was somewhere near the field. "Can you hear me?"

"No," came the reply, "no engine noises." Charlie told them he was going to circle and change the prop pitch and to listen for him. This he did.

"Can you hear me now?"

"No, still no sound. You are definitely not over this field."

Olsen quickly figured his position, feeling that he had probably over-corrected to the left and was probably also south of the field by now. After making a heading correction he began to let down, and down, and down, and still he saw nothing below. At five hundred feet he gave in and went back up. He repeated this procedure three or four times, each in a slightly different location, each time going a little lower. Still he had no luck, so he decided to make a big circle, then bigger and bigger, hoping for a brief opening in the fog. Still nothing. It was now or never, he thought. He was about out of gas.

He started back down, determined to take it all the way down— five hundred feet, four hundred, three hundred, two hundred. . . . Then he saw a faint orange glow coming up off his left wing. At 150 feet he broke out and saw something burning. A farmer must have been burning off a field. At any rate it sure looked good. He leveled out and continued under the low overcast, passing a huge silo almost at his altitude. Hoping to be near a town, he began a wide circle to the left, occasionally passing ragged wisps of fog along his path. Suddenly he spotted a highway with car lights and a railroad track running parallel. He turned and took up this new heading south and followed the highway. After about three miles, the small town of Whatley appeared off his nose, and he flipped on his cockpit light and looked at his map. Sure enough he was off course 180 degrees, so he spun around, corrected thirty degrees, and headed straight for Spence Field ten miles ahead.

After a while he called the field again and said that he thought that he was approaching from the southwest. "Can you hear an engine noise now?" he asked and cycled his prop.

Silence, then . . . "Not yet," came a reply. Charlie continued on until runway lights were visible over the nose of the plane.

Just as he reached for his hand mike to let them know that he had the field in sight, a voice cracked over the headset, "We hear you. We hear you. It's a wet runway, just bring it on in the way you are coming, you are cleared to land."

One or two more guys were already down and they had followed the same procedure as Charlie. One guy said that he broke out at less than a hundred feet and almost went in. There were about twelve planes lost on the flight that night, and three or four pilots were killed. Charlie had known a couple of them.

On May 20, 1942, Olsen was among those cadets at Spence Field who had completed their Air Corps Advanced Flying School Training and graduated as second lieutenants in the U.S. Army Air Corps. With the war on, civilian travel was hectic and sometimes very time-consuming. Ofttimes people would be stranded for long periods of time at bus and train stations. Both gasoline and tires were rationed, and highway speed was reduced to thirty-five miles an hour for the duration of the war. Private cars were not what they used to be, and there was no chance for new ones should they wear out before the end of the war. Automobile manufacturers were now tooled up for war production. Consequently, few of the new second lieutenants had families present for the ceremony. The few people attending were mostly from the surrounding area, since some friendships had been made during the young men's stay at Spence Field. For the most part they just pinned their new wings on one another, not at all like in the movies being cranked out by Hollywood at the time.

All of them had completed the required training in the PT-17, BT-13, and also the AT-6, which carried them through Primary Training, Basic Training, and Advanced Training. Second Lieutenant Charles Olsen was now ready for his fighter. But then came the disappointment. The U.S. Army Air Corps did not have one for him.

I graduated from the T-6 and they didn't have any fighters for me to go to, no openings at a fighter command. So I had a choice of going to bombers or ferry aircraft, or instructing back in Basic Training. We had drawn lots for the few openings at various fighter squadrons and I lost. I asked for a fighter squadron again anyway, but it didn't help. Someone had said that I could teach and they needed instructors and besides I didn't want to be assigned elsewhere and lose my chance of getting into a fighter command somewhere.

They told me that I could instruct and wait for an opening in a fighter squadron so after graduating from training command class 42-E, I was transferred to Cochran Field at Macon, Georgia. And I waited.

Consequently I was side-tracked for a few months, acting as an instructor while my classmates went on ahead to pilot training for pursuit or fighters, or they went to bombers or some similar fate. I was one of the very few that went back to the training command.

Charlie would occasionally hear from his old instructor, Forrest Dines. He was curious as to how his ex-students were doing, trying to keep in touch. Charlie would answer him back and tell him how it was going and how he wanted a fighter. Forrest would write again and fill him in on several of his classmates. He told Charlie how important his work in the training command was to the war effort and tried to encourage him. He would add, "Do you remember so and so? Well, he got his fighter and I just learned that he was killed in the Philippines." After a while the letters stopped coming, Forrest probably having been transferred elsewhere.

Olsen instructed English, American, and Chinese students in the fine art of flying the BT-13:

I had English in the morning and Chinese in the afternoon, and I didn't get any fonder of flying students. I had trained to be a fighter pilot, to shoot and to drop bombs. I had practiced through the whole training command thinking that I was going to go out with a fighter squadron in some fighter command, and here I had graduated and they had put me teaching a bunch of students. The same old crap every day—you take off, this is the left rudder or this is the right rudder, you slip it this way. Pretty soon it's monotonous. Not that they don't have to be taught, but you figure now look, I've put in my time. Everybody should have to teach these monkeys three to six months, and then they should be able to do something else. There were other things, too. You had this dinky little field, some little bitty field in the middle of Georgia or Alabama and nothing around for miles. They had a western movie one night a week if they didn't have something at the PX. In other words, if you wanted a malted milk you had to go to Little Rock or Mobile to get one.

It was nothing at ten o'clock in the morning if somebody wanted a malted milk or a good cup of coffee to go out and get into the damn plane and crank it up and go to Little Rock. If you wanted a certain type of sandwich you'd go over to Atlanta and get the sandwich at such and such a restaurant. We didn't always land at a military base either, hell no, we landed anywhere we wanted. Remember the war was going on. We had number one priority. There wasn't that much going on in those days. Airlines were few and far between. You would call up Atlanta tower and give your army aircraft number and they would give you wind direction and you'd go right on in. They'd give you the runway and tell you where to taxi. You didn't have to have an excuse other than to go get a chocolate malt.

Every month Olsen put in a formal request for transfer to a fighter command. "I kept asking until finally they said they had an opening at Drew Field, Tampa, Florida, for advanced fighter training in P-39s, and I said, 'Fine, I'll take it.' I finished up with my class in about a week and went to Drew Field on June 30, 1942."

Here at Drew Field Olsen checked himself out in the Bell P-39 Air Cobra:

I went over the cockpit checklist for the P-39 and that was it. There was a Capt. Lance McCall, a guy with a mustache. He waxed it so it looked like two matches sticking out. I sat in it while he looked in and we went through a cockpit check, started the engine and dropped the flaps and so forth. I got familiar with the plane and then flew it. You could check out any fighter like that. The P-39 had a tricycle landing gear. You couldn't nose it over with that long nose wheel up front so it went like a kiddie-car.

Even now when I think of the P-39 the first thing that comes to mind is that overpowering smell. Most airplanes have some aura of oil and gasoline, but not the P-39. It had the most peculiar odor I ever encountered. It's like an immense amount of old burned gas and oil in a very small area. It leaked a lot of oil. It was unique among fighters of that time not only for the rearward position of the engine and the tricycle gear but for the automobile-like doors on either side of the narrow cockpit. The plane was too vulnerable. It tumbled and was too erratic. It had a wide wing, a squat tail, and was too perfectly balanced with the engine in the rear behind the pilot. I tumbled once. Couldn't get out. I was pulling up from a dive at about eighteen thousand feet and had just pushed the nose over into a weightless turn towards level flight when it happened. The plane went completely out of control, actually tumbling end over end. All the forces acted on the exposed flight controls out on the wings and tail, transmitting back to the stick between my knees and it began ricocheting violently about the narrow cockpit.

I tried to bail out but could not jettison either door while trying to contend with the flaying control stick. It was behaving like a heavy double-bladed ax literally beating me to a pulp. It was impossible to escape the plane. I was desperately trying to get hold of the stick and it almost pulled my arm out of the socket. I kicked all the rudder that I could and nothing happened. I was losing altitude fast. No way a human could have held onto that stick, the force of the thing tumbling, the stick flopping—I chopped the power, then applied full power, tried everything. Suddenly at about twelve hundred feet altitude the stick stopped, and I grabbed it and put on the power and finally went forward and came out into a normal dive. I recovered at about eight hundred feet.

I went up again to about eighteen thousand feet and flew around for a while. I was nauseated, really sick. I had been foggy most of the time, but I remembered tumbling because I could see horizon, horizon, horizon. I had been lucky. I watched from a high vantage point one day as a less fortunate pilot failed to recover from such a predicament as he tumbled from several thousand feet and crashed into the water below.

We didn't call it tumbling in those days or understand what caused it. After this they placed restrictions on maneuvers in the P-39, and a factory representative came over to debrief those of us that had survived the experience. I don't know the final outcome from all of this. I suppose they modified the plane, made some changes in the design because they were later used in the war, especially by the Russians. Maybe that's why they gave them to the Russians—I don't know.

Yet with all its uniqueness and problems, Charlie liked the P-39, especially for aerobatics, even though many pilots had a bad time with it. They were racking up those P-39s pretty good when Charlie arrived at Drew Field. Men were in various stages of fighter training. Ironically the great majority of these wrecks were not from tumbling and whatnot while flying the aircraft but from landing too hot.

I guess this was because it was so easy in a P-39 to come in real hot. It was so smooth and pilots would get preoccupied. Vision was good and the plane was so easy to land. You could never nose over with that tricycle gear nose wheel out in front, and so they would come on in and set their little kiddie car down and get a kick out of steering it even at two hundred miles an hour. You would have to work at it to ground loop a P-39. This one guy got killed when he went under a big oak limb. It just took the canopy off. They removed what was left of him and set the wrecked plane right by the flying shack. I don't know whether they did it to impress us or not, but it was right where everybody gathered. The operations officer would say, "Now go out there and look! This is what you hot shots get for coming in too goddamn hot."

Charlie looked into the smashed cockpit and he could see some of the man's teeth and jawbone, brains, and hair still in the plane. Sometimes there was more than one wrecked plane stacked there. It was the shock treatment. Most of the wrecks were usually from landing accidents. A few were from flying into high tension lines. In later years Olsen had additional recollections about the wrecks:

I'll tell you how bad it was at Drew. We flew every day and every Sunday there would be hundreds of cars lined up outside the fence. Civilians—watching for the crash. One day a guy overshot. He came in too hot and saw he wasn't going to make it and he dumped his flaps and tried to go around. He settled right on the tops of all the cars parked there and wiped out about eight of them and himself and a few other people. After that the military saw to it that nobody could come near there again. When you landed too hot, you wouldn't stop. Sometimes the brakes would fail and you'd keep going and you couldn't turn or would blow a tire—then BOOM— you'd cartwheel or flip over on your back and wipe yourself out.

It made an impression on you seeing all of these planes torn up! It impressed me. In the first place I didn't like the idea, I mean I saw a lot of guys get killed before, six or eight or ten in school I can remember. And that night flight, when all of them planked down all over. I started noticing that it wasn't the accidents per se. It was the finality of the accident—mistakes were permanent. It seemed like every time they had an accident in a P-39 the pilot was killed. Out of ten accidents, they lost eight or nine pilots. Whereas in training, if you had an accident, you didn't necessarily get killed. I noticed that some of them would go out in a P-39 and they wouldn't come back. They would go out and rat-race or go on maneuvers and the next thing you'd know, an hour or two later they didn't show up. Then another hour or two later we'd get the report. Somebody went down.

They spun in, tumbled in, or crashed, or something happened. Some days we lost two, some days three, some days one, some days none. I know that when I was at Tampa that four or five people were killed whom I knew personally.

At the mess hall one morning at breakfast I was looking at a guy sitting close by whom I didn't even know. He was just sitting there quietly eating his breakfast and he began to change. It was a visual change and I thought he became whiter than the rest of us. There was something about his appearance that became unnatural. I don't know what it was. He looked rather pale and all neat and proper as if he was being prepared for something. I then had a premonition that he was going to die. He was killed that same day. I figured that it was my imagination or something, but it bothered me. I had about forgotten about it until the same thing happened about a week or so later. I was at breakfast again and we were sitting and talking and eating, and I looked up across the way and saw this neat-looking pilot, his face so pale, and this strange sensation came over me once more. He looked extra clean-shaven and polished, his clothes were so neat. I tried to shake the feeling, but when I returned from flying that afternoon I was astounded to learn that he too had been killed. After that I ate my breakfast almost in seclusion trying not to look or talk to anyone. I would just eat my breakfast and go out to fly.

Charlie spent less than sixty days in fighter school. Eleven of his group were assigned to the Panama Canal Zone, Fifty-third Fighter Squadron, Thirty-second Fighter Group and were to report for duty by August 4, 1942.

During World War II, the Allies considered defense of the Panama Canal to be of major importance. The canal was protected by the United States Army and Navy and operated by American civilians who called the Canal Zone home. Like the military, these "Zonians" proudly, almost religiously, flew the Stars and Stripes.

Civilians in the Canal Zone all worked for one employer—the Canal Zone Company. They were members of a unique society, belonging to a socialist state unlike any other in the world. They enjoyed the benefits normally attached to socialism or Communism, without the typical drawbacks such as high taxation for the productive class and oppression. Everything was provided for them—health and sanitation, fire protection, police protection, schools, shelter, all aspects of civil government, and each head of household had a well-paying job.

The Canal Zone Company was designed and structured by the United States government to put ships through the canal, and it charged only such fees as were necessary to cover its maintenance and operation costs. Over the years, as the company developed, it became necessary that some form of government be established to care for the needs of the civilian workers, and the company served in that capacity as well. The chairman of the Board of Directors of the Canal Zone Company was also appointed governor of the Canal Zone, who from the beginning was always a general officer of the Corps of Engineers. The chairman was traditionally secretary of the Army. His original function was to serve as the direct representative of the president of the United States.

This closed society functioned in a most tranquil environment. It had no unemployment, no social welfare problems, and very little crime to contend with, because the company had absolute jurisdiction in selecting its employees and all had one common goal, the operation of the canal. If a person became unemployed, he was expelled from the Canal Zone. If a person retired from the company, he had thirty days in which to pack his family and belongings and leave. If a person misbehaved, either Panamanian or American, he went to the federal prison at Gamboa or was deported.

A person in the Canal Zone during World War II worked in either a civilian or military position, but both classes functioned as a team, operating and protecting the Panama Canal. In 1941, all businesses and other facilities within the Canal Zone were operated by the United States government, and they were quite modern and well maintained.

There were three methods of travel from the Pacific side to the Atlantic side of the Isthmus other than by ship. One was by plane, a second by the Panama Railroad, and the third by a single isthmian highway.

There were two major United States Army airfields within the Canal Zone—France Field, near the city of Cristobal on the northern Atlantic side, and Albrook Field, near Balboa on the southern Pacific side. France Field stationed the Curtiss P-40 and Albrook Field the Bell P-39. Only a single street separated the Canal Zone's

Balboa from Panama City, the capital of Panama, and the Canal Zone's Cristobal from the Panamanian city of Colon.

There were various country clubs and golf courses within the Canal Zone for both the military and civilian personnel, but the bars and restaurants appeared to get most of the business of airmen who were off duty. The cost of Canal Zone entertainment, food and drink, was quite modest, there being no profit motive. Life in the Canal Zone in 1941 was pleasant, but it lacked the hustle and bustle, the billboards and other advertisements, and the competitive atmosphere so much a part of life back in the States.

Heavy jungle growth filled with snakes, parakeets, monkeys, sloths, and jaguarondis was evident everywhere in the Canal Zone. It was kept in check by the constant vigilance of natives who kept it cut from around buildings and other structures, using only their long machetes. Otherwise, the jungle with its humid climate, disease, and parasites would re-claim the area, erasing all trace of human endeavor, as had happened with the Inca and Mayan cultures. For the most part, these grass-cutting machete experts were colorful and friendly people. Yet, on occasion, having the temper of their ancestors, they were known to confront one another using these handy weapons.

During World War II, the Allies considered the Canal Zone vital to wartime shipping and speculated that the Axis powers might view it as a prime military target. There was an endless parade of cargo and warships, sometimes stacking up for miles into the huge freshwater Gatun Lake, waiting for passage through the locks. Gatun Lake was the only place in the world where an oceangoing vessel could be "washed down" by fresh water, and deckhands generally enjoyed the passage while slinging a mop.

Both Atlantic and Pacific entrances to the canal were heavily guarded by the United States Navy, with mines and antisubmarine nets always in place. Overhead Navy PBMs and PBYs droned continuously, on patrol looking for German submarines. Ships of Allied nations would be met at sea and maneuvered into the locks and through the canal in a manner not to divulge the true locations of the mines to the enemy. Navy vessels would escort them initially to the first locks, opening and closing the antisubmarine nets as they passed.

The importance of the canal in shipments of war materials during

World War II is indisputable. The Axis powers were almost certainly aware of its significance. It was probably due to its distance from Europe and the formidable nature of its military protection that the Canal Zone never came under any significant attack during the war with the possible exception of some submarine activity.

As of early 1942, America, the sleeping giant, had barely risen and was faced with the huge, complex task of fighting a war on two fronts while supplying the other Allied nations with enough war materials to sustain their existence until the tide of war could be turned. Priorities depended upon where one stood at the time. Initially, the United States' attention was turned primarily towards the war in Europe, and England and France received the bulk of American aid, transported across the North Atlantic by air and ship. The China-Burma-India (CBI) Theater received some troops and supplies by a South Atlantic route. Along the way, aircraft were stationed in such places as Puerto Rico, British Guiana, Panama, Brazil, Trinidad, and the Ascension Islands.

Pilots of the patrolling aircraft felt they had the most boring jobs of the war. But from 1941 to 1943, given the German U-boat harassment in the North and South Atlantic and the Japanese Navy's activities in the South Pacific, getting troops and war supplies to European and Asian fronts was a most difficult logistical problem. The pilots in Panama had double duty. They had to contribute to the protective war umbrella along the South Atlantic shipping lanes as well as protect the Canal Zone itself. They were stationed primarily at France Field at the northern terminus of the Canal Zone on the Atlantic side.

On the afternoon of August 1, 1942, a Boeing 307 Stratoliner carrying thirty-two passengers landed at Albrook Field near the Pacific exit of the Panama Canal. Some of the passengers were civilian employees of the Canal Zone Company, which operated the canal, but the majority were uniformed officers, some of whom were brand new fighter pilots from Drew Field in Florida. The pilots sort of grouped together for a moment after disembarking as each man surveyed the surroundings. For most of them, this was their first duty outside the United States. They had known one another only very briefly back at Drew Field, but already friendships were beginning to develop, which can happen rather quickly in the service. All that the men demanded to know of each other was whether or not one smoked, possibly where a guy was from, whether or not he drank or played cards, and other minor details. Most of the emphasis was on the present and what lay ahead for them and not on anyone's past.

Charlie Olsen lit an Old Gold cigarette from the company that boasted "not a cough in a carload" and took a panoramic view of the horizon.

"So this is Panama," he said, speaking mostly to himself but audibly enough to be heard by 2nd Lt. Tom Cotton standing next to him. Charlie was not particularly impressed. With the exception of the rolling green hills, a few palm trees, and some double-decked houses, he thought to himself that it would easily pass for Louisiana, or at least for Georgia or Alabama. On the other hand, Tom Cotton immediately wished for a movie camera to record the event. It was certainly different from Powder River, Wyoming.

Tom Cotton was a Gary Cooper type of individual, rather calm and soft-spoken. He was the type of guy that Charlie felt comfortable with. He made friends easily, everyone appreciated his company, and they generally listened when he finally got around to saying something. Tom chose his words carefully, rarely speaking in haste. This probably accounted for a mannerism which he developed that consisted of brushing across the bottom of his nose with a forefinger, then smiling a faint little smile that could have any of several meanings, such as, "I just had this humorous thought but I'll tell you later," or "I don't believe a word you are saying but go ahead and tell it anyway."

This smile had been nurtured on fertile ground at various military schools prior to his enlistment and now possessed great virility. It was very infectious too, frequently catching on with other fighter pilots having tendencies in that direction should they hazard his company. Tom never appeared to start anything, yet he was always suspiciously present when it happened. Looking back on his fighter-pilot years, one yearns to ask him, "Will the real Tom Cotton please stand up?"

After a few moments one of the men asked one of the base personnel for directions to the Army shack and the group, each shouldering fifty-five pounds of GI gear, wandered over to report in. Each man was assigned a room at the Bachelor Officer's Quarters and after stowing his gear and settling in, it was nearly time for chow.

They had stayed up practically all night the night before leaving Miami—whooping it up, playing cards, and drinking. Now all of them stretched out on their bunks for a little shut-eye before going to chow, all except 2nd Lt. Curtis G. Johnson, that is. He had managed to get enough sleep on the plane coming down, and he busied himself by showering and shaving. He carefully pulled the comb through his coal black hair and patted the last unruly hair in place. As a final gesture of approval, he brushed his mustache with his forefinger and winked at his reflection. "To hell with chow," he thought. He was going to hit the city lights and see what was cooking in Panama City. Curtis was a good-looking lone wolf with Spanish features. He was more interested in his personal appearance and pursuit of the fairer sex than wasting his time playing stud poker all night with the boys. He was the kind of guy who comes to mind when one recalls the story about the new second lieutenant just graduating from flight school who bought up the entire PX's supply of pilot wings. When an opportunity presented itself in the form of a good-looking girl, he would make her a present of one of the wings at a tender moment, saying, "These are my first wings, the ones that Mother pinned on me the day I graduated. They mean a great deal to me, and I want you to keep them for me until I return." There are a few grand-mothers who to this day still cherish a pair of those "first" wings.

After chow, fed and relaxed, the men returned to the Rec Room of the BOQ and began to lounge around some of the tables. Olsen, Peterson, and Connelly started dragging up chairs for a four-handed poker game. 2nd Lt. Robert M. Peterson ran a hand over his short crew cut and started shuffling the cards. As he did so he glanced at the one unoccupied chair at the table and hollered, "Hey! Anybody else want in? Harrison?"

"Nope, I'm going to hit the sack in a minute," replied 2nd Lt. William C. Harrison, Jr. He was a lean figure of a man with a narrow face. Bill was from somewhere in the Midwest. He was a very nice guy, one that always obeyed the rules. Olsen and 2nd Lt. William S. Connelly started dividing up the matches, including a pile for the un-occupied chair since they had confidence in Peterson's persistence.

"How about it, Vidovich?" Peterson continued.

"Naw, I'm broke, count me out," replied Harlyn S. Vidovich, likely of Greek descent, short and stocky. Harlyn had the darkest beard and eyes imaginable, with big bushy eyebrows. He looked mean and tough, yet when he spoke his voice belied this first impression by revealing a most pleasant and friendly personality.

Peterson banged the deck of cards on the table, punctuating his impatience, adding a couple of choice words. He was rough-spoken, was in fact like a diamond in the rough, since he was well educated. Perhaps a better description would be that he was "rough as a cob," a scrapper. He began dealing out four hands face down around the table, and without looking up he said almost in despair, "OK, Gan!"

Second Lt. G. W. K. Johnston, III, quickly slid into the empty chair and began the attempt to sort out his hand. Gan Johnston was quickly becoming the character in the bunch. He was huskily built, had a round face with a Bob Hope ski-jump nose and a broad mouth. He was likable but had rather peculiar or humorous mannerisms such as when he tried to smoke and play cards at the same time. Though it was a rather simple task for most coordinated pilots, Johnston had difficulty handling a cigarette while fishing out a card from his disarrayed hand. He never seemed to make a concrete decision whether to keep the burning cigarette with its long ash in either hand or put it in his mouth. Such little traits were unsettling to his poker-playing cohorts or to those that drew him for a wingman on occasion. His most irritating mannerism, however, was that he generally won at poker.

Across the room a short distance, four other pilots were engaging in conversation. Tom Cotton, 2nd Lt. Roy J. Veazey, and 2nd Lt. Bruce Boylan were prying conversation out of 2nd Lt. William S. Epperson. Epperson was a lot like Tom Cotton, even in appearance. He had a narrow face and was also very good-looking, very distinguished. If you met him once you could later pick him out in a crowd of a thousand people. Epperson was brilliant. He knew much about everything. He could discuss almost any historical subject such as the history of the Panama Canal, which he was being encouraged to talk about at the moment. He later became the source of much information about the countries through which this group would travel on their way to the Far East. He was so well informed about different countries and their customs that some of the men figured that he must have lived in some of those places or that his family was a member of the diplomatic corps. It was either that or he read a lot and had total recall.

Back at the poker table, Peterson and Connelly began to squabble about the ante. They were a pair those two—both physical, short, and husky, and both Yankees. Peterson often kept a chip on his shoulder and was prone to invite someone to knock it off. Connelly too had ideas of his own, was rather opinionated. Since in addition they were both built like weight lifters, it was only natural that Connelly and Peterson would sound off occasionally. When they did, 2nd Lt. John D. Long generally got up and left the room for quieter quarters, which he also did on this occasion. He decided that it was quieter in his room where he could finish the letter to his wife. J. D. was probably the only fighter pilot in the entire U.S. Air Corps that wore pajamas. Due to his quiet manner and extreme politeness, it was suspected that he had been reared by a couple of old maid aunts or perhaps a grandmother, who had given him strict supervision that required him to get up at a certain time, eat formal meals, and be polite and formal at all times. This of course was probably not the case at all. J. D. was tall and good-looking, as all Texans are, and because of his height and stern manner, fellow pilots never overtaxed his patience. He was extremely reserved, a trait which was even reflected in his flying. If a bread roll came flying over your way during chow you could bet it didn't come from J. D. Long. You would be more apt to suspect Cotton, Olsen, Peterson, or Connelly.

Bruce Boylan was captivated by Epperson's historical account of the Panama Canal. He hung on every word, being only momentarily distracted by Peterson's elation when he connected with an "inside straight." Bruce was a Fred Astaire type who smiled all the time. Always friendly and agreeable, he was never prone to argue. He was a good listener and definitely one of the guys. He was not the kind of a pilot who would fly inverted or rat-race at low altitudes, that is unless somebody asked him to, which they frequently did. In that case he would perform with the best of them. He did not lack confidence. Generally when left alone he followed the rules, flying by the numbers unless he got very bored.

On the other hand, Roy Veazey's attention was torn between Epperson and the poker table. Short, dark, and very humorous, "Vese" was a typical Louisiana Cajun. About the time that he became interested in Epperson's history lesson, something would happen over at the poker table, and he would have to go over and look at the guys' hands, although Peterson would hide his. Everything was always funny to Veazey. He rarely ever took anything seriously. He was a good mixer and was liked by everybody. He was the kind of a guy whom you could always count on to help you out whether you were in trouble or otherwise. He simply enjoyed the hand that life had dealt him, and if that is not characteristic of the French Cajuns of Louisiana then nothing is.

Actually there were few differences among these men in matters that counted most. All of them were college-educated, had volunteered for the Air Corps, and were destined to become closer friends.

Owing to Gan's streak of good luck at the poker table and the extent of Panama's captivating history, the scene continued until the wee hours of the morning, although Harrison and Vidovich went to their rooms relatively early. The next morning the group was broken up and assigned to various squadrons around the Canal Zone.

The Canal Zone was very small in its total land area, and France Field was proportionally small for an airfield. It had one maintenance hangar, a wind sock, and a very short shell strip that stuck out into Limon Bay like a pier. It was home base to the Army's single Canal Zone P-40 squadron.

Approaching midmorning on a typically beautiful Panamanian day, one with deep blue sky and puffy white clouds here and there as if added by an artist's brush, a group of newly assigned pilots began to drift out to the flight line. Captain Shapiro, the flight officer, stood near a few parked P-40s, shifting a batch of papers back and forth from hand to hand. He was of Italian heritage, having black hair and a stocky build. His beard was so heavy that he had a five o'clock shadow by 1:30 in the afternoon, and patience was not exactly one of his virtues. His burly hand selected a page as he waited impatiently for the approaching men who were taking their time looking over their new duty station as they walked.

In addition to the men coming over from Albrook Field on the Pacific side, there were a few that had recently joined the P-40 squadron—2nd Lt. James Anning, 2nd Lt. John D. Glover, and 2nd Lt. Curtis Scoville. All three were worthwhile candidates for a poker game or rat race. Jim Anning was another thin-faced perpetual smiler who would show you his teeth at the slightest provocation. He even slept with a smile on his face. He laughed all the time and thoroughly enjoyed everyone's jokes. His hair, tossed up and back and rather unruly, made him look like a high school or early college type.

Under all circumstances he was one of the bunch, and you could never dare him to do anything that he would not do.

John Glover was one of the good-lookers. He cultivated a very small pencil mustache like "Smiling Jack" and was similar in appearance to Charlie Olsen, being of medium size, thin, and neat. Glover belted a few "blue moons" with the girls on occasion because he liked the ladies and they liked him. He had a pleasing manner with women but was well liked by everyone. He never found an excuse to raise his voice and was a very competent pilot.

Curtis Scoville had black hair and combed it straight back with a little dab of oil. He had an elongated nose and face and was quite convinced that he was the world's greatest pilot. He was very quick to be doubtful of others' exploits with an airplane unless he was involved in the incident himself, in which case he would verify everything that was said. If there was any doubt about his ability as a pilot, all one had to do was to ask him.

The men were not moving fast enough for Shapiro, who wanted to get his next bunch of pilots checked out in the Curtiss P-40 fighter. So he started his muster as soon as a few got to within earshot.

"Anning?" he queried, and from the direction of the approaching men came the reply, "Over here." The men quickened their steps.

"Cotton?"

"Yo."

"Glover?"

"Here."

"Johnston? . . . Johnston?" Shapiro raised his eyes from the roster, and he looked over at the men and then glanced back at the roster.

"Second Lt. G. W. K. Johnston, III?"

"Here, Sir," replied Johnston quickly, closing up the rear.

"Long?" Shapiro continued.

"Here."

"Olsen?"

"Here."

"Peterson?"

"Ho."

As Captain Shapiro continued the muster, Charlie's attention turned to a nearby P-40, and he ambled over and patted the large protrusion beneath the engine cowling. He had never even seen a

P-40 before. He had read all the specs; it had an Allison engine and all that stuff. It was certainly different from the P-39s he had been flying. He was immediately impressed with the tremendous nose sticking out in front. He had been so used to his "kiddie-car" P-39 with the tricycle gear, in which he could easily see over the trim nose. This Curtiss P-40 was quite unlike his old Air Cobra. You could steer the P-39 with just your feet at the most breathtaking speeds and have a panoramic view of the scenery as well. He remembered how easy it was back at Drew Field to taxi the Cobra. He would jump into the Cobra and taxi across the field just to go get a pack of cigarettes at the PX. He would park it and go get whatever he wanted and come back and get in and scoot back across the field. But this P-40 had a nose and spinner of such tremendous proportions that it seemed to stick out about two miles in comparison.

It was Tom Cotton's first introduction to the P-40 as well. Like Charlie, he had flown P-39s at Drew Field but personally did not care for them. Yet he immediately felt an attraction to the Curtiss P-40. A little grin came across his face as he brushed the side of his nose with his forefinger and kicked the P-40's tire.

In one nimble bounce Jim Anning sprang from the big main gear tire, spun around in midair, and seated himself rather pretentiously on the leading edge of his chosen P-40. He just sat there during the rest of the muster, grinning from ear to ear. He was a hotshot pilot and he knew it. He did not care which end of the plane the propeller was on. He knew he could fly it and he was anxious to go.

By the time the last "here" was spoken, Charlie was sliding into his new "office." "God, I can't even see out," he hollered out loud to the others. "I'm going to run into the first thing I come to. I'm going to cut somebody up and not even know it."

By now all of the men had selected a P-40 like cowboys going through a remuda. Each was going through similar experiences and having similar impressions, except for G. W. K. "Gan" Johnston, III, who just sat in his P-40 cockpit and admired all the switches.

All set, Charlie cranked up his P-40 and gunned it and slowly started to roll in the soft shell surface, noting it was a very big ship. It felt bulky and stout and was very noisy, quite unlike his old Cobra, which sounded like a refined stitching machine, its engine being behind the pilot. Soon they were all rolling and Cotton grinned his approval of the sound of his engine. It was like a reliable old washing machine, he thought, one that would never quit.

They all got off without difficulty and climbed for altitude to check out the P-40's idiosyncrasies. If you wanted to know a plane's stall speed, you did not ask anyone. You simply took it up and stalled it. You felt the ragged edge of flight in different configurations, altitudes, and airspeeds and noted characteristic warning vibrations preceding a stall so that you could recognize them at low altitudes where recovery time is critical. In general you just wrung it out to get the feel of it.

After about an hour, the P-40 began to grow on Charlie except for that heavy nose which always wanted to fall through. He was supersensitive now about a plane's pitch axis after flying P-39s, ever since Drew Field and the unsuspected tumbling. Charlie figured that he could certainly forget about tumbling in a nose-heavy P-40. After about an hour of familiarization, Charlie headed back to the field. Taking off had been conventional but coming down proved to be nerve-racking. He took one look at the short field down below him and felt that it must have shrunk since his takeoff. In fact, he was not entirely convinced that it was the same field. "Man, it looked short, about eight hundred feet at best. The older I get the shorter it was," he related in later years. "At any rate, it was damned plenty short with nothing but water at both ends. I don't know who got down first out of our group because I was just concerned with me." The field pattern was rather busy at the time he entered to land since in addition to Charlie's group the field was experiencing its normal traffic for the day. In addition, the morning check-out pilots were finishing their landings.

"I took my turn to make my landing and feeling no particular pressure as I had plenty of gas and could stay up for sometime if I wanted to," Charlie recalled. He made one low pass at about 120 mph to size up the field, which he noticed was not getting any longer. Back at altitude again, he began to notice that the others in his group were coming around and that nobody else was getting down either. But after his initial pass, he felt that it would be no problem for him. So he made a brisk left turn and dropped his gear and flaps smartly and turned on final approach for the short runway at about 110 mph.

"Beautiful," he thought, as he set it down. "Well, almost." By the time he had it going straight, he noticed that he was halfway down the short runway and decided that it was not the place for him to be at that speed. He gunned it. "What the hell," he thought. "I might as well go around again."

Most of the earlier group had shut down their engines now and were sitting in their parked planes listening to their radios and watching this last group of the day come in. In somewhat competitive spirits, they were wondering how this last group would fare.

As Charlie came around for his second attempt, he noticed that the field was devoid of any crash trucks or dead bodies left over from the first group's check out. So he figured that he could make it down too. He repositioned himself in his seat and looked out over the long nose as he came around on final. This time he was a little slower and slightly higher than on his first attempt. He figured that he would have to slip it and crab slightly to compensate for a crosswind which he had to reckon with now. But for some reason the plane was not getting down like he wanted, and he figured that without ordinance or belly tank it was just lighter than he was accustomed to. Besides, this was a P-40E model and it was known to float a little. So he scratched his second attempt too, gunned it again, and picked up his gear and flaps and climbed out for his third try.

Once again he found himself too high on final, but he was determined to put it down this time. He landed in a nice three-point altitude, but promptly saw that familiar scenery coming up at center field again. He might salvage the landing, he thought, and he might not. It could easily become a wipe out with a ground loop or nose over, or worse, he might roll right into the drink.

Coming around the fourth time he tried dragging it in from away out over the bay, but that did not work either. Ballooning up and down, he finally gave it up without touching the runway. On his fifth and final attempt, he put it on and it stuck. He had gotten up high and made a short turn into the field and slipped it all the way down to the very beginning of the threshold next to the water, where he chopped the power and straightened it out just before he greased it on. Even then it rolled for a most uncomfortable distance. But nearing the end of the runway, he knew he had it made. When he taxied off the strip, he saw that he had at least fifty feet of unused runway left.

Taxiing into the flight line Charlie recognized Shapiro's voice on the radio as he spoke to those remaining pilots circling to land.

Charlie learned that Long, Anning, and Cotton were still making passes. Shutting down his engine, he slid back his canopy and unbuckled his shoulder harnesses and seat belts. He was dripping with sweat. Like the rest of the guys already down, he removed his headset from his crumpled ears and hung it on the throttle quadrant. It was getting near dark now and there was some concern about the planes remaining in the pattern. Then Cotton got down, followed by Peterson. Finally one by one the rest came in—all except G. W. K. Johnston, III, who kept making pass after pass until it was nearly dark. On one of his aborted landings he just barely staggered off the end of the runway and everyone stood up in their cockpits along the flight line and started to holler, "He's going in. He's going in. He's not going to make it." But he simply clipped off the wind sock with his left wing and proceeded to mush out over the bay until he finally gained enough air speed to try it again.

Soon his buddies became so concerned for his safety that they suggested to Shapiro that someone with P-40 experience go up and bring him in. Let him fly on Johnston's wing and bring him in in formation, they suggested. Shapiro replied, "If I do that he will never learn to land the goddamn thing."

By now it seemed like everybody was talking to Johnston over their radios trying to help him in. Finally Shapiro picked up his mike and spoke in a firm but slightly peeved voice:

> Johnston, you are going to be all right. Just drag it in, Johnston, just drag it in. Bring it around and slowly drop flaps and gear. Hang it on the prop and come down to about eighty mph about five feet over the water. Don't touch that goddamn power whatever you do. Go back and make a long approach. Bleed off your airspeed and maintain eighty. Get back there about a mile. I don't care if you get plumb back to Gatun Lake, just fly it on in across the water, and when you cross the very beginning of the runway whop off all your power and hope for the best.

He put down his mike and turned to one of the men standing close by. "God, I hope he makes it, we need the airplane. Go get the biscuit gun somebody." He made it all right, doing just as instructed. He hung it on the edge of a power-on stall and then dropped it in. When he completed his roll-out he saw nothing before him but water. He used up every inch of the runway.

After that they flew submarine patrols almost every day in their new P-40s. They would get out over the Caribbean Sea for a couple of hours or more and go out towards the Atlantic Ocean and meet everything coming in. If it was a commercial airplane, they would meet it, making sure it was actually an airliner. Any unknown vessels would also be met as well as a lot of bogies that proved to be only false alarms.

Frequently around the card table at night the conversation would settle upon combat and what it would be like the first time the enemy was encountered. Eventually the squadron got a firsthand description of combat one day when Wing Commander Donaldson, fresh from England and battle with the German Luftwaffe pilots, visited the field. "He was fantastic," Charlie remembered.

> We watched him come in over the field upside down, inverted. He wasn't one foot off the ground with his antenna. Why his prop wasn't cutting grass I don't know. Then he would slow roll his special built P-39 almost dragging a wing in the mud. He would hold that thing in that position—inverted—for maybe halfway across the field and then whip it up and slow roll it and then go back up. He'd do outside loops, English bunts, and then break away, jetting between two buildings and all kinds of stuff. He was an old man— almost forty-two.

After his demonstration, the guys gathered around and someone asked, "What does it feel like when you meet the enemy for the first time? What do you do first? What happens?" He answered:

> Fellows, you go up there and get on somebody's wing and you stay there. Try not to wet your parachute when it starts happening. When the shooting starts you are going to become an observer. You're not going to be a pilot any more. You're going to see all these guns, ammunition, bombers, fighters, and you are going to see angels, stars and stripes, and even moons. All this stuff is going to start taking place like a bad nightmare and you are going to be there. If you are able to fire your guns, you'll be lucky. If you get a shot and shoot one down you're going to be the greatest pilot in the world.
>
> Shooting is like getting a knot in your throat the size of a baseball. Your mouth is dry and you think somebody took all the moisture

out. It feels so dry you think you're sucking in solid cotton and plaster. Then there's that persistent basketball in your throat. You're not going to be able to move or think. You're going to be taken away by the vastness of it all. Then when you come back into this world, you're going to be a better pilot.

Each would soon learn for himself that Donaldson was absolutely correct. Sometimes even going on patrol or answering an alert could be exciting, as Tom Cotton found out. Cotton later explained:

One night there was a heavy rain. We were on alert status, which meant we had to get right out into the air, all eight ships. It was still dark out, early in the morning. The mechanics had been working on my P-40, which had been pulled into the revetment, but hadn't finished their work. They labored into the night but were gone when the alert went off. Nobody knew that they had failed to complete the hooking up of the throttle linkage. Some phony radar signals came in from the Pacific side instigating the alert. The minute the alert horn went off, the armorer, who was also unaware of the unfinished repair work, jumped into the plane and got it started. Then we came roaring out in a mad scramble in this station wagon and fell off the fenders and everything as we ran and jumped right into the planes, snapping our parachutes before letting the brakes go.

As I recall, I was in number two position—wingman in four-plane flight formation takeoff. The runway was narrow. Actually we operated with tactics similar to those devised by Chennault, but we'd use four planes for takeoffs on a runway spaced only for three. At the far end of the short runway was the seawall. The last guy in the flight had to be airborne before he got off the runway or he would drop right into the bay.

I remember seeing the lights on the wing tips of the leader. As I started down the runway with him, I noticed I was creeping ahead and tried to pull the throttle back, but it kept sticking. I started riding out because by now our wings were beginning to overlap. Finally I pushed it square through the emergency war gate position to the firewall end of the quadrant, then quickly tried to pull it back. Unfortunately it stuck in this full open "war emergency" full power position.

I suddenly became a solo performer in this formation takeoff. I was shooting up high in an effort to get out of the second element's way. They moved right up on the leader and didn't even see me because it was raining so hard. I knew I was right above them, but I could not see where they were. About that time my engine blew up. I was in a vertical bank at the time and all I could see below was the breakwater on the edge of the runway. I thought, "If I can get into the ocean it will be no sweat." So I did, right into the water, nose down and in half-inverted position.

My P-40 was one of the old B models with the ring sight outside the windscreen, with no gunsights inside the cockpit. It was a big cockpit. When I hit the water, the prop and throttle quadrants were shoved right into the instrument panel by my left hand and I was thrown into a corner, then the plane hit bottom, nose in the mud.

It was dark down there. I thought, "Geez, I'm running out of breath. This isn't the right way to drown." So I just took a big inhale of water and I could feel it going right into my lungs. I felt better. I don't know if it was the remaining compressed air or if I became some sort of fish. But I felt like I was ready to go again and reached up to pull the canopy back. But there was no canopy.

So I reached up in the back to get hold of this structure by the oil tank, and all that was there was shattered plexiglass. When I did that I severed two fingers, one hanging on only with the skin. I gave a big yank to get out of the seat which had been crimped when the wing came over the canopy on initial impact. As I did, the parachute came open. I remember passing the tail on my way up and seeing a light coming from the surface before I finally passed out.

The light was from the crash boat which had come out to find me. They had circled the scene and were on their way back when I came bobbing up like a cork. I was unconscious. Next thing I remember is that this boat hook was under my shoulder and they got me up to the side, pulling me up with wet parachute dragging. They dislocated my shoulder in the process, which immediately brought me back to life. I tried to say some uncomplimentary things to the men on the boat, but every time I started to talk water spewed out. It came out of my lungs and my stomach. I remember flashes of a Navy chief standing there in his white uniform. I was grabbing onto him and I thought, "What a funny thing. His shirt's all covered with blood. What a messy fellow he is." But the blood was coming from my hand. The end of the finger was dangling down, bleeding profusely.

They were going to roll me over a barrel and I objected to that. That was sort of an artificial respiration technique. They would roll you over a barrel, back and forth in an effort to pump out the inspirated water. I was breathing and talking rather excitedly, spouting water all the time. They put me in this old hard-sprung ambulance and took off through the jungle. That's when I thought I was

going to die. I guess the excitement had sort of worn off as we were
driving to Fort Gulick Hospital. The road was rough and here I was
in this bouncing machine. I guess it was an extreme case of pleurisy
which made my ribs feel like they were all broken.

Then they rushed me to the emergency ward where they were
going to take x rays. They put me on one of these tilting tables and
started cranking me up. They got me up too high and I said, "Doctor, you'd better not put me higher."

Doc said, "This'll take just a minute," and he gave the handle a
swing and I pumped another gallon of seawater all over his machine.
He didn't seem to appreciate that. Then they rushed me to surgery
where a Chinese surgeon looked at my hand. He sutured the finger-
tip back on and the other severed places. Did a wonderful job. He
started shooting me with morphine as he sewed. The next thing I
knew I was in bed on an inclined board, with my head at the bottom
and my feet up, which I didn't relish. Consequently, I wasn't a very
popular patient.

Charlie Olsen was one of the eight pilots in the same formation
scramble. Olsen remembers:

I heard somebody say on the radio "He's going in," but I didn't
know who it was. I called the tower and they confirmed it was Cotton, saying they had just fished him out, but he had drowned and it
looked like he was a goner but they were still working on him.

As soon as I returned from patrol, I jumped out of the cockpit
and asked about him, expecting the worst. I was told they had re-
vived him and he was over at the base hospital. I rushed the distance
to his hospital room, quietly opening the door not knowing what
drama lay beyond. As the door swung open, I saw Cotton standing
in his shorts, high as a kite, pinning the wet contents of his wallet to
a string he had rigged across his room. With a sheepish grin, he separated the last two wet bills and pinned them to a string to dry.

While Cotton was hospitalized, Charlie had been transferred out
of the P-40 squadron to the Pacific side of the Isthmus back to P-39s
at Albrook Field. During his duty at France Field, Charlie and a few
other pilots of the P-40 squadron had managed to acquire a rather
sizable boat about twenty-two feet in length, which they had fitted
with an inboard motor taken from a nearby Hudson automobile. It
was an old boat and Charlie did most of the woodwork during its res-

toration. After scrounging around the Navy yard they managed to find a propeller and shaft necessary to make the boat seaworthy. It had been a lot of work, and now that they were transferred from France Field to the other side of the Isthmus, they wanted that boat to help fill their leisure hours. They had heard many stories while in Colon about the jivaro headhunters who inhabited the jungle near Panama City, and they wanted to venture upriver in their direction to see if they could get a few shrunken heads wholesale. Actually, they were more interested in hunting, but the shrunken head idea intrigued them to some extent. The problem was that they had no way of getting their boat across the Isthmus to their new duty station. So they decided just to fly it over.

Nobody seemed to care what they were bent upon doing, least of all their new flight officer at Albrook. "How are you going to do it?" he asked Charlie, probably in complete disbelief.

"Well, we will just secure the motor and hull on a couple of the P-39s and fly 'em back," replied Charlie.

Three P-39s took off from the fighter base near Balboa and flew north to France Field for the boat. Upon landing at France Field the three pilots quickly proceeded to separate the converted Hudson engine from the ex-Navy hull. They placed the engine on a bomb-buggy and wheeled it over to one of the waiting P-39s. Here they slung the engine from the belly tank attachment on the Cobra with surprising ease. But the twenty-two-foot hull was an entirely different matter. After much effort they finally secured it in the same location on the belly of Charlie's plane. The third P-39 was to be the chase plane on the return flight, a flight which happened to be rather low and slow over the jungles of Panama, Charlie watching the plane carrying the engine and in turn its pilot watching Charlie carrying the boat hull. The chase plane was close behind watching them both. None of the three men appeared to be concerned about aerodynamics or weight and balance. They just sat there in their cockpits grinning like opossums as they flew their prize possession back to a small fighter strip near Albrook Field. But they had provided for one safety factor— their precious cargos could be jettisoned like belly tanks should the need arise.

Until they landed, no one paid any particular attention to their activity, except possibly the natives below looking up and seeing three United States Army aircraft flying overhead with this unusual cargo, landing gear fully extended during the entire trip. Back at Albrook Field, it surely must have been another story, as one can only imagine the strange appearance of these three aircraft approaching and the amazement of their flight officer. The quicker the incident was forgotten the better for all concerned, he must have thought. After all, they had told him what they were going to do.

Shortly after landing, they had the engine back in the boat and were dragging it down the street to the nearby river where they checked it out and found that all was fine. It was none the worse for its brief flight across the Isthmus. But it was over a month and a half before the men resumed their aquatic adventures, what with flight training and gunnery practice. Preparations were finally completed for their long-awaited hunting trip up the Rio Bayano River into the land of the jivaro headhunters.

As they traveled upstream on their three-day expedition, the trip proved disappointing for most of the men, though it was somewhat eventful for two of them. The jungles were surprisingly devoid of visible game. Even a headlight hunt at night along the riverbank proved disappointing. On the second day, pulses did quicken as they rounded a bend in the river and saw an area which they figured the headhunters had cleared. In the very center of the clearing, there stood a man-made idol or monument fashioned from stone. Dangling like wind chimes from the tip of the structure were fancy-colored, feathery plumes dancing in the wind. Decorating the structure were strips of shiny metal-like bands of gold or silver. At last here was the tangible evidence of the mysterious jivaro headhunters. Strangely enough, not one in the party volunteered to go ashore to investigate. As a matter of fact, the subject never came up. They just stared and continued to motor right on up the river, keeping well within the middle of the stream.

Near midafternoon, the party put ashore to camp at a suitable location some distance upstream. A couple of the men decided to try hunting close by, which was rather dangerous since they were now indeed in jivaro country. They promptly got lost, having wandered too far into the jungle away from camp. As it grew dark, one of them fell from a twenty-foot cliff, severely spraining his ankle and injuring his knee.

With darkness approaching, Olsen and the others back at camp became gravely concerned for the safety of the two "asses" who had wandered off and gotten lost. They began to shout, and hearing no reply, they fired their rifles three times in a row as a signal of distress. They knew that the two men could be hopelessly lost.

They built a huge bonfire in hopes that at least the men might be able to see the glow in the black night, but this also failed. So they loaded the boat and headed downstream since every indication was that the men had headed that way. At least they hoped so, for upstream the river branched into many tributaries, and a search would surely have been in vain. South then, was their only hope for rescue. Enthusiastic at first, the men in the boat renewed their shouting and firing until they grew hoarse and tired. Then they devised a system whereby they would travel downstream for ten minutes and then stop the engine to holler and fire their guns and listen. Time after time, they repeated the procedure, but the only reply was the sound of the wind and the lapping of the water against the sides of the boat.

Finally, they gave up the search because their own safety was now at stake. Near morning the tide would go out and the river, which flowed into the Pacific Ocean, would be drained quickly of navigable water, leaving them high and dry on a muddy bank. Yet they decided to try one more ten-minute trip downstream.

Suddenly, one of the men stood up in the boat and said, "Listen, I think I heard something." Everyone listened intently, hoping, and then they heard eager shouts of relief from the lost men. Rounding a bend they sighted the two men comfortably seated on a log next to a crackling campfire. The words that greeted these two men from the approaching rescue vessel were mixed with shouts and gestures of contempt, but deep down everyone was sincerely relieved to find them safe. Quickly they brought them aboard and headed upstream. It was getting near daylight and they were alarmed to see the low water level in the riverbed. The tide was going out quickly. Now, rather lost themselves, they managed with considerable luck to find the particular branch of the river which communicated with the canal and their way home. As they passed through this last segment of the river, the water level became so low due to the outgoing tide that all but the injured man had to abandon the boat and push it by hand the remaining distance. The next morning the boat was for sale. That was the last time any of them ever used it.

None of the pilots knew of anyone who had personally encountered a headhunter, but they all heard one rumor (which still persists

AVG P-40 is refueled near Rangoon for ferry flight to Tongoo. (Tex Hill collection)

AVG repair crew patches up a P-40 under camouflage net. (Tex Hill collection)

Patriotic "Panda Bears" of the Second Squadron of the AVG. (Tex Hill collection)

The famous "Hell's Angels" Third Squadron of the American Volunteer Group. (Tex Hill collection)

AVG pilots (from left) Pappy Paxton, Pete Wright, Freeman Ricketts, John Newkirk, Tex Hill, Henry Geselbracht, Jr., and Gil Bright. (USAF photo)

Pilots scramble at Hengyang in early 1944. Charlie Olsen is second from left in the light-colored flight suit.

Tex Hill and crew plan mission beneath the wing of a P-40.

AVG pilot John Newkirk and his crew chief, George Brice.

A Chinese guard maintains vigil at entrance to Kweilin cave housing the net command. The sign was intended to keep civilian population out during air raids. (USAF photo)

Tex Hill and company plot progress from inside cave. (USAF photo)

Allison P-40 engine, desperately needed by Chennault's pilots, awaits flight over the Hump. (USAF photo)

A captured Japanese Oscar waits to be dismantled and shipped to the United States. (Tex Hill collection)

Crew chief Charles Chaney (left), Squadron Leader John Newkirk (center), and Tex Hill (with flag on back) study map. Pilots wore the flags to identify themselves to Chinese in case they were shot down over enemy territory.

AVG pilot Freeman Ricketts in plane showing early handmade gunsight. (Tex Hill collection)

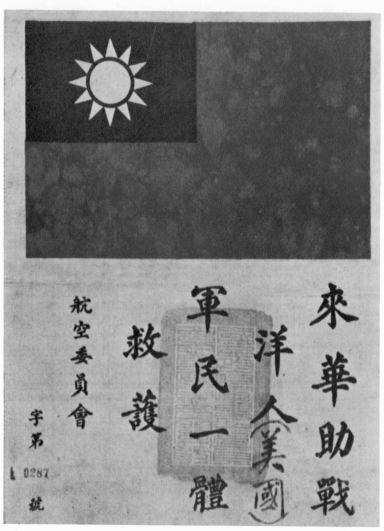

Chinese-American flag worn by airmen on their jackets to identify themselves as American pilots for Chinese, who often guided them back to American bases. (Tex Hill collection)

in the Canal Zone to this day) that a decapitated pilot was found south of where the monument had been sighted. He had belly-landed his plane in a clearing and was found still strapped in his seat, but his head was missing. It was likely that he was killed in the crash, it was reported. But there was no evidence of the kind of impact on crashing that could have severed his head, nor could it be located. Credit was naturally given to the jivaros, who were known to inhabit the area.

The jivaros themselves were no rumor. Charlie and the others saw many shrunken heads in the black market area of Panama City, mostly consisting of animal heads, but some human heads were discernible, there being no mistake about it. Their workmanship was fascinating. The secret process of head-shrinking, fruitlessly researched to some length by the medical profession in earlier years, was thought to be a procedure whereby the bones were carefully removed and the soft tissue shrunk and dried by hot sand and some drying method which allowed the retention of the proportions and the relationship of the original features. The decapitated pilot story was supposed to have occurred a year or so before Charlie arrived in Panama.

Charlie Olsen in later years had additional reminiscences of the Panama episode:

At Rio Hato flying P-39s again, we found we didn't like them anymore after flying the P-40s. We could fly the P-39s for fun, although they had a lot of things wrong with them. We used to go out for cannon practice and shoot with 37 mm guns on the coast, hitting sharks or trying to find something else to shoot like an old abandoned car. The P-39 had a lot of minor things ailing it, like the bladder brakes which were constantly going out. They would get hot and the rubber would burn. This brake problem was the cause of many accidents.

One time I cut a revetment down for this reason. The roof of the structure had a kind of peak in the center to accommodate the large four-bladed prop while the rest was just barely above the wings. It was so low that a person would have to stoop to walk on the wings while under cover. The purpose of the revetment was, of course, twofold—camouflage and to protect planes from the torrid tropical rains. It also served as a place for the ground crew to service the craft. Scattered around the perimeter was the usual equipment used for this purpose including fifty-five gallon drums of high octane gas. The floor of the revetment was about nine feet below the ground surface level. It sloped gently upward to ground level to enable a pilot to taxi a plane out under its own power. Planes were routinely taxied out by the pilots up this incline. Young hot-shot pilots feeling their oats might be inclined to depart from this confinement like a hairy-legged tarantula who had been drowned out of its hole.

One day I answered an alert. It was dark, about four in the morning. We had a couple of unknowns coming in and orders to go out to meet them. I ran to the revetment as the engine was being warmed up. Someone threw me a chute and I jumped in the plane. They gave me a signal to come on, and I pumped the brakes to make sure they were working. They were. I revved her up and she started moving. About that time, my right brake went out. It just collapsed as she was moving. The plane started turning left and I couldn't stop it. I swerved around and the prop cut the whole revetment down. The prop was coming right around at the crew chief.

He was hanging onto the pitot tube near the leading edge of the wing for dear life, trying to avoid the rotating prop. That was the last thing I saw before complete blackness. I cut the engine, and it came down, the wood, beams, everything. After a moment that seemed an eternity, they were digging me out, and all that I could think about were the barrels of gasoline which were stacked all around. I was very glad to get out of that situation, and so was the crew chief.

As I was filling out the report about the revetment, the squadron commander, Maj. James K. Johnson, who was known for his roughness and compulsion for accuracy, came by. I was expecting the usual chewing out when he said, "Don't worry about the report. The right brake went out. Just fill it out that way." After he left, I asked what was the matter with him and was told that he did the exact same thing about a couple of months before.

It was at Albrook when I first brought in a P-39 at night. As I lined up I could barely see the runway. It was raining, yet I was at the right height and everything. The lights were very dim on the field. You couldn't see a damn thing. I turned on final and dropped my gear and flaps. All was well until I hit my landing light switch to lower a retractable landing light into the slipstream beneath the wing. Then it happened. At this awkward moment the additional drag caused the plane to flip on its back. I was upside down. I quickly checked the field first and gunned it and rolled back over, barely clearing the trees as I gave it full power.

It was instant reflex action that meant life or death to many pilots. I will never forget an incident which happened much later in Kunming when a bunch of fighter pilots and a flight surgeon were sitting at this long table at the mess hall. On it was a china pitcher with water in it. One fellow said, "Pass me that water please," and another man picked up the pitcher. As he did, the handle separated from it. Down came the pitcher and water splattered all over the table. The only person who got it was the flight surgeon. He was drenched. Everybody else was up from the table before the pitcher hit. Whether we heard the popping sound as the handle broke or watched the motion as it separated from the body, in an instant everybody but the doctor was up and away. The pitcher hit and the water splashed. The men calmly picked up their plates and moved down the table and started eating again, all except the soaked surgeon, who just sat there and looked at the rest of us in disbelief.

There was a lot of boredom at Albrook, and the fact that the men had to practice gunnery so much did not help. They would shoot wooden floats that looked like rafts and that were anchored offshore for target practice. They would go out there and see how well they could shoot, but it got awfully boring for them after a while. They would rather have stayed in and played bridge or poker. Olsen later recalled:

> We got to fooling around shooting targets upside down one day and started to make side bets on the guy who would make the most hits. The pilots would get up speed and come into a slow roll just before reaching the target, roll inverted . . . pop . . . pop . . . pop . . . and then turn back over and go. Usually they would dip as they came out of the roll. They were pretty sloppy sometimes. One guy went in and we lost him.

They lost more than one pilot as a result of boredom and carelessness. The grass around the field at Rio Hato grew about four feet high and on occasion the pilots used to mow it with their props, sometimes while in formation. After Flight Officer Donaldson's visit, some of them would get a crewman to place a white cloth on top of the tall grass and then fly down inverted and pick up the cloth with the antenna mast which stuck up a few inches above and behind the rear portion of the canopy. "I never did that," Charlie later confessed with a grin. "I simply couldn't get low enough."

Coming off patrol, pilots would occasionally lower the landing gear and one after the other bounce the wheels off the tin roof of the maintenance hangar while circling to land. Years later, when asked why a pilot would want to do this, Charlie answered with a grin, "Just to let them know we were coming in." Thus it can surely be said of some ground personnel as well as instructors that their existence was one of hours and hours of boredom punctuated by moments of stark terror, such as when they ran from the building or jumped through the windows.

But a base commander could, and frequently would, sit a pilot down rather abruptly for having displayed some extraordinary feat of airmanship. A base commander was the undisputed lord and master of his domain and held the power to immediately transfer a pilot to some undesirable duty station as punishment, often on impulse alone. Generally this punishment was of a temporary nature, depriving a pilot of his beloved fighter long enough for him to think it over. It proved the best way to get his attention. It was the change in flying status which smarted the most.

Possibly Tom Cotton could express the feeling most eloquently, given the chance to describe his six weeks of duty on the beautiful Pacific Island of Galapagos about a thousand miles from the mainstream of life. This temporary additional duty (TAD) was awarded Tom for having cut the CO out of the traffic pattern over Albrook Field one day. Likewise Jim Anning, always a good man to make an example of, received the wrath of his commanding officer on one occasion for having performed a mini-air show over the alert shack of a nearby fighter strip, which culminated in a slow roll right over the shack.

"It wasn't so much what I did but how I did it," Jim related later. "It was a very sloppy slow roll." The next day they drew names out of a hat to see who would have to fly copilot on a patrol bomber flying out of British Guiana, and Jim lost. Later in China he was to learn that his name was the only one in the hat.

But Jim did not care. He just grinned all the way to Guiana and continued his education. He learned rather promptly that one does not buzz the brown, muddy waters of tropical rivers without the danger of going in. He found that it could be accomplished, however, if he carefully kept an eye on the shoreline for reference or if a little ripple was evident on the surface of the water. "Otherwise you can't tell how high you are, or more important how low you are." It was particularly dangerous flying low over the wide mouth of the Amazon River where the shoreline was not visible on either side.

Another lesson Jim learned was that it could be extremely dangerous to buzz army nurses sunbathing on an isolated beach. One low pass would send most nurses bouncing effeminately into the shallow water seeking cover, a very distracting scene for a lonely pilot, while the remainder quickly armed themselves with coconuts for his second pass, some of the nurses having been through a "buzz job" before. There is no sight so lovely as to entice a pilot to fly through a barrage of coconuts a second time.

Olsen almost made the list of distinguished pilots on September 14, 1942, just by walking by the alert shack at France Field, or at least it started that way. The flight officer called him over and informed him that he was to fly three or four dignitaries across the Isthmus to Albrook Field before dark. One was a congressman, another a senator. They were accompanied by a couple of inspectors who were touring the Canal Zone.

"What the hell am I going to fly 'em in?" Charlie asked. "All we've got here are P-40s."

"You see that plane over there?" remarked the flight officer. "It is a V-77 and will carry a pilot and up to four passengers."

"That kite?" moaned Charlie.

"Yes, that kite," replied the flight officer. "Now get with it. Here they come now."

With this Charlie walked over to the Stinson just as the mechanic was moving the wheel chocks. As the party boarded, Charlie walked around the plane displaying a rather disapproving look.

"I wondered if the thing would really fly," Charlie later reminisced. "I'd never seen one before."

Charlie climbed in the left seat of the Stinson, oblivious to the dignitaries, who were deeply engrossed in their own private conversation. However, Charlie began to get their attention when he began his cockpit preflight check. As he fumbled around, obviously totally unfamiliar with the location of all the switches and levers, the passengers' conversation gradually began to wane, and then utter silence fell over the group when Charlie stuck his head out of the cockpit and hollered to the mechanic, "How do you get the parking brakes unlocked?"

By the time he had followed the instructions, the mechanic had his head stuck in the cockpit and was starting to show Charlie where the master switch was. Just then Charlie accidentally dumped full flaps. "Bam!" came the noise. One passenger started for the right door and Charlie could just smell the sweet sea breeze of the Galapagos Islands should he botch this mission. But somehow he managed to calm his passengers down long enough to get airborne and deliver them to the other side of the Isthmus.

Another officer, remembered only as "Pinky," owned a beautiful little ocelot which he would walk on a leash. Although ocelots are beautiful little creatures and often go through long periods of docile behavior, they can also suddenly go berserk at the slightest provocation and become the most savage and aggressive mass of animal tooth and claw imaginable. Hence they are frequently up for adoption or worse after a display of temper, which was the case with Pinky and his ocelot. Most pilots didn't want to have anything to do with the "savage little beast."

But Pinky could handle the ocelot, or at least he could until the time they were out for a stroll one day and happened to pass a locomotive. The engine sent out a jet of steam which startled the ocelot and sent him straight to Pinky's back to the top of his head where it promptly anchored its claws into his scalp. Ocelot stock bottomed out when Pinky grabbed for the cat and almost donated ten fingers in the process. With Pinky trying to dislodge the cat from his bloody scalp and the cat trying to hold on for dear life while fending off the groping hands, a scene erupted which defies description. After that the ocelot mysteriously disappeared, never to be seen again.

It was difficult for Pinky to salute the CO the next morning, with his head shaved and sutured and each finger bandaged. "How in the hell am I going to explain your condition to an inspecting party?" the CO bellowed. "An ocelot did it? What the hell were you doing with an ocelot?" Such problems frequently led to temporary additional duty elsewhere, and in Pinky's case it lasted until his wounds could heal.

Liberty in Panama outside the Canal Zone was about the same on both sides of the Isthmus. Panama City was a bit more refined perhaps, being the capital city. There was a dance pavilion and everybody would go dancing. There were the regular nightclubs with the usual female entertainers. The most beautiful girls came from Costa Rica. They were a purer strain of Spanish, having light skin and blue eyes with fair hair. A lot could also be said for the Panamanian girls, darker in skin tone with raven black hair.

At most bars, "B" drinkers would come and sit at one's table and drink "blue moons" which were nothing more than Coke in a shot glass, though they cost much more. They would keep one company and were skilled at asking the kind of questions that a soldier liked to hear, such as where was he from and what was it like back in the States, questions about personal or intimate subjects that a guy away from home never tired of discussing. The guys would go in to town and have a few drinks and horse around, generally going through the marketplace if it was during the day or at night going from bar to bar just to see what the action was on that particular night. It was great except when the fleet was in. Then all the prices would go up. There were steak places, places to get something to eat different from the food at the chow hall.

After a long night on the town they would return to their quarters on the field, which were the big houses previously occupied by dependent families before the war, buildings still referred to by enlisted men as "married pukes' quarters." Two pilots would share an apartment, like Peterson and Olsen, so living accommodations were very nice for the pilots.

Since Panama was one of the trade centers of the world where ships of many flags would cross through the canal, there appeared in the various shops and marketplaces articles of trade from the four corners of the world. It made shopping most interesting, particularly since the prices were very low compared to Stateside. Various articles could be purchased at bargain prices by the men, such as Chanel No. 5 and a diamond engagement ring, which Charlie bought for Lucille, his girl back home. Fine lacework and jewelry of all descriptions were frequently sent back duty-free to the States to family and girlfriends. Mail came fast by the Boeing 307 Strato Liner which flew down daily from Miami.

"Looking back on Panama," Charlie said later, "it was good duty, but living there for over a year began to get old. Things were happening all over the world and we were all anxious to go to where the real action was. But Panama was an excellent training area for a pilot."

In his memoirs, *The Way of a Fighter,* Chennault referred to the Panama-trained P-40 pilots as the kind of men he sought for the American Volunteer Group. He could never get enough men of this caliber. These Panama postgraduates became some of the finest pilots ever to fight in China skies. Whether their interim exposure to the P-40s in the Canal Zone was a part of a military plan or just good fortune, these men were afforded a better opportunity of becoming proficient at handling the shark-tooth fighter than any other group sent into combat before them.

Elsewhere, and a little later in the war, replacements were sent into combat directly from the States with as little as two hundred hours of total flying time. They were able to handle their planes in normal flight but were no match in savage combat with an experienced enemy. Consequently casualties were high during such transitions. This was not so for the Panama P-40 pilots who later flew the same planes in combat. They had flown the P-40 for long hours during patrol and had expended thousands of rounds of ammunition during gunnery practice. They had their ranks thinned of the careless and unfortunate through training accidents long before entering combat. By the time the Panama pilot emerged from France and Albrook fields in the Canal Zone, they were, as Chennault later described them, "Expert fighter boys with ample experience in long range navigation, dive-bombing, and close formation flying."

Charles Olsen had chalked up 783 hours in the air between the time he entered the service in November 1941 at St. Augustine Field and the end of his Canal Zone duty on November 2, 1942. Olsen and Cotton had developed a close friendship that would endure for the remainder of their lives. They had polished their two-plane "Panama" routine to a razor's edge and were chomping at their bits for combat. They talked about going overseas to the CBI theater. Whenever anybody left Panama, they always seemed to wind up there. Though the men were always shipped out under secret military orders supposedly not knowing their destination, word filtered back to Panama from the men arriving in China via mutual friends in the States. So the remaining Panama Pilots were pretty certain of their destination—Kunming, China. It was comforting too, for this was the kind of combat for which they were trained.

Waiting can be a nerve-racking experience, and Olsen felt that things were happening for everyone but himself. He was still a second lieutenant and was beginning to see some pilots that he had instructed back at Greenwood, Mississippi, who now outranked him, and he longed for combat.

Days passed and his Canal Zone duties failed to appease him and he became nervous and on occasion even irritable, showing little patience. He had absolute confidence in his flying ability. He knew that there was nobody at that base who could fly the P-40 any better than himself, including his squadron commander.

A lot of the fellows did not engage in rat-racing because they were not that confident in their flying ability. They would not dare come in ten feet over the runway and roll it over because they knew they were liable to go in. They would rather fly straight and level and shoot their gunnery and as far as anything risky or anything that would test their flying ability close to the ground, they did not want anything to do with it. Those pilots who dared to test their ability and failed were no longer with them. Those that did and survived were outstanding pilots and felt invincible. Olsen, Cotton, Epperson, Peterson, Boylan, Anning, Scoville, Veazey, and Glover were such pilots, and that is why they seemed kind of raucous to the rest. They felt confident that they were good enough to do anything with that airplane, and so naturally they were the ones who would attract the attention.

Cotton and Olsen became a natural element, a team both on the ground and in the air. If Cotton did not want to think up something he would let Olsen fly ahead and do it, knowing that he could do anything that Olsen would do. "Besides, if you flew with Olsen," Cotton recalled in later years, "the safest place was behind him anyway."

CHAPTER 5

The Twenty-third Fighter Group: 1942

From stations all over the nation came trained enlisted men to Langley Field, Virginia, to form a cadre for the Twenty-third Pursuit Group I. These men were selected for their experience and ability so that the new pursuit group could be organized with a minimum of difficulty.

On March 2, 1942, the Twenty-third Pursuit Group I (renamed the Twenty-third Fighter Group shortly thereafter) was officially organized. Maj. Robert A. Culbertson was designated as detachment commander. Culbertson, a tall, broad-shouldered, athletic-looking officer with dull gray hair and steely blue eyes, began the difficult task of organizing the unit for overseas duty. Many of the hundred or so recruits had only a few days' service, but they had been ordered from units at Langley Field to complete the detachment.

His adjutant was Maj. Peter C. Borre, a short, stocky, optimistic Italian with a full stentorian voice. He promptly established a system of discipline, teaching all the new men military courtesy, basic drills, and other matters of importance to soldiers in a theater of operation.

On March 17 the detachment boarded the *USS Brazil,* a thirty-thousand-ton luxury liner owned by the Moore-McCormick Lines. The men still did not know their destination. Until sailing time, the men accustomed themselves to their quarters and discovered just how far they could go before the military police stepped in. At 1600 hours on March 19, the *Brazil* was put to sea and the "anchor pool" was divided among the participating winners. There were no thoughts of the tiring trip ahead and no worries of enemy submarines that day, since a majority of the men were confirmed landlubbers and the ship was a novel experience. It was a cool, clear morning filled with screaming gulls, tug whistles, and the roar of patrolling B-25 bombers. Recently glaring headlines had told of the bold attacks of enemy subs along the Atlantic coast, and the watchful eyes of the North American bombers were welcome.

After following a drunken, zig-zag course, which they were to employ the entire cruise, they docked at San Juan, Puerto Rico. To many the beautiful little Caribbean isle was a symbol of adventure, but to others it marked the first leg of a long journey away from their loved ones. To all it meant that they were one step closer to the wily "Jap" whom each and every soldier and nurse aboard knew had caused this abrupt change in their lives. From San Juan, the *Brazil* steamed toward the far-off African coast under conditions ideal for a summer cruise, but because of reported submarines, rough weather would have been welcome.

Under the protection of a Canadian cruiser and a small aircraft carrier which employed a few "scout" biplanes, the men arrived safely at Freetown, Sierra Leone, in west Africa. After moving into the harbor through the intricate minefields, they dropped anchor in full view of the sprawling little city, sweating in the tropical heat and surrounded by mountains covered with dense growths of tropical vegetation. Within these beautiful surroundings were anchored over two hundred ships of all types, sizes, and flags, just in from the Atlantic. A huge Short-Sunderland flying boat of the Royal Air Force droned overhead, keeping a watchful eye on every side. Daily the RAF fighter command pilots flew their Spitfires and Hurricanes, keeping alert against surprise attacks from the Axis units which were occupying French provinces to the north.

From this busy harbor they sailed once more into the lonely wastes of the Atlantic. Every person aboard the ship was christened into the court of Neptunus Rex as they crossed the equator. The occasion was honored by an extravagant program including costumes and make-up borrowed from the nurses, acting and singing, and a very smelly event which consisted of throwing rotten eggs. The Twenty-third's Major Borre was in the leading role of King Neptune. Gaudily dressed, he strutted about the deck, stripped to the waist, his torso covered with trinkets and paint.

In April, after thirty days afloat, the entire complement of military personnel was permitted five hours of shore leave in Capetown, Union of South Africa. What can happen in five hours in a seaport accustomed to such travelers so long at sea? One can only imagine the sordid details of fabricated stories these young adventurers must have told during the next thirty days at sea.

Then they sailed around the Cape of Good Hope into Port Elizabeth. Following their visit to these outposts of civilization in the southern hemisphere, they sailed through the Mozambique Straits just before the Battle of Madagascar and docked at Karachi, India. It was May 16. After having been nearly sixty days afloat, the passengers found that terra firma looked mighty good, and there were oaths that never again would they board another Army transport with their long chow lines and constricted quarters. At Karachi, for the first time since leaving the States, they saw the American flag flying in the breeze. Many freighters were lying at anchor along the docks, bringing supplies, men, and equipment for the war machines of the Far East. The following day an advance detail left the ship for the cantonment at New Malir to prepare food and sleeping facilities for the men on board, who were to disembark the next day.

The detachment was assigned to "C" area of New Malir. The area, like the other areas in the cantonment, consisted of a few block buildings with facilities such as beds of weak construction, with woven rope serving as mattresses. Although windows were of glass, they were useless since the heat necessitated that they remain open at all times, and great quantities of dust blew in and covered everything with a thick coat. Winds were continuous and with no vegetation to hinder it, the dust filled the air throughout the daylight hours. Offices were set up and duties assigned to the noncommissioned officers. Under these adverse conditions of no fuel, no stoves, and continuous dust, Mess Sergeant Ray Sell rapidly gained the name of having the finest "mess" in the cantonment.

The first real labor performed by the unit was digging slit trenches to furnish protection to the greater part of the command and also for medical facilities and gun emplacements. The lack of work, the utter desolation of the country, and the continuous dust storms blowing in from the Thar Desert all combined to give every man a very bad first impression of India. But as the men encountered the Indian belles in Karachi, their impressions changed abruptly.

On June 13 came orders from the Tenth Air Force in New Delhi for an advance detail of nineteen men to proceed by Trans-India Ferry Command to Kunming, China. These men landed in Kunming on June 15. Meanwhile personnel of the Fifty-first Fighter Group, the Sixteenth Squadron, who had also been in Karachi awaiting assignment, were likewise transported over the "Hump" to Kunming.

The Twenty-third Fighter Group was officially activated on July 4, 1942, at Kunming. Because Kunming was in a combat zone, a ceremony befitting the occasion was out of the question. But the new Army Air Force pilots flew several formations for the benefit of newspapermen and photographers. The original organization included the Seventy-fourth, Seventy-fifth, and Seventy-sixth fighter squadrons with the Sixteenth Fighter Squadron attached. Never before had a fighter group been activated in a theater of war.

Valuable lessons in tactics and techniques gained from over a year of combat against the Japanese Imperial Air Force were taught to the "green" pilots and crews of the Twenty-third by certain men of the AVG who volunteered to remain in China for a period of fourteen days. They were Freeman I. Ricketts, John Petach, Jr., Arnold W. Shamblin, Robert H. Neale, Robert H. Smith, Peter Wright, E. W. Loane, R. C. Peret, Lewis J. Richards, James H. Howard, Charles R. Bond, William E. Bartling, John J. Dean, Matthew Kuykendall, Einar I. Mickelson, Albert E. Probst, Camille J. Rosbert and John R. Rossi.

In addition, many of the AVG personnel consented to join the U.S. Army at ranks commensurate with their abilities. These men formed the nucleus around which the group was built. They included Lt. Col. Thomas C. Gentry (Chief Surgeon); Majs. David L. Hill, John M. Williams, Samuel B. Prevo, Edward F. Rector, C. B. Adair, Frank Shiel, Jr., and John G. Bright; Capts. Charles W. Sawyer and Roy G. Hoffman; 1st Lts. W. H. S. Davis, Ernest O. Bonham, William A. Sykes, Donald Rodewald, Roland L. Richardson, Edward J. Harris, Jasper J. Harrington, Donald Bell, and John Engle; 2nd Lts. Elton V. Loomis, William H. Towery, Arvold Miller, Carsen Roberts, Joseph E. Lussier, and Marlin R. Hubler; M. Sgts. Robert P. Rasmussen, George R. Bailey, and Eugene R. McKinney; T. Sgt. James H. Musick; and Ens. Alex Mihalko.

Each enlisted man was assigned duties by Squadron Leader A. E. Olson of the American Volunteer Group. Working with crews of the

"Flying Tigers" helped each man become familiar with his job as soon as possible so that the Twenty-third Fighter Group could quickly become a viable replacement for the disbanded AVG.

The detachment of enlisted men arrived at Kunming on June 16, expecting nothing but wilderness and bad facilities. What they actually found was quite different.

The airdrome lay at the north end of the Tien Chih Lake, which spread its muddy waters over 150 square miles and was surrounded by the seven-thousand-foot peaks that form the foothills of the great chain of mountains which make Tibet seem a land of mystery. The city of Kunming, teeming with refugees who had left their homes due to the Japanese invasion of Burma, was just three miles from the entrance of the field. Kunming was surrounded on all sides by innumerable rice paddies. Its lifeline, the Burma Road, could be seen winding snakelike into the distant mountains to the west. Before the fall of Rangoon, Kunming had been the northern terminus of the Burma Road supply line. But at this time, Burma had fallen into the hands of the enemy, so the road became only a path for the thousands of Chinese refugees who were continually trudging into the city.

The detachment suffered its first casualty on July 3, the day before its official initiation. Pvt. Marshall F. F. Brown was accidentally killed as he and Franklin Wamsley were working on the wing guns of a P-40B at the Kunming airdrome. Brown was standing in front of the ship while Wamsley was working in the cockpit. Guns were set on the firing position through error, and the trigger was accidentally pressed, two .30 caliber slugs hitting Brown in the temple and killing him instantly. The first casualty of the Twenty-third Fighter Group was buried in the local cemetery on July 5.

Col. Robert L. Scott, a tall, lean, easy-going Georgian who had been fighting with the American Volunteer Group, was transferred from the Assam-Burma-China Ferry Command to become the first commanding officer of the Twenty-third Fighter Group. From early childhood he displayed an adventurous spirit. At the age of thirteen he was determined to fly. He saved seventy-five dollars and attended an auction where some used airplanes were being sold. He would bid on every plane until someone else bid beyond his financial resources. Finally, the leading buyer at the auction walked over and remarked, "Son, you buy the next plane and after that don't bother me. I'm buying an airline." Young Scott flew his old crate for two years before his parents found out about it.

Born in Waynesboro, Georgia, in 1908, Scott as a young man traveled all over the world in freighters and tramps looking for the right girl to marry. But he finally found one in Fort Valley twenty-seven miles from his hometown. They were married in 1934 at West Point, from which he had graduated two years previously.

After flying school, Scott flew the mail for several months when the Army was handling mail contracts. In 1935 orders came for duty in the Canal Zone with the Seventy-eighth Pursuit Squadron. Here he was continuously in trouble because of his love for flying. In ten years he had flown over seven thousand hours in all types of aircraft. During May 1942, while flying in Burma, a combat zone, Colonel Scott logged 214 hours.

While in Panama, he made several flights to the States while ferrying Martin B-10 bombers and P-12s. After this tour of duty in Panama, he was assigned to Randolph Field, Texas, for two years and was then appointed flight commander for the instructors' school. Assignments to other flying schools followed as well as a part in a picture called *Keep 'em Flying,* with Abbott and Costello.

Bored with continuous training center duty, he wrote many letters to general officers of the Air Corps and finally secured assignment to a flight of B-17 heavy bombers under secret orders to bomb Tokyo. On his thirty-fourth birthday Scott was at the controls of one of the bombers as the flight crossed the Atlantic on its way to Japan.

Scott later explained:

My whole idea before the war was to figure out a way of getting into active combat. And when first I started my crusade to get out from behind the desk, I was fortunate enough to get an assignment to a B-17 outfit which was to bomb Tokyo from the west while General Doolittle came from the east. Ours didn't materialize because ships were stopped at Karachi for training where they were worn out in Karachi dust.

All of us—thirteen four-engine crews—were sent to form the Assam-Burma-China Ferry Command at Dinjam. Our job was to form an airline for delivery of strategic goods and war materials into China and Burma and for the evacuation of British wounded. We worked at this for some three months. We delivered eight thousand wounded British soldiers out of Myitkyino and Lashio and then dropped two million pounds of rice to the Chinese Fifth Army in the area near Putoo or Fort Hurtz.

We were flying these unarmed transports five hundred miles from Dinjam to Kunming and two to three hundred miles to Myitkyino and thence down to Loi-Wing and Lashio. We were within Japanese-controlled air. The pilots were pretty jittery about flying them over there with Zeroes all over Burma. So to kind of bolster their morale, I got one P-40 from General Chennault and flew daily strafing raids and observation trips against the Japanese.

Scott's first encounter with the enemy was on May 3, 1942.

I caught a Japanese bomber, a Mitsubishi Army-97 and I burned it up after three passes. I admit my tongue stuck to my teeth from fear the first time I saw it, but I soon realized the power I had at my command. I merely had to press a trigger, and I had six .50 caliber guns which would destroy anything in their path. I turned and strafed a Japanese troop column which was on the road near Lashio.

Scott flew many hours over Burma in a C-47, using it as a bomber, and was among those aiding in the evacuation of Burma. He was continually in hot water from headquarters for his rebel tactics in accomplishing solo strafing and bombing missions over occupied Burma.

On one occasion in May 1942, Scott took off in a newly-arrived P-43A to test it at high altitude. On gaining altitude he decided that instead of staying above the field, he could just as well fly above the nearby Himalayas and enjoy the scenery and still get the same results. He attained an altitude of forty-four thousand feet, flying directly over the highest mountain in the world, Mount Everest, at an altitude two miles higher than its peak. He photographed in color the upper reaches of the greatest rivers in the Far East and flew over the forbidden city of Lhasa. Once again he was reprimanded as a result of this flight. But by his aggressive actions, his flying ability, and his love for combat, he made himself the logical choice for commander of the Twenty-third Fighter Group when the time came.

The Seventy-fourth, Seventy-fifth, and Seventy-sixth squadrons were counterparts of the old AVG First (Adam and Eve), Second (Panda Bears), and Third (Hell's Angels) squadrons. Maj. Frank Shiel, Jr., an AVG ace, took command of the Seventy-fourth Fighter

Squadron, with headquarters in Kunming. A former reserve officer in the Army Air Corps, Frank had served with the Twenty-third Composite Group, which was known as the Army's demonstration group. While in this group he flew all types of aircraft. He had served in the First Squadron of the AVG in all campaigns.

David "Tex" Hill, who was to become a major on July 18, was himself an AVG ace, and he was the first commander of the Seventy-fifth Squadron. He had become an AVG "Flying Tiger" in 1941 and had been designated commander of the AVG's Second Squadron, for which the Seventy-fifth was the counterpart. Tex Hill had already made a name for himself. He was in the first aerial battle against the Japanese following the declaration of war. He had already fought in Burma, Thailand, Indochina, and China. As an AVG he was credited with twelve planes shot down and many more probables. He was the first American to fly a Japanese fighter, an I-97 captured at Chengtu. The tall, lean, easygoing Texan, who always wore cowboy boots, proved to be an excellent commander.

The Seventy-fifth was stationed at Hengyang, in Hunan Province, following the organization of the squadron at Kunming. Hunan is along the Hunan-Kwangsi railway near the junction with the Canton-Hankow line. The area had been under merciless bombardment by the Japanese Air Force for two years without opposition until the "Flying Tigers" arrived in June 1942 and made a contest of it.

The airdrome was located north of the city and across the river. This river, the Siang Kiang, flowed northward to Japanese-held Tungting Lake and afforded a colorful pageant to the members of the group stationed there. Hundreds of sampans sailed up and down this miniature version of the Yangtze daily. The river provided cheap transportation for supplies moving up to the fronts and for the coal that was mined in the vicinity. Because the city itself was not much higher than sea level, the heat became so unbearable and facilities for food and water so poor that upkeep of a hostel was difficult.

Kweilin was home base for the Seventy-sixth, under the command of Maj. Edward F. Rector. There he and his men sweated in the heat along the Hunan-Kwangsi railway amid hundreds of square miles of rocky buttes. The buttes towered hundreds of feet above the valley floors, making landings and takeoffs extremely dangerous. The temperature rose to over a hundred degrees almost daily. Protection for the ground crews, supplies, and equipment was readily available in the hundreds of caves that punctured the huge buttes.

Rector was also a former member of the AVG, having joined in July 1941 when he resigned as a member of a dive-bombing unit on board the *U.S.S. Ranger*. Rector was also in the Second Squadron, which was composed largely of former naval cadets. Upon completing training as a member of the American Volunteer Group in Toungoo, he was sent to Kunming. There, in his first fight, he shot down one of ten Japanese bombers which came near the base. Later transferred to Rangoon, he participated in more than twenty-five fights and got five Japanese planes to bring his total to six. He was one of the six pilots who raided Chiengmai airdome in Thailand, destroying twenty-two planes and damaging ten more.

The Twenty-third Fighter Group lost no time in making its presence known to the enemy. Two days after the AVG was taken over by the Twenty-third, Major Hill led a two-element, four-plane fighter escort of white-nosed P-40s for five B-25 medium bombers on a raid of an oil refinery at Canton. The flight took off from Kweilin, despite a low ceiling, and fortunately the cloud formation over the target had broken up enough upon their arrival to permit the bombers to make their run at five thousand feet. They scored direct hits on the warehouses. (While assigned to Hengyang, the fighter squadron frequently operated out of other bases to confuse the enemy. The leaders also frequently made up flights with pilots from various fighter squadrons, depending upon the size of the effort and the number of planes available.)

Thirty miles out of Canton on the return trip, while the bombers fled to safety, the fighters intercepted a flight of Japanese Nate pursuit ships. In the ensuing battle, a "Jap 97" made the mistake of appearing in Major Hill's sights. A single burst from his guns caused the enemy to fall in a tight spin from which he never recovered, finally crashing onto the ground. John Petach, who had also been an AVG flyer, accounted for a second kill when he shot down another eager Japanese pilot who attempted to divert Petach's attention from his unfortunate comrade. The second "97" spun out into a cloud and was not seen again. The two planes were later confirmed by Chinese intelligence. The entire flight of fighters and bombers returned without mishap to Kweilin.

On July 10 four white-nosed sharks led by Petach roared into the air from Hengyang to strafe river boats in the Nanchang area and bomb Linchaun, a city which changed hands often. The Chinese there had seen nothing but enemy planes over their heads for the past two years, and it was expected that this mission would cause a tremendous boost to the morale of the Chinese. This proved to be correct, for by taking advantage of the confusion created by the surprise air attack, the Chinese Army was able to recapture the city.

Petach, who was leading the flight, had previously warned the other members of the flight regarding the strength of the enemy's position. He cautioned them not to fly low over the target because of the heavy antiaircraft installations there. As the flight came over the target, Petach dove to six thousand feet to lay his bombs directly on the target, which was the most prominent building in the entire town. It housed the personnel and communications of the Japanese headquarters. He made his attack in the face of intense antiaircraft fire. As he pulled out of his dive, he was caught amidships by a burst of 20 mm fire, which forced him into an outside spin which was followed by structural failure of the left wing. The ship burst into flames and Petach was killed instantly.

Following right behind Petach in his dive was Arnold Shamblin, another former AVG pilot. He dropped his load of destruction in the face of concentrated Japanese fire, but then was hit and forced to bail out. The men believed that he survived but was taken prisoner by the enemy. Both Petach and Shamblin were under voluntary contract with the Army to remain in China for only fourteen more days after the termination of their contracts with the AVG on July 4. Under this agreement, they were only required to participate in airdrome defense. They went on this disastrous mission at their own request.

The same day Lt. Henry P. Elias was piloting one of the four P-40s on a raid of shipping on the river at Hankow. The bombing mission was successful, but on the way back he and other members of the flight were attacked by a superior force of Japanese fighters. Under fire from one fighter, he skillfully executed a difficult shot from a quartering position, destroying the enemy plane.

On July 16 Tex Hill led four fighters escorting five B-25s on a raid of docks, warehouses, wharves, and the Japanese concession at Hankow. With American pilots giving protective cover at eighteen thousand feet, the bombers went over the target at twelve thousand. All the fighters carried bombloads too, except Hill's, which went unloaded in anticipation of interception by the enemy. Bombs were dropped upon the target with excellent results. Six fires started, one of which was visible for thirty miles. Although fighter opposition was reported taking off immediately after the bombing, the Twenty-third's fighters were unable to make visual contact with them.

Upon returning to Hengyang, they discovered they had landed during an alert, so all bombers and fighters immediately took off again. But it was bad news for one B-25 crew, who had to bail out to safety when defending AVG pilot Freeman Ricketts accidentally shot it down, mistaking it for a Zero. "Ricketts had probably never seen a B-25 before, as it was one of the first ones in the area. He didn't know it was one of our own and he was not the first or the last to make a similar mistake," Tex said later.

By July 20, General Stilwell's ground forces had reached Imphal in Assam Province, India. A day later the Japanese launched their offensive in China's Chekiang Province on the east coast near Shanghai, which they followed by an effort to consolidate control of Burma.

On July 21 Maj. John R. Alison was officially transferred from the Fifty-first Fighter Group at Karachi, India, to the Seventy-fifth Fighter Squadron at Hengyang. Tex Hill watched a lone P-40 touch down at the far end of the Hengyang airstrip, sending up a geyser of red dust. It was a good landing and well might it be, since the pilot was Alison—"Mr. P-40" himself, Tex's new deputy commander. His reputation had preceded him. Tex was glad to see Alison and the new Curtiss Warhawk, both of which were welcome additions to the battered Seventy-fifth. For Alison, it was the conclusion of a long and difficult journey that had originated back in England in the spring of 1941.

Major Alison towered every bit of five feet, five and a half inches and looked more like an office boy than one of the finest pilots in the CBI Theater. Continually in need of a haircut, he was a quiet, easy-going, efficient man, who had an absolute dislike for anyone who prevented his squadron from fighting. He was a pint-sized edition of Colonel Scott. Both men had a fanatical love for combat.

Alison was an extremely valuable addition to the group because of his previous training. He was sent to England with the first P-40s to teach the RAF the tactics best suited for this fighter. After a period in Britain he was ordered to Russia to teach the Red Air Force the characteristics of the Curtiss fighter. Later he went to Iraq and Iran as a military observer, and then he was assigned to Karachi. Then came his transfer to the Seventy-fifth Squadron at Hengyang. He would soon prove his value to his new unit.

Lieutenant Elias got into the scoring column on July 26. Eight fighters from the Seventy-fifth and Seventy-sixth squadrons led by Tex Hill took off from the Hengyang field loaded with eighteen-kilogram fragmentation bombs. The target was Nanchang airdrome and rivercraft in the Kiukiang area. Tex had trouble almost immediately after takeoff with a faulty fuel system and so his plane and another fighter returned to the field. But the flight continued under the command of Major Alison. The enemy came up to meet the sharks and interrupted the bombing briefly.

During the ensuing battle, a voice came over the headset saying, "Hey, Elias, who's that flying formation with you with his wheels down?" Elias glanced over his shoulder and there was a Japanese I-97 Nate on his tail, firing at him. Elias got his guns in position and fired three bursts, but the Nate disappeared only to return immediately astern of the P-40 again. Elias found a convenient cloud into which he took cover and again turned the tables to come out on the I-97's tail. This time he got a good burst into its rear and the Nate rolled and was last seen headed toward the earth in a hurry. The next day Chinese reported that a Japanese Model I-97 had crashed into the Poi Check temple near the place where Elias last saw the plane.

The enemy airdrome was covered by a low overcast, but the bombs were dropped in the city with favorable results. As the flight returned to the Hengyang field and landed, Elias buzzed the field at a terrific speed and maneuvered into a victory roll and landed. As he stepped out of his ship, someone called his attention to the fact that in the excitement of the battle, he had failed to release his bombs. A shot into those underslung bombs would have meant certain destruction to both him and his ship. In addition, doing a victory roll with a full load was not recommended.

On the night of July 28 Major Alison parted the mosquito net and climbed into his bunk, tired but happy. In the morning he would not wake up in Basra, Russia. "Clang! Clang! Clang! Wake up please. Air raid, wake up please!" came the 2 A.M. intrusion. Alison jackknifed in bed. "Where am I?" he wondered. "England, Russia? . . .

Oh, oh yeah. Hengyang." He had been in a deep sleep. He quickly rolled out of bed, threw on some clothes, and rushed out on the veranda. Down below in the courtyard he could see that some of the men had gathered around a central tall figure. It was a cloudless night with a full moon. Alison joined them, and they stood silently, listening in the stillness of the night for the distant sound of aircraft engines. Hill explained that the warning net had plotted the approach of enemy bombers headed in their direction. The airfield was nestled in the bend of the river, which made it easily identifiable on a moonlit night by Japanese bombers. They might make it to Hengyang or go on over to Lingling—there was no way of telling.

Finally they heard a faint hum which grew steadily into a roar as the bombers passed over the field. There was no question that they must have seen the field with that bend in the river that almost drew a silver circle around the airstrip. Then the first bomb exploded down on the field among the dummy P-40s which had been provided for just such an occasion. Then another and another came as the bombs completely missed their target. This prompted criticism from the men that they should have done better since they were not molested by fighter interception. These comments turned on a light somewhere in Alison's head as he was watching the bombers' exhaust stacks glowing in the darkened sky, quite visible from below.

"If they come over tomorrow night," he said out loud, "I'm going up and get 'em." The others were impressed. No one had tried night interceptions yet, since the P-40 had no equipment for night fighting.

"I'll go with you," said Ajax Baumler, and then a few of the other pilots said that they would also give it a try.

During the next day, July 29, the men prepared for the first night interception. They estimated that the bombers had come in at around eight thousand feet, and the time had been two in the morning. Of course they could not be sure that they would return that night or duplicate the time and altitude, but it was a starting point. If the Japanese did return and do it the same way, the Americans figured to be at about twelve thousand feet so as to have a little altitude advantage, which would necessitate that the warning net give them at least ten minutes to get up that high before the bombers arrived.

That night the men had everything ready just before retiring. They laid out their clothes so that they could dress rapidly in the dark. They had alerted the driver down below to sleep with one foot in the cab and had carefully parked their P-40s at the foot of the runway to facilitate immediate takeoff. They were all ready—now if only the bombers would come. Just before hitting the sack, Alison looked up from the veranda into a clear black sky. The moon was not up yet but all conditions looked good.

One A.M. came and all was quiet. Then it was 2 A.M. and Alison slept well. Then once again came the noise—"Clang! Clang! Clang! Wake up please. Air raid!" There was that Chinese kid again beating on that tin can with a spoon. He had hardly gotten started when the men were running for the truck, some dressing as they ran. The truck driver raced for the field, and as they neared the first P-40 he slowed sufficiently for Alison to hit the ground on the run. The driver then went ahead and delivered the rest of the pilots to their waiting planes.

Alison hit the wing in short stride and bounced up to the cockpit and slid open the canopy. Once inside he noticed that the moonlight was sufficient for finding all the seat belt and parachute attachments. The rest was completely routine. Almost without looking he opened the cowl flaps and cracked the throttle. Then almost in one continuous gesture he screwed into his seat, wiggled his rudder pedals and ailerons, rubbernecked a quick preflight check, and hit the master switch to energize the inertia starter. Upward it whined as he looked above through the open cockpit in search of exhaust stacks, thinking, "Altitude, altitude, I've got to get up there." Then he shoved in the starter engager, and the P-40 shuddered, coughed, and then emitted a deafening roar. The stillness had gone out of the night. Alison applied full war emergency power and started his roll just as he saw the six exhaust stacks on Ajax's P-40 spew fire, lighting shark teeth and a cold, menacing eye. As the airspeed indicator passed through a hundred mph, Alison pulled back on the stick and his P-40 left the runway. At the same instant he retracted the main gear and felt the plane mush as the huge wheels rotated sideways increasing drag momentarily before being tucked into the wheel wells. He executed a "fighter dip" as he climbed out into the darkened sky, beginning the prearranged climbing left turn, with the others now following suit. Upwards they climbed. They had to reach altitude before the bombers arrived. They went to eight thousand, nine thousand, then reached a layer of haze. Finally they circled at twelve thousand, and Alison found that visibility was not as good as he had hoped. Where were the bombers, he wondered. They should have been there by now. He listened to the cracking noise in his headset as he looked for the other P-40s. He could not see them either.

"Three twin-engine bombers just went over the field," came the report from the field operator. The static was so bad that he could hardly make out what had been said. "They are traveling from north to south," continued the report. "It looks like they're making a turn now and are coming back."

"Good," thought Alison, "they've made a practice run not anticipating what we have in store for them." He rubbernecked all around as he crossed the field himself from east to west. He should have been able to see them to his left, but he could not see anything. Then the thought struck him—maybe they were not below him at all, maybe they were above at a higher altitude. He looked up and sure enough there they were.

He grabbed his mike. "I see them. They're above me and I'm climbing into position. Watch the fireworks." Baumler and Elmer Richardson were both close by. By now the bombers were heading due north at fifteen thousand feet, and he had reached their altitude. Then it happened—they banked right and started a turn. Alison banked too and turned with them. The bombers continued through a 180-degree turn until they were heading due south again. The only problem was that now he was between the bombers and the moon. Quickly he slid over to converge on the left trailing bomber in the three-plane "V" formation, but it was too late. The rear gunner in the right rear bomber had already picked him up.

Thump! thump! thump! He started receiving hits from the bomber on his right. Yet he continued to press the attack on his target. Closer and closer he converged on the left bomber, all the while taking direct hits from a very accurate rear gunner in the right rear bomber. He opened fire on the left bomber determined to get his victim before becoming one himself. In one second his guns had spewed a thousand rounds at the bomber, but then the P-40 shuddered, having taken hits in its engine. Alison began to feel a sudden loss in power just as the left bomber started an erratic turn out of formation, belching smoke and flame heading down into the path of Ajax Baumler slightly below.

With his P-40 stricken, Alison quickly banked right to take on the right rear bomber before losing altitude. The bomber began to outdistance him until finally it began to bank left. Behind him Alison attempted to close. But the P-40 didn't have it, the engine had sustained too much damage. It handled roughly and its power was sporadic. Pushed too far, it began to trail smoke and oil. It was now or never—Alison fired and held the trigger down and in a few seconds the bomber was engulfed in a bright orange mush of flame, as it exploded and pieces separated and started plunging to earth.

Just then Ajax flamed the first bomber, which had been crippled by Alison. Down on the ground the men were treated to a spectacular fiery display that was unprecedented—Two Japanese bombers falling at the same time, lighting up the China sky. Then a bomb exploded down on the field as the remaining bomber concentrated on delivering his load.

Alison advanced the throttle but the engine hesitated, then ran roughly, about to seize. Slowly the P-40 gained on the Japanese bomber until it came into range. Then for the third time Alison squeezed the trigger and with deadly accuracy exploded the final bomber in a ball of fire. He saw the crew bail out as some chutes opened, others did not, some burned, others blossomed.

Down below Alison saw a faint glow just before his second bomber hit the ground, then the last one suddenly exploded in a ball of orange flame as the wing tanks ignited. Then his overheated engine seized, to be followed by a deafening silence known only to single engine pilots. He was going down, down in unfamiliar terrain at night. Instinctively he lowered the shark's nose and started the downward spiral to the field, if he could only find it. Nine thousand, eight thousand five hundred—it was getting awfully quiet, with only the sound of the slipstream rushing over the stricken ship as Alison skillfully played off altitude for airspeed. Downward he spiraled, looking for the field. There was another explosion which briefly lighted up the night as Ajax got his second bomber.

Alison, distracted only for a second, slid open his canopy for a better view. Two thousand, fifteen hundred—it was time to consider whether the altimeter was set for field elevation or sea level. The ground would start coming up pretty fast now. Eight hundred feet and he squinted to make out the runway. Now it was "Airspeed, altimeter, runway. Must not stall. Airspeed, altimeter, runway," he said as he lined up on final approach. He had only one chance at it because there was no power up front for a go-around should he screw up his first approach. Whoof! Fire leaked back from the engine cowling—his engine was on fire. Then he saw the first part of the runway shoot past below him. He was too high and too hot. He was not going to get it slowed down in time to land on the short runway. Instinctively he shoved the throttle full forward, but of course there was no response. He pulled back on the stick to gain some altitude and a precious little bit of time to figure where he was going to put it in. He was running out of altitude and airspeed and a place to land all at the same time. Just then he spotted the river. That had to be it. At least it was flat. He pulled it over the one remaining obstruction in a last desperate payoff in airspeed for altitude, then mushed into the river beyond. The first bounce was not too bad but the second one threw him forward, and he struck his head on the gunsight protruding back into the cockpit as the plane rapidly lost its forward momentum. It then abruptly stopped and rapidly started to sink. Alison piled out of the cockpit just as water began to cascade in. He started swimming towards the near shore next to the town across the river from the airfield as the P-40 sank below the surface, engine sizzling and spewing steam.

As he climbed out on the far bank he was confronted by three armed Chinese soldiers pointing their long bayonet-tipped rifles at his stomach. They were about to shoot him, thinking that he was Japanese. "Hey, I'm an American!" he yelled, but it took more than that. It was some time before the guards lowered their rifles, since they were not at all sure they could trust this very short stranger in the night.

The soldiers detained Alison for the remainder of the night, but close to dawn they paddled him back across the river to the landing near the hostel. As he bid them good-bye and started up the bank, the field came under another bombing attack and a bomb dropped on the landing killing one of the Chinese. Alison narrowly escaped injury. As he neared the hostel he heard P-40s scrambling for takeoff and found a few pilots watching the early morning raid. They were delighted to see Alison since they had witnessed his fiery crash into the river and had given him up for dead.

In a few minutes the sky was bright blue again as the men watched the P-40s reach their fighting altitude. Then they spotted about forty Japanese fighters across the sky and watched as the two fighter formations closed the distance between them. It would be ten P-40s against forty Zeroes—that seemed to be about even, the guys figured. Out in front, Tex Hill led the sharks, their glistening white teeth still quite visible from the ground. The men on the ground had a grandstand view as Tex led the charge. Over in the Japanese formation a single fighter was seen to take the lead as if "called out" by the Texan as the two fighters converged. Firing continuously, they streaked by one another. Then the Zero started trailing smoke at about seventeen thousand feet. He turned and twisted over the field. Now down to about twelve thousand feet, he apparently realized that his ship was gone, and perhaps wounded, he abruptly turned his aircraft into a vertical dive and plunged for the field after the code of the Samurai, making a suicide dive into one of the parked planes, or so he thought. But all he had selected for destruction was a dummy P-40 which he missed by several feet. It was the first kamikaze attack on record.

Johnny Alison and Ajax Baumler had shot down four of six Japanese bombers that night in what was considered the pioneer night interception adventure in that theater. Alison was awarded the Distinguished Service Cross for his initiative. The Japanese had figured that they would send in the bombers at night and catch the P-40s on the ground, and then the next morning send in a wave of fighters sufficient to mop up what was left. But it did not work out that way since planes from the Seventy-sixth and Sixteenth fighter squadrons had been dispatched to aid the Seventy-fifth, and the twenty-minute morning fight that erupted was the largest aerial fight of the war in that theater. It did not turn out at all as the Japanese had planned.

Despite the overwhelming numbers of the Japanese planes, the Twenty-third fighters swung the balance in their own favor by their resourcefulness and superior flying ability. Maj. John Bright and Lieutenant Druwing each turned in a good morning's work. Bright met a formation of approximately fifteen mixed fighters at nineteen thousand feet. From rear quarter in a shallow dive, he attacked the tail of a Japanese flight that was flying in a loose formation of three. He made a two-second pass at a Zero, and the enemy did a wingover and nosed down. Druwing, who was close by, followed one down, got in several strikes, and saw it crash into the ground.

Then a Zero got onto Major Bright's tail and he climbed for altitude, escaped, and turned on a "97" fighter from its rear. The pilot turned and came at him head on before Bright got him and he pulled up sharply and went into a spin with white smoke pouring from his tail. Major Bright attempted to follow him down, but still another Zero got on his tail. He got away from this plane in the nick of time.

Against waves numbering twenty-three and thirty-two fighters, another group of seven ships came through without loss. Major Bright, Capt. Edmund Goss, Lts. Henry Elias, Dallas Clinger, John D. Lombard, and Mack Mitchell each got one. But Mack pulled off the stunt of the day.

Nine Zeroes of the latest type spiraled down out of the sun and proceeded to strafe the airdrome. Mitchell immediately dived from his extreme height, attaining a tremendous speed and passing through the Japanese top cover at thirteen thousand feet. He attacked one of the Zeroes that was strafing three P-40 planes on the ground. These planes were undergoing repairs and although under concealment, the enemy had discovered their position and was trying to destroy them completely.

At approximately 480 mph, all guns firing, Mitchell almost collided with one Japanese pilot who failed to see the P-40 streaking toward him. Mitchell pulled straight up and did a steep wingover, returning to the attack. Then three other Zeroes stopped their strafing activities as soon as they saw him and turned on him. But Mitchell skillfully evaded the fire of the more maneuverable Zeroes and streaked for the northwest, with several enemy planes on his tail.

After hedgehopping for a while, Mitchell finally gained some altitude but then the Japanese planes turned away. He got one of them. For this action which saved three repairable P-40s from complete destruction and action performed against superior enemy numbers at a low altitude, Mitchell received the Silver Star.

But he was not a "lone ranger" in the sky that day. While he was fighting his own battle, Lt. Dallas A. Clinger was winning the Distinguished Flying Cross for shooting down one plane, damaging three others, and scaring away a plane attacking his flight leader by threatening a head-on collision, all the while under enemy fire.

En route to Kweilin from Kunming, Colonel Scott was flying solo in his fighter when he heard about a "Jap 97" bomber in the vicinity. Years later, Scott told the story.

The first real encounter I had with the Japanese after taking over command of this group was on this flight to Kweilin. I had emerged through broken overcast over the railroad that would indicate I was near Kweilin. In just an instant I received word from the ground that Japanese airplanes were coming up on the Canton-Hankow railway. I decided that even though I had only eighteen gallons of gasoline left I would try to fly into these ships and attack what I supposed to be one single observation ship.

At 11:25 on that morning I saw one twin-engine bomber coming toward me. I turned my gun switches on and made ready to attack him when I noted two Zeroes three thousand feet higher as convoy. I hesitated momentarily because General Chennault had warned me that to attack a bomber was pretty bad but with fighter escort my chances would be slim. But I attacked anyway and in my eagerness I was going too fast. I couldn't bring my sights to bear for a head-on run. I nosed down and went by the bomber and pulled back into a chandelle and came up on his tail, but once again I was moving so fast I couldn't get my sights centered.

The Zeroes by this time were firing at me and I decided that I had to do it now or never. So I made an attack on the bomber and shot it down with about fifty rounds of ammo. One of the Zeroes got into my sight and I got a good burst at it. Later on it was confirmed. I had shot down a Mitsubishi Army 97 and a Zero. I don't know what happened to the other one.

Others scored as well or scored probables. Lts. Martin Cluck, Dyer, and Robert L. Liles got a probable each. During this entire action, the Twenty-third lost no planes and the Hengyang field got away with light strafing.

July 31 was the third day of continuous Japanese air raids on Hengyang. They strafed the field badly, but in return the Twenty-third retaliated by shooting down four Zeroes and two bombers. Pilots of the Twenty-third were awarded one Distinguished Flying Cross, two Silver Stars and two Purple Hearts for the day's fighting.

Cluck, the Seventy-fifth Squadron Intelligence Officer, received a report after the day's fighting that the Chinese had located some Japanese pilots working on their ships, which had been shot down, and attempting to take off again. Whenever the opportunity arose, Cluck always tried the almost impossible feat of getting to a downed Japanese pilot before the Chinese had killed him. So he jumped into a jeep and headed for the hills. Upon arrival he was told that the Chinese had taken away the pilot's gun and the papers he carried. That infuriated the wounded pilot, and he grabbed the gun back, wounding three Chinese and with his dagger wounding still another. The Chinese then shot him. By the time Cluck had arrived at the scene the pilot was dying. The lieutenant identified himself as an American pilot and offered the Japanese pilot a cigarette. The dying man smiled in acknowledgment but was too far gone to talk. He definitely understood English, but died before Cluck had any opportunity for communication with him.

Cluck then checked several of the wrecked planes, getting much valuable information from them, and brought guns and other accessories from them to the airdrome. He reported that the Japanese soldiers in the vicinity all wore full dress uniforms and the Samurai sword, which defined the bearer as a member of the warrior class. On several occasions it was noted that the Japanese pilots shot down were of very high rank. Another notation Cluck made was that at this time many Japanese pilots were wearing parachutes. He also observed that bomber crews, when bailing out, were armed with submachine guns that were American-made. These they used to fire at troops or peasants on the ground below as they descended. One of the pilots who had crashed near Hengyang wrote a note saying, "I was shot down by an American P-40 fighter and shot by Chinese who left me here to die." To whom the note was intended is not known.

During August 1942, American pilots, with an exuberance dampened only by the rain which fell heavily throughout the month, carried the battle to the enemy in a series of a dozen raids. On August 3, twelve P-40s dive-bombed Liuchwan. After leaving Hengyang and refueling at Siuchuan, American planes appeared over the city. Three flights of four planes each made their runs from different directions, one flight from the west, another from the south, and the third from the east, thus hitting the Japanese from all directions. Eight direct hits were scored, causing many fires. One pilot dropped his five-hundred-pound bomb directly on Japanese headquarters, killing many high-ranking officers.

Lieutenant Cluck went below to strafe a boat and reported a direct hit on a dock which blew pilings and debris high into the air. Two more hits straddled the main thoroughfare of the city. Bombs hitting the west gate of the city killed several hundred Japanese troops, according to Chinese intelligence reports. There were several boats along the river which were strafed thoroughly. The Americans wondered why there was no fighter opposition. The reason was that the

Japanese were expecting an attack on Nanchang. But five minutes after the American planes left Liuchwan, the Japanese arrived in force—too late.

Five days into August the Japanese made their way back over to Hengyang using their celebrated "flying circus" tactics. This maneuver involved a circling and weaving formation which moved slowly forward, looking for combat. Each plane in the formation rolled, spinned, and looped doing Immelmann turns and other maneuvers. Of course this was a very difficult formation to attack, but the flexibility necessary for offensive tactics was limited. In addition, a great deal of fuel was used.

The Japanese fighters came over Hengyang at 6 A.M. It was estimated that over fifty of their planes were in the area. The fight was scattered and most of the action was not visible from the ground. A formation of eight P-40s led by Major Alison went upstairs to intercept. They made two attacks, with five planes in the first wave and three in the second. Diving out of the sun, the first attack passed through the enemy's top cover at seventeen thousand feet and came out at the bottom, five thousand feet below.

One enemy plane was shot down near Hengyang and there were many more reported probables. Two Zeroes attempted to strafe the airport, but as soon as they appeared over the field at about fifty feet, the makeshift antiaircraft force of caliber .30 machine guns, Bret guns, and pistols burst loose and hit one of the planes. The other turned tail for home, but the pilot of the damaged plane decided to earn a place in "seventh heaven" and dived his plane into a barracks for Chinese soldiers. He evidently mistook the barracks for the field headquarters since it was the only permanent building in the field. Lt. Lee N. Minor was killed in action. He was hit from astern unexpectedly and thus became the first pilot to give his life in the Army Air Corps in China.

In a second raid of Tin Ho airdrome in Canton, seven P-40s went out with five B-25s to repeat the blasting given the Japanese on August 6. Fragmentation and incendiary bombs were used with excellent results on docks, the airdrome, and the harbor installations.

On this day Capt. Charles Sawyer won the Distinguished Flying Cross. After the bombing mission was completed, the Americans observed enemy fighters climbing to attack. Leaving the remaining members of his flight as top cover for the bombers, Captain Sawyer single-handedly attacked six enemy fighters. One enemy plane was destroyed in flames and fire was directed against three others. The rest of the flight engaged other Japanese fighters. Lt. Patrick Daniels became separated from his fellows and was forced to run from three "Japs" on his tail. When two of the ships gave up the chase Daniels turned on the remaining Zero, got his sights on him, and sent him down in flames crashing into the hill.

On August 9, American fighters carried out the fourth raid of the month against the city of Haiphong in Indochina. The targets were docks and warehouses and many bombs hit their mark. Daniels, who the day before had a close call over Canton, participated in the action and won himself the Silver Star. He dove in and strafed the entire dock area of the city in the face of heavy antiaircraft fire, thus furthering the results of the bombing, and more important, keeping the Japanese fire-fighting forces from extinguishing the flames started by the bombs.

The Americans did not ease up. They were back the next day carrying out bombing missions against Hsinning, near Hankow, with fourteen P-40s. They again caught the Japanese short with little antiaircraft fire encountered and no aerial opposition. They hit docks and warehouses hard and strafed hangars. Huge fires from oil tankers were left burning. They did this by diving from eight thousand feet down to two thousand before releasing their 550-pound demolition and incendiary bombs. Seven high explosive bombs hit within the walls of the city and two large warehouses received direct hits. All aircraft returned safely.

August 17 was moving day for the Seventy-fifth Squadron, and a little bit of action was thrown in for good measure when a Japanese observation plane came over to have a look-see at the goings-on. The Seventy-fifth was on the way to Changyi from Hengyang and had stopped over at Kweilin when an enemy plane was reported coming over. Four planes went up to intercept and the action was particularly noteworthy because two of the ships were P-43 Lancers getting their first and for some time at least, their last taste of combat.

One of the Lancers, with Lt. P. B. O'Connell at the controls, contacted the Japanese plane and opened fire. The guns jammed, but not until one bullet had gone through the enemy's propeller. O'Connell tried to radio for assistance, but his radio would not work either. At this time Lt. Burrell Barnum in another P-43 took up the chase. He gained during climbs, but lost distance during the dives. The Lancer was not fast enough to overtake the Japanese plane, and it was necessary for Barnum to fire at long range. He kept up the chase until the enemy plane was over his home airdrome at Canton. On his return Barnum reported that the P-43 was no faster than the Ki. 45 Japanese fighter at twenty thousand feet, though it was probably faster at higher altitudes.

Changyi, the new home of the Seventy-fifth, lies in a small mountain-locked valley just eighty miles northeast of Kunming. The cool air from the mountains, light rains, and improved eating facilities helped the pilots after enduring the heat and dryness of the Hengyang area.

Chinese citizens sometimes expressed support for the Americans who came to their country to help fight the enemy. The citizens of Tung-yen in Kweichow Province held a mass meeting on August 18 to celebrate the third anniversary of the Chinese Air Force Day. They also saluted the Americans in a declaration:

> The ruthless bombardments by the Japanese of our unfortified cities have been fortunately and effectively checked by your highly esteemed Air Force. Your brilliant and unsurpassed bravery has not only driven the Japanese into the sea and killed them in the air, but also signaled the final victory of the United Nations. We beg to pay you our deepest admiration and highest respect on this grand occasion when all day celebrating and rejoicing on the Third National Air Force Day.

At a party given to the members of the Hengyang station by the people of Yunnan Province, General Chao Heng-ti, chairman of the People's Council, gave a short talk to the few Americans remaining there after the bulk of the squadron had moved to Changyi.

Lieutenant Mikeworth lost his life on August 22. A Chinese farmer reported that his plane began to malfunction and spun into Tien Chih Lake. Neither plane nor the body was recovered, so it was never determined what caused the final accident.

After fifteen days of heavy rains and bad weather in general, the fighters took up where they left off, bombing Lashio on August 26 in the first of two raids on the important center held by the Japanese. Five American pilots in fighters and three B-25s participated in the first raid. The P-40s went into a string formation to strafe the field while the bombers got in their work. Lt. Patrick Daniels and Maj. Edward Rector flew up and down the field making passes at parked planes. They got one apiece and two other planes were badly damaged. Colonel Scott strafed a hangar, then turned on the streets and buildings of the town. While he was engaged in this, some Japanese soldiers started firing on him with rifles. He whirled on them, killing twenty and scattering the rest. Major Rector, in addition to his other activities, also strafed a train, giving it a thorough going-over. All of the Twenty-third's planes came home safely. They encountered no fighter opposition, and the only antiaircraft fire was with small arms by Japanese troops.

On September 2, 1942, a flight of sixteen P-40s carried out an attack on boats along the river in the Nanchang area. The planes went out in two waves of eight each. The object of the sweep was to attack rivercraft engaged in hauling rice to the front and evacuating personnel from the area on the return trip. The Japanese got short warning of the attack so their defense was disorganized. They fought in small groups instead of in the usual larger formations.

Tex Hill's flight opened the attack when he spotted a fleet of Japanese sailboats and junks. He and his men strafed them heavily, many of them capsizing while others burned out of control. Japanese spilled out into the water. The second flight went on to the north of Poyang Hu and spotted a number of steamers hauling rice barges. The fighters fell on these targets enthusiastically and diminished the food supply for some Japanese soldiers' mess. Maj. Frank Schiel of the Seventy-fourth Squadron led an attack on two river steamers near Poyang Hu. One steamer was sunk and there was a heavy explosion on the other. The rice barges were a total loss, for once the Americans strafed them, water seeped into the valuable cargo and caused the rice to swell and sink the barges.

Japanese pursuit, although disorganized, was active. Two planes went after Scott and almost got him. But he turned on them, shot one down, and drove the other away. Lieutenant Elias, however, was not so lucky. He was intercepted by three Japanese planes. He got one before they got him, setting his plane afire. He bailed out, but the remaining two Japanese machine-gunned him to death as he floated to earth.

Other Americans continued the mission. Maj. Bruce Holloway

strafed a warehouse and set it afire, then gave a railway station a thorough going-over. Lt. Clyde B. Slocumb, Jr., strafed a train, an eight-car affair with troops aboard. He immobilized the locomotive in the attack and riddled the cars where the troops were riding.

The fighters went back to Nanchang in the afternoon, giving the enemy no rest. One of them made a direct hit on a hostel reported by Chinese intelligence to be the residence of Japanese officers, leaving the place in shambles. The American planes then fanned out over the city of Kwan Yun Man, scattering fragmentation and incendiary bombs. A river warehouse was destroyed, and approximately a hundred Japanese were victims in the streets. Two enemy aircraft were spotted, but they did not attack. They apparently had had enough for the day.

The Japanese flew over the American airfields the morning of September 3 at 7 A.M., taking fierce and crafty vengeance. Thirty-nine I-97s in seven waves attacked Hengyang, then Kweilin, and then Lingling. They used different tactics this time, meeting the pilots of the Twenty-third at high altitudes, making half circles of the fields at six thousand feet. When they met American fighters in force, they refused combat and seemed instead to be looking for stragglers and planes being serviced. But what they were actually doing was making an effort to destroy planes on the ground. The Japanese hoped to keep the Twenty-third on the alert with succeeding waves and wait until the planes ran out of fuel. Then they would dive on them while they were on the ground refueling.

Major Hill came into contact with the enemy's first flight of twelve planes at 8 A.M. He sat on a Zero's tail while Capt. Ajax Baumler made a quarter attack on it. So the unfortunate Japanese pilot was hit simultaneously by twelve caliber .50 guns. Lieutenant O'Connell caught a straggler and put some damaging fire into its left wing, but was in a hurry for another target and could not stay to see the plane spin down.

Meanwhile Lt. Martin Cluck was supposed to go on a reconnaissance mission to Canton. But his P-43 nearly caught fire at a low level. He was all but ablaze when he ran out of oxygen and let down to the uncomfortable height of a thousand feet over the airport where the Japanese were making strafing runs. With his plane riddled, Cluck decided the safest place was on the ground, so he landed the plane while the enemy made a target of him. Rather, he almost landed, for almost as soon as the wheels were on the ground, Cluck was seen forty feet ahead of the plane pulling away from it toward the shelter of an eight-inch-deep irrigation ditch. Some of the men recall that it is amazing how deep an eight-inch ditch can be when one is being strafed. Not one bit of Cluck's two-hundred-pound physique could be seen above ground. With enemy bullets kicking up the dirt at his heels, he suffered only minor bruises.

American losses for the day were one P-40 burned on the ground and Cluck's P-43. The enemy lost one thanks to Hill and Baumler, and Chinese intelligence reported that six fighters failed to return to their base at Canton. The Japanese' new tactics were not yet reversing the tide in the air war.

Lt. Burrell Barnum staged a one-man show in the sky on September 6. He had been ordered to remain at the Hengyang airdrome until two ships had been repaired. Upon hearing the news that waves of Japanese aircraft were coming in, Barnum took off in one of the serviceable planes that happened to be nearby. He then staged his one-man attack, making a series of runs towards the enemy fighters and preventing them from effectively observing and strafing the Hengyang airdrome. During the four-hour attack, this lone American pilot was in the air three times against a total of thirty-nine Japanese planes. At no time was he outnumbered less than five to one. With a single fighter he delivered repeated attacks against anywhere from five to nine planes, and although none was confirmed as destroyed, he nevertheless delivered harassing and effective fire against the numerous enemy aircraft.

Two days later Lt. T. R. Smith downed the first Japanese observation ship in the war. Many American pilots had attempted this feat, but the speed and altitude of the observation planes had enabled them to escape time and time again. Smith, from an altitude of twenty-four thousand feet, made repeated dives upon the enemy plane, thus attaining the momentum necessary to come up on the observation plane, even with its excessive speed. He finally got three bursts of fire into the Japanese plane, causing it to slow up. So suddenly did it falter that there was almost a collision. Turning his fighter, Smith gave him the works with one final burst, and the observation ship spun into nearby Tien Chih Lake.

Maj. Bruce Holloway flew over Hanoi on September 15, noticing many parked airplanes in the airdrome. He circled Hanoi twice and on the second run received a bit of antiaircraft fire. He took photographs of the city and docks, and of the airport at Haiphong, which seemed deserted. He noted a great deal of activity at Gia Lam airdrome with bombers and fighters on the fields.

On September 22 Major Holloway made a high altitude reconnaissance through heavy weather into Burma and examined traffic on the Burma Road from Lashio north to the Salween River. Reporting that many enemy trucks were moving, he volunteered to lead a flight against them the same afternoon, knowing he would have poor flying weather over some of the worst terrain in the theater.

He made his attack under heavy antiaircraft fire and aided in the destruction of from twelve to twenty trucks, a staff car, and a sedan. He received several hits in the fuselage of his plane, but nevertheless continued his attacks until forced to head for friendly territory. As he reached a ridge to the east of the Salween River, his engine froze. He landed his plane, wheels up, in a rice paddy. Major Rector, also on the mission, attacked the concentration of Japanese trucks along the road with heavy antiaircraft fire in his direction. He hit many trucks loaded with Japanese troops. Following these attacks, he continued on through heavy rain to strafe the barracks at Chefant. He was under heavy ground fire all through this attack, but he stayed with it until his mission was accomplished.

On September 23 Lt. Martin Cluck of the Seventy-fifth Squadron was killed at Hangyi when his Ryan primary trainer crashed on the airdrome. He was returning from Kunming in the two-seater, approaching the field in a slow roll at a very low altitude. A handbag which was in the front seat jammed between the seat and the stick, and he was unable to recover from the roll. His ship dived full speed into the ground. Cluck was intelligence officer for his squadron. He was recommended by Colonel Scott for the Purple Heart on the basis of his conduct at the Hengyang airdrome one day during the previous July when he remained on the field directing fighters to safe landings among the bomb craters with the headlights of a truck despite continuous bombing of the field by waves of enemy planes.

Major Scott became an ace on September 25, and many of his fellow pilots also distinguished themselves as expert fighters the same day. Major Rector led ten fighters escorting four B-25s to bomb Gia Lam airdrome at Hanoi. This field, located in good position to attack

Kunming, was an excellent airdrome with a concrete-surfaced runway and numerous taxi strips.

Apparently the enemy was well warned, for when the American fighters and bombers came over the airdrome, there were twelve twin-engine I-45s and four single-seated fighters waiting in the wings. Dispersed on the field were a number of dummies which the Japanese hoped the Americans would strafe. None of the pilots of the Twenty-third took the bait. As the bombers made their run, the action opened in a fierce dogfight. One I-45 started the ball rolling by going head on for the bombers. Major Rector's flight peeled off to get him, and Lieutenant Daniels won the honor of zooming up under the I-45's tail to shoot him down in flames.

From this point, the action scattered all over the sky. It was then that Scott recorded the kill that made him an ace. Engaging three of the enemy who were diving on the bombers, he fired on the leader, who immediately turned away. The colonel went after another. Firing bursts at him, Scott saw him start smoking badly and going out of control. Scott then turned on the third one, got in several bursts at him, but lost him in the clouds.

Meanwhile Major Rector was all over the sky encountering flights of Japanese fighters. After his flight disposed of one that was attacking the bombers, Rector engaged two more I-45s that were climbing up to get into the fight. He leveled off on the first one and shot him down, but the impetus of his attack carried him past the second plane, which then attacked him. So Rector pulled away and promptly ran into a couple more. He was then far behind the enemy lines and near the extreme operating range of his fighter plane. He then directed the other members of his flight, by means of radio, to guard the bombers closely as they proceeded back to Kunming. Thus, fighting a single-handed rear-guard action in which he twice fought off two flights of enemy fighters, he gave his less-experienced pilots a chance to break combat with enough remaining gas to reach their home base safely.

Lieutenant Marks was leading one flight of P-40s. They went after two enemy planes which were attacking the bombers. Marks' third burst caught one of the Japanese planes, which then exploded in the air. Pieces of wreckage enveloped Marks' plane and ripped away his aerial.

Lieutenant Krippner shot down an enemy ship and left it spinning away in flames. Lieutenant Javitz fired several bursts into a flight of three planes and saw one of them dive away with a stream of smoke pouring after it. On the flight back, Javitz spotted a six-car freight train. He dove and strafed it from end to end, but due to his shortage of fuel, he was unable to stay around to see the extent of the damage. In addition to bombing Gia Lam, the bombers on their way home dropped bombs on Lao Kay.

The next day Lieutenant Wellborn and Lt. Walter J. Daniels flew along the road from Tengchung to Mangshih. The weather was extremely bad. Nearing Lingling, Daniels fired on what looked like warehouses. Next the two fighters flew back up the road strafing barracks and cars along the way. Then they gave the many gas drums they saw along the way short bursts to see if they were full. Apparently all were empty.

While Daniels was pulling out of a dive, Lieutenant Wellborn observed a tank firing at him. He made a pass at it, knocking turret gun and gunner off. It was probably the gunner of this tank that shot Daniels in the shoulder.

On September 27 the Chinese at Changyi held a ceremony in expression of sympathy to the Twenty-third for the loss of Lieutenant Cluck. The colorful affair with flowers and Chinese rituals was held in the Army compound. Following talks through a Chinese interpreter, Major John Alison expressed his thanks to the assembled Chinese for their thoughtfulness. Captain Baumler took color photos of the ceremony.

The same day six fighters flew to the Salween area to strafe truck movements along the Burma Road. This flight flew to Mangshih but could not attack due to the weather. Lt. Malcolm G. Groseclose had prop trouble and Lieutenant Marquette developed engine trouble. Both remained at Yunnanyi. Four planes completed the mission, which was a flight over upper Burma.

October was a slow month on the China front, but there was a raid on Hong Kong on October 25 and a dogfight accompanying it, which proved the highlight of the month. Scott later told the story:

> We heard there was a million tons of shipping which we subsequently found out was destined for the Solomons. This was in Victoria Harbor, which is of course between Hong Kong and Kowloon. We planned for many days to go down and destroy the shipping, but

weather held us back. We also had to remember that our first objective was the defense of the ferrying command. We couldn't leave the ferry terminus at Kumning entirely unprotected.

Early that morning we took off from Kunming, flew five hundred miles with ten bombers and twelve fighters to Kweilin. This was in Kwangsi Province. We arrived there, gassed and bombed up, and took off just after noon for Hong Kong. Our run was straight down toward Port Macao, and then we turned to the south and went across the water down to Kowloon docks. I saw the bombs explode, covering the area. We were at eighteen thousand feet. We had seven fighters to protect the ten bombers, which we soon found were not enough. Just as I finished taking pictures of the bombs hitting the docks, I said to myself "This is a soft job. No Zeroes."

We had made our turn to go back to the base when I saw them coming up. There were planes stretched all the way to the water, Zeroes climbing so steeply that it made me wonder. There were probably twenty in that one flight, climbing at an angle of seventy degrees. This permitted them to get to our altitude of sixteen thousand feet in four minutes. I remember moving down for my first attack. I saw Tex Hill off to the right, over in a half-roll, pull back on the stick and gain speed for the attack. I hadn't known how to do that. He taught me something there. Too eagerly, I shot at the first Zero, but I saw Tex get it because he got to it first. I reached in and tried to get the second but I think Hampshire got that.

Scott was right in his recollection. One of the Japanese planes got on the tail of a B-25, and although he was fortunate enough to shoot down the first B-25 in the theater, his good fortune was immediately followed by bad in the form of Capt. John Hampshire, who had heard the bomber call for help. He sandwiched the Zero and sent it spinning to earth minus part of its wing.

"I got the third Zero," Scott continued, "and then shot the fifth down as they climbed to our altitude. Lieutenant Shea of the Seventy-sixth got the fourth. From then on I can't remember much because things happened too fast." Antiaircraft was fairly heavy, but of course they concentrated on the bomber formation. As a rule Japanese failed to shoot fighter ships directly, opting for the larger target, the bomber formation. Scott continued:

We were moving too fast for them. After all the objective of the mission was to bomb. If they could shoot a bomber down, they destroyed it. Hill and I fought all the way down to the water's level. We shot down—at least the entire squadron of ships shot down—nineteen Japanese ships that day. Tex and I strafed the main street of Kowloon and also White Cloud airdrome on our way back. We came in thirty minutes after the others and we had been given up for lost. About the most amusing thing on this was after we had fought over Victoria Harbor and just about run out of ammunition, I saw one more ship to the right. He evidently saw me at the same time because we moved over to attack one another and then I saw it was Tex. I was glad he recognized me, too. The attack that we made that day did more damage than any other to date and had been planned by Chennault for a long time.

A long-planned mission on Canton began on November 22. Scott later told about this mission too, along with several others that immediately followed it:

Canton is about eighty miles from Hong Kong and all the Japanese transports' task force appeared to be staged from Formosa to Hong Kong. We had heard that two shiploads of Japanese fighters were being unloaded at Canton so we decided upon the mission. But the day of this mission, we told everyone we were going to Hong Kong, figuring that the leak would mislead the Japanese. Now we had to wait for weather again, but on November 22, we took off from Kunming with our largest fighter force, thirty-six P-40s and twelve bombers. We were able to take off from Kweilin, our eastern point of departure, with twenty-four fighters and ten bombers. This may not sound like a large formation in other theaters, but to us in China it was very large. First of all, General Chennault had planned this attack to surprise the Japs. He left word to be passed around that we were going to Hong Kong directly, but that afternoon we struck Hongay down on the French Indochina coast.

The bombers sank a twelve-thousand-ton ship that might have been an aircraft carrier. We went in and strafed the coal mines along the Hongay shores and also the power station there. We sank some more small boats which were evidently carrying officials. We sank a ferry in the river and we came back to Kweilin.

We had lost no ships in the flight down, but one was lost in a crash landing on the way back. That was a big worry with us in China. It's not so much the Japs you have to worry with, but the maps were pretty poor, the terrain was always bad, and the weather rough. It was hazardous to the young pilots as they had a pretty tough time coming back if they got separated from the formation.

The next morning the Japanese thought we were finally coming to Hong Kong. Instead we struck Sanchow Island with a bomber flight of nine, escorted by seven fighters. This was November 23. We blew up three of the four hangars at Sanchow Island. The P-40s, each with two fifty-kilogram demolition bombs, bombed the boats and harbor installations and finished with a strafing session on the boats. No antiaircraft was encountered. A large freighter was last seen burning at the stern and Lieutenant Gordon was forced down out of gas and landed on a six-hundred-foot strip. Spending two days cutting down trees which obstructed the field, Gordon showed the first signs of having worked since leaving Colorado, by blisters on his hands. But the hands gave out before he chopped down enough trees and on takeoff the wheels hit an obstruction damaging the gear so that the wheels could not be put down. This necessitated a wheels-up landing at Kweilin, but he managed this damaging only the propeller.

We blew up three of the four hangars at Sanchow Island, as I said before. Two of us went down and shot up ships on the water, but generally there was little air activity. We got back about one o'clock and took off late that afternoon on our second raid of the day and struck Canton's Tin Ho airdrome. I've never seen as effective bombing as the bombers under Captain Holstrom that day. We moved in to the north of our target until we hit the East River, then made a ninety-degree turn until we were due south of Tin Ho. We then made another ninety-degree turn as the antiaircraft fire became pretty heavy. We made a straight run toward the target. Our fighters began the squirrel-cage tactics that we had developed long before, to ward off any Zeroes that would come up. But for some reason, the Japs didn't want to ride us that day and they kept their ships on the ground. Those that we saw take off headed north, south, east, and west in all directions. The bombs of the bomber flight—ten ships—covered at least 65 percent of the building area of Tin Ho. The report came back very favorable of the number of ships they had destroyed on the ground—at least forty-two. We fighter pilots just had the ride for we were not intercepted that day.

The next morning, the twenty-fourth, we made a dive-bombing attack at Canton. We used twenty P-40s, ten for top cover and ten with fragmentation bombs on the wings while the bombers had maintenance. We hit the docks at Whangpoo and damaged an airplane factory in Canton. We planned some good trips later than this, but our hearts were a little saddened because on this flight we lost one of the most offensive-minded fellows that came under my command—Lt. Patrick Daniels. He was shot down or else his bombs exploded on the way down.

That night six P-40s each loaded with two fifty-kilogram demolition bombs raided river and airport installations at Hankow. The raid was successful with all planes returning safely. Major Alison picked up a few holes from trying to observe the burst of his bombs. Captain Baumler, for his part, picked up a stray Zero that wanted to fly in formation with him. Baumler later recalled:

At first the radial engine made no impression upon me, but a second later I noticed the large propeller spinner and immediately decided that one of us was on the wrong formation. I reached for the ground about the same time that the Jap pulled up. He then followed me, but I lost him in a quick turn. Lieutenant Blackstone said that antiaircraft fire sure looked pretty from the distance. The next morning we surprised the Japs again. Instead of going to the east toward Hong Kong and Canton, we went to the north.

We landed at Hengyang and struck Hsinning up toward the Yangtze. We bombed the town which was filled with Japanese soldiers over the heaviest antiaircraft we had seen. We were not intercepted nor do I believe there was any attempt to intercept. We came back to Hengyang, bombed and refueled and took off immediately and struck Poyang, a walled city up toward the Yangtze. This time we saw even more antiaircraft. We saw perfect bombing. Every single bomb dropped from twelve B-25s landed within the city walls of the very small city. Warehouses and fuel dumps exploded. This was important because it was the direct transportation line between the Japanese on the Yangtze and those at Changsha. Changsha was the most southwestward point they had advanced in China at the time. We went back that night prepared to take off the next morning, finally, to fulfill our attack on Hong Kong, but instead the general decided we would wait around to worry the Japs.

That night the Japs went in with nine bombers again. We shot down every single one. We captured one pilot. He proved to be of interest and we worked on getting him back to the States. After resting Thanksgiving day, November 26, we took off the next morning on a raid we had come east for—the main show not to Hong Kong, but to Canton. We had closed the post the night before, and the word had traveled back from Kweilin through Japanese spies—

Koreans, Manchukuans, and such as that, that evidently this was the day, because we had resorted to secrecy. Eagerly we took off as though we were going to Hankow, which is in the opposite direction from Hong Kong. After ten miles we made our turn to the right and went straight toward Hong Kong. But just as we reached East River, we turned right again and then turned again after we got south of Tin Ho airdrome and found an eight-thousand-ton freighter in the East River. This was sunk with five direct five-hundred-pound bomb hits from the lead formation led by Colonel Morgan. On the left, the second flight of bombers sank another six-thousand-ton freighter. This was led by Holstrom. You could see many of the hundred fighters that were around this freighter blown above the ship. The other four ships under a flight commander whose identity I have forgotten hit the docks at Whangpoo. We had just passed over the first target and were heading across Tin Ho airdrome when I saw the Zeroes. There were at least forty of them.

We had reported to us later that there were forty-five. They had taken off from Kaitak down at Hong Kong, from Tin Ho and White Cloud airdromes at Canton. These Zeroes were rapidly gaining altitude on our bomber formation, but this time we had the largest fighter force we had ever used in China, twenty-two P-40s.

We were able to strike the Zeroes while they were four thousand feet below the bombers or at least part of us did, because I ordered the right echelon to go down and intercept the Japanese below the bombers while we closed in to safeguard anything that might come out of the sun. In a few seconds, we had shot down at least five Japanese Zeroes. Within one minute, there were twenty-nine Zeroes shot down and burning somewhere around Canton. We don't know what happened to the remainder of the forty-five. Only one ship was seen away from Canton and it was shot down by Colonel Holloway. Anyway, out of twenty-two ships that we had taken in, we had lost none in combat. However, we did have two pilots become lost and have to land en route to Kweilin. Our confirmed victories that day were twenty-nine. Also, many times that number of enemy planes were destroyed when our bombers sank the eight-thousand-ton freighter. One estimate is that there were five hundred Japanese fighters on board. We didn't quit but General Chennault sent about half of us home to Kunming, and the others he sent down with the bombers once more to hit Hongay and Haiphong in French Indochina.

Maj. Tex Hill said good-bye on November 30. After eighteen months in the east with the AVG and the Army, Tex was getting a well-deserved rest in the States. He called the squadron together for a farewell talk, and those who knew him knew he was not a man to waste words. He said what every man who worked for him hoped that he would say—"If possible, I would like to return to the Seventy-fifth after my leave." On December 1 Maj. John Alison became the new commanding officer of the Seventy-fifth Fighter Squadron.

The boys were eager for one last punch at the Japanese before 1942 passed, so on December 31 eight of them attempted to provoke the enemy at Lashio down in Burma. The idea was to strafe the occupied airport at Lashio and entice a few Zeroes into the sights of the P-40s. But the weather played favorite to the Japanese and obscured his lair. They had a good flight, although they failed to find Lashio.

CHAPTER 6

The Panama Pilots'
Long Road to China

Approaching the end of 1942, Thomas Cotton was on rest and recuperation in Guatemala City after the near fatal accident that occurred when he ditched his P-40 into the Atlantic Ocean. Concerning that time, he recalled, "To say that I rested much is an exaggeration as I was making the rounds of legation row and having a great time with some of the other pilots from the Canal Zone. Suddenly we were ordered back to the Canal Zone. For what reason, I had no idea."

Meanwhile, back at Panama, Charles Olsen was hearing a lot of scuttlebutt going around. It was November, just four months after the AVGs had disbanded and their combat operations had been taken over by the newly-formed Twenty-third Fighter Group. Charlie later related:

A couple of fellows said that Chennault had asked for us. He wanted men from Panama, those who had experience in jungle training and had at least 250 hours of flying time in the Curtiss P-40 fighters. Word was out anybody who was transferred from Panama would go to China. It seemed logical, too. In Panama we were a long way south of the North Atlantic air route which led from the United States to Europe, up through Greenland, Iceland, and over the North Atlantic Ocean to England. Here in Panama, we were already part of the way along the southern route to the China-Burma-India Theater.

The southern air route led from the States to South America, then across the Atlantic over the central part of Africa and up to India. "But knowing the army," Charlie continued, "we couldn't be sure where we would go. It seemed with our P-40 training and geographical location that Chennault would be the one to get us, at least we hoped so."

On February 28, 1943, orders were delivered to the following men: Charles J. Olsen, Robert F. Dersch, Thomas T. Higgins, William O. Moran, William S. Epperson, Harlyn S. Vidovich, Curtis L. Scoville, John D. Long, Thomas Cotton, James A. Anning and Altheus B. Jarmon. The orders stated they would proceed to Walter Field in the British West Indies, accompanied by only seventy-seven pounds of equipment. Nothing was mentioned about where they were going, but they all assumed the destination to be China under Chennault, to take up combat duties where the disbanded AVGs had left off.

On that long road to China, when time and opportunity permitted, Tom Cotton wrote a series of informative letters to his grandmother in Wyoming, who was concerned about her grandson's role in the coming air war. Tom's grandmother was named Ella Henschke, and as a young woman she had gone to Wyoming from Indiana as a kind of mail-order bride. The trip to the territory then was made by stagecoach. In Sheridan, she married Tom's grandfather, Thomas M. Cotton, who was then the first newspaper publisher in northern Wyoming. After his early death, she married Herman Henschke, a prominent retailer. She was in her nineties when Cotton wrote to her during the war, and she died soon after his return, at the age of ninety-three.

Tom's words to his grandmother were carefully chosen to be informative but not alarming, dwelling mainly upon the humorous, day-to-day aspects of his life at the time. Later, when he was in combat against the Japanese, Tom's letters dealing with the dangerous aspects of war were tactfully worded. Pointed questions from his grandmother were answered rather matter-of-factly, and though he was never patronizing, he managed to play down the unmentioned but ever present possibility that he might be killed in action.

On March 5, 1943, Cotton wrote his grandmother that he and the other pilots from Panama were en route to Trinidad, where they would remain for about a week, during which time they would receive shots for typhus, cholera, and other diseases. Then on March 13, he addressed a letter to her from Walter Field, Trinidad:

Just had my last shot in my arm today which completes my series and just about makes me immune to all the diseases that man can invent. From the feeling in my arm the last week I wonder if the disease would not have been better.

This has been quite the life. Here about two weeks ago we had been flying like mad and dreaming for the day when we would have nothing to do. Now we have had nothing to do for the past week, getting up in the morning when we want to eat, take a walk or go back to bed. Now we are all sort of wanting to get busy again although we won't admit it. Our trip seems to have bogged down here for a while while the planes get here. So we just sit. No mail has reached us here as it is all addressed to Army Post Office 3764, wherever that is. So I don't have any idea how you are getting along; but I hope that you are fine.

I would have given anything to have a movie camera along with me since I joined up. There is a lot that couldn't be photographed, owing to the war; but there have still been things that would have made very interesting material.

On the morning of the seventh day, they boarded a plane which flew them across the Amazon River to Natal on the eastern side of Brazil, where they were issued gas masks and other equipment. Here they waited two more days for a "China clipper" to fly them to Africa. Cotton once again wrote his grandmother on March 18.

This evening is probably the last one in the Western hemisphere for a while. We have been traveling by plane for the last couple of days and have reached the jumping-off place. From here we take one of Pan American's giant clipper planes for the "dark continent."

The people here in Brazil are interesting in comparison with some of the other countries we have visited. The natives think the world of the American soldier. I have been called everything from "Uncle Sam" to "my very good friend." Two of us were wandering through the streets this evening and found everyone wanted to bid us good evening and good luck. One little boy not over three years old ran away from his mother, grabbed my hand, kissed it, and ran back to his mother.

Most everyone speaks Portuguese which is similar to Spanish so we have a slight speaking acquaintance. The food is bad for us as we are not used to eating everything cooked in rancid butter. However, the natives seem to love it. Perhaps the most interesting trip down was the crossing of the Amazon River, which is ninety miles wide at its mouth. Both sides of the river have dense jungles that end hundreds of miles into the interior. The rate of exchange from native to U.S. money and vice versa has us quite baffled. Each time we land we are in a different country with a different rate. Sometimes we make money and sometimes we lose it.

It has been said of fighter pilots that during their leisure hours they sometimes partook of whiskey and carried on other related activities. Some of the men were sitting on the veranda of the hotel at Natal one evening, minding their own business, when a huge figure of a man strolled up and engaged them in conversation. He stood about six feet four inches tall and weighed about 260 pounds, or so it appeared. It was Quentin Reynolds, the famous war correspondent, himself a resident at the same hotel. He was also awaiting transportation to North Africa. After a while he gathered up members of the group to show them where "the action" was. It was later obvious to the men that he knew his way around Natal.

In defense of the young pilots of Panama, it should be stated that there was not a lot to do in Natal, since they had already seen the sights during the day. So they followed this famous world traveler to a most exotic, shall we say, "USO house" in the dark sector of the city, a three- or four-story building called the American Bar. It backed up to the waterfront and was not a place frequented by the upper crust.

From the street the men could hear the boisterous activity on the top floor, which they were informed was the dance hall. The rest of the floors had convenient rooms where ladies kept their personal effects and conducted other business as well.

The party worked their way up a flight of dimly-lit stairs, the air heavy with the aroma of a place lacking in sanitation. After several more flights of stairs, walking over and around bodies of various descriptions sitting and lying on the steps, they broke out into a crowded smoke-filled room on the top floor. The scene could have been put right into a Hollywood movie. There were people of every description, male and female, including officers and enlisted men of the various Allied nations. It really was not a very comfortable place to be, Cotton recalled.

The party worked their way across the crowded dance floor to a vacant table.

"Definitely not a Chanel No. 5 crowd," Olsen remarked, as they sat down and ordered a round of drinks. They had scarcely received their refreshments when some fellow staggered over and proceeded to make a nuisance of himself, whereupon Reynolds slowly rose to a dominant height and proceeded to backhand his opponent clear across the dance floor. Immediately, as if they had been waiting all evening for the cue, the crowd erupted into a swinging melee.

"I figured that discretion was the better part of valor," Tom later recalled, "so Olsen and I decided that we would adjourn to the hotel veranda." They literally crawled toward the exit, trying to maintain as low a profile as possible to avoid any flying missiles. Going down the stairs taking several at a time, they managed to build up considerable acceleration before hitting the street, which was fortunate because surprisingly, the lethargic occupants of the stairway had also come to life and were trying to get in on the act.

Making their hasty exit up the waterfront street toward a lighted section of the city, Tom cast a furtive look over his shoulder and saw people crashing through glass windows on the top floor and heard them splashing into the water several stories below. They left without Reynolds. Apparently he was still back there enjoying himself.

Bright and early the next morning the men were rousted out and informed that a "clipper ship" had arrived and they were scheduled to leave on the return flight. By now each man was down to about forty-five pounds of accumulated government-issued equipment. As they boarded the plane, there sat Quentin Reynolds looking none the worse for wear. He just grinned, as if to say, "You missed all the fun, but there will be a couple more stops along the way."

The twenty-hour nonstop flight to Africa was uneventful with the exception of the failure of a load of fresh eggs to make it through a stretch of rough weather. Each man had a private stateroom so they really traveled first class. At midnight the clipper landed at Fisherman's Lake in Liberia with a hull full of weary travelers and a bunch of scrambled eggs. Olsen later recalled their arrival:

> It was black as hell. It was close to one o'clock and raining by the time we got separated from the clipper and found our way to the

barracks next to a little jungle airstrip. We were told not to get too comfortable because we were going right back out again if the weather cleared.

Even though it never cleared, we found ourselves assembling near a fully loaded C-47, which had been flown over by the Air Force from Accra. It was parked at the very end of the runway. From what I could see, it wasn't much of a field. It had been cleared out of the jungle and had tall trees around it. The base of the short strip was soggy and a metal mat had been placed over the surface of the entire length of the runway to stabilize the soft sod for takeoffs and landings of the heavy aircraft. The pilot, a full colonel, came over to talk to us. "You got to lighten up. We are already twelve hundred pounds overloaded," he said.

Cotton and I looked at one another and then at the plane. I noticed that the colonel had parked it carefully with the main wheels just on the very edge of the metal mat with the tail sticking out somewhere in the jungle, completely off the runway. I thought of the words of an old pilot who said there was nothing less useful than the runway behind or the altitude above. This old bird colonel was definitely putting every inch of available runway in front of him for the short-field takeoff. We had come a long way and were getting a little tired.

There is nothing like a midnight transfer out in the middle of nowhere to ruffle your feathers, and I could hear a few muffled sentiments as the eleven of us threw away all of our GI equipment, gas masks, rifles, even our .45s. We threw away everything except our clothes and we stripped them down to the bare essentials. Just before boarding, I took one last look at the tail of the plane stuck into the jungle and threw away my camera.

Inside there was little room for us to sit down. There was a tremendous amount of cargo and ammunition aboard. We no sooner got squared away in our seats when we felt the left engine start. I was looking out at the rain when the right prop began to turn. Then, boy, he revved 'em up. The old colonel, I thought, was never going to stop revving. The sound was so deafening, one couldn't hear himself shout. He must have held those engines wide open for fifteen minutes before he turned the brakes loose. He wanted to make damn sure they would get him over the trees at the end of the runway.

We started to roll. In a moment the tail came up as the plane raced down the runway on the two front main gears, splashing through puddles of water and soft earth. We were sitting with the plane in a normal horizontal position only a brief moment when the tail abruptly lowered at the moment of truth just before lift-off.

I'm sure that if holding one's breath is of the slightest benefit in weight reduction, the eleven of us made quite a contribution as the old gooney bird groaned and flexed its wings near the very end of the runway.

Weight of the cargo transferred from the wheels to the wings, and I not only saw but felt them flex as the C-47 struggled to become airborne. I looked out my window and saw the tops of the trees pass uncomfortably close to the underside of the wing as we just barely cleared the jungle.

Olsen looked at Cotton and managed a faint smile and chuckled to himself as Tom briefly closed his eyes in an upward glance and brushed his nose with the side of his forefinger. They were close friends now, Cotton and Olsen, and as in close formation flying they seemed to communicate without actually speaking.

Still the men did not know the route they were taking, or for that matter, the certain destination. They had an idea they were going to North Africa, and this proved to be right—eventually. The first leg of the African tour, however, took them to Accra on the southern edge of the Gold Coast, the plane making frequent quick stops, letting off and taking on passengers. It was a mail run until an engine was lost en route. At one time they were going to ditch the airplane in the jungle, but they threw out quite a bit of baggage and mail and so were able to remain airborne and continue.

At Accra they boarded a plane of a little more sophistication, a C-54 (or DC-4) with British markings. It carried a couple of high-ranking British officers, one of whom was Gen. Jan Christiaan Smuts, "The Lion of Africa," who was on his way to North Africa. This flight, which later terminated at Khartoum in Sudan in the upper northeast corner of Africa by the Red Sea, made several stops. Two of the stops were British outposts, one at Fort Lamy and the other at El Fasher, which Quentin Reynolds knew extremely well.

While en route over the flatlands of Africa, General Smuts called Olsen forward and asked him if he was interested in Africa. Olsen remarked "Yeah," in that slow southern drawl of his which meant, "Well, not particularly." But Smuts continued anyway:

We are going to drop down and fly over one of the most interest-ing sights in all of Africa, a huge pigmy village. I find it fascinating —those little people are quite clever. They are extremely resourceful in that they travel out in all directions from this huge village in hunting parties like spokes in a hub, searching for food. They are quite careful, however, not to overtax the nearby game, causing it to flee the area and thus become out of reach.

They march out some distance, then hunt on the return trip. Therefore they do not have to carry their game as far. Quite frankly they are cannibals when necessity dictates. When game is scarce or nonexistent, they hunt neighboring tribes in the same manner, killing the elderly and leaving the younger ones to repopulate. They are careful not to disrupt or frighten the other villages to a point of driving them away.

Charlie became more interested and upon returning to his seat he saw what appeared to be miles and miles of thatched straw huts scattered in all directions as far as he could see, but not a single pigmy. They must have remained out of sight, fearing the sound of the low-flying four-engine plane.

Arriving in Khartoum, General Smuts continued to North Africa, but the pilots remained for a few days until they could get a flight over the Red Sea to Aden on the southern coast of Saudi Arabia. From Aden they flew along the southern coast of the Aden Sea, then out into the Arabian Sea crossing the Tropic of Cancer. They landed at Karachi, India, which is now part of Pakistan.

New P-40s shipped from the States were being assembled and test-flown at Karachi before being ferried by transit pilots to various places where the Tenth Air Force was stationed as well as over the Himalaya "Hump" to China.

On March 28 Tom Cotton wrote his grandmother:

We arrived this afternoon at a place called (CENSORED) somewhere in India. The only consolation is should I continue any further, I will be getting closer to home instead of the usual, farther away. This isn't a bad place, no fighting or trouble, except for the heat during the day and the cold at night. There is a lot of desert country with camels, caravans, etc. I don't know how long we will be here; but this is the first opportunity to write.

At Landhi field, Cotton and Olsen caught up briefly with Jim Anning and G. K. W. Johnston, III, who had somehow managed to get ahead of them on the trip over from Panama. But their reunion did not last long, for Anning was soon to fly out in a C-47 for Kunming.

Meanwhile Cotton and Olsen were delayed and given the annoying task of test-flying some of the newly assembled P-40Es. The problem was that their qualification records had not yet caught up with them from the Canal Zone. When informed of their assignment and learning that he and Cotton were to be subjected to a basic indoctrination course on the "new fighters" being assembled there, Charlie was heard to utter something about a snafu. The company commander was not taking any chances with transit pilots like Cotton and Olsen. Without the proper P-40E qualification papers, he felt it was safer for him to assume the two were inexperienced fighter pilots fresh from the States. Cotton later recalled:

> They had some personnel to put us through this so-called "transition" which consisted of reading the book and getting into the airplane. We protested and told them that we could fly a P-40, but they didn't choose to believe us. Olsen was somewhat annoyed by the time we got to the parked planes and had picked us a pair. I noticed they were simply the later "E" model P-40s which had some electrical modifications in the cockpit. Olsen, rather disgruntled, had his head in the cockpit of the next plane over from me when the young flight officer in charge began to speak to the group.

"Now, men," he began, "these are new model P-40s. . . ." From Charlie's cockpit came the remark, "I only see two more switches!" The flight officer continued, for all intents and purposes unaware of Charlie's running commentary on his talk. He gave the group specific instructions to go up and make gentle banks and turns—just to feel the new ship out. He also stated they should come in not lower than a thousand feet over the desert and to lower the landing gear on the final and so forth—very basic instructions. When he had finished he walked over to Tom Cotton's plane. Tom recalled:

> I listened to his discussion of the circuit breakers, being quite interested in the newer model, while at the same time sort of keeping my eye on Charlie. Charlie was explosive and high-strung, and I knew what was going through his mind. He was getting fidgety and wanted to go fly as it had been a long time since we had had a pair of fighters up.

To put things in proper perspective, however, it should be stated that since Olsen and I had thrown all our uniforms away, we had previously gone into town and acquired a couple of beautiful uniforms—bush jackets, shorts, embroidered wings, and jungle helmets. It didn't appear to bother anyone as we seemed to be enjoying civilian status anyway. Yet I guess it must have been a little difficult to take either of us seriously.

When the flight officer finished with me and started over to Olsen, I knew what was going to happen. Before he got his mouth open I heard Olsen say, "I don't care. Just show me where the damn master switch is." Slightly annoyed, the flight officer replied, "All right, there it is! Now go out and kill yourself."

For a fleeting moment Tom wished that the flight officer had not said that to Olsen because he knew this was the beginning of trouble. Yet by the time Tom managed to pull a couple more inches of slack out of his seat belt and brushed the side of his nose, that devious little smile reserved for such occasions had already crystallized.

They took off and Cotton flew wingman to Olsen. It was just understood that he would. It was like in Panama. They were an element again, a team. As they climbed out from the dusty field, Cotton tucked it in tight. He recalled later:

> It was great to be back in the air, master of a fighter. Olsen and I had been pretty hot pilots or at least we thought we were, having had all that extensive combat training in the Canal Zone in P-40s.
>
> We went over the desert and got to doing our regular Panama routine. After a few loops and stuff, I felt confident to tuck it in even tighter. Now our wings were overlapping, with my left wing just behind the trailing edge of his right wing, and he could have almost reached out of his cockpit and touched my wingtip. The wingman in this position doesn't have much chance to see what's going on when he is in real tight. He just follows the leader and with a guy like Olsen that can take some doing.
>
> In a little while, I did notice that we were getting down sort of close to the ground, which didn't come as a complete surprise. I glanced up ahead and saw this little fighter strip coming up rather swiftly and by now we were on approach at about three feet off the ground going like hell. Then Olsen gave this little signal.

Black smoke belched from twenty-four short stacks and Karachi sand whipped into turbulence in two long parallel swaths. At the same instant both fighters rolled inverted in remarkable precision, Olsen to the left and Cotton to the right, so they could "better inspect the strip for pot marks and imperfections, and to just dust it off before landing."

After a short distance down the field, inverted to assure themselves that the field was safe for landing, they rolled back over and climbed out to prepare for their usual landing. Cotton continued:

> I tucked it in on the climb-out, and as we came on around we both retarded our throttles, letting our airspeed bleed off. Back on short final came another signal from Olsen, and we both slow-rolled again and as we did we popped our gear and flaps and landed. It was a rather snappy procedure, if I do say so myself, and you had to have your head up. Besides, we felt sort of obligated as we knew that our close formation Panama routine must have attracted some attention down on the ground. As we taxied up to the flight line, we found that what we had attracted was the CO, who came screaming out in a jeep just as we shut down our engines. He got us up before the gathering and really chewed us out, wanting to make examples of us. He told us all the danger we'd placed ourselves in and stated that our planes were too valuable for this "smartass" type of flying. He then turned to Olsen and asked him point blank, "Olsen, didn't you see the black scepter of death riding on your wing tip?" Olsen replied, "No sir, that wasn't the black scepter of death. That was Tom Cotton."

With this the CO lost control. As the group burst into laughter, he threw his swagger stick to the ground and stomped off. Olsen and Cotton found out later that he had gone straight to his office to cut their transfer orders.

April 4 was a day that was much more typical of their stay in Karachi, as Tom Cotton's letter to his grandmother that day shows.

> Dear Grandmother,
> I asked the first sergeant a while ago what day it was. First he said it was Sunday, which I knew; but then he said it was the fourth of April and this is unbelievable. Time is very hard to keep track of when there is no change in climate.
> Right now it is pretty hot. I have not seen much of interest so far. We are not in a town so all the mysteries of India are still hidden as far as we are concerned. Not much to talk about as people here

don't talk much about anything. I doubt that I will be in this spot long but cannot say as of yet. No mail has reached us now for over a month. The magazines are four or five months old so we do not know what has happened. One thing, the food is much better. We all got a slight case of diarrhea some time ago, but are over it now.

Some new Army nurses arrived a short time ago so we have a few parties and some social gatherings. The distance between the two camps makes it difficult so we only see them once in a while. All in all everything is rather dull at the present.

Tom

Thirty-five years later, one of the pilots who was present at that first "social gathering" with the nurses expanded on the subject:

It was in the spring of 1943 that the seaport city of Karachi, India, received a shipload of P-40E fighter aircraft destined for combat in eastern India and with the Fourteenth Air Force in China. From the boat, these plane parts were transferred east to a nearby Landhi air base where they were assembled and scheduled to be flown to their final destination by American fighter pilots. These pilots had just recently arrived from the Panama Canal Zone. Nearly two months in transit had begun to tell on them. Little or no actual flying had left them exceedingly restless, a situation which was compounded by the desert heat and the boredom of their existence. This inactivity breeds a devil—he was becoming quite evident at Landhi.

The Karachi officers' mess was as formal as its gardens surrounded by the high white stone walls. Thirsty fighter pilots soon found that the elite members of the mess frowned heavily on their presence in the building. Quite improper and out of place were these uncouth interlopers with their poor dress, coarse language, and equally coarse actions, the officers thought. The feeling was mutual as the young pilots anxious to reach combat could not stand the pomp and ceremony of those officers with their swagger sticks, neatly pressed shorts, handlebar mustaches, bravely fighting the war at mess over tea and gin tonics.

The oppressive heat from the nearby desert made tempers flare and very soon the fighter pilots moved out to their own little converted hotel on the eastern outskirts of town near the desert. The group had hardly settled into their rooms when word came that a boatload of American nurses had just arrived in Karachi and would be detained there awaiting their assignments. It was the next best thing to going into combat, or maybe better—this word that female companionship was within reaching distance. Moth-eaten paperbacks were quickly laid aside as the group scrambled to make the quarters presentable. Obviously, these new nurses must be given a welcome reception, and the Landhi ex-Panama pilots were going to do it! Perish the thought that these young lovelies should ever be lured to that unbearable, unspeakable officers' mess within the city.

Two of the more diplomatic and probably better dressed pilots were dispatched immediately to extend the invitation and arrange transportation. Others eagerly applied themselves to the preparations. A large aluminum GI mess tub was to be the punch bowl. Many bottles of orange gin and other spirits were stirred in vigorously with peach slices and ice and soda water. One pilot casually noted that the final mixture was beginning to dissolve the inner lining of the tub, but his fears were quickly put to rest by a friend who said, "Hell, that's not going to hurt anybody." Roommates were tossing coins to see which one would have to move his bed out of the individual rooms to the long porch or nearby desert. This was a precaution made in case either should wish to converse more privately with his anticipated guest. An old windup phonograph and some badly bent records would furnish the musical background. No detail was overlooked as the dining room was magically converted into an entertainment center.

Heavy engine noise accompanied the return of the two pilot envoys. They had requisitioned a snorting half-track desert vehicle, and it was now completely filled with singing U.S. nurses. Heaven and its angels had arrived. The half-track's motor, now drowned out by the noisy exchange of greetings, was hardly half unloaded when it became horribly evident that the new guests far outnumbered their hosts. With no ready solution to this problem, the pilots suggested that everyone proceed with much haste to the festive hall where all problems would be solved by human nature.

And so it went far into the night past the promised time when all the girls were supposed to be returned to safety. The phonograph had long run down. The bright desert moon silhouetted many human-like forms weaving about over the sand, some by twos and many singles, all wandering out in the night. The moon was gone and the sun was yet to light the skies when some unnamed pilot realized that this harmless, well-intended social event could well turn into a military incident should not the guests be returned to their ranking housemother posthaste. Unfortunately, when a count was taken at the hotel many were missing. The combination of the happiness, drinks, and possible sadness of being one of those not chosen by a pilot had led many individuals out into the night. The half-track was placed into immediate service for this important search and return mission, with its searchlight manned by one pilot and another gearing the tracks around the dune.

It was on this last rescue mission that the half-track having returned most sick or far-too-gone-to-care victims, rounded a sand dune and caught one of the pilots and his well-endowed companion in a form of mortal combat. Face to face they sat in this little wind-carved theater. He was vigorously attempting to remove her slacks from below while she equally vigorously was trying to recover them with a firm, strong hand on her belt. The violent tug of war oscillated between down and up and every "up" tug not only recovered her objective but also added many pounds of drifting sand into her waistline. When it became evident that the struggle was no longer private, in fact was literally in the spotlight, the last two remaining missing persons were loaded aboard, one very disgruntled pilot and one very much suddenly overweight Florence Nightingale. All accounted for, the mission was accomplished and all returned to point of origin.

If the success of the reception could have been judged by the immensity of the following two-day hangovers, it was the greatest in the history of Landhi air base. Fortunately or otherwise, the word got out, plane assemblies were speeded up, and orders were quickly written to send this group of unwanted pilots off on their way. To specifically identify individuals in this escapade is impossible since the author also had his first cup of that Ching Pao juice that night.

Landhi field was nothing but a flat airport with lots of modern-looking buildings, their floors raised about eighteen to twenty inches above the ground among clumps of cactus and white sand. It was a mile or so to the ocean. During the day the men continued to receive and service all the P-40s arriving at the field. They checked them out, making them combat-ready, and ferried them over the Hump. But Chennault could not get enough of them since the Tenth Air Force was also collecting pilots and planes. Yet most of the planes Olsen and Cotton saw made it to China. As planes became available, some of the pilots would ferry them to places east. Consequently, the Panama group began to break up, with most of them making it to Kunming before Charlie and Tom.

Occasionally a combat pilot would come through on his way back to the States or to pick up a new plane to fly back to Chennault.

They would explain to the new fighter pilots what the Japanese could be expected to do in combat and warn them about various things, adding that they would find out more when they too got to China. Olsen remembered meeting an AVG pilot at Landhi on his way back to the States. "He told me he bailed out and his parachute opened the last second. As he hit, he drove his shinbones right through his kneecaps. Besides that, he was on fire and the cartridges started going off in his backpack." In the meantime, the instructors gave the men silhouettes of different Japanese planes to look at. Olsen remarked to Cotton as he halfheartedly examined a model that he would like to see the real thing.

Olsen later recalled highlights of his stay in India:

Actually, life was not bad at all at Landhi field. There were about twenty excellent cooks to feed the dozen of us. It was impossible to eat all they put before us. We looked rather insignificant in a mess hall designed for three hundred. The cooks put a platter holding fifteen or twenty steaks, ten chickens, several kinds of dessert—strawberry shortcake, pie, cake, ice cream, and milk. You could eat yourself to death.

One of the mataharis turned one of his castles into a club for us. We could drink and dance, and everybody spoke the King's English. It wasn't like being in a foreign country at all. It was more like being at home or better yet, the Riviera. A couple of pilots went out in the blazing sun on the ocean and took off their shirts. They quickly became hospital cases. The next day all of their skin came off. No way to wear a harness and parachute with that kind of sunburn. So from then on the commanding officers said anybody that got sunburned automatically went to the brig.

So we played poker instead. There was this old Hindu that would walk around every night with his oil lamp and club in hand. We didn't know what he was doing there in the middle of the desert, a million miles from nowhere with no visible enemies. Finally we called him one night and asked him why he was walking around with this club. He said he was trying to keep the snakes away so they wouldn't come into the barracks. "What kind of snakes?" we asked. He said cobras.

"Wait a minute!" I said. "You can't tell me there is a cobra out there! All there is out there are acres of white sand with one clump of cactus about as big as a washtub and over there another big clump about as big as six washtubs, nothing else, not even a blade of grass. Here we are, sitting on a cement pad. We have a screen door with windows and there aren't even any insects. Just how many snakes do you think there are around here?"

"Plenty!" he said.

I said we would give him a rupee if he could find one. "How long do you think it will take to get a snake?" I asked him.

"Not long," he answered.

"If you get one, we'll give you a rupee and if you get more than one, we'll give you five rupees," we told him. He left rather quickly. It seemed as though we had a deal.

He didn't walk more than thirty feet away to the first cactus, and we watched him poking around with a stick. We heard a bunch of thrashing, pounding, and banging. And pretty soon he comes back with a great big snake about five feet long. It was two inches around, dirty-looking, blackish-brown in color. It wasn't a cobra, we thought. Anyway, it didn't look like a cobra to us.

"That's no cobra," I said.

"Oh yes it is!" the Hindu replied, taking the head and spreading the hood. As he stretched the skin, two butterfly eyes appeared on the back side of the hood. We gave him a couple of rupees and he left. In about fifteen or twenty minutes, however, he was back with more snakes, waiting for his money. He liked the deal. We said we had enough.

Our latrine was about a block or two away from our barracks. We would go walking over there in the pitch dark and sometimes due to laziness would just go over to one of the cactus clumps instead. This was up until the old Hindu enlightened us as to what was lurking in those cactus clumps. The cobras remained in the shade out of the direct sunlight during the day, coming out only during the cool of the night. The direct sun would kill them in a few minutes. To be sure, we were not pussy-footing around at night in our drawers anymore. We were careful where we walked, using a Coleman lantern and went all the way to the latrine the few nights we stayed after that.

On April 19 Cotton wrote his grandmother:

This week just the same as last week. No mail and very little to do. I am enclosing a picture of myself and two other friends that was taken here. The one in the middle, Olsen, has been with me since we were in Tampa, Florida, some time ago. Epperson, the one on the other end, is Olsen's roommate, or rather was. He has more than since moved on since we arrived. I also expect that we will be moving out sometime soon, possibly to China, Burma, or other parts of India. No one seems to know.

On April 29, 1943, Cotton and Olsen, and their remaining associates were transferred briefly to the Tenth Air Force. They were sent via P-40s to Dinjam in Assam Province in the northeastern corner of India near the foot of the Himalayas on the Brahmaputra River near Tibet.

Back on the ground at Dinjam, Olsen and Cotton found that the cactus clumps at Landhi were not the only place pilots had to watch out for the cobras. Olsen later recalled:

At Dinjam we had to walk from the barracks through some tea fields to get to the jeep's parking area. From here they would drive us to the airfield in the valley where the planes were parked. The tea fields were so dense that you couldn't see the ground where you walked and the bushes and shrubs were about waist high. During the day you could grope your way through the areas that had recently been picked and could see the ground and watch where you walked. But at night, if you were late coming back from the airfield, you couldn't see where you walked.

We were vulnerable to the cobra from waist down. We heard stories about a big cobra dropping a woman picking tea the day before we got there. Later two other workers also got knocked off. One doesn't walk very far after a cobra hits. We read statistics in the *World Almanac* and we figured with those odds at least one of us was going to get hit. We didn't. I was reluctant to walk through the tea field at night though, and didn't want to do it any more than I would want to walk through a Louisiana swamp at night with my eyes closed.

We were in Dinjam five days though it seemed like a month. Every day was the same. I remember the first one especially. Early in the morning they took us out to the hardstand, which consisted of big pieces of rock covered with gravel and sand. The plane was parked on the stand; otherwise it would sink into the sand. There was a little ramp to the runway and nothing else on the field. The planes were spaced about three miles apart to where you couldn't see the next plane. The jeep driver would drop me off before daybreak. He gave me an old book or magazine to read and a canteen of water.

We were briefed. When daylight came, we were to get into the planes, crank them up, and check them out. Also, we were to turn on the radios to be ready for alert and just leave 'em on. I was one of the first pilots out of the jeep that morning and got to my plane about thirty minutes before daylight. Man it was cold!

There were about two flights up there for a group of about eight or ten in my squadron, so there was a number of planes scattered about but out of sight. I was so cold that I got right in the plane and started the engine, warmed it up, turned on the heater, and stayed inside until the sun eased over the horizon and it got daylight. Then it started getting hot and I got miserable again. I left the radio on, climbed out of the plane, and crawled under the wing into the shade. The sun moved pretty fast and as the shadow of the wing moved, I would have to keep changing positions in order to be protected from the direct sun.

A little later in the morning the blinding glare became so intense I had a hard time finding enough shade to keep from scorching. It seemed like the time out there was a hundred hours. I'd look at my watch and it would say ten o'clock in the morning. What seemed like fourteen hours later, noon would come. About ten till one, I would see a great dust storm as in the distance the jeep swept the sand into a cloud of dust. The driver pulled up and said, "How is it going?"

"I'm cooked. It's a hundred degrees in the shade and I'm getting sunburned."

"Put a handkerchief over you, or a towel," he said.

"I don't have any," I answered.

"Bring a sheet or something with you tomorrow," he said. He gave me a sandwich wrapped in wax paper and a cup of tea. He asked if my canteen still had water in it and then said good-bye. The dust storm followed him on to the next plane. That was it.

I stayed there all day, and just before dark, I saw the turbulence come up again. This was repeated every day. The jeep would come up with two pilots sitting in there and I would join them. Maybe a mechanic would jump out and do something to the plane; but he would soon be back on the jeep. We would go down a hill and pick up another guy. We would get to the edge of the tea field about dark and then have to walk across it.

We always made it through the tea field as quickly as possible, since it was a scary situation every time. As soon as we got to the barracks we would shower to cool off, eat, shoot the bull, maybe play a few hands of cards, and go to bed. Next morning at four o'clock we would get breakfast, cross the tea field, get into the jeep again, and go to the planes.

I got off the ground only one time. I was going through my morning ritual under the wing, trying to follow the shade when the radio cracked, "Squadron. Let's go! We got a group of unknowns coming in from the south." There was nothing spectacular about the takeoff, just a lot of dust, and I climbed to about five thousand feet. I saw the rest of my squadron below as I circled. Then I got to looking around to see where the hell I was. I had never been off in that desert before. We all looked around but never made contact with the unknowns. They must have turned back.

Earlier at eighteen thousand feet in that same air space a few days back, Jim Anning and company were bound for Kunming in the cargo section of a C-47. Jim had been freezing to death for the last six hours, alternating between standing and sitting in a bucket seat which had not exactly been designed by an orthopedic surgeon. The seat was simply a canvas web about eighteen inches wide attached at both ends with enough slack to accommodate one's posterior extremity and in a short time capable of inflicting excruciating pain.

The gooney bird had been bucking strong headwinds flying over the Hump, and the normal five-hour flight was approaching seven hours. At that altitude the interior was cold and uncomfortable, and the sustained lack of sufficient oxygen in the rarefied air had most of the passengers now retching in dry heaves, having long since vomited the contents of their stomachs. A couple of the young GIs had already given up even the ghost of self-respect and were lying in vomit on the cargo floor retching in agony. Jim felt sorry for them, but he wasn't in too good a shape himself though he had not vomited. As he watched the vomit collect into a small stream and trail towards the nearby cargo doors where it was being sucked through a crack into the slipstream, he remembered someone telling him earlier that one ship had to turn around and go back to Dinjam because it could not overcome the strong head winds. He thought that some of the GIs would die or at least suffer permanent brain damage from lack of oxygen if they did not land soon.

Finally, after over seven hours of misery, they landed at Kunming, and the plane taxied off the runway. Anning recalled, "I remember that the only ambition that I had at the moment was to get off that goddamn airplane. I remember one of these guys had actually fallen out of the plane when they opened the cargo door—I mean, just fell out. Some of them were hugging the ground, no humor intended. It was pathetic. Three or four of them said they'd never leave China if they had to go by air. Poor kids, there was no way out except by air."

The next morning, Anning wandered down to the Seventy-fifth Fighter Squadron alert shack to meet the alert pilots, sprawled over the furniture taking it easy. There was no one there to assign him yet so he wandered out to inspect one of the war-weary P-40Bs which the squadron had inherited from the AVG. He climbed up on the left wing and slid back the canopy and looked into the cockpit. There was an aroma of human sweat. It surely showed signs of human habitation all right—worn places on the throttle quadrant and rudder pedals where hours and hours of boredom punctuated by moments of sheer terror were literally ground into the bare metal. There was a standing joke about these old AVG planes—their engines were so worn, it went, that a gentle breeze would windmill the props.

"Hey, Anning," came a voice.

Jim turned and saw a familiar face, it was a Sergeant Wilson whom he had known in the States. Wilson was accompanied by a young "one striper" named Goldsmith, and the two were introduced by Wilson. As the men were talking, pilots suddenly started running for their planes to scramble for takeoff.

"That's strange," said Wilson. "Kunming hasn't been attacked in a long time, since the AVG was here. Come on, we'd better get to the slit trenches over by the wind tee."

The three of them, accompanied by another pilot named Wood, headed for the shallow trenches near the end of the runway. Jim noticed how the place had come alive with people running to battle stations or for the slit trenches. When they arrived near the wind tee, Jim took up a position next to a Chinese guard in an old yellow uniform shouldering a rifle with a long fixed bayonet. He was already standing in his trench. He noticed the guard grinning at him, he thought as a gesture of recognition, until he stepped into his slit trench. It had been used as a latrine by one of the Chinese. Jim stood in the shallow trench with Goldsmith nearby. Wilson and Wood were a little further down. Just then a truck full of Chinese soldiers drove up, and a couple of men jumped out and started for the wind tee. They were going to carry it off the field so the Japanese bombardiers would not be able to see which way the surface wind was blowing in calculating their bomb drops. Someone had just given the Chinese guard standing next to him a cigarette, and Jim lit it for him. Anning later recalled what happened next:

> I heard a noise, the whistle. It was just a reflex, I went down in the slit trench, crap and all, just as the first bomb went off a few feet away. Shrapnel hit Goldsmith square in the chest and he fell in on top of me. Wilson and Wood were also hit as the three of them had been standing when the blast occurred. It blew my hat off and about thirty feet down the runway. It was the first in a string of bombs that fell mostly in the nearby city, killing two to three hundred civilians as well as a few Americans on the field.

Jim was in shock from the concussion and horrified by all the blood and from being pinned down by Goldsmith's body.

> I remember the first thing that I saw when I came up was this soldier from the truck walking around in a daze with no clothes on, just his sandals. The blast had completely torn off his clothing. Then I noticed the Chinese guard lying dead next to me, and for a moment I stared in fascination at the cigarette clinched in his teeth, still burning. Wood had taken some shrapnel in the arm, but Wilson was pretty much OK. And they both came over and we rolled Goldsmith over and saw the torn hole in his chest. We were all pretty much disoriented and confused from the blast. Someone gave me some sulfa pills, and I started shoving them into Goldsmith's mouth trying to make him swallow them. I don't know why we did it—it was stupid. We were desperately trying to help him—until someone came by and took him to the hospital where he died of course.

They took Jim too, since they had noticed that he was in shock and bleeding from one ear. It was quite awhile before Jim wore a smile again—he had felt the nearness of death.

It was not long before Olsen and Cotton joined Anning and the others in Kunming. One day back at Dinjam, Olsen recalled later, "The CO told Cotton, Long, and me not to go out to the hardstand. Long was not in my squadron, but he had come from Panama. 'They got some P-40s coming in, K models. Go check them out. You are

going to China if they are in good enough shape,' the CO said."
Olsen remembered later:

> God, we were tired of that place. I went over there and got into
> one of the planes. It had no flaps, no brakes, and was running rough
> on one mag. "Hell, it's perfect," I told the CO. "Runs like a Rolls
> Royce. Beautiful! Man, that plane's got some power," I lied. Cot-
> ton's plane was about the same. They were new P-40Ks that had
> been assembled somewhere in India or Africa off of a ship, and God
> only knows who assembled them or the shape they were in. Al-
> though they had never been shaken down, we were ready to go with
> them.

The Tenth Air Force wanted men to stay, but Olsen and Cotton
did not want to be delayed anymore. So they gathered up their things
from the barracks, tiptoed through the tea field, and headed for the
operation shack. There was little briefing. Actually they were simply
told that they would not have to navigate and that there were no
good maps to give them. There were no navigational aids for a flight
to China. You just picked up a compass heading from where you
were and went. Olsen continued:

> It was high country en route. And one really had to climb up to
> get over the mountains. One didn't fly over Everest, however. It was
> over twenty-nine thousand feet high and you went south, off to the
> side of it. They told us that it would be very simple to get to China.
>
> They had a B-25 going over to Kunming. He had made the trip
> before and had a navigator on board. All we had to do was to tack
> onto the B-25, which was fast enough for all of us to stay together
> going over. He was to get us over the Hump, down into the valley
> beyond, and line us up where we could make contact with Kunming
> net.
>
> I don't really recall any contact with the bomber pilot until he
> walked up to us and said, "Come on, let's go!" He got up and we
> followed, tacking onto him. Anyway, we went—Cotton, Long, and I
> and a couple more P-40s for a flight of about five fighters and the
> B-25. It was Cotton's birthday, May 2. No one was particularly in
> charge of the flight. We just all went along together. It was a non-
> stop flight as there was no place to land while going over the
> Himalayas.
>
> These mountains were high, but so were we, and even though I

was raised in the Louisiana swamp country, I was not particularly impressed with the view as we passed over. My mind was on what would happen in China, though I was not unaware of what actually lay below me should I have the misfortune of going down. I could see Everest off to the left in the distance, and it was pretty high. Other than that we were looking down at the terrain, and it was not too impressive. We droned along behind the B-25 for several hours, and then we began to notice that he started weaving back and forth, left to right, and then he started circling. With this we knew the damn guy was lost.

We also knew we were in trouble so we gave him a call. He informed us that he was apparently off course as they were not picking up checkpoints and the area was unfamiliar, but they would circle and should be able to pick up something soon. We circled and fooled around with him for thirty or forty minutes and he didn't pick up a damn thing. He had a lot of gas but we didn't and it was critical for us. He could even go back to India if he wanted, but we had already committed ourselves. We passed the point of no return. Fortunately, I was plotting my course all along and I called Cotton and Long. We talked it over and I said I thought I knew where we were.

We knew the sun rose in the east and set in the west and we had been going in the right direction for a long time. But I thought we were a little far north. At this time I calculated we were going to end up in Nanking or somewhere near. If we ever got over this mountain, I thought we should just go and take a little more southerly route. At least we should get over the mountains, I told them. If we have enough gas we can make our destination, and if not we can just bail out and stay together.

The bomber called and said he thought he could pick up the checkpoint soon. We told him we did not have the gas to fool around, and he understood. We probably had only another thirty minutes of gas, and we should have been over the Hump but were not. The bomber pilot said maybe he should go south, pick up the river, and if he did, he could give us a call. We told him we were going to fly southeast like we had been flying when we first started, and he wished us good luck. We flew on and finally let down through an overcast and found we were real low. We checked what maps we had, called in, and we thought we heard Kunming answering. But it was a little town which sounded like "Yunnanyi." It was off to the right as we were north of it and you could see the town off in the distance about ten miles away. He told us that his field was under alert and expecting an attack as Kunming had been under attack earlier, but they thought Kunming was clear. We got on the net and called CL-7 and they answered. It was Kunming. The field had been expecting us much earlier. We did not ask or receive any altimeter settings on the elevation of Kunming field. We told them where we were and that we had broke out and we could see a small field on a river to the right about ten miles. He said that was Yunnanyi.

"If you look straight ahead you will see us pretty soon," he added. We saw mountains first and then the field and beautiful Lake Kunming at the same time. We called them back and told them we were low on gas and were coming in for a landing with no standard approach. Were we clear? We were advised to land towards the lake which was not our preference. That was the opposite direction from our approach, and it would take longer to circle and land than would a direct approach. There was only one runway. I knew Kunming was in the mountains but I didn't realize that it was so high—almost eight thousand feet. To make matters a little more interesting, I wasn't sure that half of the stuff on the plane worked. I wasn't sure that the airspeed indicator worked nor even the altimeter. All I knew was the engine was still running and that I had a stick and bare rudder and that was all I needed to get down. But the field was deceptive as hell and the lakes were deceptive too because they were actually bigger than we thought.

We came running around a little anxious. We didn't go too far out on our turn so that if the engine conked we would put them in the field. We came down fast on the approach and dropped down. When we came in on the downwind leg, everyone peeled off about the same time. Somebody was on the inside of me. He came on in first and then I came in, indicating about 130 mph, which at that rare altitude must have been about 230 mph across the runway. Somebody landed on my right. There was nothing systematic about it. We just tried to get down before we ran out of gas. We came in all together.

I floated for what seemed like forever over the runway and thought I would never get down. I was ready to throw out an anchor or something. I floated for so long and finally got so low that the bottom finally fell out and I dropped the last four or five feet. I had experienced short fields in Panama and I wasn't worried. As the lake came up I decided that if I was too close and was apt to go off the end, I would go ahead and ground loop it. I knew that I could not go around again. I was committed to land on this pass. I had been reading zero on the reserve tank for fifteen minutes, having already exhausted both wing tanks. I taxied up to the operation shack about the same time as Cotton and Long.

Some guys came out of the alert shack, and we saw Anning and some of the other men that we knew who had gone over ahead of us. Someone said, "That was a beautiful landing, Olsen."

"Yeah," I said. "Try it without brakes or flaps sometime." It was a good reunion. Soon we were all grinning and laughing and discussing the whereabouts of the B-25 pilot. We learned later that we beat him over but he landed safely somewhere to the south.

We had finally arrived in China. It was May 2, 1943. After all these months of delays and waiting, we had finally arrived in a combat zone. We knew that we would finally see some action. We had been waiting for this for a long time. I was looking all around to see what Kunming was like. As a matter of fact, all the time I was landing, I was looking the field over.

CHAPTER 7

The Twenty-third Fighter Group: January–October 1943

The year started off with a light raid on Burma on New Year's Day with seven P-40s from the Seventy-fifth escorting eight B-25s to the Japanese base. Nothing was seen except the airport at Sweabo, which furnished one target. The enemy stayed out of sight.

The year's first big hit day came on January 16, when Lt. James W. Little and Lt. Mack Mitchell were on patrol out of Yunnanyi, and the Japanese tried another run on the airport. Little made contact with the enemy and on his first big run against the Japanese tried to "bomb" the Zero. Not satisfied with just shooting the unfortunate enemy with his guns, Little pressed the bomb release button, but the Japanese plane was saved because there were no bombs on the plane. The second Japanese to cross his sights was not so fortunate. It was a head-on pass and the Zero lost. It burst into flames, flipped in the air, and just missed the P-40. With plenty of Zeroes, time, and ammunition left, Little sought another fight and found it, shooting down this Zero, too. On the way home he radioed the soon-to-be-classic phrase, "There are two bastards who will not get home." Lt. Mack Mitchell did not make contact, but what Lieutenant Little left, the Sixteenth Squadron took care of. The score for the day was seven Zeroes and one Japanese bomber to one P-40.

On January 20 it was moving day as the Seventy-fifth changed bases from Changyi to Yunnanyi, and it was a change for the better. The food had been below par at Changyi since the Sixteenth had moved in and overcrowded the place. The bad weather was also getting on their nerves. Moving day was uneventful for everyone except Lt. Mack Mitchell, who was flying a P-40E when the oil gave out. So he bailed out and walked to Kunming with a scratch on one ear.

Six days later Lieutenant Blackstone failed to return from patrol out of Yunnanyi. He "went visiting" and came back ten days later.

Capt. Edmund R. Goss and Lieutenant Gross were to bomb the bridge across the Nam Sang River on February 11. Lieutenant Gross failed to return. Captain Goss witnessed the crash and gave a report.

My first approach to the target was a dry run, and after going over the bridge I started to pull up in a slow climb. Lieutenant Gross was off to my right, and when I started to turn left to go back to the bridge, I saw him starting to dive. I dropped the nose of my ship to ascertain what he was diving on, and I saw a troop convoy of about ten or twelve trucks. Lieutenant Gross was diving on the convoy, and I saw him open fire on the leading truck, which had not stopped. When he began firing, I could see troops disembarking from the rear truck in the convoy. I was approximately five hundred yards behind Lieutenant Gross when I saw a sheet of yellow flame envelop his right wing. He was then about two hundred feet above the ground in a dive of about thirty-five degrees. He made no attempt whatsoever to pull out of his dive before or after his ship caught fire. Lieutenant Gross made no attempt to jump, but was in his ship when it crashed.

Members of the Seventy-fifth ended February with many reconnaissance and gunnery practice runs to Burma. On February 28, the Japanese did a little practice of their own, and Capt. Jesse Carney was their target. They scored a near bull's-eye, hitting his engine. He had to crash-land behind the Japanese lines with a 550-pound demolition bomb attached to his belly rack. The men had always told Jesse that the bomb was not supposed to explode in a crash landing and for some reason he apparently believed them. The three other P-40s left their greetings with the enemy, and the men thought Carney had also been left with them, although he was seen running from the crash.

About ten days later, there were rumors that Jesse was walking out. Twenty-two days after he crashed, he came back with a beard, strange and interesting tales, and a bad case of halitosis from too many eggs. He had traveled by night through the Japanese lines. Once he had unknowingly holed up with two "Japs." They were asleep and he jumped into their dugout for concealment. Jesse wondered why his heartbeat had not waked them up. After a few days on his own, Jesse found some helpful Chinese, who took him to Paoshan, the edge of civilization.

Three days later Capt. Burral Barnum and Lt. John Tucker put in their time over Burma. Captain Blackstone and Lt. Greg Carpenter went over to destroy the remains of Carney's plane. The Japanese gunner was a sharpshooter, and he got another hit on Carpenter's engine. Greg bailed out but cheated the enemy by escaping, though it was not easy. The Japanese who were chasing him and his Chinese helpers shot one of the Chinese. Carpenter then ran a three-legged race trying to hold up the injured Chinese and run. When they were separated, the Japanese tried to bribe the Chinese to turn the American pilot over to them, but their bribe was an insult—eleven worthless Japanese-Burma rupees. Greg counter-bribed with eight-hundred Chinese dollars. The Chinese were good businessmen and showed Greg the way home.

During this time there was trouble among the big brass. General Stilwell arrived at Kunming on the morning of February 28, followed by General Bissell in the afternoon. On the same day, a February 15 issue of *Time* magazine arrived, dropping a bombshell. It aired all the enmity and bitterness among Stilwell, Bissell, and Chennault. The story said, among other things, that Chennault was willfully violating Stilwell's orders in an attempt to bring his ideas before higher authority and that opportunities to destroy key Japanese air bases were being lost through obstruction on the part of General Bissell. General Chennault denounced the article as "complete fabrication."

President Franklin D. Roosevelt personally authorized the reorganization of the China Air Task Force (CATF) as the United States Fourteenth Air Force. The War Department objected, influenced greatly by Gen. George C. Marshall.

For a long time strained relationships had existed between General Chennault, who was supported by Generalissimo Chiang Kai-shek, and General Bissell, who was supported by General Stilwell. Glenn McClure wrote in his book *Fire and Fall Back:*

> More important than the lack of coordination resulting from the 2200-mile distance between General Chennault in Kunming and his immediate superior, General Bissell in Delhi, was the lack of cooper-

ation between the two men which predated the 10 March 1943 activation of the Fourteenth Air Force by many years.

Making matters worse, from Chennault's viewpoint, was the fact that Bissell had been promoted to general one day ahead of Chennault, thus giving Bissell seniority—with all the privileges that such seniority offers. Historians report that Chennault believed that the timing of Bissell's promotion was a conscious act on the part of General Stilwell, the theater commander, to keep him in check. Bissell had been Stilwell's air officer before being sent to Delhi to command the Tenth Air Force.

On the other hand, historians also reported that Generals Stilwell and Bissell feared General Chennault's close relationship with Chiang Kai-shek which could and did, result in out-of-channels communications "over their heads" by virtue of the direct correspondence conducted between Chiang Kai-shek and President Franklin Roosevelt.

Under the reorganization, Maj. Gen. Claire Chennault headed the Fourteenth Air Force, and its original combat components were the same as those of the CATF—the Twenty-third Fighter Group with its Seventy-fourth, Seventy-fifth, and Seventy-sixth squadrons, plus the Sixteenth Fighter Squadron attached, along with the Eleventh Bomb Squadron. In the next fourteen months it would grow to include four fighter groups, two bomb groups, one photo reconnaissance squadron, and a troop carrier squadron.

The mission of the Fourteenth was based on the old policies evolved by the CATF—to defend its own lifeline over the Hump; to ferret out and destroy Japanese aircraft and troop concentrations; to destroy the enemy's military and naval installations in China; to smash and disrupt Japanese shipping along the China coast and beyond and on the numerous inland waterways of China; to destroy enemy supplies and military installations in Indochina, Thailand, Burma, and Formosa; and to encourage Chinese resistance and provide all possible aerial support to their ground forces.

To accomplish this mission, Chennault would take advantage of his interior positions—strategically located air bases forming a rough semicircle stretching from near Ichang to Hankow and down to Canton and Hong Kong with the Japanese concentrated around the rim of the semicircle or beyond. Theoretically such a battle position gave tactical advantage to the Fourteenth, and, if he had had a sufficient quantity of planes, men, and supplies, Chennault could have blasted the enemy out of China. Since this was not the case, however, Chennault had to rely upon jabbing tactics to cause the Japanese as much damage and confusion as limited supplies would permit.

Indeed, to a great extent the story of the CATF in China is a story of supply. The supply problem set the China Theater apart from all others, limiting activity and sometimes even stopping it completely. Every item necessary to maintain and operate an air force had to be flown into China along the five-hundred-mile air ferry route from India over the towering Himalaya Mountains where bad weather and enemy action were a constant threat to success. The situation was such that the Fourteenth never received more than fifteen thousand tons of supplies a month and up to mid-1944, often less than half that amount. Therefore, its limited forces were never more than barely sustained at full operational strength and often they suffered telling shortages of equipment and personnel.

But the disastrous Hump was only a part of the supply line pathway, and Kunming was a long way from America. Every piece of machinery, every American soldier, every drop of gasoline, every bullet and bomb, everything the Fourteenth used from paper clips to blockbusters came over the supply line. From America to the docks of Calcutta was the easiest part, and that included a ten-thousand-mile convoy trip. Calcutta was the second city of the British Empire, a seaport whose docks should easily accommodate American shipping. From Calcutta supplies traveled six hundred miles north to the air bases in Assam Province. In Calcutta acres of jeeps were stored in a park, all ticketed for China. But this did not mean that they arrived there. Warehouse facilities were jammed, and the overflow laid in the open, exposed to the burning sun in the dry season, drenched in torrential rain during the monsoon. All the vehicles and equipment awaited shipment to the north, but there was no road to Assam. So they used oxcart, truck, river barge, railroad, and air transport, and in no set system. What moved by rail one day was reduced to river barges the next. River barges on the Brahmaputra River took forty days for a single journey. The Assam-Calcutta Railroad was not built for heavy traffic. In peacetime it hauled tea crops to the docks and carried planter's supplies back to Assam. But during the war it carried heavy supplies for British, Chinese, and American armies in Burma in addition to material for the Fourteenth in China. China waited for equipment, and waited and waited. Ammunition rusted and rubber hoses rotted while the Fourteenth Air Force patched up and waited for some more.

Broad gauge track began to disappear about 180 miles north of Calcutta on the railroad. Time-consuming transfer to narrow gauge then began. Not even a box of K-rations could be shipped from Calcutta to Assam in the same car. The workers had only one electric crane to transfer the heavy equipment. The rest was exchanged by hand. And then the bottleneck began. Five hours was the average time for twenty-four drums of gasoline to move from broad to narrow gauge boxcars. Even tank cars had different capacities, and their contents had to be transferred. Trucks were transferred by laying planks between the cars and driving them across from broad to narrow gauge.

Then the ferries across the Brahmaputra were the last bottleneck along the line to Assam. One carried personnel and the other rolling stock. Cars were pushed aboard and in less than one hour were on the far bank. Then they were unloaded again and were off to Chabua, three hundred miles away, twenty-six hours on the fastest passenger train, or several days by freight if all went well. At Chabua things began to pick up. The airport and its satellite fields was the great hub of activity in upper Assam. Here the freight was loaded, inspected, classified, and stored. But all China had to fight for the supplies. The fraction of the supplies going to China went in transports, crammed to the fuselage.

Then came the Hump—five hundred miles of the worst flying country in the world. Everything else was easy, compared to the Hump. As one climbed up off the field at Chabua, he could see the dead end of India sealed off by the sixteen-thousand-foot Himalayas. The men had to top these peaks to get to China. To the north were the snow-laden Tibetan peaks, rising up to twenty-five thousand feet. To the south were the Japanese, below barren, frozen wastes and jungle-filled valleys inhabited by headhunters. There is no summer on the Hump. Snow always crowns the peaks. Ice hangs heavy on the clouds. Black monsoon storms sweep up from India, screening the peaks, bringing terrific turbulence which flipped fully-loaded transports on their backs. The worst up and down draft in the world slides around these slopes. Japanese fighters also prowled the Hump, looking for easy game. There was a heavy toll on freight. Casualties among transport groups flying the Hump were often higher than many bomb groups sustained in combat. Many cargoes earmarked for China rusted on these peaks. It was a tough job delivering goods to China—four hours of sweating it out each way, looking for Japanese planes if it was clear and taking chances with the weather if it was not. Then finally the pilot would break out over Lake Kunming, nestled in a broad valley, six hundred feet above sea level—the gateway to Free China. This was the home of the Fourteenth and the back door to Tokyo. It was the end of the line for the Hump pilot. Then he went back to India for another load and the Fourteenth took over.

Kunming was the first base of the Fourteenth. One of the first jobs of its pilots was to defend their airfield and keep the Hump route open, just as their predecessors did. Who were these men who did the job? There were, of course, some of the original "Flying Tigers" of the American Volunteer Group—former Army, Navy, and Marine pilots who came to China as civilians on a strictly business deal. They had been paid five hundred dollars a month in salary and a five-hundred-dollar bonus for every Japanese plane destroyed. In the five months after Pearl Harbor, they got three hundred enemy planes and lost only twelve of their own pilots.

From these original "Flying Tigers," the newly-organized Fourteenth Air Force got some of its planes, a number of its pilots, its insignias, its commander, and a great tradition. The planes were battered P-40s, with .30 caliber machine guns, which would be museum pieces at any other front. The pilots were battle-wise veterans who joined the Air Force as majors.

In the beginning, until reinforcements and more supplies arrived, Chennault and the Fourteenth had to hold operations to limited strikes at the enemy when circumstances permitted. For the months of March, April, and May, the supply situation was so bad that the Eleventh Bomb Squadron operated only six days.

On March 15 twelve B-25s bombed the power plants and railroad yards at Lao Kay, while later in March a single bomber carried out a secret five-hour reconnaissance flight over Mandalay, Burma. Only one mission was flown in April, and that was on April 24, when nine B-25s struck successfully at Namtu, Burma. In May missions were flown on the fourth to Haiphong and on the eighth to Canton. On the latter mission, the squadron suffered its only loss in three months when a B-25 exploded on the bomb run apparently due to premature detonation of its frag bombs.

Though bomber action was reduced as the Fourteenth began operations, fighter action was not. On March 22, Lt. Roger Pryor of the Seventy-fifth led one flight of heavy bombers over Lao Kay. Each plane had a 550-pound demolition fused bomb with a Russian twenty-six-second delay fuse. Direct hits were observed over the target, but the delay must have been for twenty-six days. The bombs were all duds. Evidently someone forgot something—perhaps the ordnance men at Kunming, who loaded the bombs. But the men found out one thing on the mission. Anything bigger than an anthill can be hit by low level bombing.

A couple days later four P-40 pilots tested some "skip bombing," the planes going over the target about fifty feet. The bombs were Russian, the fuses were Russian—twenty-six-second delay fuses. The first two bombers dropped the 550-pounders right on the nose. Lt. William E. Grosvenor was the third man. His bomb hit ten feet from the bull's-eye, but something went wrong and the bomb detonated prematurely. The plane was about forty feet from the action. At first it seemed to continue in normal flight for about five seconds. Then it spun in from about five hundred feet as Grosvenor parachuted. Bill was amazingly lucky that he had not been injured in the explosion even though his plane was riddled. One aileron was blown off, the wing was full of holes, and the plane was burning. When all this was happening, Bill was forty feet from the ground. Once he had survived the initial explosion, only his quick thinking enabled him to escape.

Bill recalled the story in later years:

> Our target was a small radar station. Dive-bombing was not accurate enough, and John Alison, after reading all the military poop, decided skip-bombing was the only answer. Problem was that we were using old Russian bombs and fuses. At twenty to thirty feet, some delay was needed to enable one to escape the blast. Also the military poop stated that many British flyers were killed trying to bail out by turning their planes upside down and were found trapped inside the crashed plane.
>
> We were discussing this problem the night before when Johnny said there must be an answer. Why not bail out on top? The big question was, would one escape the tail vertical stabilizer? The added advantage would be that the ripcord could be pulled immedi-

ately since the pilot would be cleared of the falling plane. There were interesting arguments back and forth.

It was decided the next day that we would skip bomb the target. Our armament officer was so worried about the Russian fuses that he persuaded General Chennault to delay the mission until the afternoon, until the fuses could be tested on our bombing range fifteen miles from Kunming.

Everything seemed to work fine until I went in and the fuse did not delay. I was stunned by the concussion, but luckily the plane was heading up. As my eyes opened, I realized that the wings were full of holes and the engine was on fire. Being so low on the ground, I had no choice but to use Johnny Alison's technique—open canopy, roll stabilizer forward, undo seat belt, jerk stick forward. Since I am lefthanded, I put my right hand on the ripcord. Without Johnny Alison's previous night talk, I would not have been able to think fast enough to escape. The jerk of going out immediately opened the parachute. Three swings and I was down—life saved by John Alison and the armament officer.

As I was gathering up my parachute rather in a state of shock, I felt a gun in my back. I turned around and saw many Chinese with guns jabbering at me. I thought that since we were behind our own lines fifteen miles from Kunming, the plane must have killed some of them, which accounted for this unwelcoming situation. They finally calmed down and I offered them some pipe tobacco and gum and all seemed well at the moment.

Suddenly a jeep roared into view, drove up to me with the driver saying get the hell in. We raced off with the Chinese guns blasting and missing us because of my astute driver. When we were out of range I noticed that he was a high-ranking colonel in the Chinese ground force. He was Gilbert Stuart, an Australian volunteer commanding Chiang Kai-shek's ground forces against the Japanese bandits. Gil Stuart was such an able commander that the Japanese and Chinese bandits had a price on his head. He was spying on the bandits when my plane crashed, and he realized I had landed among them. He knew there was a price on his head and yet drove across country into their midst, risking his life to save an unknown pilot. I had no idea my life was in real danger until he told me that I would have been killed if my small Luger pistol had been seen under my leather jacket.

Johnny Alison met us when we got back to the squadron and said, "Bailing out that way worked, didn't it Bill?" And I answered, "Thanks to you."

There would be no more skip bombing until we had American fuses. No fun walking back three hundred miles in enemy territory. Alison later wrote the Air Force personnel to promote the idea of bailing out on top. I had the opportunity to thank Gil Stuart again for saving my life when he came to our house in Rhode Island with a mutual friend. We saw Gil and Virginia, his wife, many times while they were in the area. He has since passed away, but I will always be grateful to him.

On March 31 the winter lull of the Seventy-fifth was broken when they moved their headquarters to Lingling. On the next day, April 1, 1943, no sooner had the alert crews rubbed the sleep from their eyes than nine Zeroes were plotted by the net. Having had no opposition in this section for some time, the Japanese did not bother to reconnoiter the Hengyang or Lingling airfields. At their leisure, the nine Oscars strafed Hengyang and headed toward Lingling. For the first time, the Seventy-fifth had more planes than the Japanese on a flight, but for some unknown reason two of the nine Zeroes got away. Capt. John Hampshire sighted the first "Jap" and sank it, bringing his victory score to seven. Three other Japanese planes were simultaneously set afire. The fight was called after the first round, for there were no more Zeroes. Five of them were confirmed immediately, and only two of the Japanese flight were plotted to Hankow, where they would be able to tell how they had smashed the Seventy-fifth again.

"Hamp" remained the high man in the squadron by getting this one. Capt. Elmer W. Richardson, Lts. John P. Tucker, Vernon Brewer, and George W. Lee each broke into the scoring with one each. There was so much fighting to get at the Zeroes that too many probables were claimed to list them. But it is probable that the Zeroes that got home never flew again. Tucker got on the tail of one enemy pilot, set him afire, and then fired an additional eight hundred rounds at him for practice. He followed this by doing a victory roll over the field.

Capt. Burral Barnum failed to return. His body was found near his plane, which was entangled with parts of a Zero, indicating that he had a midair collision. This was the only sure way the Zero can down a P-40. Captain Barnum was one of the original members of the squadron, having joined at Hengyang the previous summer.

On April 8, the Sixteenth Fighter Squadron, which had recently moved to Kweilin, ran a successful ten-plane mission at Fort Bayard. During the middle of the month, the Seventy-fourth Squadron was running regular offensive reconnaissance missions along the Burma Road from Yunnanyi.

The weather had been good only for the rice and ducks since April 1, but the Saturday before Easter, April 24, brought a change. The Japanese brought their entire clan this time, but regardless of their numbers, they had courage to come over two hundred miles for a fight when they knew the warning net was plotting all their moves.

This time the high school boys of the Fourteenth were left at home, for all the men who went up were strictly well-educated in aerial combat. Fourteen P-40s intercepted the Zeroes ten miles southeast of Lingling. The ensuing fight lasted for fifty-five minutes over the field and longer on the Japanese planes' way home. The Japanese had a "squirrel cage" working well and it probably saved a few of their skins. This was a defensive tactic similar to the "Luf-berry"—when one of the Zeroes was attacked, the other two or three would try to get a few shots at the attacker. None of the American boys was caught, but it saved a few Japanese lives by preventing the P-40s from staying around too long. "Hamp" jumped his score by two with one Zero and one twin-engine fighter. Maj. Edmund Goss added one more Zero to his total, as did Lieutenant Lee and Lt. Charles Gordon.

A twin-engine plane came down to drop a leaflet the text of which read:

> We express our regrets to you men who have taken great pains to come to the interior of China. We of the Fighter Command of the Imperial Japanese Air Force take pride in the fact that we are the strongest and best in the world. Consequently, we express our desire as sportsmen to hold a decisive air battle with you in a fair and hon-orable manner. We then can prove to you the spirit and ability of our Air Force. With hearty wishes for a decisive battle, Fighter Command, the Imperial Japanese Air Force.

But the Japanese were not victorious that day. They started out with at least twenty-five planes. The Seventy-fifth had fourteen. The Japanese left five of their planes with the Fourteenth. All of the American planes returned home safely.

On April 26, after almost a week of feinting attacks at Yunnanyi and turning away without attacking, thereby forcing defending fighters up to waste limited fuel, Japanese planes came again in toward the base at Yunnanyi. The warning net reported their approach, and then a short while later they were turning back. The defending fighters stayed on the ground. This time, however, the enemy quickly reversed direction again and struck the base, catching twenty P-40s on the field, destroying five and damaging others.

Two days later enemy planes feinted at Kunming in the same way with twenty bombers and as many fighters and then came in to be met by only two P-40s. The alarm came at 11:15 A.M. The warning net had failed and the base did not get the report until five minutes before the bombing started. Casey Vincent was one of the two men who met them in the air. Vincent later recalled:

> I ran out and took off. The bombs started dropping just as my wheels left the ground. I picked up another fighter on my wing and climbed. The Japanese were at twenty-four thousand feet, so we didn't have a chance to catch them.
>
> We then went out to intercept another flight reported to be coming in from Lingling. It turned out to be Johnny Alison's planes who had given chase to the Japanese . . . I saw from the air that a Japanese bomb had hit our Operations Building, which meant our fighters were no longer being controlled. I landed immediately to assess the damage. Col. Don Lyon had been killed. General Glenn had a slight injury from a bomb fragment. Our telephone lines were out . . . Many Chinese were either maimed or killed. And we were just about out of gasoline.

Vincent and his companion along with a high wind were just enough to throw off bombing, and the target was saved a pasting as most of the bombs fell on one side of the main installations. But the ground crews were servicing planes when the first bombs hit. There was little or no time to seek cover and three of the ground crew were killed and many wounded. Little has been said about the ground crews in writings of the past. To civilians these men were the ones who maintained the planes, but such a view does not give them nearly enough credit, for they did much more. "Other than servicing the planes, they sometimes manned the antiaircraft during bombing raids and performed countless other less interesting tasks. This was one day that they performed many of those tasks and the pilots lost some good friends," Vincent said.

The big fight took place a hundred miles southwest of Kunming, led by Col. John Alison, whom the Seventy-fifth still regarded as exclusively its own. The following men scored: Major Goss, one Zero confirmed, one Zero probable; Captain Hampshire, two Zeroes confirmed, two Zeroes probable, two bombers probable; Captain Blackstone, two Zeroes confirmed, one Zero probable; Lieutenant Pryor, one Zero confirmed; Lieutenant Mitchell, one Zero confirmed; Lieutenant Tucker, one Zero probable; Lieutenant Griffin, one Zero confirmed. All of the squadron returned to base safely.

On May 2, the date Charlie Olsen, Tom Cotton, and company arrived at Kunming, others from the Seventy-fifth Squadron flew over Hunan Province. Again they did not have long to wait for the Japanese. At 9 A.M. between thirty and forty Japanese planes were in the Lingling area, but they did not stay long. After the first contact with the American squadron in formation, the Japanese ran for it, though some of them did not run fast enough.

Two Zeroes were confirmed near the field immediately by their fires. Thirty miles northwest of Hengyang one lone Japanese plane was getting away when eight P-40s intercepted him. Lieutenant Gordon went after him alone while the others watched. The Zero seemed like a sitting duck to Gordon, who was still coming up in the pilot's blind spot. He hit the plane, but it did not burn. Instead it reversed its direction and unknowingly, until it was too late, flew into the seven waiting P-40s. With all the shooting at the Zero by the seven, it was lucky that no P-40s were shot down as well. The entire flight played with the Zero until Griffin set it afire, a little reminder to the Japanese that they had written the rules of this game on December 7, 1941.

One group of Zeroes that had not contacted the P-40s was leisurely strafing Changsha on their way home. The Seventy-fifth had sixteen airplanes in commission, manned by seasoned pilots. John Alison recalled later:

Sixteen P-40s with expert pilots against only forty-seven Zeroes seemed to us to be kind of unfair for the Japanese, because in the early days of the war we had often been outnumbered as high as ten to one. On this day we were all in good spirits and anticipated giving the Japs a resounding beating.

I positioned the sixteen airplanes above and to one side of our airdrome at eighteen thousand feet. I don't know what happened to the Japanese formation, but only ten or fifteen Zeroes came forward on reconnaissance. They crossed the airdrome about eight thousand feet below us, and I thought it must be a trap. I waited for a few minutes until reports from the warning net indicated that the rest of the formation was not going to commit itself, and then we attacked. Either my aim was poor or the Japanese pilot I engaged was skillful because I failed to score after expending considerable ammunition.

Everyone scored in the melee. Then five of our pilots assembled on my wing, and I started north to take on the main body of the formation, which according to reports, was retreating toward Hankow. Flight reports told of about five or six Zeroes claimed in the action. Hampshire came up on my wing, reported on a kill, and said I'd find the wreckage one mile off the north end of our runway. And there it was when we went out to investigate. This was Hampshire's sixteenth victory. Although his life was to end a few short minutes later, I was able to confirm his seventeenth victory before a lucky or a skillful shot by a Japanese pilot put an end to his career.

As I led my small formation north there was lots of excitement and chatter on the radio. Hampshire was betting I'd never overtake the Japanese. About a hundred miles north of our airfield we encountered a thunderstorm and let down to about four hundred feet to pass underneath it. I saw three Zeroes hugging the earth ahead and making for home. As we bored in, Hampshire went underneath and pulled up in front of me while I was firing, and we both missed the enemy leader. But his two wingmen, who were tucked in tight, hit the ground simultaneously. It was a spectacular start, and I had been so intent on the three sitting ducks that I missed seeing a larger formation of Japanese above us. They attacked, and there was adequate confusion until it was over a few short minutes later with six Zeroes down. We formed up again to return to base.

When we counted noses, Hampshire was missing. We'd been fighting over the edge of a broad river which emptied into a lake near the city of Changsha. One of our pilots said he'd seen a plane dive vertically into the lake; another one contradicted this and claimed an airplane that looked like a P-40 had landed in the water near the riverbank. There was some confusion as the pilot who saw the aircraft go straight into the water insisted it was a Zero, while the pilot who saw the aircraft land in the water insisted it was a

P-40. Some of the confusion was cleared up shortly after we landed at our own base. I received a message from Chinese command post in the Changsha area which was brief and shocking. Brutally translated into English it said simply: "American pilot landed in river. Hit in stomach, guts running out. Send doctor quick."

I don't have the talent or the understanding to explain the feelings of John Hampshire's friends. One of his most devoted friends was our flight surgeon, Ray Spritzler, who announced that he was going to John's assistance. Someone suggested that we stuff the doctor in the baggage compartment of one of our fighters and let him jump out near where John went down. At this time, and under the stress of emotion, I didn't realize how hazardous such a venture might be. I consented, and we made the doctor as comfortable as possible in the cramped quarters of the compartment, which was not designed to accommodate a human being. The door was removed and a signal arranged between the pilot, Lt. Joe Griffin and Ray to indicate the time to jump. A signal such as wobbling the wings or shaking the aircraft had to be used to enable the pilot and doctor to communicate.

We saw them off, and it was not until they departed into the northern sky where storms had begun to gather that I realized that this wasn't such a good idea and grew truly fearful when a few minutes after their departure we received a second message from the Chinese, saying that Hampshire had died. We tried to reach Griffin on the radio, but electrical disturbances caused by thunder squalls to the north made this impossible.

I spent an anxious hour or so waiting for them to return and finally just at dark we got a report from our warning net that a lone airplane was approaching. At this time we didn't know it, but Griffin had run into severe weather and had been unable to reach Changsha. Griffin was trying to get home before dark, for after nightfall, landmarks on the Chinese countryside vanish, and we had no radio navigation. Also in this part of China there were no utility systems and therefore, no electric lights. Our runway was outlined by a thin row of large pots fueled with tung oil. Their feeble lights would give a pilot the outline of the runway for landing, but they couldn't be seen for more than a mile. We heard what we took to be Griffin's plane in the distance, droning through the dark, and although we tried to reach him on the radio and give him directions, the intensity of the station made this impossible.

Hours passed and no report. I computed the time when they would run out of fuel, and then my heart really sank. I composed a radio message to Chennault reporting that I had lost Hampshire, but I didn't have the courage to tell him I had lost another airplane too and possibly another good pilot and my doctor because of my poor judgment. I decided to wait out the night, in hopes that before morning we would have a report as to where the airplane had crashed and that some miracle had preserved two good friends who were risking their lives for another good friend whom they couldn't save.

Morning came and still no word. Several hours after we had manned our aircraft down on the flight line I decided that I had no alternative but to let Chennault know how stupid I had been. I was composing my report when someone shouted, "Here they come!" and a fighter airplane touched down on the airfield, taxied up to the flight line, swung around, and there was Ray Spritzler's smiling face peering out of the baggage compartment.

Their story was unbelievable. Completely lost and almost out of gas, Griffin decided to abandon the airplane. But just before giving the signal to jump, he spotted a cluster of lights on the ground. Any lights probably meant a village, and Joe reasoned that there might be a telephone there and that, if he circled, this would be reported to the Chinese warning net and at least we would have a fix on the area where they had abandoned their aircraft.

As he circled the lights he noticed to his amazement a long stream of fires flare up nearby. He went over to investigate, and it was apparent to him from the pattern of flames that the Chinese below had set fire to a field and expected him to land. He quickly lowered his landing gear because there was precious little fuel remaining, lined up with the flames, and put his airplane down, not knowing whether there were any holes or rough spots or barriers, artificial or otherwise. To his amazement, he hit a smooth area and the airplane rolled to a stop without incident. When he dismounted, he found himself among friendly Chinese who were overjoyed to see him.

Joe Griffin and the doctor had wandered to the edge of Japanese-held China and came down at a small village whose airstrip had long since been abandoned as a result of the Japanese advance. Apparently the telephones, if there had ever been any, were also abandoned, which accounted for our failure to get any report on the landing.

How the Chinese realized this was one of our airplanes, I will never know, but they are smart people and when they heard the airplane circling overhead they knew the pilot was in trouble. Quickwittedly, they opened a drum of aviation gasoline and rolled it down the center of the airstrip and then set fire to the spilled gas, forming a more than adequate night-lighting system for Griffin's approach. They spent a thankful night with the Chinese and the next morning, after refueling from an emergency cache of gasoline, set out for home.

Soon after his arrival in Kunming, Tom Cotton wrote to his grand-mother:

This letter comes to you from somewhere in China, mainly to tell you I am well and happy although I didn't have time for a birthday party yesterday. In fact I was in the air most of the time and forgot it was my birthday until late last evening and then I was too tired to do anything. The most interesting thing here is the price of things. Coffee and doughnuts are ten dollars. Food is not the best. There are so many things we can't eat unless they are boiled or sterilized. But the natives don't do it and they look awfully healthy.

On May 8 P-40s from the Sixteenth and Seventy-fifth squadrons escorted ten B-25s and a formation of B-24s to Canton to bomb Tin Ho airdrome. Oscars and Nates rose to defend their field, and sixteen were claimed shot down while Chinese intelligence reported eighteen down. The bombing was very good with the main hangar wiped out and black smoke from gasoline and oil fires rising ten thousand feet into the air, visible from fifty miles away. After the Tin Ho raid, the B-24 Liberators returned to flying the Hump to stock material for future missions. On this day Lt. Robert L. Tempest broke into the scoring column with two while Capt. Elmer Richardson and Lts. James Little, Roger Pryor, and John Tucker got one each.

A few days later Cotton again wrote to his grandmother.

It has been my good fortune to be assigned to the best squadron, best food, best beds and best pilots. Most of the fellows I knew before in South America. Things are not too bad except for a few air raids, not too bad except for the first few times. After the novelty wears off, that too becomes a bore. The Japs can't hit much, so we sit around and watch and listen to the evening news broadcast from Japan to learn that we have been completely annihilated. I believe in this war the safest place to be is in the air. Every now and then the Japs bomb a small village and it makes a pretty bad mess. It isn't a pleasant sight to see. The people don't realize the danger or they get hysterical. They all mill around in the streets where several well-placed bombs wipe out everything. It makes us all the madder. I wish some people in the States would see some of the places in this war. There are things they read about but do not comprehend. Nobody knows what it is all about until he experiences the blood, the filth, the shock, and complete wreckage of war.

It was May 13 when Cotton experienced his first combat mission out of Kunming.

I had Bill Bartling's [Bartling was one of the original "Flying Tigers"] old airplane. Being a junior member of the squadron, I got the worst thing. I even used to laugh and say when the wind blew the prop turned around and I was Tail End Charlie. We took off on one of those intercepts. I took off full power right through the gate—that's the word for the end of the throttle quadrant. Then you had a space of about an inch and that was the emergency boost. We took off to about five thousand feet at Kunming. I was trying to catch up with the others, the older guys. I could see Japs all over the place, smoke and flames, like a cover in one of the *Flying Aces* magazines. I couldn't catch up. Then I got to thinking, a good fighter pilot should start looking around, keeping his head on a swivel because you never know. Sure enough, here's a Jap coming up right underneath me. I kicked it up, winged over, and I didn't realize I was riding on the edge of the stall. I never looked at the cockpit. I was just climbing, and the first thing I knew I was in a spin. So I left it in a spin so he wouldn't hit me. He obviously figured he had shot me down, so I decided it was time to get out of the spin. By now I was down to about five or six thousand feet. I had begun to spin at around eighteen thousand. I got a little concerned. A little light went on inside me and said, "Hey, you got that airplane engine on war emergency boost, prop full forward. No way you are going to get it out of a spin that way." I pulled off the throttle and came out right. There I was, alone and didn't know where I was. I had no idea except the airport at Kunming was near a big lake. The flight was gone. I didn't see anybody—most lonesome feeling in the world. I pulled back up. The Jap was probably already painting an American flag on his airplane. And I went and saw the lake at a distance and landed. I hadn't even shot my guns, not once.

The Japanese struck at Kunming again on May 15 with the heaviest raid yet on an American base in Asia. The Seventy-fifth Squadron had again moved back to Kunming, feeling that they were being taken out of the fight. But the Japanese did not give them a chance to feel this way long by bringing thirty bombers and as many Zeroes. The bombers reached the field but dropped their bombs about one mile short of their target. The Americans made contact with them just after the bombs were dropped, but the enemy had become wiser and was at twenty-five thousand feet. For some reason one of the American fighters was ordered to return and gas as if they did not know when they needed gas. This saved a few Japanese, but the other flights accounted for five Zeroes and one bomber confirmed and two Zeroes and one bomber probable. In all, fifteen Japanese planes were shot down by the Twenty-third Fighter Group. Major Goss added another to his score to give him a total of six. Lt. "Poco" Little got one Zero and divided one bomber with Lieutenant Casey. Little became top man by half an enemy plane with a total score of six and a half. Lieutenant Calvert broke into the scoring column with one Zero and Lts. Gordon and Mitchell added one more Zero each to their score.

Although the enemy's bombs missed their mark, a fair degree of damage was done, including the destruction of one B-24 and one B-25. For the second time in three weeks the Japanese had slipped through the usually dependable warning net to hit Kunming. Only the inaccuracy of their bombing had kept the Fourteenth's nerve center from suffering heavy damage.

The purpose of this strike and similar ones in late April was to give support against a Japanese ground offensive launched on May 5 against the Tungting Lake area and the upper Yangtze in western Hupeh Province. The goal of the offensive was to gain control of river shipping in that region. Deploying east and west of the lake, Japanese forces had begun pushing back Chinese troops in the Tungting rice bowl area with drives toward Changsha and the northern bank of Tungting Lake and also across the Yangtze south of Ichang in an area northwest of the lake.

Between May 21 and May 25, the offensive was in its final phase with the Japanese making good gains and still striving to attain air superiority in the battle area by hitting at all American and Chinese bases within range of the fighting. For its part the Fourteenth, strengthened by the arrival of fifty new fighter planes in May, was attempting to help turn back the main drives, bombing and strafing enemy ground positions, fighting off raiders, and attacking every enemy airdrome its planes could reach.

When the fighting along the Yangtze moved out of range of the Fourteenth's fighters at Hengyang in the latter part of May, the Chinese appealed for more air support. As a result, nine B-24s of the 374th and 425th squadrons were deployed at Hsichang near Chengtu. On May 28, the detachment dropped eighteen tons of bombs on the city of Ichang, 70 percent of them landing in the target area and damaging military and supply installations and interrupting communications along the Yangtze River so completely that a Chinese counterattack launched the following day met with complete success. On May 29 gun positions south of Ichang and west of the Yangtze were bombed in support of Chinese ground forces.

The Japanese had started a drive from Tungting Lake in the early part of 1943 with the avowed intention of taking Changsha, the Chinese "rice bin," and Chungking, the provisional capital and symbol of resistance in China. The Twenty-third Fighter Group, in trying to check the drive, was greatly impeded in its operations because much of its effort had to be devoted to protecting its precariously held forward bases. But the men of the Twenty-third bombed and strafed enemy ground positions, fought off enemy raiders, and attacked every Japanese airdrome within striking range.

Japanese plans for the entire operation revolved in large part around the city of Yochow on the northeast corner of Tungting Lake. As a railhead and river port, Yochow served as a collection and distribution point for the enemy forces in the whole region. It also stood as a guardian over rail, river, and lake traffic between Hankow and Ichang. As a result of its importance, the Twenty-third made Yochow its top priority target. On May 28 twelve P-40s of the Seventy-fourth Squadron dive-bombed Yochow while twelve more Warhawks carried out an even heavier attack on that city. In those two raids, the "Flying Tigers" destroyed a locomotive, an entire train, and the Japanese headquarters. In all, about two hundred of the enemy were killed including a lieutenant general who was arriving by train from Hankow to direct the offensive in the Yochow area.

On May 30 Tom Cotton wrote his grandmother again.

Uneventful week. Monsoon season makes it unpleasant. You asked me if I had been in a fight. We make visits on the Japs now and then and sometimes they come over to see us. These calls not being social, are very irregular and done when the least expected. Yes, I expect to be home before the war is over. The largest tour of duty here runs about a year for a pilot. Yesterday we had an unexpected visit from Captain Eddie Rickenbacker, the famous pilot of World War I. He flew here as a special envoy from the secretary of war in Washington. In his talk to the flying personnel, he recounted his experience in the Pacific Ocean when the plane in which he was riding ran out of gas and landed in the water. The coincidence of the whole thing is that somebody had written me the same story when I was in Panama. He stated that when they had been adrift for seven days without food and water, that they prayed and it wasn't long after that, a seagull came and lit on his head, thus saving the crew. They spent twenty-one days on a small raft.

On May 31 the B-24s again attacked Ichang. During and after the bomb run the formation engaged in a fight with up to forty Oscars. The battle lasted fifteen minutes, and when it was over, the bomber gunners had claimed twenty enemy fighters destroyed and five probables, setting a new theater record for the number of planes claimed by heavy bombers in a single engagement.

For operations over the Yangtze-Ichang area, some of the Liberators had six to eight .30 caliber machine guns installed in their bomb bays and aimed forty-five degrees downward. These guns, fired remotely from the cockpit, made the Liberators the first such ships in the Air Force.

The Seventy-fifth was part of the May 31 attack on Ichang, too. Colonel Alison had orders to return to a fighter pilot training field, but he wanted to shoot down a few more enemy planes so he stayed around the area for a few weeks. He took Lt. John Tucker and Lt. Don Brookfield and started looking for a fight. Heading a squadron of Chinese pilots and escorting the B-24s, Alison found the fight near Ichang. He set one Japanese plane aflame and suddenly realized he was being followed. In fact, the tracers passing him seemed to mark a one-way path. His plane was being riddled by a Zero who waited too long for the kill.

The P-40 could not pull away because the rudder was partially shot away and the remaining part was flapping in the breeze, slowing the plane up and causing a rapid increase in Alison's pulse. Just as Colonel Alison said what he thought was his last amen, the Japanese plane turned away, but not of his own will. One of the Chinese pilots had noticed the Zero on the tail of the P-40 and had sandwiched it. Fate was kind to Alison, for although the Zero was no longer there, neither was all of his P-40. He made it to Lindshanan and landed on two flat tires. Believing he had used up his luck for this year, he went off to train a new fighter group to oppose the Japanese. While the colonel had been the target for a Japanese pilot, Brookfield and Tucker had found a few targets themselves. Both were kept quite busy and could not determine the full results of their fire, but each one got a probable.

June marked the real beginning of the monsoon season in China, and as a result the 308th Bomb Group carried out few combat missions. Instead it concentrated on ferrying in more gasoline, bombs, and other supplies from India. The Eleventh Squadron flew five missions in the first half of June and two the last half, both on June 21 in support of Chinese troops.

The Fourteenth's fighters attacked railway and waterway transportation targets in the last two-thirds of the month, striking at rail facilities and lake traffic at Yochow in the northeast corner of Tungting Lake and flying sweeps over the Yangtze. On June 6 Cotton took advantage of the lull in fighting in the air and wrote home again.

> One of my friends brought a small terrier with him from South America. The dog was born an aviation enthusiast and now has logged some 50 hours of flying time. Although his time in service is much shorter than his master's, a call for Major will bring him running. Also sometimes the commanding officer. Having been born in Peru, he understands Spanish as well as English. Since Major is flying with the fighter pilots, it only seems fitting that he should have a parachute. Government regulations state that all flying personnel must have parachutes, and it doesn't say anything about dogs not being flying personnel, so this past week, we spent our days devising a chute for Major. The squadron parachute department did a beautiful job and it has been drop tested with a bottle of water where Major should have been. The results were excellent but there is nothing left but for Major to try it. So far he has not made any statements on how he feels about it all.

On June 8 nine P-40Ks from the Seventy-fifth escorted some B-24s for the purpose of bombing Haiphong near Hanoi. No opposition was encountered. But Major Goss led another escort of ten P-40s also to Haiphong. The weather was acting up, which made it difficult for the P-40s to keep in contact with the bombers. Finally, the fighters and bombers became separated. Although they had lost their escort, the bombers went into the target area alone. On the return trip, Colonel Knowles crashed into Lt. Therial B. Morton. The collision put both ships out of commission and forced the pilots to bail out. Morton's ship crashed into a mountain only a few seconds after he bailed out.

The next day Bill Grosvenor, being a bit nervous, decided to go down to Haiphong and see if he could determine the damage done in the June 8 raid. The weather was with the enemy, and he could not get through to his objective. At least he got a little flying time and practice, and he needed it, since fighting was slowed down during monsoon weather.

Later in June Tom Cotton wrote a long letter to his grandmother in Wyoming containing the following comments:

> The mail situation is very bad with none coming in. China is rather a dirty place. I should say this part of China is dirty. The majority of the people live in poverty, that we never see in the States. America's poorest people are well-to-do in comparison. Disease is rampant among the Chinese, making things worse. We have Chinese pilots in our squadron now. They are just as intelligent and educated as we are. They come from the Jap-occupied territory and have been trained in the States. They are back to get their homes and families from Jap control. They tell me in parts of China, where they used to live, it is as nice and clean as it is in the States. We haven't seen much action lately and have been thinking of different ways to win the war.

The little fellows from Japan tried their luck again on June 29, but as usual they were not successful. Some of the Twenty-third's planes had moved to Hengyang and at the time of the first alarm at 9:43 A.M., there were only five ships in commission. Lieutenants Casey and Aaron Liepe took off to intercept what was believed to be a reconnaissance mission. But the Japanese were out in full force, for at 10:06, a second wave was reported and a third followed fifteen minutes later. At 10:29 the remaining three defenders took off. Unfortunately Casey had engine trouble and had to return to the field. At twenty-five thousand feet the P-40s went into action with Captain Grosvenor coming through to take top place in the honor roll for the day. He was lost from the other three ships and although he was only a lone fighter against approximately thirty bombers and Zeroes, he attacked doggedly and succeeded in slapping one Zero down and causing one bomber to drop its bombs far short of the target. After this he tried landing with a flat tire but immediately found his landing gear collapsing. The other three planes landed in Kweilin.

Although the month of July started quietly, it developed into a veritable well of activity with the Japanese Air Force sustaining losses on all counts. On July 4 the squadron celebrated its first birthday, and Cotton described the celebration in a letter home.

> The Fourth of July and the birthday of the Fourteenth Air Force. Celebrating with a large dinner tonight. This morning Chennault awarded medals for bravery to some of the older pilots. The squadron is flying a pretty show formation for Chinese morale and looks great from the ground. During this formation, the Seventy-fifth Squadron, led by Johnny Alison, came zooming across the field, making the generals run for cover. They pulled up abruptly before some large poplar trees near the hostel and did a half-roll right through the trees. On landing, they told Johnny that was some pretty precise flying he was doing. But he told the fellows around me that it was not intended as that. When he pulled away sharply, he inadvertently did a snap roll and the plane just happened to go through the trees vertically and rolled out on the other side.

On July 7 twenty-two P-40s, consisting of sixteen from the Seventy-fourth and six from the Seventy-sixth, escorted bombers to Canton. After laying their eggs in the target area, the bombers left for home. Intercepting Zeroes were engaged by the fighters and as usual were given a severe trouncing. Scores for the day: Col. C. D. Vincent, two Zeroes confirmed; Capt. J. M. Morrison, two Zero probables; Lt. W. B. Hawkins and Lt. T. P. Bennett, one Zero probable each. Two American planes were damaged and crash-landed, but both pilots returned.

On July 8 the Sixteenth Fighter Squadron attempted several missions but had to turn back because of inclement weather. Lieutenant Calvert of the Seventy-fifth went on reconnaissance to Lao Kay but was forced to turn back due to the weather. Bombers escorted by

P-40s raided Hanoi and Haiphong. Antiaircraft fire created a Zero scare and some pilots dropped their belly tanks. Lt. Poco Little's belly tank did not hold enough gas so he belly-landed at Mengtzu because the landing gear failed to work. Lt. George R. Howard folded a landing gear in the same field while Lieutenant Cotton came through and made a successful landing.

Tom Cotton later told the story.

On our flight to Indochina as a bomber escort, we were to meet the bombers just prior to the target. Then we would go to the target —a maximum range for us—drop the bombs and come back. Due to the usual lack of communications, when we reached Tungting field, the bombers decided, instead of attacking from the usual north-south course, to go over the gulf and come back over Haiphong and Hanoi, which I suppose was to confuse the Japanese.

This created a problem for us fighter pilots inasmuch as we were at maximum range and even with no combat, we would be fortunate to return to our home base. We did go with the bombers on the run, and as we came off the target we realized it was not possible to get back to the home base at Kunming. We started to go to a friendly airfield on an island but found it was insecure for landing. Therefore we headed back to Kunming hoping we could find an emergency field along the way. On the river near Haiphong, there was a base called Mengtzu with an airfield. When I left, the two other planes— Little's and Howard's—that remained with me toward this destination, hoped that we would be able to spot the airfield before we ran out of fuel.

We did find the town of Mengtzu and the airfield. However, on making a low pass, I found that it was completely flooded. And it was reported there were large ditches dug in all parts of the field, except on the runway. But it was impossible to tell where the runway was, because of the water. There was a compound, manned by an American intelligence unit. They were on a microphone on the roof of the compound trying to tell me which way to land. There was a Chinese operator on the inside at the transmitter and every time the American boy on the roof tried to tell me what to do, and how to land, the Chinese boy would break in and tell me in Chinese. Consequently, I was getting nothing but a large howl on my radio.

I made one pass across the field to see if I could make out the runway, and as I pulled up I saw my first element leader, Lieutenant Little, go sliding in on the mud. He hit one of the ditches, it went up on its nose and settled back. I made one more pass and by this time the fuel pressure lights were burning red which meant I had about two minutes of fuel. And the wingman always uses more gas than the leader being on the outside of the turn. Lieutenant Howard had to go in—he had no other choice. He took another route across the field and went in with the gear up, hit a ditch, and went sliding up in the field. By this time I had determined a probable place where the runway was, since they had both landed where it wasn't. I therefore took a chance, put down the landing gear and came over the edge of the bamboo in a full power descent through the mud on the runway. The plane started to tip over but righted itself. One airplane out of three got down intact. The Chinese immediately got there and covered the planes with bamboo and hid them from the Japanese intelligence.

We were taken to a hostel where we were given rooms, a beautiful place on a compound with a lot of tropical birds flying around. There was a large three-story house, the top floor manned by the naval radio station which was part of Chennault's network. Living accommodations were on the second floor and the first floor housed the kitchen and, lo and behold, one of the best cooks ever.

Charlie Olsen left for a Haiphong escort mission at 4:45, twenty minutes after Cotton. "It was a well-planned mission," he recalled.

We passed Haiphong, but we went on to Hong Kong and the Kowloon docks. We had some bombers with us also, some torpedo bombers, skip bombers, B-25s rigged up. They were going to drop these torpedos and blow up the shipping. We had some B-24s we had to protect, too. Ben O. Cline and this other fellow who I have seen on the movies many times, used to ride with the B-24s and take actual movies of the flight out the door. They were scared to death. I guess I would have been too because they knew these bombers were very, very slow. If they didn't get the fighter protection, they were like sitting ducks. Not that they didn't have gunners and all, but they would just buzz around and make like a bee and you couldn't take care of them from all sides.

But the fighters could ward them off and make a pass from the front and sides and they could get shots, too. Anyway these two Hollywood fellows were there. I was on somebody's wing. Bombers were about twenty-two thousand feet. I saw a beautiful clear sky. Bombers were all in the group, circling around, dropping down to twelve to eighteen thousand to make bomb rounds. They passed

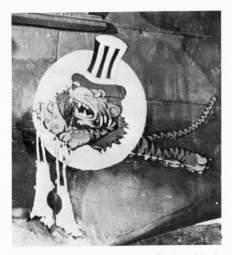

This unofficial emblem of the 23rd, painted on the fuselage of a P-40, depicts America's entry into the war: a tiger jumps through a Chinese sun while holding a torn Japanese flag in its claws.

Polish ace Maj. W. C. Urbanowicz joined the 23rd briefly. (Tex Hill collection)

Damaged Curtiss P-40 bellied in after overshooting the runway. (Wiltz Segura collection)

Tex Hill's Mustang P-51, named "Bullfrog," had its spinner painted red, white, and blue to represent the three squadrons he commanded. (Tex Hill collection)

Appropriately named B-24 bomber. (Dr. Jones Laughlin collection)

Seventy-fifth Fighter Squadron commander Major Tex Hill exits alert shack at Hengyang early 1943. (Tex Hill collection)

Seventy-fifth Fighter Squadron pilot Wiltz (Flash) Segura. (Wiltz Segura collection)

Col. Tex Hill at the 23rd Fighter Group headquarters Kunming 1944. (Tex Hill collection)

Bomb craters pit runways at Kweilin just prior to evacuation of the base.

Three generals gather for a strategy session: Gen. "Hap" Arnold (left), Gen. Joseph Stilwell (second from right), and Gen. Clayton Bissell. (USAF photo)

Beautiful landscape of China as it appeared before the ravages of war.
(Tex Hill collection)

Community rice harvest at Kunming. (Tex Hill collection)

Gasoline drums destined for forward bases such as Hengyang were transported partly by land and partly by river. (Tex Hill collection)

Masses of Chinese labor to complete an airstrip at a forward base. (USAF photo)

July 4, 1942 formation ceremonies of the Twenty-third Fighter Group from the original First, Second, and Third AVG Squadrons. (USAF photo)

Lt. James Anning and Lt. Curtis Scoville ham it up between missions. (Jones Laughlin collection)

75th Fighter Squadron pilot Tom Cotton. (Jones Laughlin collection)

Howard Samuel and fellow pilots fly combat cargo in a final push for Kweiyi. Note P-40 escort fighters behind plane at center. (Howard Samuel collection)

Lt. Marvin E. Balderson's plane, "The Virginian," after it crashed at Changsha. (Jones Laughlin collection)

down—no action—very quiet. Everybody was alert. I was the last fellow out in this echelon stack, out on a long line, and I looked to my left over my shoulder and saw this great big red spinner. Big radial engine, tacked on with me, flying right in formation with me, about a hundred feet away. Beside him were six, eight, or twelve stacked around him. All these big spinners with big red balls. They tacked on with us, all these Tojos and brand new Zeroes. God I didn't know what to do. I couldn't believe my eyes. This was the first Jap I had ever seen this close.

I pushed the button and said, "Zeroes!" And everybody started looking and asking, "Where? Where? I don't see any. Identify yourself."

I said, "Olsen! Olsen!"

They said, "Where are they? Where are they? Low? High?"

I said, "One o'clock flying in formation with us on my wing, about eight or twelve of them."

About this time, everybody disappeared. I was all alone. I dove out, but they didn't do anything. They weren't interested in us. They were waiting for the bombers, apparently. When I saw those things there I almost died.

On July 12, while attempting a reconnaissance mission to the west, two P-40s of the Sixteenth became lost in the overcast and crash-landed near Yunnanyi. Both pilots were uninjured. Fourteen P-40s of the Seventy-fourth, escorted bombers to Canton but never found out the results of their efforts because of the weather. Two P-40s, piloted by Gordon and Tucker of the Seventy-fifth, strafed positions within enemy lines. Lieutenant Tucker's plane was struck by small fire antiaircraft and he parachuted to safety. He returned to the squadron six days later. After bailing out one mile inside Chinese lines, he walked and rode horseback to Wenshan and then went by air back to Kunming.

On July 12 Tom Cotton wrote to his grandmother. He told her the reason he had not written for a while—that he had been downed at Mengtzu. He also mentioned other things:

I have met many interesting people here in China. For instance, an Irish gentleman who has spent his life in China as a part of British Customs. Quite an old man but young in his way. I am staying in one of his houses in the compound, used for such emergencies as mine. He does not expect to return to his homeland. He has been here too long for that. The people who live here in the interior of China have been away from their homes for so long, they have a tired, wistful look on their faces. They seem to know they will never return to their homes and civilization. On the light side of our life is our Chinese cook Charlie. He believes himself to be a very good American. This he proves by trying to master the English language. He does very good except he places the emphasis on the wrong syllables, and the American boys don't help much as they taught him the opposite meaning for some things. He comes in and complains that he has prepared the poorest dinner in his life. Everybody laughs and says it certainly is. He thinks, of course, that bad means best. . . .

When I did return to Kunming some ten days later, they disassembled the two damaged airplanes and drained the rice paddy and made my plane flyable. It took about eight days to carry gasoline down to Indochina from China for sufficient fuel to get my airplane back.

On July 13 it was bad luck again for the Seventy-fifth, when Lt. Gan K. Johnston's P-40, while on a mail run, developed trouble, forcing him to hit the silk. Several hours later, footsore and happy, he walked into the base.

Lt. Bruce Holloway on July 20 led six sharks of the Seventy-sixth on a very successful strafing mission down the Yangtze River area. The pilots destroyed a 150-foot water launcher, a hundred-foot launch, three locomotives, and other rolling stock. After having sent out a recon ship to Lashio in Burma, four P-40s of the Sixteenth dive-bombed Tengchung and installations along the Burma Road. Also on July 20, Tom Cotton wrote home the news that his buddy Charlie Olsen had given his girl Lucille an engagement ring. He also asked for a small motion-picture camera, which was unavailable in China unless, of course, one was a millionaire.

Attempting to raid American bases at Lingling and Hengyang, the Japanese suffered another costly setback on July 23. Attacking enemy planes in the vicinity of Lingling, Seventy-fourth pilots Jeffreys and Kinsey destroyed one bomber and damaged one Zero, respectively. The Seventy-sixth intercepted Japanese in bombers and fighters over Hengyang and exacted a heavy toll. At 5:45 A.M., the squadron was alerted and took to the air. The flight had just attained altitude when the enemy came in. A fierce engagement followed with Japanese planes crashing in flames over the entire area. Taking to their heels, the Japanese fled in wild abandon. Then in the afternoon, they were back again over Hengyang and once again were beaten with heavy losses.

Score for the day: Lt. Jesse Williams, one Zero confirmed, one probable; Lt. W. C. Bonner, Jr., one confirmed, two probable; Lt. Richard J. Templeton, one probable; Lt. George G. Ferris, one probable; Lt. Bruce Holloway, one confirmed; Lieutenant Sher, two confirmed, one probable; Capt. Martin Lubner, one confirmed, two probable; Lt. John S. Stewart, one confirmed, one probable; Lieutenant Masters, one probable; Lieutenant Manbeck, one Zero confirmed, one probable and one bomber confirmed, one probable; Lt. T. P. Bennett, one confirmed, one damaged; Lt. G. W. Lee, one probable; Lieutenant Stewart, one bomber confirmed, one probable; Lieutenant McGuire, one bomber probable, two damaged; Colonel Knowles, one bomber confirmed; Col. Casey Vincent, one confirmed; Maj. Norval C. Bonawitz, one bomber probable; and Lt. T. Y. Cheng, one bomber confirmed. It was a big day for Chennault's men, but one of the American planes, piloted by Lt. Wayne G. Johnson, crash-landed and the pilot suffered slight head wounds.

The Japanese came back again for punishment on July 24 with the Seventy-fourth and Seventy-sixth squadrons playing the perfect hosts. Nineteen planes of the Seventy-fourth intercepted the enemy flights over Lingling and Kweilin. Lts. Robert M. Cage, William O. Morin, and Kinsey each confirmed a Zero, and Lieutenant Hawkins got one Zero probable. Of eight Zeroes intercepted over Kweilin, only one returned to Canton. Major Bonawitz, who confirmed two bombers, was forced to crash-land and as a result sustained slight injury. Lieutenant Barnes was killed. Lt. Minnack was shot up and crash-landed, sustaining no injuries. Lt. T. P. Bennett was on a cross-country flight putting time on his ship when he intercepted and confirmed a Zero. Capt. Robert E. Smith, piloting a P-38, was attacked from above and shot down by two Zeroes. He bailed out and was rushed to the hospital by the Chinese. He was badly burned about the face and hands and also suffered from shrapnel wounds above the chest and legs.

In the Hengyang area the Japanese were intercepted by the Seventy-sixth. In the first pass on the bombers, Captain Miller confirmed two of them and Lt. John Williams wrote a finish to another. Three Zeroes were sent crashing in flames, two accredited to Lt. William DiStefano and one for Lt. Bruce G. Boylan. What bombs the enemy were able to drop fell clear of all target areas, coming down harmlessly in the hills and rice paddies.

The next day the Japanese came back with their bombers and fighters, and again they returned to their bases badly mauled for all their efforts. Intercepting them over Kweilin, Lieutenant Spurgin of the Seventy-fourth confirmed one Zero and Lt. Paul Herring of the same outfit got one probable. In a running fight near Hengyang, Capt. Martin Lubner shot down one Zero and Lt. John S. Stewart and Lt. Glen Beneda each got one probable Zero. Flights from the Seventy-fourth and Seventy-sixth escorted bombers to Hong Kong and Hankow where enemy installations were heavily plastered. No enemy fighters attempted interception and all American planes returned safely.

July 26 proved to be a fatal day for H. L. Lee, who was flying a mission along with four other pilots. Escorting bombers to Hankow, they were intercepted by approximately thirty Zeroes. In the battle which followed Lt. Jones confirmed one Zero and two probables. Lee was seen to dive out of formation with several Zeroes on his tail. His fate was unknown. Maj. Elmer Richardson, the group operations officer, leading the fighters, also confirmed two Zeroes in his fight. The bombers laid their eggs and all returned safely to their bases.

On July 27, the Chinese-American Composite Wing (CACW) was activated in the Fourteenth Air Force at Karachi, India. The wing was led by Chinese aircraft officers who were to act as group, squadron, and flight commanders. Its combat units were the First Bomb Group (B-25s) and the Third and Fifth fighter groups (P-40s), each group having four squadrons and each unit receiving its numerical designation from the Chinese Air Force. Training began in August and the first units moved into China for action by October.

At the beginning of July, there was an important tactical development when General Chennault designated shipping and port installations as primary targets for the Fourteenth. As an immediate result, eight of the nine missions flown during the month by the 308th Bomb Group were directed against such targets, especially in the area of Haiphong, Indochina. The 308th flew the first of these missions on July 8, hitting dock installations and ships in the harbor at Haiphong.

It was a tough mission for a Liberator named "Mudfish" and its crew. On takeoff the plane struck a steamroller, shattering the nose-wheel gear so that the wheel was left dangling in the air. The pilot, Captain Carp, elected to continue the mission although the plane would easily be spotted as a cripple. All the way to the target area, a gunner tried to disengage the wheel but without success. Finally, near Hanoi, he made one last desperate attempt. Lowering himself without a parachute through the gaping hole in the fuselage and hanging by both hands, he jumped on the wheel until it broke loose. He then successfully climbed back into the plane, and Mudfish made a normal and uneventful bomb run.

Mudfish then turned for home, and all crewmen elected to remain aboard while Captain Carp attempted a landing. By the time they reached Chungking, all movable equipment had been piled in the rear of the plane to lighten the nose as much as possible. The crewmen also wrapped themselves in flying equipment to cushion the shock of crash landing. Then the pilot turned in for the landing and at the last moment shut off all engines to minimize the chance of fire after the plane hit the ground. He touched Mudfish down on two wheels and, as it responded to his touch, held the nose up until speed was lost. The nose came down and the plane dragged along and came to a stop—without excessive damage or injury to the crew.

By the end of July the Eleventh Bomb Squadron, which during the month had lost three B-25Cs and two B-25Ds, had eighteen B-25 aircraft on strength, while the four fighter squadrons of the Fourteenth were down to only sixty-four P-40Es, Ks, and Ms, of which slightly more than half were at the eastern bases.

The Eleventh Bomb Squadron entered the campaign against enemy shipping July 27 when six B-25s attacked a large transport vessel off Stonecutter's Island, Hong Kong, but on this first venture, all bombs missed.

If the Eleventh Squadron's start on anti-shipping operations in July was ineffective, the 308th made up for it. During July the Liberators claimed four thousand tons of enemy shipping sunk and another thirty-five thousand tons damaged.

On the last day of July, Lt. William S. Epperson lost his life. Enemy bombers and fighters attempting to raid Hengyang were intercepted by the Seventy-sixth and a flight of the Seventy-fifth. Epperson was diving on a Japanese bomber formation when he met with misfortune. His three fellow pilots of the Seventy-fifth went a long way to avenge him. Lt. Charles Gordon had one bomber confirmed, one Zero probable; Lieutenant Calvert, one bomber confirmed, one Zero probable; and Lt. Chris Barrett, one Zero confirmed. The Seventy-sixth pilots also scored, Lt. MacMillan having one Zero confirmed and Lt. Donald Hedrick, one Zero probable and one bomber probable. Besides losing Epperson of the Seventy-fifth, Lieutenant Krippner of the Seventh-sixth crash-landed, sustaining a slight head injury.

Bill Grosvenor was grounded the day of the fight because his plane had been shot out the day before. Later he recalled the day of Epperson's death:

> We thought the Japs would come over the next day to avenge their previous day's losses. As operations officer it was my duty to schedule who would fly. Many times as a junior officer, I was outranked and my plane was taken over. I promised myself not to do this to someone else.
>
> Epperson was a great pilot and a wonderful guy. Somehow he had a premonition of death, but I did not realize his feeling when he offered me his plane, and remembering my promise to myself, I said he had better go up. If only I had accepted his offer, I would not have been on the ground watching his P-40 spinning down, the pilot almost pulling the plane out the last second. Later I found out that it was Epperson. If only I could have known what was going to happen, but perhaps it is better that we don't.

Air operations for the first half of August were all but stopped by bad weather and heavy rains. When the skies began to clear up on August 13, the Sixteenth Fighter Squadron resumed offensive patrols over western China and Burma. A week later, six escorted B-25s struck at Tin Ho airdrome, Canton, and placed their bombs in the revetment and hangar areas although they were under continuous attack throughout the bomb run.

At 9:15 A.M. on August 20, forty Zeroes attempted a fighter sweep on Kweilin and were intercepted by fifteen P-40s of the Seventy-fourth led by Col. Bruce Holloway. In the brief aerial combat which followed, Capt. Arthur Cruikshank destroyed two Zeroes and Lt. Jess Garrett damaged another. Captain Jeffreys and Lt. Y. K. Mao were both shot down and crashed in flames.

In the afternoon Col. Bruce Holloway and Maj. N. C. Bonawitz, leading a flight of P-40s, escorted several B-25 bombers to Tin Ho airdrome at Canton. Intercepting Zeroes over the target, the men added to the score for the day. The day's score totalled: Captain Cruikshank, two Zeroes confirmed; Lts. Paul Herring and Kinsey, one Zero each; Lieutenant Holloway, one Zero confirmed, one probable; Lt. Hendrickson, one Zero probable; Lt. L. W. Smith and Lt. Jess Garrett, one Zero damaged each.

The next day the Japanese switched their attention to the American base at Hengyang, where they were intercepted over the field. In the fierce aerial battle which followed, the Japanese were the losers with five Zeroes shot down and possibly four others damaged. The 449th, coming up from Lingling just as the Zeroes were fleeing for home, gave chase and probably destroyed three other Zeroes. This time Col. Bruce Holloway and Lts. Richard Templeton and Calvert got one Zero apiece, and Lieutenant Williams scored two. Four more probables were credited to Burbank, Edmund Goss, Schultz and Holton.

On the same day Hankow was the target for seven B-25s, fourteen B-24s, and a P-40 escort. The P-40 escort ran into trouble when its planes had to be scrambled to defend Hengyang, but eventually a full twelve-plane escort was readied and joined the medium bombers. Meanwhile the B-24s from the 374th and 375th squadrons, failing to make rendezvous with the other aircraft, flew on unescorted to strike at the Hankow dock area. While on the bomb run the Liberator formation underwent a vicious frontal attack by Oscars of the Twenty-fifth Sentai (wing), in which the Sentai commander, Maj. Toshio Sakagawa, shot down the lead Liberator of Maj. Bruce Beat. The other B-24s, still engaged, persevered to the target and dropped their bombs, scoring a perfect bomb pattern along the entire length of the dock and warehouse area. One of them, however, was badly damaged and later crash-landed with three dead and two seriously wounded.

As the bombers turned away from the target, Oscars of the Thirty-third Sentai entered the battle, and attacks continued for a period of almost thirty minutes. When the last fighter finally withdrew, ten of the dozen remaining Liberators were badly damaged, with one man killed and four wounded. The bomber gunners were credited with claims of fifty-seven enemy planes shot down, thirteen probably destroyed, and two damaged. But they actually shot down no more than a few of the attackers, and the high claims merely reflected the ferocity of the action. Concerning this mission, Chinese intelligence later reported that one thousand drums of gasoline and many buildings were destroyed, with fires still burning on the following day, and that a headquarters building where a meeting was in progress was demolished, killing three Japanese generals, four colonels, and a naval commander.

Reaching Hankow after the departure of the Liberators, the escorted B-25s successfully carried out their strike on the airdrome there, placing 78 percent of their bombs on the target area and destroying one plane on the ground. There was no air opposition.

On August 24, the Fourteenth went after Hankow again, this time dispatching fourteen B-24s and six B-25s, fourteen P-40s and eight P-38s. Colonel Holloway led the flight of P-40s, which was composed of pilots from the Sixteenth, Seventy-fourth, and Seventy-sixth fighter squadrons. The Mitchells hit Wuchang airport, across the river from Hankow, with good results and no losses. On the way to the rendezvous the seven B-24s of the 373rd Squadron had run afoul of bad weather and had to return to the base, so that left only seven Liberators of the 425th Squadron to bomb the Hankow airdrome. After bombing with good results despite having no escort this time, the B-24s were heavily engaged by some forty Oscars of the Twenty-fifth and Thirty-third Sentais. These Japanese shot down four B-24s, destroying one, and badly damaged the remaining three, and also claimed two P-40s in the forty-five-minute air battle, although no American fighter planes were lost. Three Oscars were shot down, including the plane of Maj. Akira Watanabe, sentai commander of the Thirty-third, who was killed in action.

The three surviving B-24s made it back to Kweilin with two dead and six wounded aboard. Next day, they flew home to Kunming, but on the way one of the Liberators crashed, killing ten of the twelve men on board. So the disastrous mission ended with the 425th out of action for some time to come.

But the remainder of the 308th Group carried on, flying two more missions by month's end without loss. On the last of these, a bombing mission to an airdrome at Hanoi, eight of the twenty-two escorting P-40s became lost on return and ran out of fuel. Six pilots abandoned their planes by bailing out, and two made forced landings, one of which resulted in a seventh P-40 being destroyed.

In spite of the bombers' bad luck, Holloway's men destroyed ten

Zeroes and added three probables to the score. Lt. William Hawkins and Capt. Arthur Cruikshank of the Seventy-fourth were high scorers for the day with two Zeroes destroyed and one probable each. Lt. John S. Stewart of the Seventy-sixth also had two Zeroes confirmed.

With unabated fury the Twenty-third Fighter Group's squadrons carried out numerous dive-bombing and strafing missions on enemy ground targets and shipping, beginning on the first day of September. Lts. Lynn F. Jones, Jess Garrett, and Kinsey of the Seventy-fourth, while on a strafing and dive-bombing mission on the Bay of Hong Kong, attacked a troop transport, leaving it sinking. Then, concentrating their gunfire on another boat, they caused heavy damage to it. Turning their attention to ground installations, Lt. Garrett on one strafing pass probably destroyed a large transport sitting on a concrete runway. Exhausting all their ammo, they returned safely to their bases.

A flight of the Seventy-sixth, led by Capt. Martin Lubner, carried out a highly successful dive-bombing and strafing raid on shipping at the Yangtze River. Besides sinking a 250-foot tanker, they inflicted heavy damage upon a number of tugs. Leaving the river area, the flight then proceeded to Ichang where, observing an enemy cavalry detachment, they struck in force, leaving it in shambles. The flight then returned to Hengyang.

A flight from the 449th, taking off from Hengyang, proceeded northwest to Nanchang, where they wrought death and destruction to enemy barracks and installations. Leaving the encampment, the flight proceeded north and destroyed the locomotives at Tiran and heavily damaged several others. Continuing on in a northerly course, they destroyed a hundred-foot steamer, two 125-foot tugboats, and a barge attached to one of them. Heading south toward Yochow, the flight destroyed a locomotive and eight cars. Then, low on fuel and ammo, they returned to base.

The next day Capts. J. M. Morrison and Crooks and Lieutenant Bundy escorted some bombers to Lai Chi Kak. Intercepting Zeroes were driven off with Crooks and Morrison each claiming a probable. One 250-foot oil tanker was probably sunk and two fire-fighting barges damaged. The smoke from this and the previous raid extended upwards to fifteen thousand feet.

On September 4, eight fighters escorted the bombers to Tin Ho airport. They encountered fifteen Zeroes just as the bombers approached the target. The bombers dropped their eggs and dove away. In the ensuing aerial battle, Captain Crooks and Lts. Harlyn Vidovich and T. Y. Cheng each confirmed a Zero and Lieutenant Kramer a probable. Light to medium antiaircraft fire was observed but no damage was sustained with all the Americans returning safely.

While inclement weather prevented fighting on September 5, Lt. Bob Maxent winged his way into the blue that morning for the last time. He went out on the mail run and never returned. While taking off at Changyi, his plane spun and burned. The doctor who attended Maxent told his friends that he suffered no pain from the fire as he was not conscious after the plane hit the ground.

It was business as usual September 6 with Lt. John S. Stewart of the Seventy-sixth leading a flight on a dive-bombing and strafing mission to Kiukiang. They bombed and sunk a 250-foot freighter, blew up four locomotives, and destroyed a factory near Yochow. They also bombed a 150-foot freighter and a tugboat. Near Kiukiang Lieutenant Stewart spotted a Japanese transport, and he destroyed it with one diving sweep.

Two Lightning P-38s from the 449th, taking off from Hengyang, dive-bombed Shihhweiyah and made dive-bombing runs northeast to southwest. Lieutenant Bolton destroyed one foundry and damaged another. Lieutenant Helms destroyed a 250-foot boat and damaged another in the dock area.

The same day Col. Bruce K. Holloway, for many months commander of the Twenty-third Fighter Group, was relieved of his duty and assigned to the newly-activated fighter wing. Throughout the entire period of his command, he was the guiding spirit in the impressive record attained by the Twenty-third. "Capable and square, Colonel Holloway had the respect and esteem of the entire command. A leader of men, a great soldier, the colonel leaves a record unattained by any man in this theater of war," wrote one historian. He had flown more than 285 combat hours, had gone on 109 combat missions, and had recorded thirteen enemy planes destroyed in the air and five probably destroyed.

On September 9, ten fighters of the Seventy-fourth escorted a mission of B-25 bombers to White Cloud airdrome at Canton. Zeroes numbering approximately twenty in all intercepted them after the bombers had laid their eggs in the target area. In the fierce aerial battle Capt. J. M. Morrison definitely destroyed two Zeroes, Lt. Lynn

Jones racked one up, while the others listed four probables. Except for two badly-damaged P-40s, both of which were brought to safety, no other American planes sustained any damage. Capt. Byron Gilmore of the Seventy-sixth, along with two sharks, escorted several P-38s to Kiukiang where the P-38s dive-bombed and left the area. The P-40s remained to strafe the barracks at Teian and after setting them on fire returned home.

The P-38s of the 449th dive-bombed and strafed numerous installations in the vicinity of Yochow, Puchi, and Changanyi and shipping at Wusuch and Kichune, inflicting heavy damage and numerous casualties. Lieutenant Beardsley destroyed a twin-engine transport southeast of Whampoa.

Capt. Martin Lubner and Lt. William DiStefano led the fighters of the Seventy-sixth on a bomber escort mission to Hankow on September 10. They engaged intercepting Zeroes in battle, and Captain Lubner and Lts. T. Y. Cheng, John S. Stewart, Thomas Bullard, and Bonner each confirmed a Zero. All the American planes returned safely. Later on in the day, Lt. John Williams led a dive-bombing and strafing mission to Kiukiang. Numerous hits were scored in the target area and a 175-foot boat was left sinking. Williams was missing from this action. All others returned.

The next day Lt. Paul N. Bell, leading a flight of five ships of the Seventy-fourth, escorted some B-25 bombers to Hankow, with only five or six Zeroes attempting interception. They were easily routed. Lt. Paul Herring's ship, however, was damaged and he also sustained a head injury. Unable to find a landing field before his engine quit, he bailed out over Kweilinchu and was reported safe in Chinese hands. On a bomber escort mission to Hankow, a flight composed of planes from the Seventy-sixth and the Sixteenth was intercepted by Zeroes. Lieutenant Pruett of the Sixteenth took top honors for the day by downing one Zero and one I-97 fighter. Four P-38s of the 449th left Hengyang the same day on a dive-bombing mission on targets to the north. Arriving at Tayeh, their first target, they made direct hits on a large building, completely destroying it. Also severely damaged were three buildings in the barracks area. At Yengsin, the barracks were strafed, killing approximately thirty enemy soldiers as well as destroying several of the barracks.

On September 12 the Seventy-sixth successfully protected several dive-bombing and strafing missions. Lt. Thomas L. Bullard, leading three sharks to the Kiukiang area, concentrated on a Japanese rest camp. They scored direct hits in the target area, inflicting heavy destruction and casualties on the installations and the personnel. Colonel Pike led four sharks of the Seventy-sixth on a strafing mission to Yochow, in the Kiukiang area. Barracks and railroad installations were heavily plastered.

Early in the morning four P-38s of the 449th raided Kiukiang, scoring direct hits on the boats in the docks, damaging several and heavily damaging a 250-foot freighter. One Lightning proceeded to Tayeh, scoring a direct hit on the barracks there. Shortly past noon, ten more P-38s took off towards Hong Kong. Four planes were loaded with five-hundred-pound bombs while the remaining six planes acted as top cover. Arriving at the Bay of Hong Kong, they made a systematic search for enemy shipping. At the east end of the harbor, Lieutenant Gregg made a dive-bombing run on a 550-foot boat, the bomb going through the ship and exploding ten feet on the other side. Lieutenant Rockwell dove on a 485-foot boat and released his bomb, zooming away as a terrific explosion sunk the boat. Lt. Goodwin Taylor made a direct hit on a 530-foot boat with unknown results. Continuing on to Ai Cohn Island, the flight strafed a gunboat, which they saw explode at one end and burst into flames. Rockwell, attempting to nurse his damaged plane back to friendly territory, was unable to free himself from his stricken plane and crashed to his death.

Lieutenant Kramer of the Seventy-sixth led a flight of four on a strafing mission to Loyang on September 14. Two sharks turned back due to engine trouble. Reaching their targets, the two remaining P-40s strafed buildings at the Shihhweiyah mines and then continued on to Yengsin where they expended the rest of their ammunition on the barracks and returned home safely. On the same day, Colonel Pike led five sharks of the Seventy-sixth on a dive-bombing mission to Nanchang. Dropping their bombs, they proceeded to strafe the target. Lieutenant McGuire, struck by enemy ground fire, was barely able to make it over the lines where he bailed out safely into Chinese hands. Again the 449th struck devastating blows against enemy shipping and ground installations. Lieutenant Rea dropped his five-hundred-pound bomb directly on the stern of a three-hundred-foot boat which sank almost immediately. Captain Moon left a 250-foot boat listing heavily when his bomb struck not more than ten feet from its target.

The next day Lieutenant Wimmack led a flight of eight P-40s, escorting bombers on a raid to Wuchang. Zeroes attempted to intercept without success. In a short but furious battle in the air, Lieutenant MacKinnon of the Sixteenth destroyed one Zero while Lts. Robert M. Cage and Altheus B. Jarmon damaged two others. Meanwhile Colonel Pike, leading a flight of seven sharks from the Seventy-sixth, escorted bombers to Hankow. Intercepting Zeroes were engaged and in the ensuing fight Pike's plane was seen smoking badly. He was believed to be taken prisoner by the Japanese.

Lt. Col. Norval C. Bonawitz assumed command of the Seventy-fourth Fighter Squadron on September 16. Hailing from Montana, Bonawitz was a typical, ruggedly-built outdoorsman, well tried in combat.

On September 20, for the third time since the Army Air Force had been established in Kunming, the Japanese attempted to bomb the air base. Approximately thirty to forty bombers escorted by a large force of Zeroes were intercepted by American fighters, and the hills and rice paddies in the vicinity were literally strewn with the flaming wrecks of Japanese bombers and Zeroes. Sweeping low on the enemy, the planes of the Sixteenth blasted their way through the bomber formation, drawing the protecting Zeroes away from the formation.

Coming out of the sun, the Seventy-fifth exploded in a surprise sweep on the unprotected bombers, sending them to destruction below. The men of the Seventy-fifth were eating breakfast when the plot came in on Japanese planes headed in their direction. The pilots took to the air and the ground crews to the hills. After a couple of hours, all hell broke loose as the Japanese bombers unloaded their bombs on the Kunming airdrome. But the Japanese got the biggest surprise of their lives when the Seventy-fifth exploded out of the blue above them, scoring nineteen ships confirmed.

Bill Grosvenor, in recalling the fight later, said:

> I believe an interesting aspect of the story is that every day we listened on the radio to their beautiful American songs and arguments between Jack and Bill on the pros and cons of the war. That day the program was interrupted to say that Kunming was going to be at-

tacked by the vastly superior Japanese Air Force. They did not say when, but we knew that if the Japanese said so, they would do it.

As many planes as possible were greased up and repaired. One must respect the Japanese in that they had guts. As one bomber went down, another would close formation to take its place. I remember after several passes, I maneuvered too much while shooting and my guns jammed. I made two extra passes thinking the guns might work again. No luck. The Japanese did bomb their objective, but their losses in aircraft were too many for the results obtained.

The score for the day read, Capt. Roger Pryor, two bombers confirmed, two probable; Capt. Bill Grosvenor, two bombers confirmed, two damaged; Captain Gordon, one bomber and one Zero confirmed; Lt. Donald Glover, one bomber; Lt. Vernon Tanner, one bomber; Lt. Curtis Scoville, one bomber confirmed, one bomber probable, and one Zero damaged; Lt. Don Brookfield, one bomber and one Zero confirmed; Lt. J. D. Long, one Zero damaged; Lt. Jim Anning, one Zero damaged; Lt. James Folmer, one Zero probable; Lt. Henry I. Wood, one bomber probable; Lt. L. R. Lewis, one bomber confirmed, one bomber damaged (all of the above pilots were members of the Seventy-fifth Squadron); Lt. Richard Mauritson of the Seventy-fourth Squadron scored one bomber damaged; Lieutenant Farris of the Seventy-sixth Squadron scored one bomber damaged; pilots from the Sixteenth Squadron scoring were Maj. Robert L. Liles, one Zero confirmed, one bomber probable, and one Zero damaged; Lt. Jasper Brown, one bomber confirmed, one probable; Lieutenant Evans, one bomber confirmed; Lieutenant Clapp, one bomber confirmed, one probable; Lieutenant Henderson, one bomber confirmed; and Lt. Clarence Dooley, two bombers confirmed.

When the battle was over, 1st Lt. L. R. "Sad Sack" Lewis was missing from the flight. He later told the story of what had happened to him.

It was my first real fight. Sixteen of us went up there to intercept. After we saw them, we counted twenty-seven bombers and between sixty and eighty fighters escorting them. They were about four thousand feet above the bombers. We climbed into position to about twenty-two thousand feet to make our attack. We went in to our initial attack and drove through them, and we saw five to seven go down in flames almost immediately. We came in for the second pass and the fighters began to hit us. I became separated from my flight leader, Major Goss.

On the third run, I was by myself making a pass, and I was hitting a bomber and noticed tracer bullets going over my wing and diving out of the way. I didn't realize that I had used up as much fuel as I had. I was fifty miles out of Kunming by now. The weather was overcast, and I was running low on fuel, so I immediately first tried to elude my pursuer and made a landing to the north of Kunming. I had gotten on the wrong side of a mountain ridge and it was four days before I got back. From all indications in talking to the other fellows, the Japanese admitted that only two of their twenty-seven bombers had returned. I claimed one which went in. The Chinese infantry confirmed it and I have the serial number as a memento.

When I landed on the wrong side of Kunming, I landed on a road near a rice paddy. Belly-landed, due to the mountain terrain, and the plane was damaged. I removed as many instruments as possible and brought them back, but it was difficult to carry anything through the mountains. For a while I was going to bring the ammunition and some of the guns, too, but it became quite burdensome. The walk in took three days. The last day they met me with a jeep. No one else went down on the mission. With the Japanese flying their squirrel cages, it was difficult to get an accurate count. They always had us outnumbered ten to one.

On September 21, the Seventy-fifth Squadron did not fight, as they spent the day repairing the damage from the previous day's battle. Lt. Thomas F. Pugh of the 449th Fighter Squadron, attached to the Seventy-fifth, was reported to be in the hospital at Changyi. His ship was out of commission and he had been forced to crash-land.

It was on September 24 when Lieutenant Lewis walked into base headquarters and told the story about his belly-landing and the Chinese who helped him get home.

After landing, I cleared the ship as quickly as possible. The Chinese helped carry my baggage to the nearest Chinese Army post which was three miles up the valley. I told the Chinese official in the little Chinese language I knew, with pictures and map, where I wanted to go. They brought me some rice to eat and then they made me go back to the plane and get everything that was loose in there. I was still trying to get started back to Kunming, but they would not let me leave all morning. All that afternoon I was being stared at. To help pass the time away, I did a few tricks for the Chinese boys. As it was not quiet and was getting late, the soldiers made the kids leave so I could eat and get some sleep. About ten minutes after the boys left, two of them returned and wanted to see me. I had just finished some rice and meat that had spoiled my appetite, but I had to eat some eggs they gave me before I could go to sleep. I boiled them myself.

The next morning, arising early, I tried to get an early start back. Well, the Chinese can't be rushed. About 7:30 they brought me three eggs and I ate them with rice and cake they prepared along with my rations. After eating they brought me three more eggs, with me telling them in sign language that I had plenty. They seemed to know that but insisted I take these along with me.

Starting out at 9:30 with four soldiers, one Chinese coolie, and two mules, I began my journey. I was supposed to ride one mule and use one to carry my belongings. My weight was too much for the stirrups, so I broke both loose from the saddle. They would put me back on. About five miles down the trail the donkey threw me when he was frightened by a small snake.

Traveling on up winding trails and over mountains and down deep valleys, I both rode and walked. Not having ridden an animal for some time, I was both sore and tired all over. This went on for three days. While traveling, the soldiers took good care of me and gave me roasted corn, pears, and nuts along with my other food. Some of the places we traveled over looked like scenes from jungle pictures. Some places the trail completely disappeared for stretches of fifty or one hundred feet. I was in a couple of rain showers the second day and had to wade through one creek nearly waist deep.

At night I would sleep on boards covered by a thin cloth supported by boxes two feet off the floor. I had a blanket for cover. Every night before I would go to bed the soldiers would bring me warm water to wash my face and hands and warm water to wash my feet in. After four days I was able to send a message back to my squadron and speak to someone who knew English. It took me a six-hour ride in a jeep to get back to my squadron on the last day. The fourth night I spent with some missionaries. They fed me, made it possible to get a good warm bath and then a good night of sleep. The Chinese magistrates gave me a chicken which the missionaries prepared for me. I was happy, but was tired and a little sore. It was great to get back with my squadron and I was eager to contact the Japs again.

October proved to be the quietest month in the history of the Twenty-third Fighter Group. Extremely inclement weather seriously curtailed all operations. Except for the mission to Haiphong on the first day of the month and a few escort missions and interceptions, there were no other operations.

October 1 was not a red-letter day in any sense of the word. Sixteen P-40s from the Seventy-fifth with eight of the Twenty-fifth's P-40s undertook to escort twenty-one B-24s to Haiphong. Three of the planes were forced to return because of engine trouble, and Lieutenant Wang of the Chinese Air Force, who had been attached to the group for some time, crashed into the side of a mountain and was killed instantly. Over the target, the bombers hit their mark, and the target areas were really blasted. As the formation turned away from the target, about ten Zeroes jumped it. A flight of them dove down through the element being led by Lieutenant Brookfield.

Lt. Henry Wood, who was on Brookfield's wing when the fighting began, was nowhere to be found after it was over. He was reported by Major Brady of the bombers to have made a head-on pass with a Zero, shooting it down in flames, and then to have gone down smoking himself. He was taken prisoner by the Japanese, and the story of his experiences will be told later in this book.

Lt. Jimmy Chen of the Chinese Air Force was also lost that day. Tom Cotton later recalled the story of Chen:

> Lieutenant Chen was flying on my wing when the formation left the target area. He remained in his position for approximately fifteen minutes. When my flight turned back to protect two straggling bombers, Lieutenant Chen was missing. More about Chen later.

Thus in one day, we lost three brave men. The two Chinese pilots, who were trained in the States, were favorites and proved in combat the fine spirit of cooperation between the Americans and the Chinese. The men feared that Wood was either killed or in the hands of the enemy—either case a bad one. Capt. Bill Grosvenor, Lieutenant Brookfield, Lt. J. T. Opsvig (449th), and Lieutenant Wood, all scored with Zeroes confirmed. Curtis Scoville damaged another.

Now to continue the story about pilot Jimmy Chen. As we proceeded out of Kunming we were flying up above an overcast to meet our bombers which were coming in from India. As we cleared the top of the clouds in this very mountainous terrain, one of the Chinese pilots (other than Chen), signaled he was having trouble with his oxygen mask. He signaled he was going home immediately and descended through the clouds not realizing there were mountains down in the clouds which he had climbed up past earlier. He apparently plowed into the mountain as we saw a big black cloud of smoke come up.

Down over the target area Jimmy Chen was flying the second element wing position, which was on the far side of the echelon. And we covered the tail position of the bombers, which forced us to make "S" turns as our speed was in excess of theirs. Over the target area, we experienced some antiaircraft fire, and some Japanese Zeroes were circling outside, however, apparently making no attempt to engage us in combat. As I was "S" turning the formation back and forth to stay behind the bombers, Lieutenant Chen got out of synchronization with the flight, and suddenly he became more of a problem than the Japs because when we zigged, he zagged. And he comes zooming across our flight, forcing me to make the formation move up or down to avoid him running into one of us in the wild foray. The bombers made a turn over the target, dropped the bombs and the Zeroes immediately pounced on him. And that was the last time I saw him in action. He was going down on fire and we assumed he had been killed.

It is interesting to note that a year or so ago when I was in Hong Kong, I was in the lobby of the President which is now the Hyatt Regency Hotel, when I noted a familiar face over at one of the travel counters. I went over and spoke to this Chinese. And I said, "You look like Jimmy Chen." He looked at me and said, "I don't know you," and said that was not his name. I apologized and was sitting down in the lobby reading the *Stars and Stripes,* and this gentleman sat down beside me and said, "How did you know my name was Jimmy Chen?"

I said the last time I saw him he was heading in for Indochina on fire, and I assumed he had been killed. He said, "That's right, and you were in the Seventy-fifth Squadron." And I said yes. And he said, "Oh, I remember you now," and then he proceeded to tell me the events which followed his descent and the last time we saw him. It seems on the way down he attempted to get out of his airplane and was successful except when he left the ship, the tail broke his arm in a compound fracture. He had difficulties, but once he got down, he landed among the Risi-French in Indochina. He was badly injured and required medical aid. For some reason the Risi-French turned him over to the Japanese armies. They did give him medical treatment, but sent him to a prisoner of war camp or several camps which were mainly underground. He spent his time to the end of the hostilities being transferred to various war camps in China and in the Japanese islands. Living conditions were poor, and he ate stale, rotten food, sometimes even eating rats to survive. He lived in damp caves which did nothing for his health. At the end of the war, he was down to ninety pounds.

After the war, he was returned to Taiwan and ended up in government service there, an air attaché to Canada. After a tour of duty in Canada, he went back to Taipei and entered the intelligence service of the Chinese Air Force. His duty in Hong Kong to this day is a mystery to me. His card gave an alias, stating he was the owner of this travel agency plus a construction company. He didn't say too much about his job but arranged for me to have a beautiful time in Hong Kong and other places. . . . He promised me another good time the next trip, but when I got back there was no travel agency and no Jimmy Chen.

Tom Cotton described the tactics of the October 1 battle in a letter to his grandmother dated the same day. "We operate like a bunch of bandits. We leave from our base here in China, fly way down to Jap territory, hit the Japs like a ton of bricks, and run like hell to the mountains. Please disregard any propaganda the Japs are putting out in the States. They try to do that to hurt morale."

On October 4, the Japanese bombers and fighters came visiting for the purpose of striking the Kweilin base. All their bombs missed the target area but ruined the rice crop in the paddies nearby. American fighters attempted no interception. The next day the Japanese made a return visit, but this time American pilots intercepted and drove them away. Lieutenant Cage claimed one confirmed and Capt. Arthur Cruikshank two probables.

They came again on October 6, this time trying a raid on the newly-established base at Siuchuan. The enemy fighters and bombers were met by a small flight of the Seventy-sixth who wreaked havoc with the formation, sending them scurrying home. Scorers for the day included Lt. Thomas L. Bullard, one Zero; Lt. Richard J. Templeton, one bomber; Lieutenant Lunsford, one bomber damaged; and Lt. Max Noftager, one Zero probable.

On October 7 the Seventy-fifth carried out the same type of mission as on October 1, but this time the Japanese were not so lucky. Nine B-24s were escorted to Haiphong by sixteen P-40s and one lone P-38. Once again the Japanese planes tried the same trick of diving down through the P-40s, this time picking Capt. Bill Grosvenor's flight. But their luck had run out. The bombers did a nice job on the target area and everyone returned safe and sound. Lieutenant Pruett of the Sixteenth logged one Zero confirmed and Lt. Gan K. Johnston of the Seventy-fifth one probable.

The weather began acting up again so operations were at a standstill for a few days. There was one report that even the birds were walking as it was too bad to fly. Then on October 8, the Seventy-fifth moved to Kweilin from Kunming, just as the monsoon season hit China again. One of the reasons for the move was that the men felt they would be in a better position to fight the Japanese since they flew out of the Hankow-Canton area. In later years Tom Cotton remembered the move vividly because it was his first landing in a P-40 after dark. "By luck I found the airfield," he recalled. "It was a regular fighter approach and I landed without incident. But I woke up the next morning and looked at all of the high volcanoes I had missed during the night."

On October 10 Tom Cotton sent his grandmother a long letter on elaborate stationery headed with appropriate symbols and the words, "October 10, 1943—Thirty-second anniversary of China's National Independence Day."

Dear Grandmother,

Of all the days I have spent in China, this is by far the most enjoyable one. October 10th—China's National Independence Day—is something like our July 4 at home. It is a day of celebration and festivity and merrymaking. The Chinese have donned their best clothes; streets are decorated with gay colors and national flags. School children have a holiday; the hostel in which I am staying is putting on a special menu. Speechmaking, lantern parades, Chinese music, intermingled with the incessant firing of firecrackers, bespeak the indomitable spirit of an unconquerable race.

According to my Chinese friends, it was on October 10, 1911, at Wuchang that Dr. Sun Yat-sen first ignited the torch of liberty for China which resulted in the overthrow of the absolute Manchu monarchy and brought about a republic like ours. Hence Dr. Sun is honored as the Father of the Chinese Republic and October 10 is observed as the Birthday of New China.

The picture on top of this letterhead carries an image of Dr. Sun and that of the Generalissimo setting his face toward the unfinished tasks of his devoted master. The twin red cross signs are Chinese characters for "Ten" and "Ten" which of course means the tenth day of the tenth month. So this day is also known in China as the Double Ten Festival.

But this October 10, the thirty-second anniversary of the birth of the Chinese Republic, carries an even greater significance, a double joy, because Generalissimo Chiang Kai-shek, the national leader who leads China in resistance and reconstruction, has been elected chairman of the national government. In other words, he has been elected, as we say, president of the Chinese Republic, and he is assuming office in the wartime capital of Chungking today. The Chinese firmly believe that the Generalissimo, as president of China, will lead the nation to an early victory against Japanese aggression, which will also bring final consummation to this global warfare in favor of the United Nations. So my days of returning home are not far distant.

The rest of the men arrived at Kweilin on October 11 as the Seventy-fifth moved to the new base lock, stock, and barrel. But the men were grounded due to the weather. While grounded, the men of the Seventy-fifth found various ways to occupy their time. In later years Charlie Olsen told the story of an event that occurred in the hostel in the mountainous area of Kweilin, quite a distance from the field, during the time they were grounded.

In the evening we went into the mess hall after supper, where some of the men from the Seventy-fifth were playing poker. I wasn't in the game. They had one light above them. I watched them play poker for ten to fifteen minutes and only half-heartedly put my mind to it. I looked up at the fellow sitting across from me. There was this great big spider sitting on his shoulder. It was a huge thing, almost as big as a saucer. At first I thought it was a joke. Somebody made up this kookie spider out of pipestems and stuff, so I thought. Then it moved.

I screamed, "Don't move. There's a great big spider on your shoulder! It could bite your neck." I rose and hit that spider. Swatted it off with my hand. I thought I was hitting a ball it was so heavy. He went out in the middle of the floor, and somebody took a wooden chair and bam! Smashed it down on him. We called the hostel manager. He was a nice fellow. We showed him.

"Look at this. Where did he come from?"

The hostel manager got all excited, chattering in frightened Chinese. Finally he stopped talking Chinese and told us in English that this was a big spider that lived in dark caves like a bat. And there was a cycle when they migrated. This was one of them. But when there was one, there were hundreds and thousands of them not far away. About that time we started looking around and sure enough, there was one hanging on the window screen outside, and as we looked out of the door we could see a couple crawling on the ground. But mostly they were in the bushes. Before it was over, we found dozens of them.

We got lights and went outside to our barracks, and they were in the trees, on buildings, and on the roof. Everywhere. Hundreds of them. The hostel manager was scared to death because he said they were very poisonous. We got back to our room and found two. Shot them with my .45. We searched the room. Found no spiders in our double-decker bed.

We decided to close the door. About that time, I looked at the bottom of the bed above me and there was one sitting on the bottom side of the upper mattress. I shot him. We checked the beds more thoroughly then, and every other inch of the room, locked the door, cut off the lights and went to sleep. The next morning all were gone.

A subsequent search for information on the species of spider or migration habits of any large spider in this portion of China has proven unfruitful. One entomologist suggested that the migration might have come when the caves which the spiders inhabited were flooded during the rainy season.

Cotton wrote his grandmother on October 30:

An alert came while I was reading your last letter. While I was out, a lucky bomb had blown up the house, desk, letter, and all, so I guess you will have to write the letter over again. No news is good news. If anything does happen to me you will probably get the news within twenty-four hours. Also a missing in action report may be good news. When a pilot is reported such, he is given thirty days to notify his home base where he is. All China has friendly people in territories who help people to escape. Sometimes pilots have to walk back because our flights go to great distances. Sometimes it takes thirty days to walk back. From your letters, I can see it has been almost three years since I saw you. However, some of the older men are returning, which is good news. I guess my turn will come soon. Probably the first of next year.

On October 25 Fort Bayard, a port in southern China, received a "friendly" call from two B-25s escorted by four American P-40s led by Maj. Elmer Richardson. The bombers did their little job and headed out to sea. The P-40s returned to Nanning for the night. Next morning they came back to Kweilin heavily laden with lots of bananas for the boys of the Seventy-fifth to eat.

The unsung heroes of the trail, the 75th ground personnel, arrived in Kweilin on October 28. A convoy from Kunming, less one Chevrolet truck (which took up permanent residence at the bottom of a nameless river), arrived with the personnel looking like the House of David baseball team. After shaving and eating all the food in sight, they decided that the experience was worth the trip, but never again would they venture forth into the wilds of China with motor vehicles. October went out with all crews grounded.

"Some days it does not even pay to get up," to quote Col. John Alison. On November 3 eighteen of the Seventy-fifth Squadron's P-40s undertook to escort twenty-one B-24s on a raid on Japanese-held Hong Kong. Nine P-40s had to turn back because of engine trouble and confusion on the part of some of the new pilots. Three auxiliary fields were used to land. The others came back after the bombers failed to drop a single bomb on the objective. The leather medal for the day went to Lt. Jim Anning, who was reported to have nearly landed at White Cloud airdrome in the fair city of Canton. The people there were of the unfriendly type at this time, so it was well that Jim did not actually stop there. Five miles north of Canton the mission was intercepted by about a dozen Zeroes, and during the ensuing fight Capt. Bill Grosvenor shot one down, and another was damaged. All planes returned to Kweilin although one was slightly damaged.

Earlier that morning nine pilots of the Seventy-fifth, led by Maj. Elmer Richardson, went out to try to intercept plots of enemy planes reported nearing the field. But the report was erroneous and no contact was made.

On the same day, the Seventy-fourth sent seventeen P-40s to escort bombers to Hengyang. Southeast of Canton, the mission was intercepted by approximately eighteen Zeroes. In the fierce engagement that followed, Captain Bell and Lt. Robert M. Cage each got one confirmed and Lt. Altheus B. Jarmon scored a probable. Cage's ship was damaged and he had to belly-land at Kweilin, but the others returned safely.

While American and Chinese fighters kept busy in this area, Japanese fighters were continuing to strike at transport planes flying the Hump. To counter such hunting forays, a grave concern when supplies were so short, General Chennault devised a scheme. He ordered all transports to fly the northernmost route and the B-24s to fly the southern route in loose formations of six to nine aircraft, hoping the enemy would mistake the latter for cargo-carrying C-87s. To assure the best results, all gunners were ordered to hold their fire until the enemy planes were at close range. The results of this plan were highly successful. On October 26 and 27, using Chennault's tactics, the Liberators of the 308th Squadron shot down eighteen enemy fighters without loss. Enemy interception of vital cargo flights dropped off markedly after that.

Of course the men of the Twenty-third were not the only fighters in China at the time. While the heavies were engaged mainly on Hump run operations during September and October, 1943, the mediums of the Eleventh Squadron were busy striking directly at the enemy. From September 1 through 26, the squadron flew sixteen missions—medium altitude attacks against shipping on the Yangtze, railroad yards, installations, harbor areas, ammunition dumps, factories, and airfields throughout Japanese-held China. Then on September 27, two B-25s flew the squadron's first sea sweep from Nanning. Sweeping the Gulf of Tonkin at low altitude, the lead plane, flown by Lt. Col. M. F. Taber, the squadron's CO, hit a two-hundred-foot freighter, which was being abandoned as he flew off. The second plane crashed into the sea during the mission, killing two men, but the others made it back to base.

On the Fourteenth's fighter side, operations continued at a regular pace into early October with a series of attacks on river traffic and troop concentrations and missions in support of attacks on enemy airfields. On September 14, the Twenty-fifth Fighter Squadron arrived at Yunnanyi from India.

From February 2 through the end of October, 1943, the pilots and gunners of the Fourteenth Air Force had claimed 351 Japanese planes shot down while losing sixty-eight of their own planes. They looked forward with confidence to the last two months of 1943, which would bring some of the most intense fighting of the war.

CHAPTER 8

The Twenty-third Fighter Group: November–December 1943

Throughout November 1943, the men of the Twenty-third Fighter Group kept plugging away, strafing at Liuchow Peninsula and intercepting Zeroes at Hengyang and into the Tungting Lake region. The Tungting Lake region, situated in north central China, was the scene of the most bitter fighting ever witnessed in this war-torn country. On November 13, the Japanese forces moved southward, crossing the upper Yangtze River from their old positions above Tungting Lake. The drive continued from there down the road to Lichow. Another drive was started south of Liuchow, encircling the city. Forces advanced by means of roads across the Tungting Lake to Changteh. Throughout these moves, the Chinese offered fairly bitter resistance. The siege of Changteh, for example, lasted for seventeen hard-fought days.

In starting the offensive, the Japanese had two primary purposes. The north central part of China is rich in the production of rice, and the enemy contemplated the capture of these crops during the process of the campaign. In addition, the Allies had hoped to move some trained and seasoned Chinese troops from the Tungting Lake area to northern Burma to aid the Chinese engaged in battle there. But, as the Japanese had expected, due to the offensive these troops had to remain in China in the Tungting Lake area.

Throughout the campaign, valuable assistance was afforded the Chinese troops by organizations of the Twenty-third Fighter Group. Changteh was under constant patrol by the Seventy-fourth and Seventy-fifth fighter squadrons. Nanhsien, Hwaijung, Ansiang, Kienli, and Siuchuan were bombed as well as Yochow, located at the mouth of the Tungting Lake. Food, supplies, and ammunition were dropped from planes to the gallant Chinese force. Japanese rice fields at Pailuchi, Puchi, Shasi, and Kaingling were constant targets for strafing. The railroad line between Yochow and Wuchang was under constant strafing as well as barges and sampans used by the Japanese to move in supplies and reinforcements.

On November 11 the Seventy-fifth Squadron moved to Hengyang. The next day Tom Cotton and Charlie Olsen were among the fighter pilots who went to strafe Yochow. They had already been to Sichai, where they strafed that tremendous cavalry of Japanese. Olsen recalled:

> They looked like herds of cattle. I caught four men running with my machine gun. They just disintegrated. The fellow in the back just folded over like I cut him in half. I must have severed his spine. The one in the right front just evaporated in my sights. We'd been strafing them, reconnaissance off to the north, and that was probably where they came from. We'd been up to Yochow, on the lakes, shooting up the boats earlier in the day, and I think they were getting tired of it. Maybe they had some idea to get us out of there. We were too far north.

On November 15, members of the Seventy-fifth were honored by having Polish ace Maj. W. C. Urbanowicz attached to them. He was actually on leave and joined the group of his own volition. The next day seven of the Seventy-fifth Squadron's P-40s escorted some B-24 bombers to hit some shipping and the docks at Kowloon harbor. The Japanese decided not to intercept and the mission went off with considerable success. A large ship lying in the harbor was observed being hit by bombs, but the smoke was so thick that the pilots were unable to tell whether or not it sank. The planes encountered only moderate antiaircraft fire, which nonetheless showed that the Japanese were actually there. Charlie Olsen led the flight of fighters for the strafing mission against the enemy troops, horses, boats, and rafts and made several passes in the face of heavy and accurate ground fire. His rudder control cable was severed by enemy fire, but he was able to return safely to his base.

On November 17, three enlisted men of the Seventy-fourth Fighter Squadron received soldier's medals for saving the life of Capt. John Morrison at Kweilin on the preceding August 20. Morrison, coming in for a landing, had crashed and caught fire on the edge of the runway. T. Sgt. Eugene Arvin, S. Sgt. William Barowsky, and S. Sgt. Ralph Scott had dashed out and pulled the unconscious pilot from the flaming plane.

It was back to the war again on November 18. Four pilots from the Seventy-fifth and twelve from the Sixteenth cruised up to Shihmen for just a little trick, which was on the whole successful. Four P-40s were used for top cover while eight strafed. They hit a Japanese cavalry unit on the south bank of the Shihmen River and killed thirty to forty horses. One barge with about thirty men on the south bank of the river was also knocked out. A few Zeroes were in the area but the pilots missed them. They saw some antiaircraft fire but the aim was really bad and nobody got hit. November 18 was moving day for the men of the Seventy-sixth, who went from Hengyang to Kweilin, and for the Seventy-fifth Detachment, who moved from Kweilin to Hengyang.

The Seventy-fifth and Sixteenth squadrons joined forces again on November 20, going to the Ling Ho River to strafe from Tzuli to Tsingshih, and hunting was fairly good. One flight of P-40s were to strafe with two flights to act as top cover. They proceeded downriver from Tzuli. At Maoerhyu the four strafing ships made one pass on a cavalry unit estimated at about a hundred men and twenty horses crossing the river. Troops and horses of this group of the left bank of the river suffered heavy casualties. Maoerhyu and Shihmen were smoking from former fires. Near Shihmen, four P-40s again attacked a group of horses and soldiers—forty men and fifteen horses—along the riverbank. From Shihmen to Lichow they attacked two small river boats—a sampan and another, smaller boat. Then they made one pass on a town near Shihmen, starting a few fires. There was a single-span pontoon bridge crossing the river at the first town west of Lichow, where there seemed to be a small settlement on each side of the river. The men doused this area with a bit of lead and cruised on. Lichow and Tsingshih were both smoking and Lichow was blazing as well. In the Hsutu Hu Bay, opposite the landing ground, one hundred yards off shore, the Americans attacked three boats, one boat resembling a naval lifeboat towing the other two. All three were sunk. In a repeat performance, the Seventy-fifth and Sixteenth returned to Tzuli in the afternoon and bombed the town, setting fires all over.

On November 21, thirteen ships, the lucky number for the Seventy-fifth, went to strafe shipping northeast of Changteh. Colonel Rouse of the Headquarters Squadron of the Fourteenth Air Force along with four of the Sixteenth Squadron's P-40s went down to strafe, and the rest stayed top cover. Once again it was the old story of setting sampans afire, sinking boats, and killing "Japs." No concentrations of men were encountered except those riding in boats, and an accurate estimate of how many of those who were killed was impossible. The American pilots wondered where the Japanese Air Force went—all of them except Charlie Olsen, that is, who ran into a Japanese wing commander over Tungting Lake.

He had stripes and markings on his plane, little victories on the side of his cockpit and back side, but not in front. There were three stripes on the body, which was very unusual and signified that he was a general, a full colonel, or high up on the totem pole. He could fly and he decided he was going to take me on.

When we met over the lake, I was alone. Another one with him backed off and he turned at me. I figured, "Oh, oh. I got me a pro here. He's going to come and get me and the other one is going to watch." I could almost hear him thinking. "Watch me get this '40.' "

We started sparring. He circled. I circled. He dove and I climbed. He climbed and I dove. He kept sparring. I kept waiting for an opening and he never gave me one. It was getting late and I didn't have much fuel because I was coming off an escort mission. I figured I had about ten minutes and that was all. I was going to have to quit soon or he was going to get me. I had to settle it right there. When he circled around to the left, I started circling behind him. He probably figured I had made a bad move, that I was going to try to turn inside of him and I couldn't do it. With his Zero, I was going to turn inside of him and knock him down. So he thought.

And I let him think that. We circled and I kept gunning it and he kept gunning his. I kept coming around, and he let me close in a little on him to let me think I was going to get him. He was going to turn into me. The whole time I was climbing and slowing down. Four hundred. Come in at a dive, three hundred, two eighty. I got down more like his speed and we went around the lake three times and I kept closing and closing. And just about the time I figured, "If

I close anymore, I'm going to get him and that's not likely as he is not stupid. He's going to make his move." I climbed a little higher and about that time he turned into me. He cut me off.

He figured he had me. That's what I was waiting for. I pulled up on my tail, chopped the throttle and sort of flipped it, and pushed my nose down heading in the opposite direction—right for him.

He kept coming—he had no choice. He had to face me in a head-on pass or break away. If he broke away I was going to be on his tail in seconds, shooting him to pieces and the Zeroes were pretty vulnerable from the rear. He had one chance to save his butt, let alone his face, and he knew it—he had to face me in a head-on fight, and unless he was new in the area, I'm sure that he didn't relish the thought, probably wished that he had brought his wingman with him, maybe now not so confident that he was going to fix me up. The very fact that he let the other plane stay up showed me he had confidence in himself. Yeah, he was going to fix me up all right. The thing that I couldn't figure was what gave him so much confidence because they had never fixed us up much in the past. "He must be new in town," I thought.

He flattened out now in a shallow dive and I saw his guns start to twinkle like tiny Christmas tree lights. Tracers passed over my cockpit as I climbed slightly up to his altitude holding my fire, conserving ammunition for a closer shot. By now I could see the big spinner, red cowling, and shiny pushrods. Eight hundred, six hundred yards. Converging fast now, he's still diving slightly and I'm still climbing, slower than him. We start getting pretty close now and I cut loose, firing continuously. I could see my tracers converging right smack into his engine. I see the pushrods and blue flashes up in his engine —little pieces, little glints of stuff flying away. I was concerned that if he blew right in front of me I would fly right into the stuff so I kept on his engine, not trying for his wing roots and fuel cells. Then Varoom! He pulled over me and I knew I'd got'im—he wasn't going home.

Immediately, I turned into his wingman who was still out but coming in fast. However, what ever happened to his superior behind me must have discouraged him because he suddenly broke off and turned tail. It was my suspicion that the guy I had shot was going down so I kept chasing the wingman for a short time sending a few .50s his way. I could not close the distance sufficiently to make anything count so I broke off and headed back to the lake where I had fought the commander. I kept searching and there was nothing. I had hoped that I could see something, a parachute, smoke, or an oil slick on the water, but the haze over the water made it difficult. Though I had fired on both planes and felt certain that I had finished one, I only claimed one damaged when I returned to base.

On that afternoon of November 21, eight P-40s led by Maj. Elmer Richardson made a sweep across shipping from fifteen miles east of Changteh to an area north of Ansiang, sinking and destroying much enemy shipping and killing crews. But they had some trouble distinguishing Japanese from Chinese.

The Seventy-fourth Squadron sent a fighter sweep to Canton on November 22. Planes circled the city five times, but no interception was attempted. One plane developed engine trouble on the return trip, and the pilot was forced to bail out. Once again the Seventy-fifth was out in force. At 7:15 A.M., nine P-40s were alerted to investigate plots of enemy aircraft reported nearing the field, but no contact was made. At 10 A.M., P-40s went out strafing Japanese boats and troop concentrations on the river west of Changteh. Eager beaver Bill Grosvenor led a few of the boys to strafe the Changteh area. "Ho hum, another milk run," the men said to themselves. Major Richardson led the first team up and strafed rivercraft loaded with Japanese, and casualties were heavy. One launch tried to hide under some branches used for camouflage, but it was of no use. Still there was no ground fire or Japanese interception. Maybe the "Jap" Air Force went home, considering it a bad job, some of the American pilots thought. They were living in hopes that the Chinese ground forces, aided by the Americans and their own Chinese airmen, would be able to keep the Japanese from getting rice from the famous Rice Bowl. Lt. J. D. Long led an offensive reconnaissance over Changteh but saw little of interest to him or the others on his flight. The front lines were so indistinct as to make them almost impossible to find.

The next day thirteen P-40s from the Seventy-fifth, led by Major Richardson, went on an escort mission with B-25s to Hankow. It was a hit and a return without casualties.

On November 24 Lts. Curtis Scoville of the Seventy-fifth and Wong of the Chinese Air Force pulled off a little reconnaissance over Tungting Lake area to see what they could see. There was not much to see, so they returned. But Lts. Donald Glover and Charlie Olsen had better luck. They led flights accompanied by eight ships of the Sixteenth to escort five B-25s to Hanshow. The bombers scored 100 percent hits on the target while the P-40s did a little strafing on the side, getting a few boats and sampans. Long took a couple of flights to Hanshow to look over and knock out any Japanese he could see. But he was disappointed that there was no action.

The next day was Thanksgiving, 1943—one of the big days in the history of the Twenty-third Fighter Group. Lieutenant Glover of the Seventy-fifth took a pass up and above Hanshow, shot up a few things, and rolled home. Capt. Bill Grosvenor and eight newcomers went up and supported the Chinese ground forces by knocking a few more disciples of Premier Tojo out of this world.

One of the pilots who participated in this mission was Lt. Everett O. White, who had reported for duty with the Seventy-fifth at Heng-yang back on November 12. He went on his first combat mission on November 16, and during the next eight days, he flew six more missions, strafing Japanese troops and ships in the Tungting Lake region. Then on the Thanksgiving Day mission, White was shot down by ground fire. Fortunately he escaped the Japanese, and some Chinese helped him get back to the Hengyang base. But he had lost his memory due to a head injury that gave him amnesia. From this time until April 1944, he was a patient in hospitals in Kunming, Ledo, Assam, Calcutta, and then finally Miami, Florida.

Throughout the Twenty-third's air war against the Japanese there were many crash landings and forced landings made in P-40s by pilots such as Everett White, but it is interesting to note that practically the only injuries sustained were those involving the head. The sudden deceleration thrust the head forward where it came into contact with the gunsight. The resulting injuries ranged from slight scalp lacerations to concussions and severe skull fractures. Those gunsights were soon padded with rubber sponge, but this apparently was more of a psychological than actual aid.

The newer model aircraft were equipped with shoulder straps, which, if used, helped prevent the forward thrust of the upper body. But most pilots disliked using them because they interfered too much with their freedom of movement in operating the ship, and in the excitement of preparing for a crash landing, they would forget to use them.

At Siuchuan, history was made that Thanksgiving Day when B-25s, P-38s, and P-51As streaked into the air to outwit the Japanese and make the first Allied raid on the island of Formosa a success. The strike was led by the newly appointed commanding officer of the Twenty-third Fighter Group, Col. Tex Hill, who later provided a personal account of the raid.

We'd been doing recon missions over Formosa for many months, trying to figure out how in the world we could get there because there were some very lucrative targets. The main target there was at Chiachiku, which is just south of Taipei and has now been renamed by the Chinese. It's called Sinchiu. At that time the Japanese name was Chiachiku. The fields there showed very heavy concentrations of bombers and fighter airplanes. As a matter of fact, the recon that was made prior to our raid, just the day before, showed a hundred plus bombers on the field as well as 112 fighters. We moved into a place called Siuchuan the evening before. Casey had called me in and said that we were to try and make this raid. We took everything in China that would make that long trip, which consisted of eight P-51As, ten B-25s, and twelve P-38s. I was in charge of the flight.

I was the only one who knew what we were going to do, where we were going. This thing had to be very secret because if any information were leaked to the Japanese over there, we could've lost our entire force. Because of the way our raid was set up, we would go in right on the deck so that we would be undetected. Now we moved into Siuchuan the evening before. The next morning early we got up and everybody was excited because everybody knew that something was in the air. They didn't know what it was. So then I held this briefing. Preacher Wells was in command of the B-25s, Sam Palmer was leading the P-38s, and I was leading the P-51s. The B-25s were to do the navigation. It was a pretty hairy trip in retrospect because there was a hundred miles of water there that we crossed in single-engine airplanes with no Mae West to hit a target and then a hundred miles back. That's a pretty good little risk. However, at the time we never thought anything of it because we never had had any Mae Wests and it's only in retrospect that I kind of break out in a sweat thinking about it.

But anyway, as we approached the coast we had achieved complete surprise. There was one airplane coming down the coast. It was a transport of some sort, and I dispatched a P-38, I believe it was Sam Palmer, over. But anyway, they shot that plane down, and it probably was carrying quite a number of dignitaries or high-ranking people. The fighters had been alerted just prior to our getting there, and they got seven airborne but we shot those down immediately. The Japanese bombers were in a landing pattern when we arrived and so we started in on them and started shooting them down in the pattern. And the B-25s (they were loaded with parafrags) pulled up to a thousand feet and released these parafrags. It was an ideal load because the gasoline trucks and everything were right on the field ready to receive these Japanese bombers coming in. So it was an ideal situation. We strafed the bombers that were on the ground and the trucks and then headed on back because we were operating at the extreme limits of our range. My flight time was five hours which is quite a long time on a P-51. We didn't get a shot fired at us so to speak. We all returned to base safely.

It shows that a mission, if it's well-planned and well-executed—well, you can just really pull it off. The photos taken over the target show thirty-seven enemy aircraft burning on the ground. The smoke was so heavy and the fire and smoke so intense, that it's hard to see everything. It was a highly successful raid, and it really shook the Japanese up because at that time they never dreamed that we could reach them there. We were able to pull it off, and I think there was only one bullet hole in one P-38 when we landed. Coming off the target I was really frightened because my guns had been very hot and apparently had a shell in the chamber that cooked off. When I was leaving the target it went off, and I thought I had had it. I looked around and didn't see anybody and finally realized the guns were real hot and this ammunition had cooked off in the barrels. It was a very interesting flight.

We thought about following it up. We probably could have gotten by with another raid the next day on a follow-up deal, but the weather conditions were such that we couldn't get in. So that was it.

The score for the day: Colonel Hill, one Zero destroyed in the air, one bomber destroyed on the ground, one bomber probable on the ground; Capt. J. M. Williams, one bomber confirmed on the ground, one bomber damaged on the ground; Capt. John Stewart, one bomber confirmed on the ground; Lieutenant Bell, one Zero confirmed in the air; Lt. Robert Colbert, one bomber confirmed on the ground; Lt. Donald Hedrick, one bomber probable and two bombers damaged on the ground.

Aside from these victories, numerous installations and personnel were destroyed. The forward echelon commanding officer, Col. Casey Vincent, planned and directed the successful raid. All planes of this striking force returned safely to Siuchuan. Four P-40s flew top cover for this returning mission.

Two Japanese versions of the raid were broadcast. One newscaster reported "an attempted strike on Chiachiku airdrome in which the Japanese forced the raiders to turn back before reaching the field, shooting down two American aircraft." Another enemy radio report was less modest. This broadcaster reported that the American bombers "were forced to jettison their bombs before reaching the target and all except one were shot down." Such extremely distorted claims were additional proof that the Japanese had been severely jolted.

Siuchuan was not the only place of action on November 25. Some of the men from the Seventy-fifth, including Charlie Olsen, Tom Cotton, and Wiltz Segura, went to Hanshow on a strafing mission at about dawn. Cotton recalled:

We had this projectile which had a delayed fuse on it. We could set it. We were strafing down the side of the river, picking off sampans, and this guy fired it right at the waterfront, where some ships were docked. The projectile went completely through the ship, down three blocks through the houses, and exploded somewhere downtown.

Some guy had an old civil war cannon. And as we came down low, around the banks of the river, I saw him light the fuse of this old cannon and run. And there was this big billow of smoke all over the water.

I was told we had to turn off at another place before we got to Hanshow because it was a hot area. I was preoccupied and when I was to pull off to go back to our base, we were right over the airport at Hanshow, and they were waiting for us. The whole place lit up with small arms and antiaircraft, and smoke filled the airplane. I got hit right in the middle of the airport. It was so cold outside and there was a big mountain right behind Hanshow and I thought, "If I can just get to that mountain, I can stand a chance." But I knew that I wouldn't stand a chance if I got down on that airport or anywhere in the immediate vicinity. So I gave it the gun and started climbing up and prepared to jump out of the airplane. I told the flight to go home. And I started disconnecting my radio and everything else, cranked back the canopy, and stepped partly out of the airplane.

And I looked down and said, "Man, that's cold down there, snow and everything else." I looked up and there was my flight, an echelon on my wing. They were staying right with me. I thought and I knew the reason why—they didn't know how to go home. So I got back in and plugged everything in and said, "I told you to go home."

One of them pipes in and said, "Aw, we just wanted to see you jump." And then the smoke went away. I made it in, barely. I thought I would have to belly it in several times since I had run out of oil. And it was getting red-lined, the temperature up, but I came in and landed and taxied up to the line. My crew chief was a wonderful guy. They had an alert, Jap fighters coming in behind us. He said, "I'll fill it up with oil and it will last another fifteen minutes."

Meanwhile Wiltz Segura had his first combat experience:

We were just past the city called Changsha by Tungting Lake. There were supposed to be some troops crossing the lake, hauling supplies in small boats. It was a strafing mission, and we used eight airplanes, four on the bottom and four at the top. That gave us top cover in case the Japs would intercept and hold them until we could climb up and get away. I was on the bottom. When we shot up all of our ammunition, we always saved a hundred rounds and then we'd go up and fly top cover.

The Japs were in small boats on the lake. There was no place for them to hide. The troops were paddling boats like mad, and we came down upon them in a line all abreast. I picked up a boat, a sampan ahead of me. Must have been six or seven troops in it with baggage. I looked at them through my sight, coming down waiting to get them in range. Just as I pulled the trigger, I realized I'd never shot a man before. Well, all the sudden I thought, "That's the enemy. He's trying to destroy my way of life. It's like a ballgame. Let him have it." I split the boat in half, saw people jump on both sides. I blew up everything. After that, it was one after another for a year and a half. It got very impersonal after that. We were mad at them for what they were doing with our prisoners in the Philippines.

Even as the Twenty-third was enjoying success in all its endeavors on that Thanksgiving Day, General Chennault, Generalissimo Chiang Kai-shek, and others had flown to Cairo to present their views to President Roosevelt and Prime Minister Churchill. It was the first face-to-face meeting between Roosevelt and Chiang Kai-shek. Roosevelt and Churchill affirmed their support of TWILIGHT, the name at the time of the Allied plan calling for bombardment of the Japanese home islands by B-29s controlled out of Washington. This decision automatically relegated the China-based Fourteenth Air Force to a lower priority and precluded Chennault's attainment of a long-desired goal—to be the architect of the aerial destruction of Japan.

MATTERHORN was the code name selected to succeed TWILIGHT for the upcoming B-29 effort in the China-Burma-India Theater. MATTERHORN called for the India-based Boeing Superfortress to be flown out of airstrips near Chengtu, China, against the Japanese homeland. Although Brig. Gen. Kenneth B. Wolfe was sent to the CBI Theater to implement MATTERHORN, command control over the Superforts remained in the hands of Gen. Henry "Hap" Arnold in Washington.

The attempt to build up the minimum stockpile required to begin B-29 operations resulted in a reduction of Hump tonnage for the Fourteenth Air Force. Fuel reserves were already low in the eastern bases, which were a month's distance from Kunming by land lines normally employed in China. General Chennault vigorously protested the higher priority given to stockpiling gasoline for the B-29s and warned General Stilwell that the fate of China was at stake. Since the priority for project MATTERHORN came from the Joint Chiefs of Staff, Stilwell could only advise Chennault to cut back on operations to the extent needed to build up his own emergency gas reserves.

On November 26 Cotton wrote home to his grandmother:

Yesterday was Thanksgiving and I find much to be thankful for. First of all to be an American. One does not realize that until one is here, stationed in Hengyang, with the main mission to support Chinese ground armies. We are fighting north and northwest of Changsha. We call our group the Tungting Lake Task Force with missions to halt Japanese shipping on the Yangtze River, across the Tungting Lake and also stopping the Japanese ground armies that are rapidly encompassing the Hankow area. Constant periods of strafing daily, carrying supplies, escorting B-25 bombers, low-level missions on the Yangtze River, running around shooting up sampans, strafing towns and railway yards which sometimes interrupts our rest. The Japanese take advantage of a full moon for their night raids, coming down the river, and since we are at a distinct bend of the river, we are easily spied in the moonlight.

On the day Cotton wrote the letter, eight men from the Seventy-fifth, led by Lts. Tom Cotton and L. R. Lewis, took on a little more offensive reconnaissance up at Tehshan. They attacked fifteen to twenty boats and left the usual fires and Japanese dead strewn around, and also gathered useful information on enemy troop movements. Lts. Jim Anning and Charlie Olsen, with flights, escorted five B-25s to Shasi, which resulted in the usual destruction of Japanese installations and soldiers. Lts. Curtis Scoville and L. R. Lewis, fortified by the presence of their respective flights, also made a little call on the Japanese, inflicting heavy damage on some docks and boats, and killing several enemy soldiers.

The next day was a busy one for the Seventy-fifth with five missions. The first one was at 7 A.M., when seven P-40s were alerted by reports of enemy aircraft nearing the field. But no contact was made. At 8:30 A.M., eight P-40s were off to strafe the river from Taoyuan to the Tungting Lake area. Thirty small boats were shot up in this vicinity. The highlight of the mission occurred when Lt. C. K. "Casey" Wong tried to set an all-time record for number of birds killed with an airplane, the result of which was damage to the spinner and both wings of his ship.

At 10:30 two fighters went up to try to intercept a Japanese recon near the field. No contact was made. At 3:30 eight P-40s were off to reconnoiter the railroad northeast of Yochow. After successfully completing their mission, the planes zoomed back to safety. Again at 5:15 twelve fighters were alerted to investigate plots of enemy planes nearing the field, but no attack developed.

The Japanese had surrounded quite a few Chinese troops in the Changteh area, cutting off their supply lines. So on November 28 the members of the Seventy-fifth loaded up a few belly tanks with ammo and skipped them into the town so the boys on the ground would be able to keep up the good work even though they were surrounded. Maj. Elmer Richardson led this mission.

On November 29 Capt. Bill Grosvenor in his usual eager manner led eight ships up to drop supplies to the Chinese and then strafe some nearby enemy targets. It was on this mission that Lt. Warren R. Smedley observed the boiler on a Japanese steamer mimicking a shower screen by spraying steam in all directions like a lawn sprinkler. The steamer was shooting something besides steam very soon. In another mission, Charlie Olsen led his flight on a strafing mission with Tom Cotton acting as top cover for the activity below. Hunting was fairly good with an estimated fifty to seventy-five enemy soldiers biting the dust. A Japanese plot was picked up about that time, and the boys attempted to intercept but had no luck.

It seems the Chinese who were surrounded at Changteh needed food in addition to ammo, so also on this day Major Richardson's Grocery Delivery Service was born. There was a sad note in the day's activities with Lt. Curtis Scoville missing in action. Members of his flight reported that he had been hit in both oil and Prestone coolers by small arms fire, but it appeared that he had been able to glide to friendly territory.

Without a doubt the busiest and most profitable month of 1943 for the Twenty-third Fighter Group was December, beginning on the first day when the Americans went on five missions against the Japanese. At Kweilin, the Seventy-fourth sent eight P-40s to escort bombers to Hong Kong. Enemy fighters intercepted the mission but the P-40s made no claims. Ten P-40s of the Seventy-fourth went up as top cover for the returning mission. Upon landing, one P-40, flown by a new pilot named Lieutenant Bear, overshot the runway and was damaged. The pilot was not hurt.

At 10 A.M. Maj. Elmer Richardson led two flights of P-40s from the Seventy-fifth on a strafing job on the Japanese retreating from Changteh. According to the intelligence report, about 30 percent of the personnel strafed were casualties. Not content with the morning's work, Captain Lee led a couple of flights of the boys at 3:20 P.M. They patrolled over Changteh and then strafed Japanese boats in the Tungting Lake area. More columns of smoke rose into China's skies. Also on this day Maj. Roger C. Pryor and Lieutenants Brookfield and Tempest left for home.

The Seventy-sixth at Kweilin sent ten P-51s to escort bombers to Hong Kong. Two of them returned early due to engine trouble. The mission was intercepted by enemy aircraft, and during the flight two P-51s went down near the target. Captain Williams, the pilot of one of the Mustangs, was hit in the coolant and forced down in enemy territory. He landed his plane and burned it. Lt. Robert Colbert, the pilot of the other downed Mustang, bailed out. But both pilots returned to Kweilin some weeks later, having been brought through the enemy lines by the Chinese. On the mission one Tojo was claimed as damaged. It attacked the Group Commander Tex Hill, who drove it away and registered some hits on it.

A report was later filed concerning Lieutenant Colbert's return through the enemy lines to Kweilin:

Colbert was flying a P-51A as wingman for the second flight leader, Captain Williams. His flight was flying top cover, the bombs had already been dropped, and the bombers had started on their return trip. The fighter formation was somewhat strung out over the estuary when Lieutenant Colbert noticed five planes almost directly behind him. They were at first so far to the rear that identification was impossible. He did several "S" turns to try to see them better and finally identified them as Tojos, but they were too far back to fire.

Just as Lieutenant Colbert started to report the presence of the fighters to the rest of his flight, he was hit by shells coming from behind and to the right. He didn't see the plane which attacked him. His coolant, elevators, radio, engine, and instruments were shot immediately. Fragments of the shells which entered the cockpit lodged in the calf of his right leg, right knee, thigh, and right shoulder, and another small piece lodged beneath his left eye. He immediately dived away and apparently lost his attacker and by using both hands, was able to level out and head north-northeast.

Lieutenant Colbert's engine was cutting out badly and gasoline was leaking into the cockpit in considerable quantity so he bailed out just north of Shatsing. His altitude at the time he jumped was between five and six thousand feet and the speed of the plane approximately two hundred mph. The left side and top of the canopy only released when the emergency handle was pulled. Due to his injured leg and the force of the wind, he had some difficulty getting out; but by putting his left leg over the side of the cockpit and leaning out he managed to get into a position where the wind would catch him and pull him out clear of the plane. On the way down he saw his plane crash, doing about three hundred mph and exploding. The ship hit about a mile north-northwest of Tingtsum and Lieutenant Colbert landed on a small hill nearby.

When he hit the ground, he took time to open his jungle kit and remove the contents, which later came in handy. His first aid kit he left on his chute at the time.

There were about fifty workers in the field nearby where Lieutenant Colbert landed. They motioned him back further into the hills and then went on with their work. He followed their advice and walked back a little further into the low brush and sat down. A short time later two of the workers came over to him. One of them spoke a little English but could not understand any; but by means of the pointee-talkee and also his Chinese back flag, Lieutenant Colbert identified himself and explained the situation to them. They understood the pointee-talkee and also seemed very friendly. They helped him down the hill to where his parachute was. The first aid kit had by this time been ransacked. The material in it, however, was soon recovered and returned to him.

The Chinese then took him to another hill and to a small clearing nearer to their village and began to discuss ways and means of getting him out. They also brought him hot water to drink and bathe his wounds, which he then bandaged. He also made liberal use of the iodine from the jungle kit, painting the various cuts and sores of the curious who gathered about him.

They explained to him that he must get rid of everything that would identify him as an American, so all his clothing and possessions were removed except for the pointee-talkee and one ring which he refused to surrender. He was given Chinese coolie clothes and his own were taken away and hidden. A Chinese barber was also called and his head was shaved.

The process was finished by about seven in the evening, five hours after he had been shot down. At this time, about five of the Chinese moved him to another clearing somewhat north of the first, and at nine o'clock they moved him again about one and a half miles northwest to a little mud hut back in the hills. There he had a straw bed and a comforter. Two of the Chinese, one of them being the one who would say a few English words, remained with him all the time.

At two o'clock in the morning they moved again, one and a half miles further west to a cave in the bank of a stream which was very well concealed. The cave was only about seven feet long, four feet wide, and three feet high. They remained there the rest of the night.

Early the next morning, five or six of the villagers brought food—rice, sausages, and fish, which he found to be unpalatable, and oranges and bananas. He was told that the Japs were in the area looking for him but had not yet come to the village. These "Japs" were later identified to be the Red Army. The Red Army is a pretty strong force of Chinese Communist guerillas which fight both the Japanese and the Chinese central government troops.

After this news there was another hurried discussion of ways and means. As a result, plans were made to take Lieutenant Colbert out of the area by means of a bus. He refused, however, knowing that they would have to cross the Canton-Kowloon Railroad which he understood to be patrolled. He then asked them to get him in touch with the central government troops or Chinese guerillas, but they said that it was too far for him to go to reach either of them. He spent the second night in the cave.

Early the third day, they decided to try walking out, but it began to rain so they cancelled the trip and moved back to the hut instead. About nine o'clock in the morning the two guards came to him and told him there were two men coming to see him but that they were bad and that Lieutenant Colbert should not trust them. They arrived and one who spoke English introduced himself as Mr. Chung from the Chungking Special Operations Unit, which was a type of commando organization working behind Japanese lines.

Lieutenant Colbert and Mr. Chung talked for an hour and a half discussing the situation and Lieutenant Colbert came to the conclusion that he was completely trustworthy. Mr. Chung agreed that the suggestion of going out by bus was completely impossible due both to the danger and to the fact that the road had been torn up, something which the villagers did not appear to know. Mr. Chung did think that Lieutenant Colbert had been kept in the area too long and inasmuch as no plans for his removal had yet been put into effect, Mr. Chung left to talk over the situation with his superiors and promised to come back if the villagers would let him. Lieutenant Colbert gathered from this conversation that the villagers were in some disfavor with the central government because of some dealings with opium or a similar offense.

About an hour after Mr. Chung left, one of the boys went into town for food and came running back saying that the Japs (Reds) were in the town. Then Lieutenant Colbert and the two Chinese ran back to the cave where they awaited news that came to them from one of the Chinese's older brother who was an herb doctor in the village. He said that the Japs had taken the wives of three of the village officials as hostages for Lieutenant Colbert's release to them and had also burned his house. (This the Special Operations Unit men later told him was not true.)

All the next day was also spent in the cave with the Reds still searching for him. They discovered the hut and some other caves but did not detect the one in which he was hiding. That night was also spent in the cave still discussing plans as to how to get away. Again it was suggested that they get in touch with the army but the same objections were raised.

On the morning of the fifth of December, seven of the Special Operations Unit, all well armed, arrived. They were led by Mr. Chung. They explained that the Reds had left the village and that it was safe to start out. They left about ten o'clock with only one of the villagers going with them and headed for the town of Taiping, a small place about fifteen miles east.

About seven miles along their route, they heard the sound of revolver and rifle fire which the Chinese said was a fight between the Reds and a Japanese patrol. The Japs had apparently learned of Lieutenant Colbert's presence in the neighborhood and had sent out a patrol to get him.

The party made a detour around this area, went on over some hills and then called a halt. The government's men then sent the villager back saying that they could not reveal to him the methods they were going to use to get Lieutenant Colbert out. They were not unpleasant about it and appreciated the work he had done. They gave him some money to cover his expenses and one of them went with him back to the nearest village where he was to stay overnight and then return to his home in the morning. Lieutenant Colbert gave him six hundred dollars in Chinese currency at this time and had previously given him forty dollars to cover his food and other requirements.

About eight o'clock that night, two hours after leaving the villager, they arrived at Taiping. There was only one family living at this place and only two or three houses. The people, however, were evacuees from Shanghai, spoke good English and had good homes, and were trusted by the government. The people were very nice to Lieutenant Colbert and treated him to a good bed, good food, and place to wash. It was here he met Mr. Chin (Captain Wong) and arrangements were made for him to get across the railroad. Some of the government men were put out to patrol the route to be followed to the tracks, which vigilance was maintained until they were away from the area early on the seventh morning.

Lieutenant Colbert remained at this village the fifth night and sixth day with Captain Wong and the others of the Special Operations Unit and started out for the crossing about one o'clock in the morning of the seventh day. The railroad ran only about five miles from the town but it was considered to be the most dangerous part of the trip due to the fact that the Japanese have strong garrisons along the tracks and it is further patrolled by cavalry. The crossing was made at a point a short distance north of Tontaoharu, where the enemy has a strong post. They arrived without incident.

After passing the tracks they went straight east and then north but were unable to find their way and came south again. Captain Wong detailed two of his men to get a farmer to guide them to the river which they knew was nearby. They found one of the Chinese farmers near where they had stopped and offered to pay him to show them the way. He refused, possibly because he was midway through his morning meal. They persuaded him, however, at gunpoint.

He showed them the way to the river which was only about a half mile away. The farmer carried Captain Wong across while one of the government men carried Lieutenant Colbert. The stream was about a hundred feet across and waist deep. The others waded across afterwards. The farmer was then paid off and sent back with a warning to keep his mouth closed. He was not permitted to see Lieutenant Colbert during the time.

They continued to walk until about two in the afternoon and then came upon a village of Tsingkaihu where they met Maj. Won Chi Pan, commanding officer of the detachment which had found Lieutenant Colbert.

After a meal, a sedan chair was hired in the village and the whole party of seven or eight people proceeded on to a village in the area of Titcheuhwai where they stayed for the night. The party was well armed with rifles, revolvers, light machine guns, and grenades and always kept scouts out in front and behind on the march and kept guards posted at night.

On the eighth day a chair was again hired and the trip was made over the hills to Chanlung. That night the Weichow-Tanshui Garrison Headquarters was informed by telephone that a lieutenant of the USAF was on his way.

They stayed at a Chinese hotel that night at Chanlung. Some of the BAAG representatives met him there. They were nearly rubbed out before they identified themselves to the man guarding Lieutenant Colbert. They took no chances on losing him and the captain and Major Won took turns all night guarding his room. They were up the next morning and proceeded to Weichow by chair, arriving about three o'clock in the afternoon. There the BAAG doctor, Captain Van Dellin, started working on Lieutenant Colbert's leg. He was anesthetized, and then the doctor began the removal of the fragments but leaving those in the knee and beneath the eye alone.

They remained there for five or six days under the care of the doctor. They were treated royally. The BAAG took care of the Chinese's expenses while there and offered to pay them back for all they had spent on Lieutenant Colbert which was estimated to be between eight and ten thousand Chinese dollars. This was refused as all other offers had been.

On the ninth day, a wire was sent to the British Headquarters in Kweilin saying that Lieutenant Colbert had arrived at Weichow and it was believed that possibly an airplane might be sent to take him from there. This hope also caused a slight delay. However, it was seen to be impossible due to the difficulty of landing on the small strip and to the proximity of enemy operations so a wire was sent back and plans made for moving on by way of the river.

The villagers and town officials and the officers brought him many gifts of fruits, canned milk, flowers, cocoa, towels, sausages, dried ducks, and Maj. Gen. Yip Man Yu and his chief of staff, also a major general, who was in charge of that sector, gave a party in Lieutenant Colbert's honor at the army athletic club. All the BAAG were invited and other army personnel as well.

Arrangements had been made in the meantime to leave Weichow by boat the eve of the fifteenth right after the party. The group was to include Lieutenant Colbert and Major Won, who had the additional excuse of wanting to go to Chungking to transact some business, and an interpreter supplied by BAAG. The BAAG also gave Lieutenant Colbert ten thousand dollars in Chinese currency to take care of expenses.

The boat was about seventy-five feet long, powered by a gasoline engine, and could accommodate nearly fifty people in the crowded bunks lining the sides. It was pretty well filled up. They spent two days and two nights on board. The meals were prepared on the boat.

They followed up the East River to Hoyuan where they got off and stayed in the BAAG station with Captain McEwan for that night, the following day, and the following night. The last night another party was given by the officials of the town.

Arrangements were made in the meantime for two chairs, one for Major Won, who had a slightly injured foot, and they departed early on the morning of the nineteenth of December. They traveled north to Dungtap, staying there for the night in a Chinese hotel. Bus transportation was the method of travel used from there to Kukong. This journey took all day of December 19, 20, and 21 due to many breakdowns and flat tires. They stopped in hotels in small villages on the nights.

They arrived at Kukong early on the morning of the twenty-second, went to the Chinese Military Headquarters and reported to the general. Army officials there made arrangements for the train to Hengyang. Two alerts were experienced while at Kukong but the Japs did not come in. Prior to boarding the train, Lieutenant Colonel Ao, who was the air defense officer, gave a party on the floating boat on the river. After the party, about 7:30 in the evening, they boarded the train for Hengyang.

At five o'clock in the morning the twenty-third of December, they arrived at Hengyang where Major Hendrickson took a few more pieces of shell out of Lieutenant Colbert's knee. They remained there overnight and took a transport to Kweilin the next day.

While Lieutenant Colbert was finding his way back to home base, which took most of December, the fighting continued. On December 2 the Seventy-fourth again sent eight P-40s to escort bombers to the Kowloon docks. A heavy overcast was encountered over the target and no interception was made. A flight of eight more from the Seventy-fourth based at Hengyang was sent up to investigate plots of engine noise nearing the field, but no contact was made.

The Seventy-fifth made five missions that day. The most fruitful began at 10:45 A.M. when eight P-40s proceeded to Changteh to dive-bomb Japanese installations northeast of the city. The western part of the city was observed to be in flames. They bombed the northeast part of the town across the river from Changteh proper, and all bombs fell on the target area.

The Seventy-sixth Squadron and the Seventy-sixth Detachment at Siuchuan racked up six missions. At 12 noon, nine P-40s were alerted due to plots of heavy engine noise nearing the field. Contact was made at twenty thousand feet with approximately forty-six fighters and seventeen bombers. One flight climbed to twenty-seven thousand feet and shot down an I-45. The enemy bombers sneaked in under the American fighters and hit the field from 2,500 feet. Three P-40s were put out of action. Two of these were damaged so badly that the pilots hit the silk while the other was damaged but its pilot managed to crash-land on the field. Eighty-five holes were counted on the field proper and fifteen unexploded bombs as well. The flight landed at Hanchow, returning the next morning. The score for the Seventy-sixth that day was Capt. John Stewart, one Zero damaged; Lieutenant Kramer, one I-45 confirmed; Lieutenant McGuire, one Zero probable and one damaged; Lt. Max Noftager, one Zero confirmed. Noftager was forced to bail out due to his plane catching fire. Lt. Howard Bullock also hit the silk after being shot up.

The Seventy-fourth at Hengyang sent eight P-40s to patrol and strafe the Tungting Lake area on December 4. On the south shore of the lake, five sampans loaded with enemy troops were strafed and sunk with an estimated fifteen to twenty casualties. At noon, eight more P-40s were off to patrol Changteh. The flight was intercepted by six Tojos over the city, and during the ensuing fight Captain Wimmack claimed a probable and Lt. Harlyn Vidovich a probable and a damaged. One P-40 was hit and forced to land at Changsha. The pilot, Lieutenant Cousins, returned a few days later via the river and railroad to Hengyang.

At 4:05 that afternoon six P-40s from the same group escorted B-25s to Changteh. While the bombers were making their runs, seven Tojos intercepted and during the sharp conflict two were claimed as damaged and three probably destroyed. Captain Bell's plane was set afire, and he was forced to bail out at a very high speed. He managed to get out all right but broke his leg on the tail of the fast-moving ship. Although listed as missing in action for a number of weeks, he was carried to the hospital at Changsha where he received the best possible care.

The Seventy-fifth completed four missions that day. The Chinese troops on Tchshan Mountain needed some ammunition so Maj. Elmer Richardson along with Maj. W. C. Urbanowicz of the Polish Air Force took a few of the lads and dropped a supply in the Chinese compound. Lts. Donald Glover and Charlie Olsen led their flights on a mission to dive-bomb Japanese sections of Changteh with frag clusters. All the bombs fell on the target area. Capt. Bill Grosvenor, not to be outdone, dropped some ammo to the Chinese on Tchshan Mountain, putting all twenty thousand rounds of it right down into the valley.

Later, at 4:45, a couple of flights led by Glover and Olsen escorted B-25s to Changteh. During the bombing run they were intercepted by a flight of Tojos. Lt. Jack Blanco and Olsen each claimed one as a probable, and Glover and Jasper Brown each claimed a damaged. All planes returned safely to Hengyang.

The Japanese were beginning to feel the effects of the Americans' concentrated and powerful attacks on their shipping in the Changteh area. Beginning December 5, the Japanese Air Force attempted to counter the effectiveness of the Fourteenth by striking at Chinese ground forces and attacking planes and bases. That day, some twenty Japanese fighters jumped eight P-40s of the Seventy-fifth Squadron.

Lt. Vernon Tanner had his hydraulic system shot out, and Lt. Nathan Green had to land his burning P-40 in a hurry, but both survived. The Seventy-fifth had a very busy day. At 7:30 A.M., work call saw Capt. Bill Grosvenor and Lt. James L. Lee leading their flights on offensive reconnaissance and patrol up around Changteh. They strafed a few boats on the lake, which burned from the effects of the .50 caliber fire. A couple of Japanese with machine guns in a rice paddy tried their luck but no P-40s were hit. At 4:25 Lt. Tom Cotton led two flights to drop salt and ammo to the soldiers on the mountain again. No contact was made with the few Zeroes seen.

The next day at 9:30 A.M. nine P-40s from the Seventy-fourth escorted bombers to Changteh. Over the target the mission was intercepted by approximately fifteen Zeroes. The fighters attacked immediately and Lt. William O. Morin got one confirmed as he watched it crash to earth. He also claimed a probable. The others who scored were Lt. Robert M. Cage, one Zero damaged; Lt. L. W. Smith, one damaged; Lieutenant Butler, one Zero damaged. Colonel Rouse, flying with the Seventy-fourth on this mission, also claimed a damaged.

On the historic day of December 7, instead of taking it as the Americans had done in 1941, the Twenty-third dished it out with unabated fury, and it was the Japanese who were on the receiving end. The Seventy-fourth sent out four P-40s to dive-bomb Japanese installations in the Changteh battle area. Bombs were observed to land in the river and on the bank. The Seventy-fifth sent out four P-40s into the air at 8:30 A.M. to investigate plots of engine noises near the field. Then at 10 A.M. fourteen P-40s went to Changteh on an escort mission for the B-25s. After the bombs were dropped, the boys shot up the town a bit.

Poor Changteh—real estate experienced a real slump there. Next day eight P-40s of the Seventy-fifth escorted bombers back to the city again. The bombs were seen to hit in the southeastern part of the city, and there was no attempt at interception. Ding hao. But where were the Japanese?

Then in the afternoon, sixteen P-40s of the Seventy-fifth escorted bombers to egg Tehshan. Eight of the fighters were loaded with frag clusters. At the target the fighter-bombers split, one flight bombing Dehshanshih, the other hitting Tehshan, south of the river. Major Urbanowicz returned shortly after takeoff due to some minor trouble

Charlie Olsen, stateside 1944. (Charlie Olsen collection)

Flight Surgeon Jones Laughlin. (Jones Laughlin collection)

Tex Hill, during the early AVG period, wearing a Chinese uniform. (Tex Hill collection)

Seventy-fifth Fighter Squadron pilots Marvin Balderson, Walter Daniels, Joe Brown, Nathan Green and O. (Moose) Elker. (Jones Laughlin collection)

Pilot A. E. Probst at ease after his stint with the AVG. (A. E. Probst collection)

Transport pilot Howard Samuel.

Hell's Angels pilot R. T. Smith in cockpit of his plane marked with record of ten kills. (R. T. Smith collection)

Lt. Henry Wood, who was shot down behind enemy lines and captured by the Japanese. He remained in enemy prison camps until 1945. (Henry Wood collection)

American pilots return following the final mission flown by the AVG.

A multitude of humanity retreated from Hengyang by foot and vehicle after the base fell to the Japanese. (Tex Hill photo)

Shark-toothed truck is loaded on a ferry in the retreat from Hengyang. (Tex Hill collection)

Railroad stations quickly became choked with refugees after the fall of Hengyang. (Tex Hill collection)

Chinese workers plant bombs in preparation for destroying the runway at Kweilin. (Tex Hill collection)

Photo reconnaissance of forward strikes in enemy-held territory. (Tex Hill collection)

The Burma railroad supply line. (Howard Samuel collection)

A street in the old downtown section of Kunming. (Wiltz Segura collection)

Pagoda at Hengyang towers behind ferry. (Wiltz Segura collection)

and then took off again in an attempt to catch the formation. Upon reaching the target, he was mushroomed between a flight of Zeroes, and it seemed it was going to take some expert flying to get out of the trap. No matter which way he turned he was looking at a bunch of Zeroes. But by some evasive maneuver, he eluded them and reached Hengyang just as darkness settled over the field. The major made an excellent landing but at the edge of the runway hit a rock pile, washing out the landing gear.

On the morning of December 10, Hengyang skies were heavy with the aftermath of night bombing. It had been a night of unrest for the men of the Seventy-fifth, awakened in their hostel beds every two hours by the drone of Japanese approaching the field from the north. The old timers were annoyed at the interruption of much-wanted sleep, but it was a different story for five new pilots fresh from fighter school back in the States. They had just arrived and were gung ho for action, without the benefit of much briefing as to the procedure. Wiltz Segura recalled:

It was midnight when the first group of bombers started coming to bomb the airfield. Five of us were new to the squadron and had never experienced a bombing raid. We naturally assumed that we would be taking off immediately to intercept the enemy. We raced from the hostel, jumped into a jeep, rode down the winding road to the field, which followed a curvature of the Hsiang River and headed for the alert shack. It was a good fifteen-minute drive because of the five-hundred-foot hills which the road skirted.

When we got to the shack there wasn't a soul in sight. The bombers had not started to strike yet as far as we could tell. In bewilderment we waited around thinking the rest of the pilots would show up soon. After ten or fifteen minutes, still no one came so we decided we might as well head back to the hostel.

As we were driving down the middle of the runway with the headlights on, we began to hear the drone of heavy engines approaching overhead. It finally dawned on us that with the jeep lights on, we were the target about to be bombed. We piled out of the jeep and started running for the slit trenches by the side of the runway, all except the jeep driver who was bringing up the rear. I had a good lead out front, running like hell, when the first bomb hit behind us. It scared us so much that the stragglers passed me like I was standing still, including the jeep with driver.

We all dove for the slit trenches and spent the next hour or so dodging bombs. During the first bomb pause, we left the shelter, which was too close to the field for comfort, and sought safety back at the hostel where the rest of the men were still trying to sleep. Much to our surprise, we were informed that our P-40s were not even equipped for night flying, much less night interception.

Hostels were purposely located away from the field to lessen the chance of men being killed during air raids. The hostel was set up on a quadrangle with a couple of buildings on the left and a couple on the right, including a dispensary. It was formerly a girls' school. Buildings were two-story, New Orleans style, with slave quarters on top. The only difference was there were no slaves at the hostel. The buildings were made out of adobe. Down the center was a tennis court which the men used during time off. Charlie Olsen recalled:

What impressed me most was it was more like a resort hotel, quiet and nice and very old. But this southern boy couldn't believe the size of the camellias. They weren't bushes like the ones in my native Louisiana. They were trees, hundreds of years old and they were in bloom, pink and red. Flowers as big as saucers. There was a mess hall at either end, barracks at both sides, and from there we would leave down the road, heading southeast to the field.

We'd get up at four o'clock in the morning and have breakfast and then drive down to the field. At the field there was basically only one runway where the action took place. We didn't worry too much about the direction of the wind because the mountains protected us from both sides.

Our planes were scattered on hardstands or revetments, or were under some kind of nets or sheds for camouflage, away from the runway. Some were fairly close, say two hundred yards, while the others were three hundred or six hundred yards away, wherever they could find a decent place where the plane could still taxi out. Most planes were at the northern end of the field, but the surface on the perimeter of the runway was pretty hard. You could taxi most anywhere.

When I got to the field this particular morning, it was still dark. There was barely a first glimmer of light. We had not planned or expected a fight. However, since midnight the Japs had been pock-marking the field, doing the usual harassing things. Before, they would drop a few bombs and then they would leave. Or they'd send a photo ship during the day to take a few pictures and then drop a bomb and go. But this time they kept coming back every hour, and we realized they were not going to let up. They were setting us up for the morning, trying to knock out the field so the fighters couldn't get off. Then they planned to come in and really clean us off using fighter sweeps at low altitude at first light.

I was in one of the first jeeps down, but not the first. The first one went to the control net, which was located at the southwest corner of the field under a railroad track. It was actually headquartered in a tunnel with a curve in it, like a sewer. A grating on the floor raised it up above the water, but one could hear the trickle of water under it. In the net were the usual phones and maps. They could talk to us in our planes or to anybody else in the area for that matter.

I had parked my plane on the north end of the field the evening before, and it was fueled and ready to fly. Cotton and Jarmon's planes were close by, so the jeep driver dropped the three of us off at the same time and continued northward to drop off other pilots. We knew where our planes were even in the darkness. Jarmon was the first one to rev up. Then he promptly rolled over a piece of shrapnel as he taxied out. It was something like a child's jack only with big spikes, a calling card of the Japs the night before. He blew a tire. Jumping out of his plane, he ran toward me and hollered, "I'm snake bit!" just before jumping into a small bomb crater. It was so small, in fact, that I could barely see it. After I got airborne, Jarmon received a direct bomb hit and was never seen again.

As Jarmon piled into the small crater my engine roared to life drowning out the other sounds. Unless you saw the bombs explode, it was hard to tell if they were coming down or not. It's like you're driving in a car down the highway and you blow a tire and lose the wheel when you're coming to a railroad track. The train is coming on. You know you are going to hit him head on, so you don't really remember if there was a flagman on the left or right. With all the noise on the field, it was hard to ascertain exactly where the bombs were hitting.

I decided the best way to get off the field was not to taxi through the bomb craters at the end of the runway. The jeep driver had told me he'd drive a straight path across the runway, and when he got down far enough he'd turn around and flash his lights on in my direction momentarily. If there were any pock marks, he'd weave and circle and try to give me a straight shot. He drove off to the southeast and I took off diagonally across the runway straight for him. I dropped my belly tank and taxied over it. With all the shrapnel flying, I didn't relish going up like a Roman candle.

I didn't use all of the runway, because I could remember the faint outline of the alert shack going by on the left. I could see the jeep's lights and little else between us. Didn't need more than eight hundred to a thousand feet to get off. As soon as the gear started retracting, I fired my guns to clear the tapes, making sure they were still functioning. Cotton was right with me. When I was rolling, he was rolling. As soon as I got three hundred feet altitude, I started turning and looking around. As Cotton and I climbed off the darkened floor, all at once I could see, as if somebody had turned on all the lights.

When I first got off, I didn't see any Japs. I knew they weren't high because I had heard some engines. Yet the net kept talking on the radio about "angels twelve" and stuff like that, meaning twelve thousand feet and that was pretty high. I knew there were bombers up there waiting and possibly even Zeroes and dive bombers. Yet I figured most fighters were a couple thousand feet at most. These bombers weren't hitting the field that good either. They used the distinctive crook in the river to navigate by on moonlight nights and simply bombed where they thought the field ought to be. I climbed to about two thousand in a couple of minutes, and the ice and mud started sliding off the windshield. I could see at last, somewhat decently. Got my gunsight on. I had all the switches on. I was ready to fight.

Japs were all over. Somebody said on the radio there were two hundred in the area. This was going to be my first big contact. All this time I had been waiting for months and months to get my hands on a chance like this. I was getting to be an old hand, going out on interception after interception, with absolutely no contact. They'd come in at us about twenty thousand and disperse, and by the time I got up there they were gone.

I knew I was going to be in a real fight that day. I was feeling pretty cocky because I had waited for such a long time. I called Cotton. "We're going to get our meat today." I turned to the left and Cotton was on my wing. I asked where J. D. Long was and Cotton said, "He got off. I know he got off. I saw him clear the runway."

"Well, at least three of us got off who know what we are doing," I replied. "What about Glover?"

"I don't know," Cotton replied. "He was on the other side of the runway."

I said let's tack on and go find something. And about that time I heard a voice calling on the radio. It was Lingling talking, saying, "They're out at Hengyang. We had better get some help up there. Calling SM7. They got a big fight at Hengyang!"

Then I heard one of the pilots say, "How about us?" And the reply was quick. "No, some of them are moving down from Hankow. You had better stay. They have gotten us into this. We are going to be part of this action, too. I think they are coming on to our field. Get up above Lingling and get ready! We'll go to Hengyang if we have to, some of us."

At this time I sighted some Jap planes. I called out, "I got three or four, northwest of the field, and I see two or three northeast of the field! And they're Zeroes! I don't know what kind. I see no bombers, all fighters." I headed toward them and when I did, they broke off.

. Another voice came in on the radio and screamed, "I see them!" Then I saw Cotton's plane cut across and I lost visual contact with the Zeroes. They just disappeared. All these planes going four hundred mph in different directions. It only takes thirty seconds and they are all gone from a given patch in the sky. In a minute each travels several miles. Pretty soon in this general confusion, a Zero dove in front of me. I don't even know where he came from. I saw my tracers hit, but it didn't seem to particularly distract him. It was a single.

I started climbing back up and heard somebody on the radio cry, "Oh God! Three of them got me bracketed over here. I'm east of the field! East of the field! East of the field at four thousand! Two or three of them got me bracketed. I need help. Help!" Cotton and I headed for his direction but encountered two Zeroes en route. One dove after me, but Cotton was behind him in a flash, raking him off my tail. And I continued in the direction to help the man in distress. It was Beauchamp, but suddenly he left us and began heading for the field. He tried to bail out, but was unsuccessful. He was the only American air combat casualty for the day.

I heard Randy Lewis call on the radio, "Okay, I'm away." Then I picked up two Zeroes in front of me. Came right upon them and gave one big burst, my blue noses hitting all over him, his wings, cockpit, cowling. The other one broke away, pulled up, and tried to go around in a tight turn to get back of me in an attempt to tack on to my tail and shoot me down. But I kept on him. I had him going pretty good when he saw it wasn't going to work and started to straighten out. Then I saw smoke and oil, a mist coming down out of him. I had hit his engine. His plane started to trail a little smoke, and a P-40 suddenly cut in front of me, I suppose with the intention of taking him the rest of the way down. That baby was mine. I had staked my claim, so I gave him a burst with my guns and when he saw my tracers coming over him he moved back out.

I gave the Zero a couple more shots. Boom! Boom! This time I hit him real good because he started spinning and going down. I followed him maybe three hundred feet. I wasn't about to follow him long enough to watch him explode. That's suicide. I'd be watching him and another Jap would clip me. So I broke off and went back up. Whoever confirmed it was on my right. I don't know who it was. After a while I got back and joined somebody else. Balderson maybe. Scared to death. Wanted to know, "Where's the fight?" Somebody kept calling, "Bombers at Angels twelve. Angels twelve, Angels nine and thirteen." I decided that I would go up and get some of that easy stuff. I wanted to get up high. I climbed up to about nine thousand looking for some bombers as the sun started to break over the horizon. Back on the ground it was still dark.

Segura had spent much of the night in the trench near the hostel. When dawn approached those on the flying schedule were given the order to go to their aircraft and stand by on the radio for instructions. It was not quite daylight when he reached his plane. He could faintly see the airplanes and vehicles directly ahead of him as he looked carefully. Later Segura recalled:

I found my plane and stood on the wing. It was freezing—a little frost made the wing slippery. I opened the cockpit and flipped on the master switch and listened through my earphones. On the radio somebody from the net was giving us plots on where the Japs were. I didn't know if any of the earlier bombs had damaged the runway or not. It was still too dark to tell. Pretty soon someone ordered, "Any of you guys that can get off the ground, get off! Japs are about thirty-five to forty miles off."

Almost immediately from off to the left came the sound of the first inertia starter as it began its upward whine, followed by another and another. Segura swallowed hard and clambered into his cockpit. He flipped the switch to energize his starter and began to count—one, two, three precious seconds, four, five—until he could hear its scream above the noise of the other fighters already coughing to life. "Now," he thought, as he pulled to engage the flywheel starter spinning up to maximum rpm and he listened breathlessly for that unique-sounding wind-down, the exhilarating prelude of a P-40 coming to life. Suddenly the plane trembled like a Louisiana racehorse receiving its mount, and the huge three-bladed prop began a spastic turn—faster . . . faster . . . faster, then slower for a brief second as the engine belched black smoke and fire a foot from its dozen short stacks. Then the three blades disappeared into a blur, and Segura was completely immersed in the sound of an angry Allison engine.

At this instant the first fighter to his left started weaving out, bouncing stiff-legged, and turned to pass in front of him. It was an awesome sight—that determined eye over the menacing shark teeth, lighted grotesquely by the exhaust stack fire. The pilot half stood in the open cockpit, his head darting from side to side over the muddy windshield looking for a clear taxi way. Each burst of power created a precise corkscrew vapor trail which spiraled backwards over the fuselage and blended into the bellowing dust kicked up from the gravel floor by the powerful prop.

There was no set preliminary order for taxiing to the runway. In a scramble pilots got their engines started and began to weave out like a bunch of locusts interwinding and making "S" turns as best they could to reach the runway for takeoff as quickly as possible. With all that dust kicked up by so many props, taxi accidents were common. And especially on cold, damp mornings like this, there was ice and mud on the windshield. This morning would be particularly hazardous if the Japanese had been successful in pockmarking the runway with bomb craters during the night. To taxi under power into an open bomb crater is one thing, but during takeoff under full power would mean a complete washout.

Glancing to his right, Segura noticed the prop on the nearest plane had just begun to revolve so he gave a burst on his throttle and his plane reluctantly began to move. He followed close behind the fighter that had just passed before him.

I could not see, the windshield was icy, and on top of the ice there was dust. I stuck my head out of the cockpit watching the P-40 in front of me. Then I saw the whole plane disappear in front of my eyes. He had taxied right into a bomb crater. I stopped abruptly and waited for another plane to come by and then followed him. And sure enough, he disappeared too. I stopped again until another came by and, thus working myself through the bomb craters, came to the end of the field. Must have lost three leaders getting there. I'm not even strapped in when I finally get to the end of the runway and someone said, "Get off the ground!"

I give it the needle, heading north, cockpit still open. Simultaneously, I'm trying to strap my parachute on and secure my safety belt. First I'm airborne and then I'm not, airplane keeps coming up and then falling off. Finally I get airborne and managed to get buckled up.

When I got off the ground, I was by myself. I couldn't find anybody. I started climbing. Thought I would run into somebody and tack onto them. I never did see any of our own, but I guess I got too high remembering what the old timers had told me about the advantage of altitude. As I passed through twenty thousand feet, I wondered if I was high enough. I had been in China for such a short time and was a very green second lieutenant. I could hear them give the plots from the ground. "There's a wave coming in from the southeast." And I'd look down and see the plinks on the ground where they were bombing the airfield. Then I'd start down and then I'd think I would be too late before I got there. So I'd climb up again.

Meanwhile the Hengyang base was being attacked. Lt. Elmore E. Bullock took off in a shark to intercept the Japanese bombers and fighters. Due to mechanical difficulties, he was forced to return to the field and land, parking his airplane in a revetment beside a medium bomber. After he had gone to a position of safety, a Japanese bomb struck near the revetment, igniting thirty-six drums of fuel which in turn set the bomber on fire. As soon as the enemy bombers had passed over the field, Lieutenant Bullock rushed to the revetment, hoping to save any undamaged equipment. Arriving there he found that his ship had been pushed to a position near the opening and that S. Sgt. Robert Yarino had started the engine and was attempting to taxi the airplane to safety. However, due to his unfamiliarity with the controls, he could not do so. Bullock climbed in and taxied to a safe distance from the blazing inferno, just two minutes before the bomber's own bombs exploded.

"Be careful. There's a wave of Zeroes with the bombers," Segura heard on his radio.

Finally I decided I had better get down if I wanted any action. I dove down to between three and four thousand feet and that was when I heard Lewis had made a head-on pass with a bomber formation. He must have knocked down about three in one pass. By now the sun was up, and I saw airplanes blowing up all around in the sky, and then they disappeared. I was so occupied with not letting the Jap Zeroes get on top of me that I went back up. Then I saw a lone airplane about ten to fifteen thousand feet, way up in the sky. I started climbing as he was getting away in the horizon and I chased him.

Finally, when I got up to his altitude, I started closing rapidly. I was wide open. Wondered if the engine was going to hold out. Got closer and closer and climbed up two thousand feet higher than him, remembering what the old timers had told me: "Don't get sucked in. They always set up a decoy out there. Just when you're occupied with him, they will come out of the sun." I was looking in the sun and all around. I was by myself, my throat was parched. Finally I got real close and was coming in fast, as the plane grew bigger and bigger in my gunsight.

In a second, something else came to my mind. I remembered someone telling me about one of our boys shooting down one of our own airplanes, a B-25. "You got to be careful. They all look alike in a fight." The warning rumbled in my head.

I thought it was kind of strange that this plane would be away from its formation. At the last second, just before I pulled the trigger and I'm coming down on him, I thought, "Now just wait a minute. I've got to be sure this is a Jap." I almost ran into him trying to pull out high enough to look at his insignia. I should have known by the single tail. Only Jap bombers had a single tail over there. We had only B-24s and B-25s with twin tails. Just as I pulled off I saw the big red ball on his wing so I rolled back and from about twenty feet I hit him right under the wing root under the right side, slid underneath him and let him have it on the other side of the wing. He flipped over, his canopy blew out, and there was a fire in the cockpit. He started going straight down and at a moment fear was replaced by exhilaration. I dove down and saw a P-40 under me.

I figured I was about twenty-five miles from Hengyang, but I didn't have any maps or previous experience to know for sure. We had taken off in such a disorganized manner that I was not sure where I was. I was so glad to see that P-40 that I dove down hoping to hook up with him. But he had seen me hit the bomber as he had been chasing it at a lower altitude. After watching my tactics and probably knowing I was green, he thought I had mistaken him for a Zero and was afraid in my excitement I would turn on him too. He made a hasty "split S" and headed out. I hollered, "Hey wait a minute. I want to link up with you."

"Not with me you're not," came his reply. Later on this pilot named Beard told me he saw me shoot this guy down and when I dove after him, he felt he would be safer elsewhere.

The airfield was bombed and they wouldn't let us land at Hengyang. I was told by the radio to go to Lingling. I didn't know where Lingling was, but I sure didn't have fuel enough to get there no matter where it was. Radio told me I had to try to get there anyway. I paused for a moment, looking around and felt a kind of emptiness in the pit of my stomach.

"Where's Lingling?" I asked.

"Lingling is south. Just follow the river."

I headed out but the fuel gauge was bouncing on empty. I started looking around for a place to land and saw a little bitty road. There were rice paddies on both sides, more like a trail than a road. I spotted a little place in the road between two curves that looked like the only possible place to get her down. I knew I would have to give it a try, preferring that to stepping over the side and bailing out. A second lieutenant just out of flying school, new to China, and just having been through the first harrowing experience of combat, I was well aware of the fact that I was by myself and I didn't know where I was, except somewhere in China.

I looked over the road. Both tanks were now empty. What worried me most was that after I let down to make my approach should the engine quit before I could set it down, I would be too low to bail out. I began to let down anyway and finally spiked the P-40 down. As I touched down, I looked out and noticed I didn't have two feet of road on either side of my landing gear. The road had appeared much better from the air. I applied too much brake and my tail kept coming up. I saw the curve coming up at the end of the short road, just as I felt the brakes going soft. When I got to the curve, still doing about ten to fifteen miles per hour, I couldn't stop. I just went over the edge of the ditch and nosed up, smashing the scoop and bending the prop in the process. All of this produced a variety of unpleasant metallic sounds, preluding deafening silence. For a moment I just sat there, somewhere in China, I thought, and in rhythm with the sound of some liquid dripping beneath the crumpled engine cowling, I began to pat myself for assurance that everything was still in place.

Meanwhile Charlie Olsen, with the sun to his back looked down and saw seven Zeroes flying in formation. Years later he recalled the incident:

Holy mackerel, what is this? I decided I could get a perfect over-head shot on the whole bunch and quickly calculated a diving angle and closing approach that would allow me to take the leader and then return and get two or three of them at once. I timed myself to dive down on them at a slight angle to take advantage of my alti-tude. They had not spotted me yet. By the time I could dive to their level they would appear as they passed in front of me and I could lead them and shoot the leader and then rake my fire back over the formation. The formation would be hidden from my view beneath my plane during the dive. I pushed over and came down on them. I must have been traveling a lot faster than they were or my angle of attack was too shallow because when the time came for them to ap-pear in front of me, they did not appear.

In about ten or fifteen seconds they still didn't appear, and then I really began to get worried. Because I knew then that we were either going to collide or I was going to find myself out in front of the whole goddamn formation. I throttled back and started shooting in an effort to slow myself down. I rolled inverted to see where they were. The instant that I did, one came out from under me. I thought my prop cut his tail, that was how close he was. All I could see was "whoosh!" a blur, as he whizzed by. I saw part of his prop and can-opy and the pilot himself. I almost got him but it wasn't the way I had planned it. He flew right through my line of fire. Hoping he'd continue to pass under me, I rolled on around and came back up in a loop, over the top, and started down the back side and got one right off the bottom of the loop. He rolled over as I hit him firing blue noses which exploded all over his fuselage. I hit him good, but being alone and without a wingman, I broke off and dove towards the river and pulled back up in a different part of the sky to get some altitude. You use up a lot of altitude during a fight because a P-40 just doesn't perform in a fight unless its nose is kept below the horizon. You fight your way down to the deck, but you don't want to be caught down there, at least not without enough airspeed to outdis-tance any pursuing enemy aircraft. These were Chennault's tactics pure and simple and they worked. As the P-40 labored for altitude, I looked around, but the formation must have got together and gone the other way. I don't know what happened to them.

After gaining sufficient altitude, I turned towards the field and heard Cotton's familiar voice on the radio saying, "I've got fifteen cornered by myself northeast of the field." I hastened to close the distance, feeling sure that he would share them with me. We shared everything, well almost everything. Tom had this cute little. . . . Suddenly two more Zeroes popped up before me, then more, about six. I got ahold of them, chasing around, and finally one of them turned back on me, made a stupid head-on pass at me, and I really hit him all over the wing and cowling. As he went by I noticed another was ahead of me so I rolled to the right. I fired. I didn't know how extensive the damage was, so I just chalked him up as damaged.

A little later I caught another one and trailed him all the way down, and I kept hitting him and hitting him, but he never would explode. He wouldn't do anything but go down. I don't know if the pilot was dead or what happened, but he just kept going down, down. He never evaded me, he just slowly descended taking hit after hit. I took him all the way down to a thousand feet, then broke off.

By that time I saw three more so I pulled up and went after one. I got him good, but counted him as a probable. I flew all around searching. An hour had gone by and now the fight was over. About this time I started seeing P-40s all over the sky. When I first went up I could shoot anything I saw. If it moved I could shoot at it. That was the way it was when you were the first one up. You knew any plane you saw was the enemy.

Charlie Olsen came in at Hengyang field, but he did not land on the runway. There were holes all over it. He came in between the alert shack and some other buildings at the east side of the field off the runway. Likewise Cotton and the rest of the old gang.

Segura's emergency landing had placed him in a predicament. Six months passed before the plane was retrieved and restored to flying condition. Segura recalled:

I was in friendly territory, although I didn't know where I was or whether or not I was in friendly territory. Chinese troops came by and picked me up. That night they put me in a train nearby, with a schedule and my parachute. Nobody on the train could speak English. There was a well-dressed, educated man sitting next to me. We tried to talk all night but communication was a problem. He was getting off at Hengyang, too. Finally he said something about French engineering. He had been in France studying locomotive engineering. I figured if he had been to France he could speak the language. Being from south Louisiana, I could also speak French. So I started talking to him in French and he answered just like that. Here we had been trying to talk for the past twelve hours with no avail and we both had a common language. So we spent the remainder of the trip in pleasant conversation.

The squadron journal of the Seventy-fifth Fighter Squadron described December 10 with the following notation:

Today was a dilly. We got warning when the Japs were sixty miles out and believe me it was a mad scramble. We had a few waves of Japs come down and bomb without material damage to any of our installations. We were treated to an attack by dive-bombers but they dive-bombed just as lousy as they bombed from high altitude, so the sum substance of the dive-bombing was two B-25s damaged that were sitting on the field. Lts. Frank L. Gray, Randy Lewis, and Wiltz Segura were credited with the bombers. Lewis made a spectacular head-on pass with six bombers and shot down one immediately and probably destroyed another. It was the show of the day. A very sad note was when Lieutenant Beauchamp bailed out too low and struck the ground before his chute opened. The squadron will not be any better by this absence, and we will miss his ready smile for many days to come. God rest him.

In later years Randy Lewis told his story of that day this way:

I got to ten thousand feet and saw the bombers were getting ready to make their run so I went to the north to head into them to get a better pass at them and try to intercept them before they got to the air base. I was calling all the time, trying to tell them what altitude they were and their location. I got no response because they were broadcasting too. They were just about over the railroad station, lined up for the runway, when I hit the lead bomber which crashed behind the hostel. And I moved over to the second one, but due to the closeness, I had to pull off, circling, and come up behind them to try to knock off another one if I could. And all of the fighter escorts they had were raining down when I ran out of ammunition. So I had to take for the river, and I went back to Lingling and landed. Very few of us landed at Hengyang. Later on in the evening we went to Hankow on a raid. I changed airplanes and had engine trouble and had to return.

On December 11 the war continued its devastating pace beginning with Lt. Curtis Scoville walking in on sore feet and sporting saddle sores from his journey with the Chinese entourage he picked up just outside of Changteh. He arrived in time to see a flight of nine P-40s led by Elmer Richardson form up over the field and head for Nanchang to catch the enemy with their pants down. Arriving there, the sharks (six from the Seventy-fourth and three from the Seventy-fifth) caught a gaggle of various Japanese aircraft in the traffic pattern attempting to land, and with their low speed and altitude, the diving sharks devastated their prey. They did it both in the air and on the ground, and all but one shark got confirmed kills. The Polish ace Major Urbanowicz polished off two Zeroes in the air in rapid succession. Richardson got one in the air and one on the ground; Lieutenant Kinsey, one Zero in the air; Captain Jones, one Val dive bomber in the air; Lieutenant Herrin, one Zero in the air; Lieutenant Spurgin, one Zero in the air; Lieutenant Mullineaux, one Zero on the ground; and Lt. J. D. Long, one Zero on the ground. All were confirmed. At the same time, seventeen other P-40s of the Seventy-fifth were escorting B-25 Mitchells that were very successful in blasting the docks at Shihshou and the town of Ansiang.

December 12 moved right along as a midmorning flight of nine P-40s from the Seventy-fourth roared into the blue to intercept Japanese planes reported to be nearing Hengyang field. They turned out to be a bunch of Zeroes whose numbers were greatly reduced when the sharks began dividing them up. Captain Lundy shot down one Zero, and Captain Jones took another and also sent one on its way as a probable. Lt. Richard Mauritson sent two home damaged, and Lt. L. W. Smith sent one. Lieutenant Gibeault crippled one as a probable and shot down another. Lt. Oren Bates damaged another. Lt. Robert L. Milks confirmed one Zero and sent another home whistling with .50 caliber bullet holes. Lieutenant Meyer shot down a Zero and got a probable. He gave the pilot of a third one something to remember him by for the trip home. The moral of it all was, no doubt, that one should not mess with the Seventy-fourth.

Two P-40s did not make it back, however. Captain Lundy's engine was hit just after he claimed his Zero, forcing him to bail out. While floating to the ground in his parachute, one Japanese pilot made an unsuccessful strafing pass at him, and he managed to land safely. During the fight with the Zeroes, the Japanese bombers continued to Hengyang, escorted by another group of about thirty fighters which squirrel-caged around in their usual manner. There were two formations of bombers and as they neared the field, another group of P-40s took off and engaged them over the field. By the time the fighting was over, the melee had drifted to the northeast of the field and out of sight of ground personnel. During the battle, Lieutenant Beaty, a new pilot from the Seventy-fifth, was up on his first mission when his plane went into a flat spin and was observed by ground personnel to crash and burn in the southern part of the city across the river.

Two P-40s were thus lost on this day, and another was damaged. Lt. Lynn F. Jones of the Seventy-fifth shot down one of the Zeroes and then landed his damaged plane in an emergency field after being reported missing. The Japanese lost five bombers, three Zeroes, five probables, and six damaged. Yet to the Americans the enemy's losses did not seem to balance the scales against the loss of one of their own.

There was considerable activity around Hengyang on December 10, 11, and 12, and this resulted in some confusion in the records regarding dates of specific operations and personal combat. In such cases pilot's logs are probably the most accurate source rather than official documents, which were sometimes completed a few days or even weeks after the actual combat. For example, on December 12, the following pilots were awarded the following official credits: Maj. Elmer Richardson, one bomber confirmed; Capt. J. D. Lee, one Zero probable and one Zero damaged; Lt. Curtis Scoville, two bombers confirmed; Lt. Nathan Green, one bomber confirmed; Lt. Charlie Olsen, one Zero confirmed, one Zero probable, and two Zeroes damaged; Lt. Jim Anning, one Zero confirmed, one Zero probable, and one Zero damaged; Lt. Randy Lewis, one Zero damaged; Lieutenant Volmer, one Zero damaged; Capt. Richard A. Mauritson, one Zero confirmed, one Zero damaged. While these credits were correctly awarded, they were not all necessarily earned on December 12. For example, Olsen's activity which is reflected here actually took place on December 10 according to his personal records, as well as those of Segura.

December 13 provided little action unless one happened to be one of the participants drawing fire. The Seventy-fourth sent eight sharks to escort bombers to Lichow to rattle a few warehouses and upon leaving the target one pilot spotted thirty sampans on the river down below. He reported the information to the net and the Seventy-fifth dispatched sixteen hungry sharks to take care of the situation. Two of the fighters who wanted to get in on the fun were from the Fifty-first. Capt. Donald Glover led the group, which quickly cleared the river of fourteen sampans, directly south of Ansiang. The P-40s came in so low that they drew small-arms fire from the ground as well as heavy machine-gun fire from the city proper, yet they suffered no significant damage.

On December 15, two flights of eight sharks from the Seventy-fourth led by flight leaders Richard Mauritson and Harlyn Vidovich, flew top cover for another eight fighters from the Fifty-first which were sent out on a strafing mission. They strafed Shihshou and along the eastern shore of the great Tungting Lake. Visibility was not good, but two large fires were observed by the men flying top cover. They were proof that down below on deck, the sharks of the Fifty-first were emulating their namesake. But all was not exactly serene and peaceful at the top cover level of five thousand feet. The men began to experience periodic engine failures which later appeared to be the result of water-contaminated fuel. To go down over the target in Japanese-occupied territory carried a very guarded prognosis indeed, and every pilot feared it. If they went down in Free China, no matter how far from their home base, they knew they had a good chance of walking in with the help of the Chinese. But to go down with the Japanese, capture or even death was possible, even probable. They feared this more than any number of Japanese fighters. Yet on this mission they all returned safely to gripe vociferously in the best tradition of the American fighter pilot about the contaminated fuel.

Next Major Richardson of the Seventy-fifth led sixteen P-40s, including nine from the Fifty-first, to strafe the airport at Pailuchi. They headed out towards Yochow and then on to Pailuchi. It was a complete surprise as they caught all the planes on the ground. Their first strafing pass was from north to south across the field and then from east to west. None of the Japanese aircraft got into the air. All the sharks returned safely, the pilots claiming the following aircraft destroyed on the ground: Major Richardson, one bomber confirmed and one damaged; Capt. Donald Glover, one bomber confirmed; Lt. Joseph Brown, one bomber confirmed and one damaged; Lt. L. R. Lewis, one single-engine plane damaged; Lieutenant Ashmore of the Twenty-sixth Squadron, one bomber damaged.

December 20 was a day to remember. The Seventy-fifth received some help on this day in the form of five new men who were assigned to their forward base. For the first time in the history of the Seventy-fifth, they had non-flying personnel specifically trained to handle their ground transportation problems. Their mission was to take care of the vast fleet of cars and trucks assigned to the squadron—four jeeps and two trucks.

On December 22 Kweilin had four alerts. At 3:30 A.M. heavy engine noise was reported southeast of the field. Three P-40s, piloted by Capt. John Stewart, Lieutenant Kramer, and Lieutenant Wilson, took off. The enemy failed to reach the field and the all clear was sounded at 6:15. Then again at 9 A.M., two Mustangs were alerted to investigate plots of a Japanese recon nearing the field. The two planes remained aloft until twelve noon. Meanwhile at 10:15, six P-51s were alerted over the field due to numerous confirmed plots from the south and east, but the enemy never showed up.

At 12:15 they were off again. The pilots, Lts. George Ferris and Shiable, were circling to gain altitude when a Japanese Ki-46 twin-engine scout and fighter plane was observed approaching at eleven o'clock and five hundred feet above. Lieutenant Ferris, the element leader, immediately closed the range and at three hundred yards fired a short burst and at two hundred yards fired another. After the second burst, the right engine began to smoke and fire came from somewhere between the engines. The enemy plane then began to dive away and Ferris managed to get another shot at the ship and caused a part of the right wing to fly off. The ship then flipped over and went spinning down. Two other Mustangs flying below saw this ship go down. The plane crashed three to four miles from the field and was immediately confirmed by the Chinese.

At Kweilin, the Seventy-fourth and Seventy-sixth squadrons combined to escort four B-24s to Canton on December 23. The Seventy-fourth sent six P-40s and the Seventy-sixth sent seven P-51s and eight P-40s. Upon reaching the target, the mission was intercepted by about fifteen Japanese fighters. The P-40s attacked from astern and slightly above. At the same time, two or three enemy fighters made head-on attacks at the bombers. Planes from the Fifty-first Group were on this mission, along with Lieutenant Wilson of the Sixteenth Fighter Squadron, who claimed one Zero confirmed. The Mustangs did not come down to engage the fighters but remained with the bombers. Lieutenant Kramer of the Seventy-sixth, in a P-40, claimed one Zero confirmed. The Seventy-fourth engaged the interceptors, and Lt. Richard Mauritson claimed a Tojo confirmed. Lt. Conrad Adams and Lieutenant Hendrickson each got one Tojo probable.

The bombers did not observe radio silence, and this foolishness nearly cost the loss of one fighter, piloted by Lieutenant Cousins, who could not contact help because of the excessive conversations on the radio. The Seventy-fifth sent down a flight from Hengyang and they acted as top cover for the returning mission from Canton.

On December 24 at 8 A.M. twenty-five P-40s were sent off from Kweilin due to plots of many enemy aircraft nearing the field. The flights were stacked over the field at different altitudes, but the enemy failed to come in. When the all clear sounded, one P-40 had to make an emergency landing due to prop trouble and crashed onto the field. Major damage was done to the plane but Lt. Robert M. Cage, the pilot, was unhurt.

At 11 A.M. nine P-40s of the Seventy-fourth and three Mustangs and three P-40s of the Seventy-sixth escorted bombers to Canton again. This mission was intercepted by approximately fifty Japanese fighters, and during the ensuing engagement, one Zero was claimed as probable by Captain Hanbeck of the Seventy-sixth and one Zero was claimed as damaged by Lieutenant Spurgin. One B-24 was seen to go down over the target with smoking engine. Lieutenant Butler of the Seventy-fourth was forced down at Chaoping. Lieutenant Zavokos of the Seventy-sixth was chased by a number of Zeroes and finally was forced to land in friendly territory, completely destroying the plane. He managed to walk in a few weeks later. All other planes returned.

The Twenty-third Fighter Group's second Christmas Day in China was spent sweating out the mail that was still in the post office at Kunming, waiting to be delivered. At Hostel No. 6, Kunming, the Seventy-sixth had cause for great joy. Captain Williams and Lt. Robert Colbert, who had been shot down behind enemy lines on December 1, had returned a few days earlier. They had a big party with everyone that liked Chinese alcohol getting in their share of Christmas cheer. At Hostel No. 3, the Seventy-fourth Squadron and Group Headquarters had a big supper. At Hengyang, many people from many parts of Hunan Province brought gifts for the Seventy-fifth

Squadron, showing their great respect and appreciation for their work during the Tungting Lake offensive. A phone call was received at Group Headquarters from the first sergeant of the Seventy-fifth, reporting that gifts were assembled all around their alert shack on the airfield. Charlie Olsen got a letter from a schoolchild at Lien Shieng Middle School, praising the efforts of the Allied airmen and signed, "Your little friend, Chang Wen-Kwaing."

On December 27 Capt. Donald Glover led some of his buddies from the Seventy-fifth on a mission to strafe Pailuchi airdrome. Glover got himself a couple of locomotives, and the whole gang concentrated on a tanker and sank it with great dispatch. Lts. Curtis Scoville and Warren Smedley attempted to intercept a "photo Joe" over the field but had no luck. Major Patterson of Fourteenth Air Force Headquarters was attached to the Seventy-fifth Squadron temporarily to replace Capt. Ramon Spritzler, who went to the Twenty-third to take over as Group Surgeon.

The Japanese pulled a fast one on the Seventy-sixth on December 30 but paid dearly for it. At 6:45 A.M. plots of heavy engine noise two hundred miles south of the field were reported. Six Mustangs and two P-40s were sent up, and the first Japanese planes were sighted at twenty thousand feet, above the American fighters. There were no contacts, but a few seconds later four more Zeroes were observed on the deck strafing the field. There were evidently three layers of enemy aircraft. They were soon contacted, and a vicious battle took place which lasted until all had disappeared from the field. The following claims were made: Lieutenant Butler, one confirmed; Lieutenant Schaeffer, one confirmed; Lt. Richard J. Templeton, one confirmed and one damaged; Lt. Wendell Stonehan, one damaged; Lt. Donald Hedrick, one confirmed and one damaged.

In addition, S. Sgt. George Spencer scored one confirmed. Spencer, a crew chief, manned a single water-cooled .50 caliber machine gun in a pit a little south of the center of the field. As one of the Japanese planes pulled up steeply from his first pass and turned to strafe again, Spencer gave the Zero a good lead and fired two long bursts totaling 125 rounds. His gun then jammed, and although he saw no apparent damage inflicted, ten mechanics who were near the field saw an enemy plane crash and blow up about five miles west-northwest of the field. It was the same direction the plane Spencer had fired on had been heading. For the Americans, one plane was strafed and burned and another one, a DC-3, was damaged. All fighters returned to base on this last sortie of 1943.

CHAPTER 9

Lt. Henry I. Wood,
Prisoner of War

On October 1, 1943, sixteen P-40s of the Seventy-fifth escorted bombers over Haiphong. Over the target the bombers made direct hits on installations and upon completing their runs turned the formation for home. Suddenly enemy Zeroes struck and in the battle, four Zeroes crashed to destruction. Lt. Henry I. Wood, pilot of one of the P-40s, disappeared in the brief interval of fighting. So read the record of that fateful day. The men believed Wood to be gone forever since he did not return to base. He arrived in China early in March of that year, a few days before the Fourteenth Air Force was activated. This was his thirtieth mission. He had downed a bomber the previous June or July in combat. Years afterward, Wood recalled all that had happened to him after he was shot down on October 1, 1943.

The October 1 mission had been postponed three separate times due to bad weather, and finally, instead of taking off during the morning, we took off shortly after noon. The mission was uneventful until we got over the target at Haiphong when the B-24s dropped their bombs. I had been scheduled to lead the right rear flight and Don Brookfield, who already had orders to go home, elected to go with us. He took the flight and I took the echelon as the element leader. Of the eighteen fighters who were doing the escort, two didn't join up. One was my wingman and one was Brookfield's. So I flew wingman for Brookfield and only two of us were guarding the right rear. We were at about twenty-one thousand feet and the bombers at twenty thousand when we went over the target.

After the bombers dropped their bombs and turned northeast, instead of heading back to base, Brookfield for some reason kept staying over the target. But at twenty thousand feet we couldn't see much but smoke, so we got quite a bit behind the main formation, about one and a half miles behind to be precise. Antiaircraft fire was hitting us all around. I took a severe hit from "AA" fire and was picking up my microphone to call Brookfield, when we were hopped by about thirty fighters. Brookfield peeled off to the left and I peeled off to the right. I dove down approximately five thousand feet, picking up considerable speed, and turned up into the last part of the bomber formation.

The last Zero had left the fighters and had gone to the bombers and it began a half roll through the tail bombers. And as I pulled up to the loop, one of the Zeroes came out in front of me, and I fired my guns. He still hadn't dropped his bamboo wing tanks, and he flamed immediately. I flew within fifty feet of him and saw his wing disintegrating as he went down. My own engine seemed to quit but I didn't think much of it, because often in a high angle of attack and after firing six .50s, the airplane tends to stall out. So it didn't immediately dawn on me that it had stopped. I just nosed over to pick up airspeed, and then I realized that I didn't have a working engine.

The antiaircraft fire had hit the tail section of my airplane. At that time the P-40's control surfaces were fabric, but the rest was metal. I could see most all of my right aileron and most all of my right elevator. The rudder was pretty badly damaged, and I didn't have good control of the aircraft. I leveled off and looked around to see if anybody was following me.

Then I dropped down to see if there were any more Zeroes. I couldn't jump because I knew they would shoot at me in midair. Next I tried everything I could think of to get the airplane engine going again, but I couldn't get it to come to life. I turned off and on all of the switches, even doing the ridiculous thing of turning off and on the gun switch.

I theorized that I had taken a hit earlier from the "ack ack" or possibly from the fighter that first fired at me, before pulling away when I dove. It must have nicked the gas line and when I fired my guns, the vibration shook it where it wouldn't feed.

Many years later Wood learned about a similar incident from another Seventy-fifth Fighter Squadron member, Charlie Olsen. Olsen said that his plane engine once quit and restarted at twenty-five hundred feet, and when he got it back to the base they found several aircraft with belly tanks full of some sort of green slime. The belly tanks had been shipped over from the United States and were not properly cleaned out before being put to use. The slime moved up to the carburetor and caused the engine to cut out. Therefore, Wood came to the conclusion that perhaps it was green slime which killed his engine rather than a hit in the carburetor.

I got low to about eleven hundred feet as indicated, and I knew I was near a small village northeast of Hanoi, probably about thirty miles from the city. And I jumped. What I did to make sure my plane was destroyed was to trim it up nose heavy, crouch down in the seat, and when I was ready to go, I was in a stooping position. I just pushed the stick forward. In theory, if you did that you would do a back flip out of the airplane. I didn't do a back flip. I did sort of an angle flip over the side. I used to dive in high school, so I just tipped my body naturally, instinctively, and it is a good thing that I did because as I turned and went by the horizontal stabilizer, it was just about two inches in front of my nose. And my feet just cleared the vertical stabilizer. As soon as I realized I was clear of the airplane, I counted two and pulled the ripcord. It is a good thing I pulled it when I did because I was almost too low to jump. I was in some low foothills, and I fell backward, forward, and backward again and on my back swing, or my third one, I hit the ground.

A wind caught the chute dragging me until it collapsed up the hill about fifty feet. My face was scratched a little. I disengaged the chute. This was about 4:30 in the afternoon and there was still considerable daylight in Indochina at the time. So I took the chute down the hill with me into a rice paddy, because I knew I was too deep into enemy territory.

I got into the paddy and laid down between the growing rice there. In about twenty minutes I could see activity come into the rice paddy, coolies, natives, and later men in uniform. I just laid real still and several times within twenty or thirty feet of me they would come by, but they didn't see me. The parachute was wadded down beside me in the water. After dark, about nine o'clock, I decided I could move. I got up cautiously. My parachute was soaked but there was a little fishing paraphernalia in there, and I took it out along with a machete, some C-rations, and a chocolate bar from the pack. I took them with me toward the little village I had seen as I was coming down in the parachute. About a quarter until ten, I came to the edge of this village, which was a compound composed of mud huts arranged in a circle. I worked my way all around the wall until I came to the entrance. Entering, I saw several people standing by a fire. Immediately a dog began to bark. And I said in Chinese, "I am your very good friend." I was hoping I was anyway.

And as I started over to these natives at the fireplace, there was an elderly man of about sixty there. He held up his hands to indicate to the rest of them to be quiet, and I walked over to him, reaching for my little booklet called a pointee-talkee. I turned my leather jacket inside out to show I had a Chinese-American flag, and I pointed to the place in the book which said I was an American pilot, to help me, that my government would pay him well. This happened the day after payday and I had a good bit of Chinese yen which I did not know was any good to them or not, but I pulled it out anyway. I gave it to him indicating that he would get much more if he could hide me and work me back into China.

He apparently knew no English but motioned to me, indicating that things were all right and took me into one of the little mud huts. They gave me some cold boiled water and scrambled eggs. I was sitting on the floor by a little table eating the eggs and drinking the water when something caused me to be apprehensive. It was a noise, a kind of dull thud. It was probably a rifle butt striking the side of the mud hut. What had happened to me was that a platoon of Japanese soldiers led by a lieutenant and a noncom who could speak some English had come to the village. They had been brought there by the people I had talked to. I had asked for the Chinese guerillas. They had sent for the Japanese troops instead.

The locals were probably too scared to hide me because they were afraid they would be killed if they were caught. I indicated from the book for them to hide me. They took me to the next room, but there wasn't any real place to hide because there wasn't anything there besides thatch rugs on the floor and a small table in the corner. I held up a couple of these rugs over me in the corner. Then suddenly, the room lit up and I could hear these gruff voices which I presumed were saying "hands up" in Japanese. I didn't move. Somebody snatched the rug. I stood up with my hands up.

I was not treated rough initially, surprisingly enough, as I had been led to expect I would be. They did take my jacket off and search me thoroughly, and the one which could speak some English said, "Never mind. Never mind."

He took me to the other room where I had been eating and mo-

tioned for me to finish. I had suddenly lost my appetite. In fact I was
so confused (and even though I had fairly good intelligence—later
I graduated with honors from college) by being treated nice, that I
asked them through the pointee-talkee what Chinese troops were
doing in this area? And there was an uproar—a sound of laughter
when one of them read it to the others. Finally the tall one who kept
saying, "Never mind. Never mind," said, "Ha. Ha. You think we
Chinese. We Japanese."

It was a big joke to them, but not to me. They then tied my hands
behind my back and put some of the troops in front of me. They
had cattails which had been dumped in kerosene which were lit and
we started traipsing through the rice paddies, with troops in front
and back of me. And it was pretty slippery trying to walk through
the rice fields and every once in a while I would start to go down. I
was afraid that somebody would shoot me in the back thinking I was
trying to escape. I had no such ideas at the time, being in the middle
of a bunch of Jap soldiers.

After about forty-five minutes or an hour we reached a road
where they sent up some flares and indicated to me to sit down.
While we were sitting there one of the soldiers took the chocolate
bar they had taken from me and offered me some. And I said thank
you to him. They all laughed. They thought it was funny since they
had taken me prisoner and confiscated my food and here I was
thanking them for offering me something to eat. In about thirty minutes, a big truck came down the road and we all piled into it. It had
an open bed with low sides. I stood in the middle with the rest of
them hovering around me. My hands were still tied. We came to a
compound which was apparently a troop training area because there
was a number of barracks. I was taken inside one of the buildings
with an extremely mean-looking Japanese. The only other Japanese I
had seen like him was when I had shot down a bomber on another
mission and flew almost into the nose of his plane before I cut under
it. And I could see the pilot's face there. I had apparently killed the
copilot and the pilot was just staring at me through the canopy.

This mean-looking fellow had on a kimono, not a uniform, and he
apparently was the man in charge. I found out the next morning he
was a captain, and he was definitely in charge of the outfit. The man
glared at me, and through one of his subordinates, he told me to answer his questions or he would cut off my head.

And I nodded my still intact head that I understood. He then
asked me what my rank was and I told him first lieutenant. He then
asked me how many planes were in my formation. I said to ask one

of his pilots who was up there on the mission. He must not have liked my answer because he became even more enraged. And he had someone tie my hands behind my back, to the back of the chair and my feet to the runner of the chair. Then he took out some paper towels and took his own neck and wiped it and removed his sabre from its sheath, indicating to me that he was going to cut my head off.

He then had someone tell me to answer his questions and I nodded that I understood and he asked the same questions again. I told him that I did not have to answer questions of this nature. He then ordered his soldiers to carry me outside where there was a big bonfire. They set the chair down with me in it, and at that moment I was convinced I was going to be killed.

I had always been told that one's life flashed before you if you were going to die. Mine didn't flash before me. But I had already done some thinking along these lines during the afternoon. I had been very apprehensive. Then I went to the compound and met the natives, and I got a glimmer of hope that they were going to hide me.

And I thought, "This is going to be rough on my mother as she has six boys in service, and I am going to be the first to go." And the last thing I thought about as he started to bring down the sword was how I used to have to wring chickens in the neck, and my mother plucked them afterwards when I was a kid. I could see me squirming around with the reflexes going and I thought to myself, "I'm not going to give him the satisfaction of seeing me squirm." So all I could think of was to stick my neck way back as far as possible so he could have a good clean whack.

Down came the sabre, stopping just an inch above my neck. He did that twice and then he said something in Japanese and untied my legs. He untied my hands from the chair but left them tied behind my back, took me over to a tree, tied my hands to the tree, and wound the rope around my whole body and the tree.

He apparently gave them instructions, "Ready! Aim! Fire!" in Japanese because they all brought their rifles up to bear and they all clicked on empty magazines. He did that twice. Then it began to dawn upon me that he was apparently just trying to scare me, that they were still wanting the information or I would already be dead.

They took me to a guard compound or jail and put me on the floor and took off all my clothes except my shorts. My hands were tied behind my back and hands tied to my feet. They laid me on the concrete floor and put a hard bag of cement under my head. I would have been much more comfortable lying flat. And then they proceeded to beat me with long sticks which looked like broom handles. Some of the officers took off their boots and began beating me too. And I lapsed into unconsciousness. Several hours later, I awakened and all of them had gone.

In this guard compound the guards were sitting along a bench with a noncom in charge, and one of them had apparently brought some incense because I had been bitten badly by mosquitoes and didn't realize it until I came into consciousness. As my awareness came back and the mosquitoes were still chewing on me, that was really the worst part so far because I couldn't scratch the bites.

Shortly before dawn, I noted the noncom in charge kept reading a big heavy book, which was probably a Japanese-English dictionary. He came over to me showing a little paper with writing on it. Looking at it he said, "You are very brave man. *My maundy* you go to New York." *My maundy* is a Chinese term meaning "later." Why a Japanese would use a Chinese word, I don't know. But that is what he said.

I had never heard of a prisoner being expatriated from Japan so I was very skeptical of what he said. And then a humorous thing happened. Just as he finished saying the words, the paper still in his hand, an officer walked in and the Japanese soldier jumped to attention. He said something which sounded like *Jejugius* and presented arms, even though they were indoors. And I could see what he had in his hand was carefully camouflaged so that the officer could not see it. I am sure he would have caught hell if indeed he had written there what he said to me and somebody had seen it.

The next morning about ten o'clock, my uniform was given back to me and I was told to dress and put the jacket on with the flag outside. I was paraded in front of a large formation of Japanese troops while the captain in charge was speaking to them. I didn't know what he was saying about me.

Later in the afternoon I was put in a truck again and taken to Hanoi. I recognized the town when we got there to the suburbs because there were a good many signs in French and English which the Japanese had not obliterated. I was taken to a beautiful occidental type building in the heart of Hanoi, led inside, and the ropes were taken off my hands. Shortly later, I was seated in a nice dining hall with china and silverware.

A very nicely dressed man in Western style clothing, a Japanese, came in speaking with an Oxford accent and told me he was sorry I had been mistreated the night before and wished to assure me this was not the Japanese' nature. But I should realize that there was a war going on and sometimes troops from the field got upset. He said I would be treated well in the future, and he just wanted to talk to me a little. He didn't often get a chance to talk with an American. I didn't believe that.

It turned out that his name was Ariaa and he was the Japanese premier for French Indochina at the time. It became obvious in a very short time with him trying to converse with me, that he was trying to discuss military information with me through seemingly irrelevant conversation. First he asked me where I was born. Where did I live? Did I have brothers and sisters? Apparently these questions were innocuous.

Then he said, "How did you like the place you were flying out of in China? Where was that?"

Of course I refused to answer the questions. And I told him in a nice manner that I didn't mind talking with him, but there were things of obvious military significance and he must realize it. After he understood he wasn't making any headway, he apologized, said he had to leave and that I would be served a nice meal right at the table I was sitting at. And again he apologized for the behavior of the Japanese. As he left the room other Japanese came into another door and immediately tied me up and hustled me down to a basement where they had made some cells by taking a large room and segregating them with four-by-fours from the floor to ceiling with an inch space between each board. They stripped me of all my clothes except my shorts, made me get down through a little door like an animal cage into one of the cells where there were four native Vietnamese, I presume. They indicated for me to sit on the floor like the others were doing with knees crossed and with my hands folded across my knees. So I sat there for a while and naturally that got tiring, so I leaned back and when I did, I was yelled at in Japanese, and a long thin stick came through the bars and I was knocked in the head.

So I learned that I was supposed to be sitting and not lying down. I was kept in this room for five days without food. I was allowed to have water twice a day. They got us up in the morning and put us to bed at six at night and allowed us water and took us to the benjo as they called it, which was the bathroom, consisting of a little slit in the floor.

At the end of the fifth day, they brought me a big fish head which was supposed to be a delicacy in that area. I still wasn't hungry enough to eat a fish head, but later on during my incarceration, I would have gladly eaten it.

The next morning after offering me the fish head in the middle of the morning, they took me out of the cell and into a room where there were a number of Japanese in a big ring on the floor and others sitting behind them in chairs. And that is where they started pressuring me in earnest about intelligence. I let them know that all I would tell them was my rank, name, and serial number. They tried to talk me into the information by being innocuous in their questioning like Ariaa had done. They felt that if I talked they would get their information. After they questioned me about an hour and a half, they put me back into the cell. That afternoon about three o'clock, they took me out again and told me that I had to talk. They were tired of talking to me in this manner, and they expected me to answer the questions. When I refused to answer, they locked the windows. There was this little device I called a windlass. They put wires on your wrists and put it around your finger and tightened it gradually, pulling the finger back until it broke. They didn't break my finger but it was very painful. And they also took a hammer and you can still see the scars on my hand where they broke the bones. This went on for several days, and after the second day, they initiated a new procedure where they had a ladder which was inclined at about a forty-five-degree angle to the wall. Then they tied me to the ladder with my head low, and they put water-laden heavy towels over my face where I would choke and gasp and eventually pass out. Then they would bring me to and ask the questions again. This went on for about three weeks.

Then they took me to an airfield where I had been on an escort mission a time or two when the B-24s had bombed them. While I was at the airfield up in a high room, but not in a control tower, there was an air raid alarm. Everybody became very excited and they were hustling me out of the building and into a truck. There were a number of trucks trying to leave the field with troops on them. No pilots were trying to take off because they apparently felt that the American planes were imminent which they were. They had not received the alarm in time. But there was a road which paralleled the runway. And as we were leaving I looked up and I could see the B-24s at a high altitude and barely make out the fighters with them.

I knew that the bombs had already been dropped and were on their way and sure enough in a matter of seconds, the bombs were dropping all around us. I had extremely mixed feelings—I was hoping that they would blast the hell out of the Japanese, but I sure didn't want to get hit. It was a real terrifying feeling to be in that situation. We continued on down the highway for several miles, got into ditches on the side of the road, and stayed there for an hour. Then we got back into the trucks and went back to the airfield. Unfortunately the bombing had not been accurate, almost all of the bombs had gone off parallel to the runway about three hundred yards from the road we had traveled. A couple of the bombs had hit the field, and one had hit a large hangar where a number of airplanes were housed, and there was considerable damage to the planes as I could see fires still burning. I could see the damaged airplanes.

Later on during the day I was put on this airplane, a Lockheed Lodestar, along with some Japanese passengers, and there were four guards with rifles and bayonets accompanying me and a Japanese captain in charge of the troops. In the course of the flight it was very pleasant. This particular officer was very courteous, and he indicated he understood English but he could not speak it well though he could write it. He showed me pictures of his children and said he had been away from home five years. He made no attempt to interrogate me for information. He also offered me some of his chow because they apparently didn't have any box lunch for me on the plane. He gave me some cheese and a sandwich and I could tell from the course of the sun that we were flying along the southern China coast over towards Taiwan. And sure enough we landed on the island.

For the first time in several weeks I had an enjoyable couple of hours, apparently while the plane was being refueled. I got to lie outside in the open on the grass near the runway. It was a beautiful sunny day and in no way was the captain in charge attempting to hamper me. I had come through some pretty difficult times in the course of the flight, from a mental condition. Several times I felt that I might have had the opportunity to get out of the seat in a hurry, run up to the front of the plane. There was a "stepover" in the Lodestar which was approximately two and a half feet high, separating the cockpit from the area for the passengers. I kept thinking that if I could really get up there and grab hold of the pilot's wheel, I could spin that plane in with everybody on board and accomplish something besides being a prisoner.

I could never bring myself to do it, but I would have never reached the cockpit if I had tried. I'd have been stabbed in the back or shot. But I had some real tough times worrying whether I should

try or not. I had been in excellent health at the time I went down.
My main activity in Kunming—I wasn't a gambler or a player of
bridge—was working out with weights and doing a little running and
push-ups and reading a good many books. My health was good at
age twenty-five and I was in top physical condition before my capture. My health had not deteriorated rapidly in their hands. After
the first five days I had a fair diet with rice in the morning with
some sort of Chinese vegetables and the same thing in the evening. I
was getting an adequate diet even though it wasn't the most palatable
one.

We eventually landed again, and I ascertained that I was in Nanking. What made me realize that was I was again in solitary but not
made to sit on the floor this time. I was allowed to walk around all I
wanted to. The room was approximately eleven feet long and five
feet wide, so I paced up and down that room most of the day. It was
right near the entrance of a large compound, and I could see into a
large courtyard.

The second day I was there a big black car came up with general's
flags on it and a man got out. I am sure it was the man they called
"The Tiger of the Orient." He was the Japanese general in charge of
that area. He simply came over and looked at me through the bars,
didn't say anything, looked at me for about thirty seconds, and
turned around and walked away.

Again I stayed in this cell for approximately three weeks because
I was making marks with my fingernails on the wooden bars, four-
by-fours, but wider spaces between them than the ones before, about
two and a half inches. One day they came in and said I would be
moved that day. They had not tried to interrogate me at all in Nanking and this morning they told me why they had stopped questioning me.

They told me they had captured a Chinese pilot named Chen who
was in my unit and that he had been badly wounded and they had
been able to get all the information they wanted. And I found out
later that what they said was true because I was taken to a prison
camp with him and he said he had been wounded—his leg had been
broken and he was shot in the arm. Apparently under the severe
mistreatment he had and the painful conditions, he told them things
they wanted to know.

From Nanking we traveled to Shanghai where I was put into a
large prison camp. At that time, it held Italian prisoners from a ship
that had been scuttled in the harbor at Shanghai. It also contained
some civilians from Wake Island, Marines from Wake Island, and

the North China Embassy Guard. It was a well-formed prison camp, and I simply was put into a cell by myself for approximately one week and then released with the general prisoners. I remained in this camp from December of 1943 until late May 1945.

Other than two bad personal experiences in the long stay at the prison camp, it was not particularly bad other than the lack of communication with the outside, poor diet, and very little recreation. We normally worked nine days and then were off one day.

My first bad experience was when I was asked to work by Maj. Luther Brown, who was a Marine major acting as executive officer for Colonel Ashhurst, who was the senior American officer in charge of the camp. Brown had ordered me to go to work in a garden with other Americans which stood within the compound. I told him I didn't feel like I or any other prisoner should work.

He attempted to reason with me, saying that he was in charge and this work was not of any particular help to the Japanese. It helped get us our own food and was of some value. It was up to him to make a decision like that, and it was not up to me as an individual to decline or accept.

I still felt it was my own individual decision and I told him so. He went over to a Japanese noncom named Neasaki, who was in charge of this particular detail. Neasaki walked up to another prisoner who had a shovel, grabbed it, and hit me on the side of the head with it as hard as he could. It knocked me to the ground. I was stunned. And when I got back up Major Brown told me he was sorry, but if I didn't work, I would get similar treatment. That was my first experience with any collaboration by an American with the Japanese. I later found out that within a small group there was considerable collaboration.

In fact volumes of information on it were filled out in Manila at the end of the war, but nothing was done by the psychiatrists or attorneys. They felt that a lot of what we said, due to living under such bad conditions for such a long time and to our mental health, was imagined. But that wasn't so. It wasn't until the Korean War that they realized that we were brainwashed and that there were Americans who collaborated with the enemy after they became prisoners.

I decided I had better go to work, that I didn't want to get whacked anymore since I was a lone individual in the crowd. Life was bearable except for the daily drudgery of going out to work on days when it was cold and sleeping in a building that wasn't heated and observing some American prisoners, including Major Brown, sleeping on innerspring mattresses with big trunks full of canned food from the Marine ship stores which they had been able to salvage in Peking. They were treated differently from the rest of the prisoners too. The reason why they were being treated differently, I found out, was they surrendered to the enemy. You can't blame them for surrendering. They were the embassy guards when the war broke out, and these people were the ones who had been fraternizing with the locals on a daily basis, the Japanese who occupied Peking at the time. And as the embassy guards, they were good friends with them, drank with them, danced with them, fraternized with them, and the Japanese gave them twenty-four hours to surrender. For doing this, they were rewarded. There was no attempt to dispose of the military hardware they had, which consisted of guns and bayonets and food. Anyway, whatever arrangements were made, the former guards kept their personal clothing, watches, trunk loads of food, and it was shipped from Peking to the prison camp in Shanghai. Their goods were maintained in a separate warehouse, and they were allowed to use it and no one else.

I found out that before I came to the camp, the Wake Island Marines, the ones that defended Wake Island, were put into the camp and Major Brown would not allow them to associate with the Peking Marines. Here was a group of Marines who had been undergoing harsh mental treatment and some of whom were wounded, and they weren't even allowed to associate with other Marines, who were the former embassy guards. It took months before Major Devereaux, who after the war became a brigadier general, was able to resolve the situation with Major Brown and get him to share some of the clothes with the other prisoners.

Besides Brown, there must have been between sixty and eighty people from the embassy guard, including several officers, a number of captains who enjoyed the favors. Major Brown allowed everybody from the former guard better treatment than the rest. It may not have been the others' nature to take advantage of the situation while fellow Americans were deprived, but Colonel Ashhurst apparently made the decision and Major Brown implemented it because Ashhurst said he was a sick man and put his executive officer in charge. Finally Devereaux apparently overcame the situation. He had been the commander at Wake Island.

Otherwise there was just minor ill-treatment when they would call a shakedown, like trying to find out why so much electricity was being used at the camp. Some of the men had been taken to town to build a rifle range on "front days." They called it Mt. Fuji, but it was just a hill. On a "front day" the Japanese would take us and mistreat us, telling us that there were severe conditions on the front. We were well protected, so we should be mistreated because our comrades were having a rough day at the front. There was a song we made up. "With a front day every day out of nine/They run a short load (we'd push cars up this hill, and we'd push a light load if we thought the Japanese weren't watching)/Then Yaza day is a day of rest/Yaza day . . . Yaza day. . . ."

Eventually, in May of 1945, treatment wasn't as harsh as usual and we received two Red Cross boxes.

Then Colonel Otaru, who was the Japanese commander at the camp, indicated we would be moved. We were transported in box-cars from Shanghai, beginning in late May of 1945, on up through Manchuria down through Korea to Pusan on the southern tip, where we were put into a large encampment with one water spigot for the entire camp.

We were kept in the camp mostly out in the open for four days, and we didn't know what we were waiting for. But apparently they were waiting to put us on a ship to take us up by rail to Hokkaido, the northern island, where they had in mind to put us to work in the mines. It was a real rough trip, and the only time any prisoners escaped en route was a time when five escaped by cutting barbed wires late at night. We were separated in two ends of the boxcar with barbed wire, and in the center of the car was the Japanese guard. There was a small window in each end with wire over it. They were able to cut the wire by putting a little commode there and placing a blanket up for a screen and fooling the guard by making him think they were just going to the bathroom there. And they were able to work the barbed wire loose and five slipped out into the night before they were discovered.

Then we left Pusan on a ship. We were crowded into the hold where we stood up. I don't know how many hours we were on there. But it must have been between thirty-six and seventy-two hours on board, and there was no room between the bodies. Then we were moved across the Tsushima Straits, into Japan proper onto Honshu island, put on small Japanese railroad cars, eighty to a hundred of us on each car, lying on the floor, under the seats, on the seats, up in the baggage baskets. They had heavy opaque screens over the windows so you couldn't see what was going on outside. But we were so tightly packed in there that there were several places we cut the screens and could see the vast devastation of the countryside that the B-29s had wrought. It was just at ground level for blocks on end close to the railroad tracks. In one place we saw hundreds of railroad cars which had been destroyed. And every now and then there was a B-29 raid and we would huddle up in the cars in some subterranean chamber. They were really trying to protect us at that time.

We finally reached the island of Hokkaido, the northern island and were taken to a small mining town called Ashamitzabetsu. At that time they separated the officers and the civilians and the airmen for the first time. I felt they were trying to protect us and give us more consideration than they ever had before, or they wouldn't have done that.

So on the third day they ordered us to go to the mines and I refused to go. I was the only one out of eighty-three of us (among them were Marines, an orderly, two Navy medics, and several enlisted men who had been put in with the officers). Brown was still in charge of the camp. I refused to go out. I was ordered to stand at attention by the Japanese this time. Brown finally lost all of his friends he had in the move, and he had been mistreated several times himself for the first time since his incarceration. So I stood at attention all day long, from when they first went out at seven o'clock in the morning, and I was still standing at attention when they returned at five o'clock in the afternoon.

They ate and I was still at attention at ten o'clock that night. Every time I moved, and I couldn't help but move, I was beaten by a particular guard standing over me at the time. He hit me with a rifle butt.

But I must have accomplished something by my tenacity at that late stage in July of 1945 because the next day, instead of standing at attention again, and instead of taking me out to the mines, they put me to work at a pookey party. Pookey was a plant very much like an elephant ear, edible if you did a lot of boiling. I was taken out with several Japanese and two other Americans, and we went out to the forest. There were streams and low mountains, and it was beautiful country. There we cut pookey. It was carried back to camp and boiled for our food. And for the rest of the time I went on pookey parties, and they made me the rice cook for the camp. So I never did work in the mines with the rest of the prisoners.

On August 14, the commandant of the camp, the first lieutenant, did not come to the camp. No one was taken out to work. No one was taken out to pookey parties, and we realized something must be going on. Three days later some lieutenant colonel whom we had never seen before came in and told us the story that the Americans had some horrendous bombs but the Japanese would never surrender. They also kidded us about being cowards for surrendering and said the Japanese would always commit hari-kari before surrendering.

But the Japanese people as a whole had given in due to the horrendous weapons, he said. And we were to wait there and see what was going to happen to us. Well, I didn't want to wait, even though I was urged by Colonel Ashhurst and Major Brown, whom I had no use for, to wait and see what would happen. I felt we should be fed better and have better care, and I talked another officer, Lieutenant Rouse, into leaving with me. We simply walked out of the camp.

We ignored the guards who hollered something to us and kept walking. They didn't do anything. We went down to the center of the little town to the railroad station and kept saying, "Sapporo! Sapporo!"

We ended up on a railroad train car, were transferred to another one and onto a third, and by the time we got to Sapporo on the third train, there was a Japanese noncom who spoke very good English and who asked us why we left camp. We told him we understood there were some American Air Force officers in Sapporo and we wanted to be taken to them. And sure enough, we were taken to a place where there were eleven men under Maj. Don Quigley, who turned out to be a squad commander of the Seventy-fifth Fighter Squadron of which I had been a member. He came to China after I did and became squad commander before he was shot down. For the next few days, we lived like kings. Quigley got on the ball and got us on tours of the farms, universities, and even a small group to church. Instead of being treated like prisoners, we were treated like tourists. And we had plenty to eat, eggs, all sorts of vegetables, good meat, things we had been told earlier weren't available. I was real glad that I had the nerve to walk out of camp along with Lieutenant Rouse, who was a bomber pilot.

After a few days, one of the Japanese soldiers said the Americans would be coming in and they would be dropping supplies first and for us to go out and mark an area where they could drop them. And they did. They dropped big fifty-five-gallon drums from parachutes with clothes and food in them. We had good food, good shoes, and uniforms again.

But some unfortunate things happened, too. I remember when I was in the Shanghai camp there was an enlisted man, a Marine who was always in good humor even though in terrible health. He almost died several times. A Captain White, a Marine non-flying officer, had marked the drop for the camp where this Marine was, and he didn't make the people stay far enough from the area. And this sick Marine and two others were standing close to where the drum came in. The parachute slipped off it, and it killed all three of them standing together. This man had been captured at the outbreak of the war, the first day of the war, and he was killed by one of our own air drops at the end of it.

Several days later we were taken to an airfield where Americans had flown in some DC-3s and some P-51s. And we were flown to the Philippines. Army Air Corpsmen were flown to the Philippines and the Navy-Marines were flown to Guam. We arrived at the Philippines September 12, 1945. There we were plainly told after we revealed all of the tales of the Shanghai prison camp personnel, not to talk about it again. We were interrogated several days by psychiatrists and by American attorneys, who were members of the armed forces and civilians, and we had to sign statements that we would not relate any of this when we got home or else we could not be taken home before we were cleared.

They didn't want any of this information in the newspapers. And they didn't want to believe us, and they didn't want us knocking any other Americans. It was all right to tell about any atrocities of the Japanese, but with Americans we were supposed to show our patriotism. Luther Brown had gone through the Naval Academy and was promoted to colonel before he retired. And nothing was ever done to him. They wouldn't believe that an American officer would do what he did. He was such a party boy at Shanghai that he had become real stout, but after getting in prison camp, he decided to take care of himself, and he slept in a private room with an innerspring mattress and worked out with weights.

I returned to the States October 8, 1945.

CHAPTER 10

The Twenty-third Fighter Group: 1944

In the latter part of 1943, the Fourteenth Air Force slowly changed from a band of aerial guerillas into a highly specialized striking force that began to take a significant toll on the enemy's two most precious commodities—aircraft and merchant ships. But the success of the Fourteenth was nearly its downfall as well. In an attempt to neutralize Chennault's forces, the Japanese launched a massive counteroffensive into eastern China against the American air bases. This offensive forced the Fourteenth into a more defensive posture, and Chennault's chance to win the war by air power no longer existed. This was not Chennault's fault. The Fourteenth had simply lost its supply priority, and even though it was finally approaching parity with the Japanese Air Force in numbers of planes by 1944, the shortage of supplies at its forward bases was probably more critical than a shortage of planes would have been.

Although Chennault had temporarily lost the initiative, his pilots continued to play a major role in disrupting Japanese lines of transportation and communication as well as an increasing role in ground support. The strength of the Fourteenth Air Force had risen by the end of 1943 to 188 fighters, fifty-one heavy bombers, twenty-three medium bombers, nine cargo planes, eight liaison planes and six F-4 or F-5 photo reconnaissance planes.

An important order of business for the Fourteenth as 1943 turned to 1944 was to improve its chain of command in combat operations. Consequently, on December 23, the Sixty-eighth and Sixty-ninth composite wings were activated at Kweilin and Kunming. The Sixty-eighth took control of combat units operating east of longitude 108; the Sixty-ninth, combat units operating west of that longitude. Both commanded mixed units, the Sixty-eighth Wing having the Twenty-third Fighter Group and the Eleventh Bomb Squadron under it and Chinese-American Composite Wing units attached. The Sixty-ninth Wing had the Fifty-first Fighter Group and the 341st Bomb Group, which was transferred with its Twenty-second and 491st bomb squadrons from the Tenth Air Force to the Fourteenth in January of 1944.

From the beginning of the year on into April 1944, the ground situation in China remained quiet, while the Japanese launched two offensives in Burma with an eye to invading India and concentrated on building up their forces in China. The weather and the tenuous supply situation limited fighter operations from western and eastern airfields during much of this time, but there was still a good deal of fighter action going on.

On January 7 Capt. Charlie Olsen (he had been promoted) took his flight and escorted B-25s to the Yangtze below Kiukiang. The bombers overshot the targets and everybody strafed. A steamer was sunk and another damaged and left sinking. Capt. Tom Cotton (also promoted) escorted two B-25s to the Yangtze River east of Hankow on a shipping sweep. They came to the river just north of Kichune and went downriver to Kiukiang. They saw a number of sailboats in the vicinity but made no attacks. They made their first attack on Hunter Island, with three passes on an anchored 250-foot steamer with smaller boats alongside. The first and third passes missed, but the second dropped a bomb that burst right underneath the steamer's bow. The pilots figured it must have sunk later. The bombers attacked a target near Kiukiang docks, but the pilots were uncertain as to what the result was.

They encountered antiaircraft fire over Kiukiang airdrome. There were no casualties. One pilot reported a landing strip across the river from Kiukiang. Several long camouflaged barracks-like buildings were seen on the riverbank near the docks. These docks seemed fairly active, and some of the docks appeared to be newly constructed. All were connected with heavy industry located in the eastern part of Kiukiang. There was no enemy interception. Pilots participating were Lts. James E. Folmer, Donald S. Lopez, and William E. Daniels, but they did not strike.

On January 9 the Seventy-fifth was out again. This time Capt. J. D. Long led a flight to strafe the Yangtze above Yochow. The next day Lt. Curtis Scoville led a flight for top cover for two B-25s on a shipping sweep on the Yangtze River. The bombers, upon entering the target area, encountered heavy antiaircraft fire with the result that one of them had to be listed as missing. Several new targets were observed on this trip and the pilots planned a visit to the area.

On January 15 Lt. Russell Rauch was piloting a medium bomber over mountainous terrain on a bombing mission toward Luzon. The weather was turbulent and icing conditions were making the trip most hazardous. As the ice began to accumulate on the ship, he ordered those aboard to don parachutes, meanwhile exerting every effort to fly out of the dangerous area. He vainly attempted to warn passengers in the rear. As the weight of the ice increased, the ship began to lose altitude, but Lieutenant Rauch skillfully kept it flying. Finally, realizing the impending danger of the plane's going out of control, he ordered all personnel riding in front to abandon the ship, still attempting to contact those in the rear. Failing to make contact with them, he voluntarily remained with the ship and gave his own life in the hope of making a safe landing and saving the lives of those aboard. But they all perished.

On January 24 Capt. Derward B. Harper was the leader of a flight of medium bombers on a mission over the East China Sea. Just as he was beginning to bomb a vessel, he was attacked by a Japanese seaplane. By skillfully maneuvering and employment of fighter tactics, he brought his forward guns to bear and shot down the more maneuverable enemy plane. On the same date, he led his flight out of an advanced staging field when the ceiling was only three hundred feet to the seacoast where they destroyed six enemy ships. On this mission his compass was destroyed by enemy fire. By using a pocket compass taken from his jungle kit, he returned his plane to base in spite of extremely adverse weather conditions. On the following day, despite mechanical trouble and knowledge that inclement weather would probably prevent a return to base, he led his flight in a well-planned attack on a heavily-armed gunboat, sinking it with one direct hit. Returning from this mission the flight was forced by fuel shortage and weather conditions to land at a base considered inadequate for bombardment type aircraft. But Captain Harper and company made it.

For the rest of the month, the Twenty-third repeated performances of hitting boats and shipping along Kowloon docks and Siuchuan. On January 25, the B-25s had another good day. They sank four Japanese boats and damaged another, all in the same general area where they had been sighting them. The weather was bad, and the Americans had to land at different fields upon completion of their missions.

On February 3, General Chennault came in to Kweilin for a visit and went out to the eastern fields the next day. Moving up to Siuchuan from Lingling in February, the 449th Fighter Squadron flew a variety of missions during the second and third months of the year.

On February 5 American bombers sighted a convoy between Hong Kong and Tokyo. Lt. Harold Rochelle was copilot of a medium bomber and Capt. George T. Grottle was its pilot. They were forced to turn back from the low-level sweep against shipping due to mechanical trouble. S. Sgt. Golden M. Gallup was engineer-gunner of the bomber, and he assisted in the successful return and landing of the ship at an advanced base. Two days later, with the bomber repaired, Grottle and crew, including Gallup, volunteered to attack Japanese shipping in a heavily-defended and patrolled river near Puchi. They made repeated attacks on six 125-foot boats and a 150-foot tanker, which resulted in the destruction of three ships.

The 449th Fighter Squadron began operations in earnest on February 10, when four of its P-38s accompanied eight Mustangs heading north to strafe Kiukiang. On the way, the P-38s encountered three Japanese Ki 45 Nicks and shot down two of them. On February 11, P-38s dive-bombed and destroyed a railroad bridge at Sheklung, a short distance from Canton. On February 12, fourteen P-38s intercepted nineteen Oscars flying at sixteen thousand feet and heading for Kanchow. Six were claimed as shot down and six more as probables in exchange for the loss of one P-38 whose pilot bailed out and returned safely to base.

Ten P-38s strafed along the Yangtze River on February 24, shooting up fifteen sampans and eight motor launches. During the mission, an Oscar sneaked in behind a P-38 and scored telling hits. The pilot crash-landed and returned to base several days later. Ten P-38s dive-bombed bridges between Kiukiang and Nanchang on March 2, scoring three direct hits with thousand-pound bombs. On March 4, four

P-38s flew top cover to B-25s sweeping the Yangtze and were jumped by ten Oscars. Three Oscars were destroyed while three P-38s were damaged, two of which belly-landed on return to Siu-chuan.

On March 10 eight P-38s escorted two B-25s on a river sweep and were jumped by eighteen Oscars, but the fighting was indecisive as no enemy planes were downed and all P-38s returned. Two P-38 pilots shot down a Nick recon plane on March 18. Then on March 19, nine P-38s and three Mustangs escorted two B-25s on a sweep of the Yangtze again. One Lightning P-38 flight blew up a locomotive above Anking and also shot up a large steamer.

Heavy bomber operations in the early months of 1944 were restricted mainly by lack of fuel. In fact, due to the demands of hard fighting along the India-Burma border, the supply of fuel in India for China ran so low in March that for a time there was not enough to load all the group's bombers if they went on a ferry mission. But in April conditions improved, and the 308th flew eighteen missions. On one of them, near Saigon on April 23, six planes sank six large merchant ships and a small naval vessel—totaling eighty thousand tons of shipping.

By early March, Charlie Olsen and Tom Cotton were both approaching the end of their tours of duty in China. On March 16 they went on a mission which destroyed a locomotive, using for the first time an air-to-ground rocket. Olsen later detailed some recollections of this period:

> They called us the Buck Rogers outfit for a while. We started getting all these supplies, these long blast tubes, and we didn't know what to do with them. We threw them around the airport, didn't even know what they were for. Finally, some ordnance officer rushed in and completely blew his stack. This was all top secret stuff, and here all the Chinese were out playing with them and hollering up and down the ends of them. So we got them all assembled and started carrying three rockets on each wing. Then we went after the trains which we always did whenever we got the chance.
>
> The boys would try to catch a train at a tunnel if possible. The idea was to bomb both ends of the tunnel and leave the train inside. The blast tubes restricted the performance of the airplane, and we didn't particularly like them. We'd usually send four planes with

rockets and four more to try to protect the slower ones with the rockets on them.

On March 10, we had a big campaign. One of the Chinese route armies was surrounded west of Changsha. The Nips had this complete army surrounded on the hill and had cut off their supply of food. We took these bamboo belly tanks and cut them open and filled them with dried beef and salt and machine-gun ammunition. It was just at the end of our operational range. We would go up there, but we had instructions definitely not to engage in any form of combat except to strafe on the way in. We'd make one pass, and they would light some smoke flares on the hill. And we'd go in at ground level and strafe right up to this cutoff point, then light up the hill and drop these tanks. Then we'd go over the hill and out.

It was exciting, because the Japs usually kept about twenty-five or thirty Zeroes on patrol over this hill because they were determined to wipe out this army. We had two or three American boys in there with a radio set, who were giving us air-ground and tactical information. There was a little incident there. The American boys with the Chinese general, before they got surrounded, kept telling him that they were going to be in a hell of a spot and to get out of there. And the general said, "No. No. Help is on its way." This other route army was coming and they would all be saved, he thought. They got worried, and finally it was quite evident they were surrounded. The general turned to one of them and said, "Well, gentlemen, to die for my country is my honor and your misfortune." One of them said, "To hell with you, buddy." We lost contact because they threw their radio sets away, got into some coolie clothes and lit out. Those three guys got out between the lines, somehow.

Well, the Japanese Army and the Communist Army were north of the river. The Communists were getting to be quite a threat, too, although they were very nice as far as our pilots went. They helped us quite a bit in getting pilots out at that time, those that were shot down.

Cotton also had some memories of this period:

We started getting bombers in. We always had the Eleventh Bomb Group, the B-25 outfit that was in China, that we escorted most of the time. And along about that time they formed the Chinese-American Composite Wing, which was Chinese-American forces comprised of P-40s and B-25 bombers. We were very unhappy about that because our airplanes were completely shot up all the time and patched with gas cans—completely makeshift repairs—and here the Chinese group was furnished with these brand new airplanes right off the assembly line. They even had computing gunsights in them. We still had the old ones. We used an old wire ring out on the cowling most of the time. All the Chinese did was wipe themselves out. Every time we heard they were coming in to land, we'd get all our airplanes clear off the field and get clear up in the hills and watch this fiasco. It was the greatest air circus in the world. They came in a very dubious formation, and then they went in every direction with no rhyme or reason. They came in, they landed, and they ran together. I remember they crashed nine airplanes one day in Hengyang.

The Chinese coolies with their ancient equipment were building a big, parallel strip next to the old big Hengyang fighter strip. One day, when this Chinese group came in, one airplane went right down the middle of one of those groups of people working on the runway. It was a closed runway. It would have been obvious to anybody else. I don't know how many were wiped out. By the time he got stopped, you'd think the people would get out and murder him, but he opened the canopy and they saw he was a Chinese boy and he was the biggest hero. And here was this carnage, a mile long behind him.

You couldn't escort these Chinese bombers because they'd shoot at you. You couldn't get close to them. They'd take off with their windshield wipers on. They had every switch in the cockpit on—the guns firing as well. It was a real harrowing operation.

A mission of March 18 was Cotton's last in China. He participated in a river sweep that day at Shihhweiyah. Charlie Olsen made his last mission on March 16 when the locomotive was destroyed. Cotton later related:

Olsen and I headed out of Hengyang shortly thereafter. We had quite an experience getting out of there. At that time the Japanese had pushed past Hankow and were heading down the river toward our place. I don't know whether Changsha had been captured at that time or not. The squadron was on strafing missions, would go up the river strafing, return, reload again, and take off all day long and into the evening. We were fighting in poor conditions. So many Japanese coming, and there was no way to stop them. The Chinese Army had been routed, and there was little or no defense against the invaders. The Seventy-fifth retreated back. We sent a caravan back to Kweilin with all the ground supplies and non-flying personnel. Took some of the Chinese girlfriends along. And it took a month or so to get to Kweilin. By the time Olsen and I got ready to leave, most of the aircraft had been flown out. It was an unusual route out. We got into a sampan down the river, where we got one of the typical Chinese refugee trains with people hanging out on the engine and roof. All seats were taken but we managed to squeeze in. We had had nothing to eat for twenty-four hours and we got hungry.

The Chinese were eating tangerines and things they had brought with them. I suggested to Olsen that we try to find a dining car, but he said to forget it. He had just looked into the kitchen as unofficial mess officer with the squadron, and I took his word for it. So we sat for another twenty-four hours starving and thinking of all the good things we were having to eat when we got to the United States.

I made a list of all the delicacies I would get when I hit home. Apple pie and ice cream were high on the list. Eventually, we got to Kunming, where we took an uneventful trip over the Hump on one of the airlift planes. We crossed India rather rapidly with very little delay and soon were back on Miami Beach. One of the first things we did was to go to the bank and find out if any of the bank drafts were good which we had bought in China. Much to our chagrin, the drafts were very good. They were a deal since we were paid in China with American money, and there was an official exchange rate of twenty to one. For one of our dollars we could get twenty Chinese. It was not unusual to get up to eighty dollars for one American dollar on the black market. Therefore, we would take our surplus cash after our deductions and go down to the black market and exchange it for our Chinese money for local use. If you went to the Bank of China, you could buy a five hundred- or thousand-dollar note payable a year from then or on demand in the Bank of China or the Chase National Bank in the United States.

So we got our American money exchanged at the black market, eighty to one, took Chinese money to the Chinese bank, and bought a bank draft payable in American money in the States at the rate of twenty to one. So roughly we had sixty Chinese dollars profit. Little did we know that the U.S. government at the time was backing the Bank of China, and the notes were 100 percent secure. Anyway, I took the money I cashed from the notes and bought me a brand new uniform, was assigned to San Amaca Redistribution Center, and went on to my long-awaited leave to Wyoming. The last I heard of Charlie Olsen was a telegram to Wyoming saying he had bought a car, got married, Ding hao, and had blown a tire.

Men were now being rotated more frequently. It was strictly an American policy. In England, for example, pilots kept on fighting because they were in such short supply. In addition, how could they be rotated and sent home when they were already home? The battles were over their own cities. America kept training new pilots and sending them to all theaters and rotating the seasoned combat pilots home. Generally it was after they had completed so many combat missions. But the final decision was left up to the flight surgeon, and he could send a pilot home for medical or psychological reasons as well.

In China, the necessity for rotation had a lot to do with living conditions to which the men were subjected. By the time they came home, many weighed up to fifty pounds less than when they had gone over. But it was not that they were no longer capable of flying or that it would have hurt them to fly another fifty missions. It was that if they were not relieved, they would become so ill that they could never be discharged from the service. They would all be on physical disability. Lung flukes, liver flukes, blood flukes, not to mention malaria, yellow fever, and cholera were omnipresent. So it was not exactly when a pilot arrived in China that determined his "tour of duty;" but rather when the flight surgeon figured an individual had absorbed enough punishment, either physical or mental. The cutoff time was around a hundred combat missions but varied depending upon the field conditions, replacements, and the need for pilots at the front.

A flight surgeon was frequently present at debriefings in an effort to ascertain the point at which a pilot should be relieved of combat. They would interrogate the men, watch their reactions and mannerisms, and contemplate their answers. They were genuinely concerned with the pilots' personal safety, but their questions were not always appreciated right after an encounter with the enemy. Charlie Olsen once recalled such a time:

> One jackass asked somebody, trying to get a little medical information, "Do you itch or do your hands sweat or do you sweat when you see the enemy?" Hell, you don't have time to think, you are too busy, you don't know what you do. And your reflexes and your feelings are different after the first encounter, after you build confidence and experience.

You don't know what to expect the first time. I guess it's like just getting married. On your wedding night what do you expect when you marry your wife and you take her to a hotel room? You just don't know how to really handle everything. You're just taken away by the vastness of it all.

I mean you've trained for combat and all of this stuff, and finally the day arrives—your first encounter with the enemy. Your whole flight arrives down at Hong Kong, and all of a sudden "Varoom" come the Zeroes, the bombers' bomb-bay doors are open, bombs and belly tanks start raining down, and you drop your belly tank. And they start hollering, "Five o'clock, there's seven of them. Look at that slant-eyed . . . look out, here come those slant-eyed sons of bitches at three o'clock and there's about eight of them. Oh, look out somebody. My God! They got hit!" Then pretty soon you see a B-24 burning and spinning in, and you know it's full of men. Then two planes collide in midair—pieces of engine falling down, wheels flying through the air. Hell, finally a Zero goes by and you squeeze the trigger and nothing happens. You squeeze it and you don't even realize you have your gun switch off.

You don't know what you do. You're not even aware that you are there. There are no sounds. You're deaf from the time the engine starts back at the field. You're really deaf, you know, to normal sounds. You've got your phones on so when they talk you hear it because the sound is concentrated, but normally your only sensations are sight and touch.

The only message you get from the engine is vibration. You don't hear if the engine is missing. You don't hear it, you *feel* it. You feel the vibrations through the stick, through the throttle quadrant, through your feet on the rudder pedals, and through your seat—the contact points with the machine itself.

The moment the thing misses three licks you feel it. You pick up the vibrations instantly when you lose rpm's. You pick it up instantly if you've got something else, if you've got a hunk of metal missing somewhere, a rip, a tear, or something in the metal. You can feel it. You know this on your first contact because you've learned this through your training, how the plane normally feels and flies.

But you are overcome by the vastness of it all only once—the first contact. After that you're conscious and you know it's going to be hell to pay and you know people are going to be hurt. I mean that's part of the game. I mean you know people are going to get killed. You expect that, I mean—you just hope it isn't you.

Doc wanted to know was I afraid. Was there fear? Yes, I was

afraid sometimes but not of the Japs. As a matter of fact I wanted to contact him. I had waited and looked for him, and when I finally saw him it was a relief. Now I can fight, now I can shoot, now I can do something. The more the merrier, man. If you had ten of you out there and you ran into ten Japs, there was fear, fear that you wouldn't get your piece of them. If you're with ten planes and you run into a hundred Zeroes, that's great. Man, just think of all of them you can get, you know, you got ten or fifteen of them all to yourself.

But you're never afraid of the fight. By now you figure that you're good enough, you can shoot good enough, you can handle the plane good enough, that you shouldn't get into too much trouble unless you've got your head up your behind. If you concentrate on one thing and forget about what's happening around you, you can get in trouble. But you take everything into consideration before you commit yourself. You see what's there. If you see four Zeroes you make damn sure there isn't eight more hiding somewhere when you go for that four.

Just like the day over Tungting Lake—there were two of them, and I made sure that's the only two there were. I wasn't going to get sucked in. I felt that I was good enough that those two posed no threat at all to me, not the slightest. I knew the commander's limits in the Zero, and I knew mine in the P-40. I knew every trick that Jap could've thought of or dreamed of, and I had a new one for him. I knew he felt pretty hot, and it kind of pleased me, you know, that he was going to commit himself and fight. That's the reason that I toyed with him. I could have taken him earlier, but he left his wingman up there, cocky-like, and came after me alone. I think that bothered the Doc. The thing that I said wrong, if anything, was that I could've finished him off quicker. Doc dwelled on that for a time, asking me more questions about fear.

I'll tell you where there is fear, gut-gnawing fear. It's going down to Hong Kong or somewhere where you're on your butt for four or five hours going down. You cross the foot of the Himalayas, and you're three hours deep in enemy territory. You fear all right, you fear that the damn engine is going to fail. You fear that the belly tank may have green slime in it and that any minute you are going to get a carburetor full of it like I did on my second escort mission to Hong Kong when I lost an engine cold at twenty thousand feet and I came all the way down to twelve hundred before I got the engine started again. You fear that the engine is going to throw a rod when you are only five miles from Hong Kong.

During the fight you don't have time to worry because you are occupied, but when you turn off the target for home it's a different story. You start checking around for coolant leaks or oil pressure drop, anything that might keep you from getting home. You start looking and feeling for structural damage that you may have sustained over the target. Because you are over enemy territory and you are afraid of going down, being captured.

It was something different than fighting over Hengyang, Lingling, or somewhere over friendly territory. I never worried about such things over friendly terrain. I never worried whether I'd belly-land, bail out, or get shot down. I figured I could handle that, just the same as if I was over my own field. That would be the last thing an experienced pilot would be worried about, a forced landing. No matter where the damn engine quit. If he's good enough, he'd put it down on the lake, on a road, in a field, anywhere necessary but he'd get it down. It's when you're way behind the enemy lines that you fear going down and not getting back. That's more or less what you worry about, not getting shot down per se, but getting shot down behind enemy lines.

I was in China for months and months before I got my first contact—I mean actual contact where I could fight somebody. Most of the time we had been protecting the bombers. We couldn't fight. We had to stay cover for them and try and keep the Zeroes off of the bombers. We couldn't take off and chase one. We just had to kind of let them come through us and try to aim at them and shoot or chase them away. All the time we were conscious, like the hen and the baby chick. So you never really got any individual fighting or anything like that. You stayed in formation and went.

But later on, like over Hengyang when I got into a fight where it was a free-for-all, and later on when I'd go on strafing missions and whatnot, you did your mission and you could go hunt for targets of opportunity, anything you could pick up. It's different. You're actually out destroying something.

After a while though, after you drop enough bombs and you shoot enough rockets, you've been through it long enough that you almost don't have to navigate anymore. You know where you are at all times and you know how long it's going to take you to go there and back, and you know where the line is, the enemy line, and where it isn't. You know what to expect when you get to this river and what to expect when you get north of here, and pretty soon it becomes so familiar that it's second nature. And that's what the fighting gets like later on as the months stretch into years.

Yet, there is one other kind of fear, where fate is the hunter. It appears suddenly, almost like a funny hysteria. I was coming back from Hankow and it was after a strafing mission. The flight had got scattered and I was all alone. During the strafing I had closed my engine coolant shutter doors before diving down, and afterwards I had climbed back up to altitude and had failed to open them again. I generally kept them slightly open during cruise. I had climbed to twelve thousand feet for the return home, and it was a clear day with a few big cumulus clouds around. It was about eleven o'clock in the morning.

I was coming on back and just cruising along, and everything looked pretty good, with Hengyang coming up real soon. I looked down and I was getting a little warm. The needle was not near the red line, but it was getting up above the green. I started looking around in case I'd picked up a hole from ground fire over the target which was making the engine run hot from coolant loss or oil. I then realized that the engine coolant shutters were still closed. I said, "Oh well, I'd better open my coolant shutters," and looked around outside and there wasn't anything. So I reached for it up forward and low in the cockpit and the harness had me, my shoulder harness. I straightened up and released my shoulder harness and then leaned forward with my head and shoulders to open the shutters when I heard a "whoof." I straightened up quickly and saw a big red meatball peeling up right at me, and he zoomed over. He had put a 20 mm cannon round right through my canopy, right where my head had been. There was a large hole right through the plexiglass from the left side through the right side and not another mark on the airplane. I instinctively dove and started looking around, but that was it. I listened to the sound of the wind whistling through those two holes by my ears, sort of distracted, and it took me a few moments to realize what had happened. He had timed me, having entered that cloud with the sun to his back and figured just about where I would be when he popped out the other side. He was able to give me a short burst, but only one round went through the canopy. He then just peeled straight up and over me and took off.

The first offensive campaign of the year in China began on April 17 when a Japanese division crossed over the Yellow River to Honan Province at night to assemble in areas along the river. Two days later it and another division, spearheaded by tanks and supported by dive bombers and fighters, started south to take the 240-mile link to the Peiping-Hankow railroad held by the Chinese. As this force got under way, another Japanese force with the same mission began driving northward toward it from the Hankow area.

Encountering no effective opposition, both forces gradually advanced and by the middle of May had cleared a corridor approximately fifty miles wide, centered on the railroad, from the Yellow River to Hankow, fully opening up the railroad from there to Peiping. By June 2, the Honan offensive had drawn to a close with the Japanese having secured their objective at a light cost.

Concurrently, other Japanese forces from the southern bank almost to the Great Bend threatened to push along the Wei River to Sian in Shensi Province. However, they were stopped short of the Great Bend and ceased offensive operations by the end of June.

On April 21 fifteen P-40s from the Seventy-fifth bombed the Hsinning barracks and strafed them with rockets. About five miles southeast of the target, a truck with about twenty men was strafed heavily. Hsinning was apparently completely surprised, for the antiaircraft fire was very light and inaccurate. At least twenty of the rockets were put into the main cavalry area, hitting buildings and bursting among horses. About two hundred horses were in the area, some being ridden by cavalrymen nearby at the bend of the river. One building was blown apart and another badly damaged. All ships returned safely to Hengyang. At 6:30 P.M., there was an alert at Hengyang. But the alert turned out to be for American planes returning from the Hsinning mission.

Two days later fourteen P-40s from the Seventy-fifth returned to Hsinning to attack the artillery post and another post at Kuanfuchow. At Hsinning four rocket planes came in for the first pass, and at least fifteen of the twenty-one rockets fired hit the target area. Following these planes were four others with bombs. Six of the bombs struck the building area and three buildings were demolished. At Kuanfuchow, two rockets were fired, burning in the middle of a herd of horses and hitting about twenty horses and five or six men simultaneously. One plane was forced to return shortly after takeoff because of fuel trouble.

On May 14 the Seventy-fifth participated in an offensive reconnaissance over Pailuchi. The planes made a sweep across the city but saw no enemy planes. So the mission swung to the east. Fifteen trucks parked along the highway were set fire by strafing. Changanyi was strafed and an oil fire started. Lt. Francis Armstrong made a head-on pass with a Zero on the Yangtze River near Yochow. The enemy was seen to smoke heavily and head for Pailuchi streaming smoke behind. He also hit another Zero, damaging it. Lt. James Focht burned out a generator on takeoff and was forced to return. Lt. Marvin Balderson knocked a hole in his belly tank with a stone on takeoff and was unable to join the mission. Lt. James C. Vargaropulos landed at Siangtan after damaging a Zero near Yochow. The rest returned and landed safely at Hengyang. The other pilots were Majs. Philip Loofburrow, Robert Denny, Donald Quigley; Capts. J. D. Long, James Anning; Lts. Leonard Aylesworth, Jasper Brown, Donald Lopez, James Folmer, William Moonan, and Paul H. Moehring.

The Seventy-fifth went out three times on May 17 beginning at 7 A.M. when they attempted an interception. One enemy plane was approaching Hengyang from the north. Two P-40s headed for Siangtan expecting the Japanese pilot to look for ships on the landing strip. But he turned back near Changsha, and no contact was made.

At 9:15, thirteen P-40s escorted B-25s to Shayang and did reconnaissance on the return trip. Bombers successfully unloaded their bombs in the target area. The P-40s left the bombers twenty-five miles southwest of Shayang. They strafed and burned seven or eight trucks loaded with gas or oil. Majs. Philip Loofburrow and Robert Denny were hit by small-caliber ground fire, Loofburrow losing his electrical system and Denny his oil system. Major Denny picked a field near Liuchow and set down on the ship's belly. On return Lt. Jesse Gray contacted enemy fighters and claimed one probable even though his gas supply was very low. The bombers and eight fighters landed at Lingling to refuel, and most of the sharks landed at Hengyang. Pilots participating besides those already mentioned were Capt. Curtis Scoville, Lts. George Howard, William Daniels, William B. Carlton, Jr., Donald Lopez, Nathan Green, Herbert King, David Rust, and William Noonan.

The morning ended with an alert over Hengyang called due to heavy engine noise following the mission back from Shayang. Eight P-40s contacted thirty enemy fighters just northeast of Hengyang. The score in the fight which followed was Lt. Francis Armstrong, one confirmed; Maj. Ira Jones, Lts. Vernon Tanner, O. H. Elker, and George Howard—one probable apiece; and Major Jones, Lts. James Folmer, Howard, and Elker—one damaged apiece. Tanner was hard hit, and since in landing at Hengyang he had no wheels, the ship was washed out.

It was back to Hsinning on May 22 when eight P-40s from the Seventy-fifth dive-bombed a highway bridge at the city. As they approached Hsinning, the top cover saw enemy fighters—Oscars and Tojos—approaching from far astern. The dive bombers, heavy with load, made their run, hitting the railroad tracks at the corner of the town and some trucks.

During the ensuing battle, Capt. Curtis Scoville confirmed a Tojo, Maj. Ira Jones claimed an Oscar as a probable, and Lt. Francis Armstrong damaged an Oscar. All planes returned safely. Scoville and Jones were attacked by four planes, at least two of which were Tojos. At forty-seven inches of Mercury and twenty-eight hundred rpm, they were able to outclimb them. Scoville was then able to get in a diving pass at the first one, who reefed into a tight turn and escaped. Scoville again outclimbed the second Tojo and dived. This one started vertical rolls and Scoville rolled with him, shooting almost six hundred rounds. Scoville broke off and Jones saw the Tojo crash into the ground. Ira Jones then saw an Oscar closing in on Scoville. He got dead astern and fired, observing the hits. The Oscar rolled over and started tumbling. It was at five hundred feet at the time, and so probably did not recover at this low altitude. Since his radio was not working, Elker did not hear plots of more Japanese planes coming in, and so he followed the Zeroes to Siangtan and came up with four damaged.

Some of the same pilots returned to Hsinning on an offensive recon mission later in the day. Lt. Moehring had a poor belly tank connection and was forced to return. The two bombing flights dropped their bombs in the western part of the city, hitting a factory on the south side of town as well as adjoining buildings. About fifteen trucks were strafed west of the highway bridge. There was no interception.

On May 26, the Seventy-fifth lost 1st Lt. Marvin E. Balderson. Jim Anning recalled the mission:

> I was the flight leader in a flight of four P-40s flying top cover near Tungting Lake. Down below us were four more P-40s on the deck strafing ground targets. Our job was to prevent any enemy aircraft from dropping down on them while they were concentrating on

their targets. I had my wingman with me, and Smedley was the other element leader with Balderson flying his wing. Smedley was more experienced than Balderson but had a tendency to get out of position. Balderson was one of those kids with about thirty or forty hours total out of flying school.

We were flying under an overcast, which was good since it protected my flight from an attack from above. However, the area was covered with a thick haze and it was almost impossible to see anywhere except straight down. I hollered at Smedley to bring the element up closer. The damn area would just get hazy at times. I'm talking about haze up to fifteen or twenty thousand feet sometimes, which makes for a rotten situation—nothing to navigate by, no landmarks visible. It was easy to get separated and our maps weren't even accurate. Those maps had blank spots saying no known data, and then there were these magnetic effects where it would swing your magnetic compass twenty to thirty degrees.

I am a believer in two elements keeping it tight anyway, not necessarily side by side but fore and aft. That way not only can the two plane elements take care of themselves by protecting one another's tail but the close-up flight of four aircraft is better protected since the two elements can protect one another by scissoring back and forth. If I looked at Smedley's element and saw somebody coming down on either one of them, I could swing over there and shoot the guy coming in. That is, if the other element is up tight. But strung out way back it was hard even to see them in the haze. Also, because of the haze, I was having trouble keeping an eye on the guys down below.

All of a sudden we broke in the clear. I think the Japanese had radar out of Hankow because all of a sudden we broke in the clear and I could hear in my radio something about Zeroes. Those radios were all static, an old coffee grinder. I looked back the best I could at those idiot airplanes, and I saw those Zeroes coming in like a bunch of hawks and I started a 180. They were coming through, so as I dropped my belly tank I called the alert to the people downstairs that they were there. They were coming through the other element, and I saw one Zero right up Smedley's tail and the other, Balderson, had a couple coming in behind him.

I knew the only way to catch them was to get up speed so I dove and my wingman followed. I rolled over and went straight down. I was supposed to do anything to make sure no Zeroes got through, which they didn't because it was so hazy that they didn't see them. I tried to orient myself—now I'm trying to find Balderson and Smedley. Smedley I never did see again, nor Balderson for that matter. I lost contact with him, too. I fiddled around there for a while but was low on fuel and had to go home. Balderson went by himself. We never heard from Smedley again, and I later learned that Balderson belly-landed at Changsha on the way back to Hengyang after running out of fuel.

Dr. Jones Laughlin, who was flight surgeon for the Seventy-fifth at the time, later recalled his own involvement in the incident:

Balderson was on his way back up from Tungting Lake country when he got back as far as Changsha. This is a town where Yale University used to have a school. It had a big wide road, with the river near the main street. Balderson came in too hot over the river and wound up at the end of the street. He never set his plane down until he got to the end and slammed into the embankment and killed himself. So they sent a radio message back with one of these little radio communications, saying they had him in a Chinese hospital up there and if he regained consciousness, they might have to operate or something for the head injury. He hit his head on the gunsight at the impact.

So it was decided I would fly up there and take some blood plasma and some oxygen and some sulfadiazine pills. We didn't have any penicillin. The whole squadron was on edge, and I don't know whether they asked me or if I volunteered to go see about him, but everybody was happy about the decision. So they radioed the message and I went.

But first let me finish the story about the accident. Balderson was scared. He was coming back up from Tungting Lake and he didn't think he had enough gasoline to get back home and he made a couple buzzes around that river. But if he would have come in and set it down right after, then he might have been OK. But he didn't set it down until two or three hundred yards from the end of the street and he banged into that damn pillbox. That's one of those things they dug into the ground where they put the Chinese soldiers and chained them in and locked them up and they had little windows to shoot back at the Japs when they came. They left them there, chained up to the post.

So someone called a plane out of the air, a China Air Transport command ship which ferried supplies to the area. So I got into this old gooney bird, a C-47. The guys started telling me all kinds of things about bailing out, how to pull the strings and slice and glide. I had never bailed out before. Everybody in the squadron was there—Segura, Fulmer, Quigley, Tanner, the chief, and Loofburrow. And so when I got on this plane I told the crew chief, "Hell, you just back up to that other side over there and I'm going to stand here and whenever the pilot gives you the signal, you just put that big foot on my butt and I'll jump. It'll just be up to me to pull that string.

I had a seat pack on. It wasn't a regular parachute, and it wasn't for paratrooping. It was a seat pack that fit in the seat of one of those fighter planes. So they got in the air and they made the run up to Changsha. They had all my stuff put into one of these belly tanks and it had a parachute on it.

The pilot told me that he was going to fly to the area, and when the wind was right for a jump, I'd go back and jump. So I got to the door and the sergeant gave me a boot. Changsha had been bombed by the Japs. It was all red brick, a city about the size of Houston. I jumped. And I started drifting right down over a big graveyard and there were smokestacks stuck up there four, five, and six stories high. I thought, "My God, I'm going to hang up on one of those damn things." So finally, I thought, "Well, those guys told me to pull on these two cords on this side and to slip air and make that thing slide." So I started pulling and I started sliding. I'd pull a little more and slide a little faster and pull a little more and slide a little faster until finally I felt I wasn't going to make it. I got so close to the ground, I thought I'd better turn this damn thing loose now and see if I could hit it. And I could see a meat wagon down there with no coloration on it at all. It sure didn't look like the familiar old Dodge.

I finally hit the ground. The Chinese were so frugal that some of them had spaded by hand a long row by the street to make a vegetable garden. I just cleared a wall and plopped right down, bingo, right into that spaded, soft dirt. I had landed just off the hard, cement street. And there were Chinese everywhere.

The Chinese were hollering, "Lady Lindbergh! Lady Lindbergh!" I had on a flying suit and I had this little old camera, a 35 mm, sticking out in front and something else on the other side and they thought I was a woman. Then I was contacted by everybody out there—the major, the army, the city council, the hospital staff, the head nurse at the hospital.

They were all Chinese nurses except one, who was an American who was associated with the Red Cross or some missionaries. That night they had a meeting at her house, and they called in all the

American missionaries. There were missionaries of all denominations there, Methodist, Baptist, Lutheran, what have you, and they all lived there. They might get $150 a month in American money, but they lived in a big house out in the middle of the river on an island and lived like kings. They had a ricksha sitting over by the riverbank and the driver gave them personal taxi service and they had personal sampans and household servants on this island. They never had it so good.

They had an accumulation of years of Chinese pottery, silk, draperies, and other treasures, and they just couldn't go off and leave it. So they wanted to talk to me to see how long it was going to be before the Japs were going to get there. I said, "My God, you should've left last week. You're already trapped. These Japs are just out ten to fifteen miles out of town, and they may be in here before any of us can get out. They may be here during the night. All of you have stayed too long. There is no way you are going to get out of here." And finally, about a week or two later, there was one padre, a Catholic priest, came walking back into Hengyang with his stick on his shoulder like a carpetbagger coming south.

This good-looking nurse wanted me to stay with her, but I thought, I don't want to get myself court-martialed like my predecessor. So I decided to spend the night in the hotel, sleeping under one of the massive mosquito bars. The next morning they had the ceremony down at the river for Balderson, who had died at the hospital. There was a riverboat full of flowers, tributes from the Chinese, all around the casket.

After the ceremony, all of the Chinese officers stood together in great lines on the riverbank. And the commander told them for all of the officers who did not have sons to get on the boat and leave. In China it was a big thing if you didn't have a son because there would be nobody to carry on the family name. So the officers with no sons got on the boat with me and we chug-a-lugged back up the river against the current. I got to the base two weeks later.

The missionaries stayed there. I heard a story later about one of those missionary ladies. She went off into the hills with a whole orphanage of kids, Chinese kids, and she went so damn far off into the hills that the Japs never got her. Whatever happened to the rest of them is anybody's guess. Except one came back. About two or three weeks later a gal came out to the base, and here it was this good-looking nurse—the one I had declined the invitation to spend the night with. She came in and wanted to get a booster shot for typhoid. And I regretted spending the night at that stupid hotel at Changsha.

As I said before, it took two weeks to get back to the base at Hengyang. One night I decided that I would go into town, and the only way you could get there from the base was to cross a railroad bridge. I started across in the old meat wagon and the air raid sounded. So I got off the bridge, turned around. The Japs came every night, and there was moonlight enough to see so they bombed about every fifteen minutes. And our boys, every time a plane wrecked, would run out to take the machine guns off of it, and they'd dig a pothole out there along the runway and set up this machine gun on a piece of four-inch pipe. So one of these Japs came in, and they were blasting those tracer bullets—you could see them go right up, bend over, and come back. And the Nip got yellow and swung off and dropped his cotton-picking bomb.

I was out there with those that were in the sick bay, and we were right in the middle of this hospital area in a slit trench. This guy straddled the slit trench with his bombs. One of them hit the kitchen, another hit the courtyard and one hit a wing which was the enlisted men's dormitory. It set eighty beds on fire and we all ran and pulled the mattresses out. Many of the men ran for the sandy hill behind the alert shack. Some of them were swimming in the river at the end of the runway.

The second offensive of the Japanese campaign to open a transportation route across China had begun even before the first offensive at Honan was ended. On May 26, strong Japanese forces with air support opened a drive in Hunan aimed southward from the upper Tungting Lake region. The right wing of the drive moved south along the west side of the lake below the Yangtze, gaining some forty miles, and then was halted. The main force drove south along the east side of the lake and made good progress, getting five divisions to the Liuyang River east of Changsha by June 10. Eight days later the Japanese overran Changsha, ending the fourth battle for this key city on the Hankow-Canton railroad since the fall of 1939.

The Japanese offensive in Hunan continued southward after the fall of Changsha, covering nearly a hundred miles by June 26. Japanese forces took the evacuated Hengyang airfield, which became the first base of the Fourteenth Air Force to be lost to the enemy.

As seventy thousand Japanese troops had deployed and come

down the Hsiang River toward Hengyang during the period from June 17 to June 25, the Twenty-third Fighter Group threw its total effort against the advancing enemy and supported an attempted stand by Chinese ground forces at Hengshan, twenty-five miles north of Hengyang. On six of the nine days the weather was adverse with an overcast arched over the river valley and engulfing the tops of the mountains on either side. Half of the missions flown had to be run through this restricted tunnel created low over the valley floor by the clouds. In spite of the clouds and constant machine-gun and small arms fire from the ground, the pilots of the Twenty-third carried out a total of 538 sorties during the nine-day period, strafing and bombing enemy forces relentlessly. Their assaults killed 1,640 enemy troops, destroyed some 780 cavalry horses and packhorses, and immediately behind the front, destroyed 377 small supply boats, damaged 372, and sank fifteen river vessels of one hundred feet or more in length.

They also damaged armed gunboats which the Japanese rushed into the area to protect their water supply lines, destroyed ninety-one transport vehicles, and damaged another fifty. They wrought extensive destruction of supplies and equipment in more than a hundred compound storage areas. In four encounters with the enemy, pilots claimed seven destroyed, seven probables, and eight damaged without loss. But all their efforts were not enough to stop the enemy or save Hengyang airfield.

On May 27 Wiltz Segura helped the war effort by shooting down a Zero near Yochow on his forty-fourth mission in China. He later recalled the events of that day:

In a strafing mission, the best thing to do was to get out without being shot. Usually the ones we got were Zeroes in the air. I was on top with a guy named Scoville. The tactic was to fly in groups of two. If the Zero got on your tail, they were so much more maneuverable than we were and were hard to shake loose. You had to point your airplane at the other guy before he could shoot you down. If you weren't pointing at him, then he was most likely pointing at you. This is why the fight was always in a circle. I didn't fly too close to my leader. In those days during the early stage of my flying, I was always the wingman or element leader, never leading the flight. If they attacked him, I could shoot them off his back. If they attacked me, the leader would shoot them off my back.

So I got way out so I could turn into this guy without turning into my own. We saw those Zeroes coming in at us, Scoville leading the mission. We were on the deck about two to three thousand feet, not much room to maneuver a P-40. The idea was to pick up speed and get out of there, then come back in and climb into him. I saw this Zero coming so I just swung wide, and Scoville said, "He's tacking on to you. Keep going!"

He makes a right turn. I turned into this guy and shot him off Scoville's tail. That's the last time I saw Scoville. When one makes a pass like that going two or three hundred mph in the opposite direction, you can lose them. By myself, I went up as high as I could, and there were Zeroes all over the skies and P-40s too. I could hear them in the air. I got up high and looked down and saw five Zeroes. I saw one lone one and went after him. I headed out and just as I did that, I saw three or four coming from behind me. I made a pass at him and we made a right turn. We were getting close to the ground. I could see the trees coming at me. I hit him but didn't knock him down. Got a piece of his tail. Just about then the tracers were after me. I threw it into a left turn and went straight down, using those few thousand feet I had left. I saw the tracers, and my plane was in a spiral, which was the hardest way for them to hit you.

I could tell I was putting space between me and the Zeroes, because the tracers were coming over my right wing. Pretty soon they were getting far back. When I got to the deck, I leveled off, then I knew I could outrun them. Once level, the P-40 could outrun them, could go just a little bit faster, especially if you had a good heartbeat in that cockpit. I got myself out and headed home.

Segura was one of twelve pilots who went on the offensive recon mission at Yochow and Puchi. The rocket ships went down to strafe as they hit east of Yochow. A convoy of about twenty trucks were seen on the road and strafed. As the planes swung south of Puchi they were intercepted by between fifteen and twenty Hamps, Oscars, and Tojos. During the fight, Lt. Oswin H. Elker was hit and sent down in smoke, belly-landing near enemy lines. He was reported missing. Lts. Walter Daniels and Nathan E. Green were attacked, and Daniels was hit all over his ship but managed to return to base at Hengyang and belly in. His plane caught fire as he landed but the crew got him out, though he was seriously wounded. Lt. Green's plane disappeared and crashed after Green had bailed out. Besides Segura's hit of one Hamp, Lt. Leonard Aylesworth damaged one

Tojo. Aylesworth noticed this Tojo following him and Lt. P. G. Coran. It was apparently alone, so he turned back upon it. The plane attempted to flip and dive away, but Aylesworth dived across him and raked him with .50 caliber fire. Other pilots participating were Maj. Philip Loofburrow, Lts. Richard Jones, David Rust, and Francis H. Armstrong.

On May 29, Lt. William Carlton, Jr., got a dead-astern shot on one Oscar on the Hsiang River. He closed to within fifty yards, and observed many hits, but had to break away before finding out the results. He claimed a probable.

June 1 and 2 were busy days for the men of the Seventy-fifth Squadron. On the first day, they participated in six missions—dive-bombing Kweiyi, participating in an alert over the field at Hengyang, dive-bombing Tien Sein Lake, strafing water traffic along the western side of Tungting Lake, carrying out a recon mission to Tangyang and Kingmen, and dive-bombing Pingkiang where the bombs hit right in town.

On June 2, the Seventy-fifth, the CACW, and the Seventy-sixth joined forces for five more missions. They dive-bombed the Tsung-yang area and the town of Shihshou on a lake north of Yuanchiang. About seventy-five sampans were strafed and left burning. Two Zeroes were seen by one of the flights flying top cover, and were engaged and both damaged by Major Van Ausdall and Lt. William Noonan. Later on twenty-two pilots struck Tsungyang and strafed a road to Tungchang. Thirty trucks were burned or crippled in a motor park. At least three hundred casualties resulted from these attacks. There were no interceptions. The pilots for these missions were Colonel Dunning, Major Van Ausdall, Captain Ploetz, Lieutenant McCutchin, all of the CACW; Maj. Ira Jones, Lts. Donald Lopez, Brown, Herbert King, George Howard, James Focht, Leonard Aylesworth, Richard Jones, William B. Carlton; Capts. Lester E. Murray, John C. "Pappy" Herbst, Slater; Lts. Richard Olney, Watts, Zavakos, Howard Bullock and Gibson.

Early in the evening thirteen P-40s from the Seventy-sixth, three from the CACW, and ten P-51s from the Seventy-sixth dive-bombed Tungchang and strafed the vicinity, causing three large fires. North of town some trucks were strafed and left burning. Lt. James Focht got hit in his oil system and had to bail out about ten miles east of Tungchang. There was no interception.

The next day the pilots moved to strafe the Shihshou Lake area from the south. They strafed some barges in the lake, inflicting heavy damage. Smoke and fire were evident as they left the scene. Also, about two hundred men and ten horses were killed on the barges. About two hours later, other pilots left to dive-bomb Pingkiang and escort six B-25s there. Ten bombs hit in the town, taking some buildings and a compound. As they left they could see smoke but no fire.

Picking was not so easy on June 4, when the P-40s set out to dive-bomb Ciah Shan Island. When they got to the target, they found their view obscured and returned to Hengyang.

On June 8 Chinese forces penetrated the outer defenses of Lungling, twenty miles from the Salween. Six days later, the Japanese began vigorous counterattacks, driving the Chinese back and stalling their advance. In order to overcome this failure, the Chinese determined on June 25 to take Tengchung, some thirty miles north of Lungling, and Sung Shan at all costs and then renew the attack at Lungling.

Subsequently, the Salween front—the offensive against Tengchung—was launched June 26 with air attacks by B-25s. In the meantime, as June progressed, the Seventy-fifth kept making offensive sweeps to Shanglishih, Siangsiang, and Siangyin. On June 18 on a river sweep near Siangyin, the Seventy-fifth did considerable damage to enemy boats, burning or damaging forty or fifty of them. Besides that, around seventy-five men were killed, two houses were wrecked, and one steamboat damaged.

Then the men proceeded to Changsha where they strafed thirty boats, setting four or five on fire. One oil or gas dump was set on fire and twenty horses and just as many men were killed. Lt. Walter Daniels received a bullet in his oil system and was forced to land at Hengyang. They continued to strike in the Changsha area on June 20, hitting boats and horses and barges.

Also on June 20 Casey Vincent at headquarters at Kweilin worried about the Japanese approaching Hengyang. Plans were made to evacuate the base. That day he wrote in his diary:

> Things really took a turn for the worse today. The Japanese are darn close to Hengyang. I am evacuating that base tomorrow. Demolition will follow soon after. I had to send George McMillan word to get ready also. I'm moving him to Kanchow soon, and then here.

God, I will hate to evacuate this place! I can't get any support from the people of the Fourteenth Air Force Headquarters. Either they don't know how serious the situation is—or they don't care. My request for six transports was refused with a very nasty wire. I sent one back saying if they couldn't trust my decisions, they could relieve me and I meant it! We are out of touch with our liaison teams in the field—no information for the last twelve hours. Apparently, the Chinese may try to make a stand at Hengyang. As for us—we'll "Fire and Fall Back."

Next day Vincent continued:

Damn, the one C-47 transport plane I have is out of commission. I had to use my stripped-down B-25 and the one Nordheim Norseman we have to evacuate Hengyang. I'm not getting any information from the field. . . . No telling where the Japanese are. I don't want to demolish Hengyang until it's absolutely necessary. The Japanese bombed twenty-five miles north of Hengyang this morning, and the first we heard about it was when they were actually doing it. The warning net has gone to hell. The Chinese plan to put up a strong resistance on the east-west line through Hengyang. General Lindsey is trying to get some information as to how far the Japanese have advanced toward Hengyang. I certainly hope the Chinese can hold them there. If the Japanese capture Hengyang and start toward Lingling, our position here at Kweilin will be gravely threatened. While writing this, I received word that the Japanese are at Hengshan, so I gave the order to get everybody out of Hengyang and demolish the place. It breaks my heart to destroy that beautiful field.

Vincent was promoted to brigadier general two days later.

In an offensive sweep from Hengyang to Siangtan on June 23, an estimated two hundred men were killed and about fifty boats damaged. Six to eight triple-deckers were strafed, causing much damage. All planes and pilots returned safely.

On June 25, the men stayed close to Hengyang, participating in four offensive sweeps in the area, a repeat performance of the day before. On the first sweep of the day at 9:40 A.M., eight planes took off for the area northeast of the city. As they passed Hengyang, they encountered nine Oscars and six Hamps and later ten Vals. The enemy was met with good results. Maj. Arthur Cruikshank confirmed two Vals and got one Oscar probable; Lt. Wiltz Segura confirmed one Hamp and damaged another; Lt. James C. Vargaropulos confirmed one Hamp, got one-half Hamp probable, and damaged another; Lt. Robert S. Peterson was credited with the other half probable with Vargaropulos; and Lt. Jesse Gray got one Oscar probable; Lt. Herbert King got one Oscar probable too. No American planes were damaged and all returned safely.

Wiltz Segura later recalled being on a mission that day out of Kweilin:

> We were going five or six thousand feet and all of the sudden somebody started spotting Zeroes. We dropped our bombs. It was overcast at about three thousand feet. After we made our first pass, somebody got on my leader's tail and I made a pass at them but I wasn't able to get a shot. I lost the formation. I never did see anybody else for the rest of the mission, but I could hear them down below. They found these dive bombers circling Hengyang, bombing the city. I saw these six Zeroes at quite a high altitude, about ten to fifteen thousand feet. I was quite a distance from them. I started climbing up to about seventeen thousand feet and headed closer. They saw me and headed toward me. I was a couple thousand above them and I felt rather secure. They came at me. Anytime you made a head-on pass with a bunch of Zeroes, only one could shoot at you at a time. Otherwise they ran into each other. Our firepower was superior to theirs. We had .50 caliber machine guns and they had .30 caliber. Our airplanes could take a beating head-on and still get away, but they couldn't.
>
> If we could get one shot and hit and get away, we would always go for the head-on pass. And even if we got hit, the engine was in front of you with a bulletproof windshield. As a pilot, I felt pretty secure.
>
> I made a pass at him, but before I got him, there was one of the pack and he started diving and I starting diving at him. Well, I could see what was happening. They set him up as a decoy. I figured I could get him before they got to me. I wouldn't make the mistake of slowing down. As long as I kept my speed, I figured none could close in on me. I had seventeen thousand feet to play with. This Jap headed down, I headed down at him. I was looking at the other five behind him. Just as we got down and I started rolling over, he started pulling up. That made my shot pretty difficult and I could never get the lead I wanted on him because he kept tightening.
>
> Just as I hit the horizon, it was time to break away. That's when

you start slowing down in a P-40. I had everything wide open, and I was close to him. I could see inside his cockpit. I couldn't stay with him around the turn. I broke off, got into a little overcast. The others were following. Then I broke out and saw them about a mile or two away. I started climbing again. They were climbing too. And they did exactly the same thing. I kept leading from way back. He put his nose down, and I put mine further than his. I got close enough in range and turned upside down. I flanked him out, so I had to shoot him at an angle. Kept computing lead from distance all the time. When I got him just right . . . Pow! Sideways. He curled over and blew up. I got my nose over the horizon and was off, the other five right behind me. I did that four times and I hit three of them that day. I got two confirmed. Just kept picking them off until they finally broke away and went home.

The rest of the day and the next it was the same thing—strafing the Hengyang area, recon at nearby towns. On the morning of June 26, there was an interception over the Hengyang field. Alerted by plots of enemy aircraft thirty miles out, fifteen aircraft went to the rescue. The interception took place about ten miles from the field. During the fight, Lt. Francis Armstrong was hit and was not seen to bail out or to crash. Lt. Donald Lopez confirmed one Oscar, and Lt. William Carlton and Lt. Donald Miller each scored hits on Oscars, causing significant damage. Other pilots on this mission were Maj. Donald Quigley, Lts. Jesse Gray, O. H. Elker, Jack L. Quinn, David Rust, and Walter Daniels, all of the Seventy-fifth; Capts. McMillan and E. J. Davis and Lt. Robert Peterson of the 118th; and Lts. Jess Garrett and Mullineaux of the Seventy-fourth.

That afternoon six sharks made another offensive sweep in the Hengyang area, strafing along the road west of the city and also strafing and bombing barges, damaging sixty of them. All planes returned. They were piloted by Maj. Donald Quigley, Lts. James Vargaropulos, Wiltz Segura, Russell Fleming, Paul H. Moehring, and Herbert King.

But June 26 also marked another step backwards. Planes had to be moved out of Lingling because of a warning net failure about one hundred miles in front of the Japanese advance. "I don't seem to be able to convince Kunming how serious our situation is," Casey Vincent wrote in his diary. "Good God, if the Chinese were fighting at all—we could have already driven the Japanese back to Shanghai. I'm disgusted, but we'll fight to the last ditch and abandon each field only when it is absolutely necessary. I tried to pin down General Pai today but could not. He will not admit that the fate of east China is sealed. We are all set for the vice president tomorrow." The purpose of Vice President Henry Wallace's visit to Chungking was to try to persuade Generalissimo Chiang Kai-shek to negotiate with Mao Tse-tung and Chou En-lai, leaders of the Chinese Communist forces. Wallace was unable to do so.

On June 27, the Seventy-fifth and Seventy-sixth dive-bombed Siangsiang and took a river sweep from Siangtan to Hengyang. The town of Siangsiang was heavily bombed with good hits and a large number of sampans were strafed along the river east of Siangsiang. There was no opposition this time. But the group was not so lucky the next day. When they went back to strafe the river near Heng-yang, the mission was attacked by eighteen to twenty Oscars as the bombers were making their run. One pass was made by four Japanese planes, but they turned away as the sharks turned in to their attack. The bombers had 100 percent hits in the target area. Thirty-five sampans were damaged or destroyed.

Chennault was in Kunming. Vincent flew to Kunming to discuss the imminent loss of Hengyang with Chennault. Hengyang controlled the main lines of communication leading from Hankow to Nanning. Even though the southern half of the Hankow-Hanoi axis was most certainly doomed, Gen. Fong Hsien-Chien, who was responsible for the defense of Hengyang, was determined to hold out as long as possible. His most important advantage was the terrain, which forced the Japanese to follow a narrow avenue of approach.

The Japanese began their assault on Hengyang itself on June 28. The city was the key hub on the north-south rail line from Hankow to Hanoi in Indochina (the line running through Changsha, Heng-yang, Kweilin, Liuchow, and Nanning) and from Hankow to Canton, and it occupied a naturally strong defensive position. Its Chinese defenders firmly withstood the opening enemy attacks, and as a result the Japanese halted operations on July 2 to await the arrival of artillery at the front.

On the first mission of June 29, four P-40s from the Seventy-fifth took an offensive sweep from Changsha to Liuyang to Liling. Lt. James Vargaropulos went down to strafe some horses and ran through a house which broke his plane apart, leaving him skidding through the ricefields to burn.

Shortly before noon, four P-40s from the Seventy-fifth took off on an offensive sweep northeast of Hengyang. Near Liling, three sixteen-foot boats were destroyed as well as thirty sampans. Some men and horses in compounds were strafed and fragged, killing fifteen horses and around thirty men. There was no opposition again, and pilots Maj. Donald Quigley and Lts. O. H. Elker, Paul Moehring, and East returned.

At high noon five more men took an offensive sweep to the Tuhsien area. Northwest of Tsaoshih, Lieutenant Coran was dropping his bombs on some sampans when they exploded under his right wing. The wing blew off and the ship exploded on the surface of the water. Lt. Wiltz Segura bailed out of his ship south of Lingling on the return trip and was seen to land safely in a river valley east of Chuanhsien.

Later Segura told the story of what happened:

> We were strafing around Kweilin and I was leading the mission of eight airplanes. We were on our way home. I had flown a couple missions that day already, getting up at three in the morning. I had a doughnut and a cup of coffee, landed and reloaded the airplane, and was told to go back out. At two o'clock in the afternoon I'm kind of weary. On the way home we get out of enemy territory. I decided it was just a matter of an hour sitting in this airplane, and I unbuckled my parachute straps, which were kind of tight, to sit down on my tailbone. I opened the belt, flying along with my head back. I was going along at about three thousand feet. All of a sudden the damn engine blew up. No warning. Pow! It just blew up. It caught on fire and that really surprised me. I rolled the canopy back and bailed out because I could see fire coming out around the smokestack and the propeller went dead—immediately. I got hit in the supercharger, the housing had cracked in enemy territory—the vibrations broke the housing. The propellant caught on fire. The firewall kept it from coming into the cockpit. As I prepared to bail out, I stood up, rolled over to fall onto the wing, but you don't hit the wing. I didn't have time to slow down the airplane. I knew the plane was really going to blow any minute, when it got to the fuel tank.
>
> As I stood up, I inhaled some smoke and I coughed and coughed. I saw those two straps dangling and I was already committed. I was falling, going out the side like that, one strap in hand. The last thing

I remember as I went out was that the slipstream caught me and I hadn't slowed the airplane down. It brought me into the tail. Lucky I had gone down head first and my legs had got caught, so the horizontal stabilizer caught me right across the calf. It flipped me like a top and dazed me. All I remember was thinking, "I got to pull the ripcord." Looked like it was hazy. Couldn't see anything. Felt like somebody was holding my hands out and I couldn't get them to the ripcord, spinning so fast, spread-eagle. Unconsciously I pulled the ripcord. When I got hold of it, it looked like it just went off by itself. I pulled it. I had not flown my own airplane that day. I had Lopez's. He was a little bigger than I was and I had his chute. The straps were loose and the buckles, too. When the chute opened, something came up and hit me in the mouth. It knocked me out.

Everything was quiet, real peaceful and quiet. Then I regained consciousness, things started opening up like a lens on a camera. Things kept flitting through my mind. I remembered the straps opened, falling out and I thought, "I slipped out of that damn parachute and I'm dead and in heaven." Thought I had died. This is what heaven is all about. It is so peaceful compared to the mishmash that had gone on a few seconds before. Then I looked up and saw that big white umbrella and could remember my first bailout. I was tired—two missions on one doughnut and coffee. It took all of the starch out of me. I didn't care if there were ten thousand Japanese on the ground. I hit that rice paddy; the wind blew me through two fields before I stopped. When I crawled over to the edge, I realized my legs were hurt. They started swelling and I couldn't walk. I sat on the edge of the rice paddy and said to myself, "What in the world is an old country boy like me doing half way round the world in a damn airplane? You know you can get yourself killed." I said to myself that this is stupid. If I could get out of this mess, I was never getting into another airplane again. Never. I was through. I sat there. All these Chinamen came out from the hills. Airplane goes down, explodes; plows the ground, ten to fifteen feet into a hole, blows up. Whatever ammunition was down there with the fuel starts cooking off. Shoots off ammo fifteen to twenty minutes and starts waking up the neighborhood. First of all a big boom, explosion, gas tanks explode, enough stuff goes forward, gas saturates ammo, ammo starts cooking off like firecrackers. Then the long walk through the paddies, the hiding out, and finally to the railroad station where my buddies were waiting for me.

On the last mission of the day at 5 P.M., two pilots, Lts. Joseph Brown and Baldwin, went to escort bombers to the Changsha area.

Baldwin returned with a rough engine, and Brown proceeded along. After the bombers completed their mission, he strafed between Changsha and Siangtan and hit three motor launches and ten sampans.

The Japanese were repairing the Twenty-third's old airfield at Hengyang, so the old occupants of that airfield were planning on a little retaliation. Since the moon was coming up bright, they planned on striking day and night.

On June 30 as headquarters was planning the evacuation of all American troops in China, the fighters kept strafing and accompanying bombers to their targets. The day began at 5:30 A.M. with eight men making an offensive sweep from Tsungyang to Tungchang. North of Tungchang, they strafed and bombed many trucks. Fifteen of these, which were carrying gas, were set afire. Twenty others were destroyed and fifty to sixty damaged. About forty persons went with the trucks. Lt. Miller picked up a bullet hole which caused a bad oil leak and landed at Lingling. All other pilots, Lts. George Howard, Joseph Brown, Herbert King, Robert Peterson, Donald Lopez, Lynn F. Jones, and James Focht, returned home safely. Some of the same pilots went on another escort mission shortly after noon escorting B-25s to strafe Liling to Tuhsien. They strafed twenty houses and compounds, and killed twenty horses in the area. The bombers scored on the target.

To keep up with the action in July, the units of the Twenty-third Fighter Group operated from many places. The Seventy-fourth, Seventy-fifth, and 118th squadrons were based at Kweilin but staged through Lingling and other fields to hit the enemy. Detachments of the Seventy-sixth operated from airstrips at Liuchow, Tanchuk, and Kanchow. Altogether the group's detachments were located at eight different fields during July.

The Seventy-fifth Squadron moved on July 1 to strafe the road northeast of Pingkiang, where they left sixteen trucks burning, twenty destroyed, and thirty-five others damaged. Just before noon they hit again at Yiyang, killing twenty persons, burning a boat, and damaging fifty more. Final sweep of the day was in the Changsha area, moving southwards. Fifty sampans were damaged and one motor launch damaged.

Operations slowed down due to bad weather on July 2, with the Seventy-fifth going on only one mission, and even that one was cancelled when the planes got about thirty miles out. The men returned to Kweilin. Headquarters worried about bad weather, since it gave the Japanese a chance to replenish supplies. In addition the Twenty-third's own gas supply was low.

On July 3 flying operations slacked again due to bad weather. The only mission which was not recalled to the home base before they got to the target was at 7:40 A.M. when eight P-40s made an offensive sweep to Leiyang. One pontoon bridge was destroyed and twenty sampans went with it. Thirty to forty compounds were damaged. The pilots were Maj. Donald Quigley, Lts. Joshua Sanford, Donald Lopez, Paul Moehring, all of the Seventy-fifth; Captain Ludman, Lieutenants Cheathan, Heine, and Frese of the Fifty-eighth.

The Poaching airfield was lost on July 4, the second base to be taken over by the Japanese. The same day Lt. Walter Daniels went off on a routine weather flight and observed the Hengyang airfield to be well pocked with bomb craters and apparently unusable. Therefore eight P-40s took off on an offensive sweep of the sea. Lt. William Carlton and Lieutenant Milam turned back due to rough engines. Ten boats were sunk and twenty others damaged. On another mission to Liling, Lieutenants Lopez and Frese had to turn back due to rough engines. Lt. James Focht also turned back but did not reach base. He was reported to have bailed out and landed fifty miles north of Kweilin. Twenty to thirty boats were damaged and two burned.

July 5 was a most successful day for both the American and Chinese pilots in the air. Eight pilots from the Seventy-fifth Fighter Squadron escorted bomber pilots, four from the Fifty-eighth and one from the Twenty-sixth, on a mission to Tungchang. Major Ludman turned back due to a bad engine. The mission was jumped by twelve Oscars just north of Hengyang. During the fight, Maj. Donald Quigley confirmed an Oscar, probably destroyed another, and damaged two others; Lt. Donald Lopez confirmed one Oscar and damaged another; Lieutenant Heine confirmed one Oscar and Lt. Frese damaged one. Lieutenant Maines of the Twenty-sixth, was listed as missing. Lt. Joshua Sanford was wounded in the foot but brought his plane home safely. Before he was hit, Sanford probably destroyed one Oscar and damaged another one.

The Japanese were also out near Sinshih. Five P-40s left base shortly after lunch on an offensive recon mission to that city. Four vehicles were burned and six to eight others damaged. One compound was hit and damaged. As the planes were pulling up from the target, they were hit by twelve to sixteen Oscars and had to leave the target at high speed. Participating pilots were Lts. William B. Carlton and James Focht of the Seventy-fifth; Lieutenants Henley and Hammon of the Sixtieth. Lieutenant Thielhorn of the Sixteenth Fighter Squadron failed to return to base.

July 6 was a busy and productive day. Two missions went to Sinshih, with P-40s escorting B-25s. The first hit included five horses and numerous barges along with ten sampans. On the second mission, Major Ludman turned back due to a rough engine. Near the target, the planes were intercepted by ten Oscars and Hamps. But there was no time to play war with the Japanese because the American planes had to hurry home due to fuel shortage. On the Hsiang River, they strafed and damaged thirty sampans on the way home.

Rumors were that the Japanese were retreating, and the Twenty-third certainly did slack off its flying operations for a few days, but not due to the rumors of the enemy leaving the area. There simply was not enough gas to carry on many missions at the time and no stockpile.

The Japanese bombed Kweilin on the night of July 9–10, unloading eight bombs, and some came very close to the base. One transport was destroyed, as the enemy kept striking for three and a half hours. The gasoline situation was still critical. On July 10 six P-40s from the Seventy-fifth made one recon run on the Hsiang River north of Hengyang. Forty troops were killed, one power launch burned, and six fifty-by-forty-foot barges and several sampans destroyed.

On July 11 Lieutenant Carlson went on a one-man mission which proved to be most productive. He dive-bombed and strafed Japanese Field Headquarters south of Leiyang, strafing a pontoon bridge and hitting a blockhouse in the process. Fifteen minutes after Carlson made his hit, eight P-40s left the home base to go to Hengyang for a recon mission. They burned two camouflaged barges, damaged twenty-five others, and damaged forty-five sampans.

By July 11, the Japanese had completed preparations for a stronger assault on Hengyang and began the attack against stout opposition from the Chinese garrison and supporting aircraft. The Japanese effort was aided by the weather when it kept the Fourteenth from providing air support for the Chinese.

Hitting boats and sampans was a most effective measure in stopping the Japanese incursion, for inside the barges and boats were the supplies and ammo necessary for them to continue the war. So the Twenty-third kept hammering away at the rivers and lakes on which the supply was moved to Japanese bases and strongholds. On July 12, six P-40s continued their hits on a river sweep from Hengyang northwards. One tug, forty sampans, and several camouflaged barges were damaged. Making the strafing mission were Lts. James Folmer, David Rust, O. H. Elker, Herbert King, Russell Fleming and Robert Miller.

On July 13 the Japanese made another attack on the base at Kweilin, early in the morning. Six bombers dropped heavy demolition and incendiary bombs. They put a couple of holes in the runway and burned a few gallons of the precious gas. The Twenty-third was now operating on a reduced scale, with fighters only. This gave the Japanese a distinct advantage, and all because the Twenty-third was literally running out of gas.

On July 14, the Twenty-third hit Pailuchi with twenty fighters, destroying twenty-three Japanese aircraft on the ground and also scoring twelve probables and ten damaged. They also destroyed almost a hundred trucks and sank many boats. Meanwhile the Seventy-fifth went on an offensive recon to Changsha. Lt. James Folmer destroyed a Val on an island fifteen miles northwest of Changsha. Seven boats were burned and thirty-two damaged, two trucks were burned and twelve damaged. Fifteen troops were casualties along with the trucks. Two more P-40s went for Hengyang. One compound was bombed and strafed but the bombs failed to explode.

By July 15 the war began to pick up with the news that some C-109s would be arriving, as well as some gas. The Twenty-third shot down ten Japanese airplanes and sank some more boats and hit more trucks. The Seventy-fifth dive-bombed targets north of Hengyang, starting a large oil fire and destroying more boats and sampans. Then they moved on to Leiyang where they dive-bombed a railroad station and compounds in the vicinity of Leiyang.

The next day they hit Hengyang hard. Lieutenant Folmer damaged one plane north of Changsha. One fifty-foot barge burned and two more were damaged along with thirty-five big sampans. Another mission dive-bombed the Hengyang area, bombing three compounds and starting a large fire. They strafed fifty compounds and five sampans. It was their old territory and they knew the target well.

The promised gasoline still had not arrived by July 19, but Chennault promised some would be coming soon. Members of the Seventy-fifth Fighter Squadron made four missions that day, concentrating on Hengyang. On one mission six compounds were bombed and forty to fifty fires started. Lt. Paul Moehring escorted B-25s to Hengyang on a second mission. Ten P-40s went on another mission to the Hengyang area, and bombing five compounds and strafing twenty more. Meanwhile Casey Vincent flew to Kunming to talk with General Chennault about the fuel supply. Vincent returned to Kweilin the next day with four new C-47s to be used to drop supplies to Hengyang.

On July 20 the Seventy-fifth carried out three missions. The first was a dive-bomb attack on the Leiyang area where two compounds were bombed and one town fragged. Thirty-five compounds were strafed but the results were unknown. Next they went on an offensive recon mission to Sinshih to the south. Fourteen trucks were burned, seventy others were damaged, and twenty-five troops were killed. Eighteen enemy fighters were sighted but did not attack, perhaps being also low on gas.

In an offensive sweep to the Changsha area on July 21, four P-40s from the Seventy-fifth killed forty-five horses and nearly as many men, and burned two trucks and damaged thirty-five. Four barges and twenty junks were also damaged. Lt. James Folmer fired on a Val that was passing under him, and it went down in flames. Next the men moved southward to Sinshih, where much the same story occurred—more horses, more trucks burned and destroyed. They strafed the Hsiang River from Siangtan to Hengyang, damaging an eighty-foot boat and fifty-five junks. It was difficult to see how the Japanese could stand such losses of trucks and boats and still continue a major campaign. Japanese prisoners reported they had no food, were going without rest, and were plagued by the heat, malaria, and dysentery.

On July 22 eight P-40s went on an offensive sweep to the Sinshih area, burning eight trucks and damaging forty, and killing thirty men and five horses. South of the city, Lt. Jack Quinn reported that his engine was bad. He was last seen twenty-five miles northwest of Lingling but did not land there. He was listed as missing in friendly territory. Four Oscars were sighted but they did not fight. Four P-40s returned later the next day and burned another truck and damaged ten others. Eight men and forty-five horses were killed. Lieutenant

Folmer saw one Tojo on the ground and went down and destroyed it.

The next few days the Twenty-third concentrated on the area from Sinshih to Hengyang, bombing villages and damaging trucks and compounds with excellent results. The Japanese offered no resistance. The Americans wondered where they were.

They came out on July 28. Eight P-40s escorted B-25s to Yochow, and the mission was intercepted by twenty fighters over the target. During the fight, Maj. Donald Quigley destroyed one Hamp and damaged one Oscar; Lt. Donald Lopez damaged one Oscar; Lt. Wiltz Segura damaged one Oscar; Lt. Vernon Tanner damaged an Oscar and Lt. Herbert King also damaged one. None of the American planes was hit.

As the month of August 1944 began, the tension and exhaustion from weeks of continuous combat were reflected upon the grim faces of Casey Vincent, recently promoted to grade of general at the age of twenty-nine, and of Col. Tex Hill, the immediate commander of the fighter pilots. If the chance that they could retain their airfields now appeared a remote one, it was certainly through no fault of theirs—or of the war-weary pilots and ground crews they commanded. From May 26 to August 1, they had flown 5,289 sorties—over four thousand of them in fighter aircraft. They had dropped 1,164 tons of bombs and expended a million rounds of ammo, chiefly in low-level strafing runs. These devastating attacks had cost the Japanese an estimated thirteen thousand casualties plus a thousand small boats, about five hundred trucks, a confirmed 114 aircraft, and fourteen bridges. Out of an overall strength of 150, Vincent's Sixty-eighth Composite Wing had lost only 43 aircraft.

The capitulation of Hengyang on August 8 simplified the task of the Japanese Ichi Go forces. Their Northern Armies by-passed the city and headed down the railway leading through Lingling to Kweilin. Japanese troops from Canton who had been scheduled to attack Hengyang from the south were turned west toward Liuchow. The drive of Japan's Southern Armies up from Indochina was not affected. The Chinese-American alert system, so painstakingly built over the years, collapsed immediately. The retreating Chinese armies and Casey Vincent's main air bases at Kweilin and Liuchow became vulnerable to attack without warning.

The American fliers tried desperately to protect the retreating Chinese ground forces. They strafed and bombed the Japanese directly in front of the Chinese soldiers and made hundreds of sorties to the Hankow area to disrupt the flow of supplies and lines of communication from the Japanese headquarters. Nevertheless, the Japanese continued to advance and the Chinese continued to fall back.

The Seventy-fifth Fighter Squadron was one of the squadrons which bore the brunt of the Japanese drive down the Hsiang River Valley. They hit lines of transportation, troop concentrations, barracks areas, communications, and other Japanese installations in a tremendous effort to stall the enemy offensive. In all eighty-nine missions for the month of August, 455 sorties, over twenty-six tons of demolition bombs, 385 clusters of parafrags, and over three hundred thousand rounds of .50 caliber ammunition were used in this counter drive. The Seventy-fifth thus inflicted considerable damage upon the Japanese.

On August 3 Lt. Vernon Tanner led nine P-40s to escort B-24s to Yochow and contacted eight Oscars as the bombers finished their bomb run. The Japanese pilots were not very aggressive, but as they got close to the formation, the sharks got in their licks. Five of the Oscars were damaged and the American planes did not receive a scratch. Lt. Jesse Gray damaged one Oscar; Lieutenant Tanner damaged another; Lt. Robert P. Miller damaged two Oscars; and Lt. William A. Smith damaged another.

Miller dived on one that was approaching the bombers from the rear and saw his bullets hitting in the fuselage. He also dived from above and behind one that was in a slight turn and pulled his guns through, hitting it in the fuselage. Smith saw an Oscar that was breaking away from a P-40 and got in a deflection shot, observing the plane flying into his tracers.

The next day Maj. Donald Quigley led eleven P-40s on a sweep of the Hengyang area. After bombing and strafing several building areas, they saw three enemy planes over Hengyang. The sharks set out in hot pursuit. Arriving over the scene, a total of eight Vals and twelve Oscars were circling just south of Hengyang. Major Quigley made two dives through the formation, confirming one Val and getting another as a probable. Lt. Buddie Baldwin attacked and scored one Oscar probable and one damaged. Lt. Joseph Martinez mixed with the Oscars, damaging one.

Martinez was jumped by an Oscar while climbing at seven thousand feet, but dove four to five thousand feet to lose it. Climbing up through the overcast again, he again spotted the Oscar, which he attacked with only his right guns working. The Oscar did a "split S" and pulled away, and Martinez made the claim. Lt. Richard Roberts was not seen after his first pass. He bailed out after running out of fuel, about seventy miles northeast of Wuchow. The sharks were running low on ammo and the Japanese were running so the engagement broke off.

Maj. Donald Quigley did a return engagement on August 5 when he went out on a weather recon to Hengyang and ran into twelve Japanese planes. Quigley found six Oscars overhead at twelve thousand feet and another half dozen underneath him five thousand feet. He climbed to the overcast, dove down through the fighters, and leveled off behind one of the Vals. He gave it a quick burst from dead astern, and it crashed and burned on the east side of the airfield.

Further damage was inflicted against the enemy's air force later in the morning of the same day. Nine sharks frag-bombed and strafed installations from Sinsiang to Sinshih. At Sinshih they intercepted about fifteen Oscars. James Folmer and Robert M. Chism each confirmed an Oscar, and Lt. David Rust scored two probables and one damaged. Rust had to dive steeply to get away from an Oscar. He zoomed up under the enemy ship, following him to the top of a loop. His incendiaries were sparkling all over the enemy plane, and from the inverted position, it fell sideways as if the pilot was losing control. Rust had to break away, and thus he claimed it as a probable.

On August 7, two patrols of eight planes each went out over the Hengyang area attempting to flush out some Japanese planes for aerial combat, but none showed up. The next day, eight sharks encountered a like number of Hamps and Oscars after bombing and strafing targets around Siangtan. Lt. Robert S. Peterson made a head-on pass at a Hamp, then turned and got in a thirty-degree shot from the rear. The plane burned and crashed to the ground. Maj. Donald Quigley found an Oscar, apparently crippled, and chased it all the way to Lukow down on the deck. He got three head-on passes and several times the plane appeared to be out of control, but always recovered right on the deck. Quigley ran out of ammo and broke away without seeing the plane go in. He claimed it as a probable. Lt. James Folmer got in a thirty-degree diving shot at an Oscar, and it dove almost vertically, skidding to the right in a cloud that was no more than eight hundred feet above the ground. So he claimed a probable too. Lt. Paul Moehring got in dead-astern passes on two Oscars, damaging both, and Lts. Donald Lopez and Joseph Martinez damaged one each. Lt. Joshua Sanford led another eight planes over Hengyang at 1100 hours on a patrol, but no enemy planes showed up so they strafed targets in the area.

Five P-40s went to attack targets in the Hsiaoshinpu area. One compound was destroyed by frags. Hengyang was bombed and strafed heavily, causing many fires. Lt. Wiltz Segura's plane was hit by ground fire and, with it smoking badly, he was seen to bail out and land safely. The plane crashed and burned. Segura later recalled what had happened:

It was my birthday and I was on my sixty-fourth mission in China that day. I was leading the flight. Vernon Tanner was leading the other flight. We were strafing troops at Hengyang when I went down pretty low. And as I came in at them, I could see the Jap troops. All of a sudden I realized there were two machine guns at both sides waiting for us. I came in right between them. I thought of pulling out. As I went, I heard the pop, pop of their ammo across my fuselage. My wingman said, "You're hit!" and I said, "I know I am. What does it look like?"

"You're smoking," he says. I was so low. They had some heavy guns on the river and somebody called out for me to be careful and not get over that position. But that was the closest way home. I didn't know how long my airplane was going to last. The minute I pulled up, I had to turn towards them. I went over about a thousand feet, trying to get enough altitude so if the engine quit, I'd bail out. Managed to get up at about three thousand feet. By this time I knew that they had hit my oil line and it was smoking. My oil pressure was fluctuating.

I broke off the mission. Otherwise, the rest of the fighters would come with you to escort you out, so when you hit the ground they would rake out the ground around so the enemy couldn't get at you, until you got a chance to hide from the crash.

At three thousand feet and about ten miles from where I got hit, seven minutes later, the engine quit. I knew I was going to have to bail out—everybody knew it. They were talking on the radio. I figured it was time to get unstrapped and told the guys I was going to bail out.

I had seen these guys in the movies get out on the wing and walk, so I decided that's what I was going to do if I had to go. Give it a try. I'm sitting there, putting the airplane in a shallow climb to slow it down to reduce the wind, getting it down to about 110 mph, which is just above the P-40's stall. I got up in the cockpit, stood up to step over the side. Just as I got half of my body out of the cockpit, I realized there was a hell of a lot more wind than you thought at 110 mph. It pushed me up against the back of the cockpit and I couldn't get my seat up high enough to get my parachute out. I was kind of hung inside the cockpit. I wasn't paying attention to what I was doing and that drag on the right side put the airplane into a slow turn and it started nosing down.

Next thing I knew I was getting pinned in heavier and heavier. I could tell. I looked back at the cockpit and saw my airspeed climbing to 150 mph and looked down at the ground and I was definitely headed in that direction. I'm kind of stuck then. Wind was too strong. I reached into the cockpit and lunged for the stick to straighten the airplane up, slow it down. At about 110 mph I was able to climb back in. I looked at the altimeter and sure enough I was about fifteen hundred feet. I decided I couldn't fool around anymore and decided to go back to Plan A. Just dive for the wing, jump head first so the tail couldn't get my head. I pulled the ripcord after counting to three.

My buddies were flying all around until I hit the ground. The plane went off about a half mile and crashed. They made a couple of passes around and didn't see any enemy activity. I gathered my chute and hid it so they wouldn't spot where I landed. I was trying to figure out if the enemy or someone else was close by. Chinese guerillas were the greatest at finding pilots, getting hold of them and hiding them. I was in a farming area.

I looked over the countryside. The thing was to get hold of a civilian as soon as you could, because they were all indoctrinated. As soon as you identified yourself as an American you couldn't miss. Brought you to local authorities who worked undercover. Local troops disguised as civilians they were, operating behind enemy lines. Officials, instead of evacuating an area, went incognito into the countryside and became guerillas. They did tremendous work behind the lines retrieving us. I saw this farmer in a rice paddy. I was black and muddy. He saw me and took off. I decided I had better get to him before he got to the enemy, so I caught up with him. He headed for this little village of two or three huts. I got hold of him, showing him my little book which said, "I'm friend. I'm American. Where's the enemy?"

He was scared. He led me to this little compound and then things really started happening. Guys that knew what they were doing and had guns. They came out of the hills and hid me in a little shack. They were hollering outside, giving orders. I couldn't tell if they were Japs or Chinese. They are opposite types, but get them together and Cantonese Chinese look like Japanese. My biggest worry was to find out which they were and make my escape before they organized if they were the enemy. I got hold of one guy and all he could say was, "Do not fear." They got hold of me and started running, trotting down a trail towards the woods.

About two hours later we came upon some troops. There a big argument developed, and I couldn't figure out what happened until we got back out about two weeks later. This was another guerilla force. It was a great honor for a guerilla chief to be able to rescue an American, and when he had heard that an American had gone down, he sent his men to go looking for me for the honor of capturing me. Chiang Kai-shek rewarded them later. We were told to let them have anything they wanted. But they wouldn't take money or anything or even food. The government apparently rewarded them very well. And I was finally returned to my base.

Approaching August it was apparent that unless some drastic reversal came about, the Japanese would overrun the rest of the American bases and isolate eastern China within a matter of a few weeks. Chennault hoped Kweilin could be saved by stopping the Japanese at a narrow pass about ninety miles north of the city. But the plan did not work.

Thousands of Chinese refugees, many already hundreds of miles from their homes, poured through Kweilin using every conceivable means of transportation. Most came to and left the area by rail. They were packed into, underneath, and on top of rail cars. Household belongings and bags of rice were stacked to the ceilings of boxcars with men, women, and children burrowed into all available nooks and crannies. Those not on the trains came and left in cars, trucks, rickshas, horsecarts, and wheelbarrows, and on foot. In the city proper, Chinese soldiers worked feverishly setting up machine-gun posts, trenches, and street barricades.

Some of the fields had no gas. Some had enough for just one more mission. In the case of others, gas was pumped from bomber tanks to keep the fighters in the air. Before enough gas reached the advanced fields, the Japanese had overrun Hengyang on August 10, never again to be halted until they had split Free China. Afterward they continued their drive south.

Still, the Twenty-third kept trying. On August 8, the day Hengyang fell, Maj. Donald Quigley of the Seventy-fifth, the squadron commander, led an offensive sweep to Siangtan where he was hit by antiaircraft fire. Forced to bail out south of the city, he was listed as missing in action. He bailed out about three miles south of the river on the Siangtan road. His men had strafed the city and damaged twenty trucks. On his first pass he had been hit by machine-gun fire, setting his plane aflame.

On August 11 five P-40s went to strafe and bomb transports from Siangtan to Hengyang. Ten Japanese and three horses were killed, one truck burned, and twenty-five others damaged. Then Lts. William Carlton and Forrest Parham safely dropped supplies to net plot area TW-9 and bombed and strafed Erh Tong, going northeast. Parham's engine cut out and caught fire, forcing him to bail out fifteen to twenty miles northeast of Kweilin. He was uninjured. The supplies reached their destination. Next, pilots of the Seventy-fifth went on an escort mission to Hengyang, fragging and strafing one compound and causing much fire and smoke to rise. That night they hit Hengyang again, burning three compounds plus assorted pillboxes, trenches, and strongholds. The Japanese were not going to enjoy peace with their newly-acquired territory.

The next morning, bright and early, the Seventy-fifth was at it again in an offensive sweep from Hengyang to the Siangtan area. This time they killed fifty troops, destroyed eight trucks, and damaged sixty others. Pilots Lts. James Folmer, Richard Jones, Joshua Sanford, James Focht, and James W. Carter all returned safely.

On August 13 the Seventy-fifth began its activities at 7 A.M. when planes strafed and bombed targets four to eight miles west and northwest of Hengyang. Chailitu was bombed and strafed, with several Japanese dying in trenches. At 11 A.M. they struck Hengyang again, killing fifteen men and six to eight horses and leaving one compound burning.

On August 14, some of the pilots of the Seventy-fifth went on a recon mission with an offensive sweep of the Siangtan-Hengyang area. Sixty men were killed, three trucks destroyed, and eight others damaged. In addition, one barge was destroyed and several others damaged. Some of the pilots no sooner returned from that mission before it was time to refuel and strafe the Pailuchi airfield. On this mission nine trucks were burned and forty-two others damaged. Two gasoline fires were started, two one-hundred-foot steamers were hit in the boilers, and one forty-foot launch was burned. Five more forty-foot barges were damaged. Forty soldiers and twenty-five horses were killed in this operation.

The Seventy-fifth returned to Hengyang again on August 15, burning more trucks, a gas dump, and twenty compounds. They were retaliating for the loss of their field, and they kept returning, making their hits without opposition in the air, until August 19. On a mission on August 16, Buddie Baldwin was hit by ground fire and bailed out twenty-five miles east-northeast of Changsha. He was reported safe, however.

On August 17, five P-40s from the Seventy-fifth went on an offensive sweep of the river near Changsha and the roads from Changsha to Chunglupu. Five forty-foot barges were destroyed and eleven others damaged. Two trucks were destroyed and eleven others damaged. Fifteen men were also killed. Four one-stack fifty-foot steamers were damaged. Just north of Chunglupu, on the west side of the road, Lt. James Folmer mushed in between two low hills, and the plane exploded and burned in enemy territory. Robert P. Miller received severe burns and cuts when his P-40 overshot the runway at Lingling, washing out the plane.

Early on the morning of August 19, the P-40s were out again on an offensive sweep from Sinsiang to Changsha. About twenty miles southeast of Yochow, one Val, eight Oscars, and an unknown number of Hamps were sighted. Lt. Joseph Brown confirmed one Val and one Oscar. Brown saw a northbound Val beneath him at three thousand feet. He did a "split S" on the Val, gave it a short burst, and it exploded. Lt. Forrest Parham saw it crash. Climbing up, Brown saw one Oscar at eight thousand feet at nine o'clock, and six to seven Oscars at ten thousand feet at eleven o'clock. But he was jumped by another Oscar and got on its tail, gave it a burst, and saw hits and smoke. Parham saw another enemy plane crash at this time and figured it was the one hit by his partner. Lieutenant Parham, after climbing to twelve thousand feet, saw a Hamp on a P-40 at ten thousand feet. He dove on the Hamp from behind, getting hits. He followed him down to seven thousand when the pilot bailed out. Lt. William W. Smith was missing after the mission.

After the skirmish with the Zeroes, the Seventy-fifth traveled to Hengyang, Siangtan, and Changsha on a recon mission. Here they returned to the old practice of strafing junks and bombing compounds. Later in the day, they dive-bombed and pinpointed the targets at Chaling. The targets were compounds, barracks, and one pontoon bridge.

They hit Hengyang again on August 20. The Seventy-fifth also bombed the town two miles north of that city and got four good hits in a compound. The next day they moved on to dive-bomb Anjen. Five planes of the Seventy-fifth joined five planes from the 118th. The Seventy-fifth's planes with the bombs left the 118th's planes at Hengyang and proceeded to the target. Six hits were scored on buildings in town and two hits on the road. Meantime, Lt. Jack L. Quinn observed direct hits made by the 118th's planes at Hengyang railroad station.

On August 25 Captain Tracy of the Twenty-third and Lt. O. H. Elker of the Seventy-fifth dropped supplies behind Japanese lines. The planes went to a point north of Shihih to drop supplies to Lt. Nathan Green, who had been shot down the previous May. The supplies were dropped successfully and both planes returned without incident.

The Seventy-fifth headed back to Hengyang on August 27 for multiple strikes in which they skip-bombed a bridge, strafed trucks, and dropped supplies. The supplies were dropped but no good hits were reported on the second run.

The last contact with the Japanese Air Force for the month was on August 29. Twelve sharks flying cover for the Twenty-third Fighter Group plus planes from the Fifty-first Group and the CACW encountered approximately thirty Oscars and Tojos near Yochow at the railroad yards. Lt. William E. Daniels was leading the flight. Returning from the target area, Lt. Robert S. Peterson and Lt. James A. Bosserman got separated from the flight just west of the lake while chasing a Zero off Bosserman's tail. Lt. Forrest Parham got on the tail of a Hamp about fifteen miles south of the target on the way in and claimed it as a probable. On the way back he damaged one Hamp and confirmed another. Lt. James Focht damaged one Oscar and one Tojo. Focht got in a damaging burst from above and behind when the Oscar did a "split S" and went beneath him for a pass at the bombers. Leaving the target Focht and his flight caught two Zeroes away from formation. Forty miles southwest of the target as he was climbing after chasing the Zero, he got above and behind a Hamp, getting a damaging burst at about forty-five degrees. Thus he claimed the Hamp as damaged.

The second offensive of the Japanese campaign of 1944, after pausing to bring up supplies and regroup following the fall of Hengyang, moved forward again on August 29. The Japanese Eleventh Army, consisting of seven divisions, started down the railroad from Hengyang to Canton, halted, and then swung its main thrust down the Hankow-Hanoi railroad toward Kweilin and Liuchow with their bases for the Fourteenth. By September 8, the Eleventh Army had advanced some sixty miles and overrun Lingling and the airfield there, from which the Fourteenth had withdrawn. The Japanese then advanced another fifty miles toward Kweilin along the railroad in September and then paused again.

The Seventy-fifth made several offensive sweeps to Changning during the first few days of September. On September 3, six compounds were fragged, causing considerable damage. Lt. Forrest Parham scored hits on a Val near Kiyang, causing a trail of vapor. The plane did a "split S" and Parham turned sharply and dove in behind it, firing a burst. The Val broke into flames and crashed. On many repeated trips, they fragged and strafed, hitting compounds on every mission.

One of the pilots of the Sixty-eighth Composite Wing was Maj. John C. "Pappy" Herbst, commanding officer of the Seventy-fourth Fighter Squadron and the man who was to become the leading ace of the Fourteenth. On September 3, he was on a bridge-busting mission to the Tsienshan area north of Poyang Lake, when he spotted two enemy dive bombers coming out of the clouds. As they came down to investigate the smoke rising from the target that had just been attacked, Pappy got behind them and shot one down on his first pass. As he went for the other, it maneuvered desperately in an attempt to make the P-51 spin but to no avail. It took many hits in the rudder and the rear fuselage and finally went down, ending up on its back in a rice paddy.

Two days later, while flying his natural metal finish P-51C back to Kweilin for modification, Pappy ran into a fight which almost cost him his life. Spotting two eight-plane formations of Oscars evidently protecting some aircraft below, he started to climb for altitude. But the Oscars apparently caught sight of him from the glare of his plane and turned into him before he could gain a height advantage. All Pappy could do as they came at him was fly head on at the leader, firing as he closed. In return, he took hits in the windshield that gave him a face full of glass. Right after that, the western formation of Oscars started another head-on pass. Again he concentrated on the leader and scored repeated hits before he had to break away. Nearly blinded by blood, Pappy fought on and as the action continued, he saw at least one parachute going down before his last gun ran out of ammunition. Then with the Oscars gathering for the kill, he slammed the stick forward and dove for the ground, faster and faster, pulling out just above the deck, and got away when the enemy was unable to keep up with him.

From September into the new year, the 308th Bomb Group continued attacking enemy shipping in the North China Sea, the Formosa Straits, and the Gulf of Tonkin. Its planes also struck at docking facilities at Hong Kong and Hankow, and carried out extensive mining operations against both river and sea traffic.

On September 4 eight P-40s from the Seventy-fifth went to bomb and strafe Lingkwantien, ten miles south of Hengyang. One hundred fifty men and a hundred horses were killed and three compounds damaged. Lt. Robert Peterson had his hydraulic system shot out when hit by ground fire. He had to belly-land at Kweilin but was uninjured.

Nine P-40s went on an offensive sweep to Kiyang, south of Hengyang on September 5. They bombed nine compounds and killed thirty-four horses. Lt. Gordon C. Bervan was hit by ground fire and bailed out about twenty-five miles north of Kiyang. He was reported missing after his plane crashed.

By September 8 the Japanese Eleventh Army had advanced some sixty miles and overrun Lingling—both the town and the airfield. The Japanese then advanced another fifty miles toward Kweilin and the men at this base were preparing to evacuate. Two days later the evacuation was in motion. Weather was impeding operations, but fighter pilots still made last-minute attempts to fend off the enemy, evacuating and hitting the Japanese simultaneously.

On September 13 things fell apart with a bang as the Chinese started retreating early in the morning. Casey Vincent ordered final evacuation of Kweilin, requesting twenty C-46s to begin arriving that night. He was moving the 118th and the Eleventh squadrons to Liuchow and the Chinese-American Composite Wing's squadrons to Peishiyi. Tanchuk was threatened. He left the Seventy-fourth Squadron at Kanchow for as long as possible even though the Japanese had already taken over the railroad there. Pappy Herbst wanted to fight as a guerilla squadron, and there was some talk about letting him have his way.

On the morning of September 14, Generals Stilwell and Chennault went to Kweilin for a last conference with Casey Vincent and the Chinese General Chang Fah-kwei. Stilwell approved the final decision to blow it and get out.

All but one or two trucks had pulled out into the dusk while the last planes were still loading cargo. Colonels, lieutenants, and majors worked alongside junior officers and GIs of all grades as they hoisted generators, tires, duffel bags, and other gear into the waiting planes. It was fully dark by the time the last load was aboard and airborne. Only two planes were left on the flight line, Casey's B-25 and a C-47 transport for his staff. Demolition began at midnight. A red glow in the sky behind the mountains to the east signaled the burning of a satellite field. Rolling rumbles came over the hills as the bombs let go in the distant runways.

The shacks and hostels at the Kweilin base were tucked away in the crannies of the Kwangsi hills. Demolition crews had set up a barrel of gasoline in each building. With a helper holding a flashlight beam on the target, a sergeant would fire his carbine into the barrel. When enough gasoline had trickled through the holes to fill the room with fumes, the sergeant would fire again and the room would explode with a roaring flash. Flames ripped through the thatched roofs and poured into adjacent rooms like racing water. One by one, the buildings went up until the whole field was ablaze.

Just before dawn, demolition men began blowing the airstrips, leaving one temporarily for the two remaining planes to use. As the gray light of morning crept over the hills, Casey Vincent and Tex Hill finished packing. They found they had a stock of six bottles of bourbon so they took it along. When they arrived near their B-25, Casey took the pilot's seat. Tex crouched down behind him. As soon as the C-47 transport carrying Gen. Tim Timberman and the staff people was airborne, Casey took off. It was 5:30 A.M. as he circled over the burning field and headed toward Liuchow. Then the demolition team blew the last runway and got out.

Through all this the Seventy-fifth continued making river sweeps, strafing boats, and hitting compounds—without opposition. Then on September 16 two P-51s and eight P-40s took off for an offensive sweep from Shaoyang to Changsha. They destroyed two tanks and fragged and strafed the targets. East of Shaoyang the mission was intercepted by ten Hamps and Oscars. Lt. Jesse Gray dove down from above on a Hamp closing from forty degrees. The plane flipped in front of him and dove steeply, and Gray dove with him, scoring hits in the fuselage before he overran him and had to pull away. The plane was at six thousand feet smoking from the back part of the fuselage and diving and flipping from side to side when last seen. It was reported as a probable. Lt. Richard Jones got directly behind a Hamp and made a level attack, scoring hits in the front wing. He claimed the plane as damaged.

Next Lt. Donald Lopez dove down on an Oscar and scored hits in the tail section, thus scoring a damaged. Then Gray sighted another one diving down from above upon the Oscar and he scored hits on its rear and fuselage, thus damaging another enemy plane. Lt. Jack Quinn, not to be outdone, made a thirty-degree deflection shot at a Hamp from behind and slightly above, scoring hits in the right wing and tail section and claiming a damaged of his own.

Lt. John Rosenbaum damaged another Hamp when he made a slight dive on it from a seventy-degree deflection and scored hits in the tail section. Lt. Louis Weber saw a Hamp diving down on a P-40 and dove in behind it and got in a five-second burst, scoring many good hits from the rear. He broke away without observing results, but the P-40 was saved.

On September 19 Capt. Joseph Brown and Lt. Ira Jones took two P-51s out to serve as top cover for the CACW to Sinsiang. Just south of Sinshih they were intercepted by four Oscars and two Tojos. Brown scored a damaged when he dove on one of the Oscars and got in a no-deflection shot from the rear, making hits in the rear part of the fuselage.

On September 21 Vincent gave the order to blow Tanchuk at noon. The Japanese had Wuchow and were only twenty miles south of Tanchuk. There was some disagreement between Vincent and

Chennault, probably caused by some "nasty wires" from Fourteenth Air Force Headquarters which Vincent had received.

While the order to blow Tanchuk was being made, twelve P-40s from the Seventy-fifth staged an offensive sweep from Ninsiang and Sinshih. Lt. Jack Quinn turned back because his engine cut out. Two antiaircraft positions were dive-bombed. Lt. James A. Bosserman called on the radio reporting he was low on gas and was heading home. Somewhat later he called and said he was bailing out. He was reported missing and was last seen going over Sinshih.

Then the mission sighted fourteen Hamps and Oscars. Lt. Robert Peterson got a seventy-degree deflection shot at a Hamp which flew through his tracers. He claimed it as damaged in the air. Next Peterson made a direct head-on pass at another Hamp and as it passed him, it burst into flames. The plane fell off into a spiral and exploded when it hit the ground.

Lt. Forrest Parham climbed above a formation of eight Japanese planes, and as they peeled off, he dove down behind a Hamp, scoring hits in the engine region. The Hamp slow-rolled and then dove with Parham following. He got in several bursts and then shot past it, knocking off his aerial post on the Hamp's wing. A stream of fuel vapor came from the Japanese plane, which dove away streaming thin vapor behind. This plane was claimed as a probable. Next Parham dove on a Hamp and scored hits in the tail, but he overshot before he could score the telling blow.

Lt. William T. Griswold saw a Hamp spiraling down out of a fight and dove in behind it just as it began to climb back up. At two hundred yards, Griswold shot at it and then observed fire coming from the right cowling. The plane slid off and fell away on one wing, still shooting flames. It was confirmed in the air.

Lt. Robert Smith saw an Oscar turn away from another P-40, and he met it head-on firing a long burst directly into the engine. Many hits with tracer and incendiary fire were observed in the engine and the plane was smoking slightly as it passed. Thus Smith claimed it as damaged. Lt. James Taylor got on an Oscar from above which slow-rolled and started down with Taylor following. He got in six bursts scoring hits all over the wings and fuselage, but the plane did not flame up or start smoking. He claimed it as damaged in the air. Lt. Robert J. Bellman got in a ninety-degree deflection shot at a Hamp and observed pieces flying from behind the cockpit. On a second

Hamp, Bellman made a head-on run, scoring hits in the engine region.

Eleven P-40s took off at 6 A.M. on September 22 for an offensive sweep from Lingling to Hengyang to Poaching. One hundred ninety-five boats were strafed and damaged and ten steam launches were strafed. A 160-foot steamer was burned and five compounds and one truck were strafed.

Then they went to Sinsiang where there was plenty of action for the pilots. Lt. Richard F. Jones dove on a Tojo that was on Lt. Jesse Gray's tail and got in a long burst, hitting it in the wings, canopy, and fuselage. Lt. Joseph Martinez, in a P-40, saw this one fall in flames, and thus it was claimed as confirmed in the air. Then Gray caught a Tojo from sixty degrees rear and fired as it turned into him, getting in a long burst in the engine, after which he saw the plane fall off on one wing.

Lt. Wiltz Segura saw an Oscar crossing between him and the sun. He shot it in the belly and it burst into huge flames, but this gave way to heavy smoke as it dove down. Segura split down on him and gave him another burst. The enemy plane began to spin and hit the ground before exploding. He then dove down on another Oscar, getting in a ninety-degree deflection shot, and as the Oscar dove away, he got on his tail. He closed and scored hits in the gas tanks, causing fuel to stream out. The Oscar spun out but Segura did not see what happened to him so he claimed it as a probable. He damaged another Hamp before the fight was over.

Lt. Joshua D. Sanford made a thirty-degree head-on approach on an Oscar as it was climbing from very low altitude. He scored hits in the engine and cockpit region, and the Oscar began smoking, fell off to the side, and dove straight for the ground.

British Flight Officer Gordon E. Willis observed two Hamps flying in string formation and turned in behind the second one, getting in a long burst, which caused it to burst into flames. As he dove away from his first kill, Willis headed west and climbed back up. He saw four Hamps under a cloud. They made a level turn into him, and he made a fifteen-degree head-on run at one of them. As he pushed off, he saw flames shoot from around the engine of the Hamp and claimed it as confirmed.

The leader of the Japanese planes made a right turn. Lt. Robert M. Chism dove on him and gave him a burst from twenty degrees. His gunsight was not operating so using his tracers, he raked his fire through the plane and back again. This plane was claimed as damaged in the air. Lt. Curtis Mahannah got in a sixty-degree deflection on a Hamp that was climbing in front of him, scoring in the engine and cockpit before he had to break away.

The Japanese started more night bombing. They bombed Casey Vincent's headquarters at Liuchow on September 27, hitting one P-51 and two tank cars of gasoline which held sixteen thousand gallons. Lack of night fighters on the American side prohibited defensive tactics over the field.

Even the Chinese General Hsieh Yueh was disgusted with the Chinese top command at Chungking. He felt that he could have stopped the Japanese south of Changsha if he had been allowed to use his armies as he wished. The Japanese soon bombed the base again, hitting a B-25.

By October 1, the Japanese were breaking Chinese defense lines just outside Kweilin. The Americans battered at the Japanese advance, trying to slow it up. Weather halted many plans, yet the Japanese continued to bomb at night, this time destroying one P-51 and damaging another.

On October 5 Vincent sent a good medium bomber mission against Samshui, the main supply base for the Japanese Kwantung drive. They shot down three Zeroes. By October 12 the Japanese had crossed the river south of Kweiyang, and it appeared they would have an easy go on to Liuchow. Kunming was still dreaming up impossible missions.

On a bombing mission to Canton on October 15, the Americans hit the wrong target. But the fighters shot down four Zeroes. They also took photos of Formosa showing the terrific damage inflicted by the Navy and the B-29s. A mission was planned for the next day against shipping in Hong Kong harbor.

On October 16 all missions were successful. Hong Kong was loaded with shipping, apparently driven there by the American Navy's attacks on Macao. Fourteenth Air Force Headquarters put the heavies on the docks as diversion while eight B-25s went into the harbor at low level. The P-51s dive-bombed shipping, accounting for fifty thousand tons or more either sunk or damaged, and lost only one P-51.

Tex Hill had this to say about the P-51 series of fighters in China:

We had the A models on that Formosa strike which had Allison engines. They were good airplanes but didn't have any high altitude capability. We later got the B's, which were quite an improvement, and I believe that I shot down the first enemy aircraft with one. I remember we had this fight over Hong Kong because I figured we were really going to eat them up down there. I had a squadron commander with me by the name of Willie Williams and a flight officer who was flying my wing and another guy by the name of Colbert.

We arrived down in the Hong Kong area and the first thing I know I see three enemy aircraft up there that I couldn't identify. I knew they were Japs but I'd never seen the type before. We called them out and turned into them, and as we pulled up into them, why, they went straight up and I could see we were going to stall out and so I bent it over. These guys came right down on top of us and shot down the three guys who were with me, and they chased me all the way down to eight thousand feet, which was the altitude I needed to get back over some hills.

I swear I believe this Jap was trying to overrun me in a dive. His tracers were really going by my head. When I got back I talked to the Old Man, telling him about this new type Japanese fighter which was later identified as a Zeke 52 or Tojo, which was another term I think they used for them. I told him, "Well, I don't know, there's a new type here. I don't know if we're going to be able to beat these guys in the air." And Chennault thought awhile and very characteristically—he had an easy solution for everything—he said, "Well, Tex, don't worry about that. Get them on the ground, then you don't have to fight them in the air." So this was a strategy that was actually used. Some of the guys went up to the airfields around Tientsin where these airplanes were congregated and just cleaned them out right on the ground. In fact, the good part of the story was that all these guys got back. Colbert had a bad bullet wound in his leg, but they all were smuggled out by the Chinese. Later we got the C's but the D model didn't come in until after I left China. As a matter of fact, I saw my first D model on my way back home. It was in French markings and that sure as hell made me a little bit hot, knowing that here was a first-line fighting airplane that the French already had in operation and we didn't have them out where we really needed them.

On October 18, 1944, Tex Hill left China for a long-awaited trip Stateside.

The big Chinese counterattack started on October 22, and the American airmen provided excellent support—until the weather went sour. Then, as fast as it started, the Chinese counterattack petered out.

On October 28, news arrived that the China-Burma-India Theater would be split up with Lt. Gen. Albert C. Wedemeyer as boss of the China Theater. Lt. Gen. Daniel I. Sultan was to take over the India-Burma Theater. Gen. Joseph Stilwell had been removed from the command. He had received his recall orders on October 18. The decision to relieve him had been made by President Roosevelt. On the last day of October, the Japanese had closed in, breaking to the Kweilin-Liuchow road only seventy miles from headquarters at Liuchow. Evacuation was planned.

The Japanese' second offensive had resumed on October 27, and in two weeks it roared forward another hundred miles, taking Kweilin on November 10 and Liuchow the next day. As Liuchow fell, on November 11, the Fourteenth's air units, which had been giving continuous support to the harried Chinese ground forces, struck heavily at Hengyang airfield. They did so with such telling effect that future Japanese operations there were restricted to army cooperation flights.

On November 7 Casey Vincent made the decision that this would be the last day for headquarters at Liuchow. He sent fighters out in the morning through overcast and started burning buildings in the afternoon. The transports did a marvelous job in the bad weather, and the Liuchow evacuation was successful, with not a single transport lost. Three fighters were missing, however.

On November 11 three P-51s from the Seventy-fifth flew to Hankow only to find that as the planes approached, searchlights were turned off. Perhaps they were shot out. Capt. Joseph Brown did not return.

The next day sixteen P-51s headed out early in the morning for a road sweep from Lingling to Hengyang and Kweilin. Twenty enemy planes were found over Hengyang. Lt. William T. Griswold destroyed one Oscar; Capt. Stanley O. Kelley destroyed one Tojo and damaged three Oscars; Lt. C. W. "Bill" Mahannah destroyed one Oscar and one Tojo and damaged another Tojo; Lieutenant Beard damaged one Oscar; Lt. Donald Lopez probably destroyed another Tojo; Lt. John D. Rosenbaum damaged an Oscar; Capt. Forrest Parham probably destroyed one Hamp and damaged two Oscars and

Flight Officer Willis damaged one Oscar. Lts. Andrew J. Gadberry, Donald K. Miller, Tiley, and Goodwin Taylor were missing after the mission.

That afternoon twelve P-51s from the Seventy-fifth participated in a fight over Hengyang field. Maj. Clyde B. Slocomb confirmed one Oscar and damaged another on the ground. Captain Parham probably destroyed one Oscar on the ground and Lt. Robert M. Chism damaged another Oscar on the ground. All planes returned safely this time.

Back at Fourteenth Air Force Headquarters at Kunming, Claire Chennault was war-weary and unhappy about the situation. The Sixty-eighth Composite Wing headquarters had moved from Kuling to Luliang, and Casey Vincent and company did not like the new headquarters, referring to it as a dusty hole.

The Seventy-sixth continued missions from November 10 through 16. On November 13 they dive-bombed the railroad bridge at Chuchow, damaging it severely by knocking two spans out with near misses. Next day they moved on to Poaching. Here several compounds were hit, causing much damage, and the town was covered with bombs. They hit the town of Nanyo on November 16. Seven Oscars were sighted over the target. Capt. Forrest Parham destroyed one Oscar, damaged another in the air, and damaged two Oscars and two Hamps on the ground. Lieutenant Rush destroyed one Oscar, probably destroyed another, and damaged others; Lt. James W. Carter damaged one Oscar.

Also on November 16, eleven P-51s from the Seventy-fifth escorted B-25s to Hengyang and Siangtan and made a road and railroad sweep over the same route. They damaged and destroyed several trucks and destroyed two hundred gasoline drums.

Almost as soon as it had taken Kweilin and Liuchow, the Japanese Eleventh Army began a drive westward across Kwangsi Province toward Kweiyang, beginning on November 17. Two days later Nanning was evacuated and demolished. The Japanese had succeeded in driving the Americans out of every base they had built between Yochow and Indochina.

The Seventy-sixth kept striking, making an offensive sweep to Liuchow to Ishan on November 22, followed by a mission to provide top cover for the CACW P-40s to Sinshih the same day. About an hour later, six P-51s escorted transports of the Fourteenth past Hengyang and on a recon mission to Siangtan and Poaching. They destroyed one bridge and started many small fires at Poaching. That night they strafed searchlights at Hankow after the bombers had already dropped their bombs.

On November 23 the Seventy-fifth flew two missions, the first an offensive recon from Ishan to Liuchow. All bombs hit Liuchow, causing much damage and starting one fire. Next they went to recon Hengyang and skip-bombed a railroad tunnel northeast of Hengshan. Maj. Slocomb damaged one Val on the ground. Lt. Edward J. Bollen, Lt. C. W. Mahannah, and Colonel Dunning (CACW) each damaged one fighter on the ground.

On November 28, the Eleventh Army drove across the border between the provinces of Kwangsi and Kweichow near Kweiyang, although it had been ordered to halt its drive at the border. The unauthorized move into Kweichow Province ended on December 3, however, as the army ran out of supplies and then pulled back to the Kwangsi-Kweichow border by the middle of the month.

On December 10, the Japanese' third offensive finally obtained its objective by linking Japanese forces in French Indochina all the way north to Peiping. The campaign had lasted eight months and opened a route extending nearly fifteen hundred miles, of which the last seven hundred miles had been wrested from the Chinese since the opening of the second offensive of the campaign in the Tungting Lake area in late May.

As 1944 neared its end, Japanese forces had completely cut off the Fourteenth's remaining eastern bases from the rest of China, and they posed a threat to move to Kweiyang and on to Kunming itself and then to Chungking in the near future.

Gen. Casey Vincent left China on December 13. Col. Clay Classen took his place as the head of the Tactical Command, Sixty-eighth Composite Wing. Wiltz Segura's last mission in China was the middle of December when he flew over the Hump for the last time. The Seventy-fifth Fighter Group's participation in the war was drawing to a close.

In the wake of the Japanese advance, tired and homeless Chinese crowded the long and bitter road to Kunming. Chaos and suffering defied description. Eighty trains waited to be routed westward to Liuchow over a single track in one day. One hundred thousand refugees jammed the railroad yards, waiting with their belongings for a train to carry them to the safety of the Kweijo plateau. Sanitary conditions were horrible. They slept, ate, cooked, and washed the best way they could near the tracks. Doctors feared a cholera epidemic if they were not moved quickly. Also waiting to be shipped were thousands of gallons of gasoline, salvaged from abandoned airfields. The few remaining guns of the Chinese, and Chinese and American ammunition, tools from the machine shops, even railroad ties—all took precedence over the people.

A captured Zero was shipped back for intelligence examination. Meanwhile the refugees clung to hope and waited. Some who were considered lucky fled by trucks—stinking charcoal burners and alcohol burners that had to be warmed and pushed to start. A truck carrying American belly tanks mingled with the mobs. The road was lined with broken-down trucks. Many were stripped of parts to keep the others going. The only way to stop runaway trucks without brakes was to run them off the road, where many of them stayed along with the equipment they carried.

Most of the homeless horde inched their way on foot, with all their belongings in bags dangling from poles. Beaten and weary Chinese soldiers mingled with the civilians, many of them without rifles or shoes. They carried sick and wounded on bamboo stretchers. Farmers and soldiers combined to carry much of the rice harvest beyond the reach of the enemy. Japanese fifth columnists helped spread panic.

All over eastern China these scenes were repeated throughout the blistering summer and the wet, muddy fall. Here again the people were uprooted, repeating once again the typical scenes of seven long and horrible years of war. These refugees had long been a favorite target of Japanese pilots. But during this long trek, Japanese airmen declined to venture into American-held skies by day. No Chinese were killed by strafing or day-bombing. General Chennault ordered special fighter patrols over railroad yards and other congested areas when Japanese air attack seemed likely. None came.

Prices rose by 500 percent over the already inflated values as food and shelter became scarcer along the way. Tiny villages mushroomed into teeming cities of bamboo and banana leaf huts. As the road wound up into the Kweijo plateau, some were literally on their last legs. Many of these people were captured by the advancing Japanese. Others were waylaid by bandits in the hills. Also on the road to

Kunming, refugees streamed past new airfields that thousands of other Chinese were building to give General Chennault's airmen new springboards for attack.

In Burma, crack Chinese divisions were loaded into transports and flown to the crumbling east China front. They had American artillery, mortars, and machine guns, and plenty of American ammo. They had proven that they knew how to use them in driving the Japanese out of north Burma, in December 1944. Col. Luke Williamson's flying coolies rushed fresh troops over from Chungking to the threatened area. The Japanese were within twenty miles of cutting the Burma Road in China and overrunning the new American airfields when these veteran Chinese troops, supported by air attack, hurled them back sixty miles off the Kweijo plateau down into the valleys of east China.

The Japanese had started out in May to take the Canton-Hankow railroad, occupy strategic coastal areas, and knock the Fourteenth Air Force out of China. When they were checked in January 1945, they had the railroad and the strategic areas, but they had failed to knock out the Fourteenth.

CHAPTER 11

Victory in the Far East: 1945

For the year 1944, the Fourteenth Air Force had used 18,033,025 gallons of gasoline, expended 9,248,038 rounds of .50 caliber ammunition, and dropped 9,877 tons of bombs. Enemy troop losses due to action by the Fourteenth were 33,450 killed. In aerial combat during the year, pilots of the Fourteenth destroyed 494 Japanese planes, while American losses were sixty-four. Overall the Fourteenth's claims against Japanese shipping in 1944 were 640,900 tons sunk, 237,050 tons probably sunk, and 396,950 tons damaged.

In January 1945, Japanese air units were still active. The Fourteenth claimed 211 enemy planes destroyed during the month. Over a quarter of that total was accounted for on January 17 when twenty Mustangs of the Seventy-fourth and 118th squadrons swept airfields at Shanghai, claiming at least sixty-five enemy aircraft destroyed, mostly on the ground. In the five succeeding months, only ninety-eight Japanese aircraft were destroyed in the air and none were claimed after June.

As the year 1945 arrived, the Chinese Expeditionary Force (Y-Force), operating on the Salween front in southwestern China was again moving forward. On January 3 the Chinese Ninth Division broke into Wanting on the Burma Road at the Sino-Burmese border. But a Japanese night counterattack drove them out, and Wanting was not taken by the Chinese until January 20, after it had been evacuated by the enemy. Four days later, on January 24, the Salween campaign ended as the Chinese Expeditionary Force halted to await relief by the Chinese army from India, which was operating in northern Burma and moving toward the Burma Road.

On January 20, a small truck convoy which had previously come from Ledo in India and used the rough Tengchung cutoff to get to the Burma Road north of Wanting reached Kunming after a sixteen-day trip from Myitkyino, Burma. Thus for the first time since 1942, the surface blockade of China from the outside world was broken.

A week later, on January 27, the Chinese Thirty-eighth Division, assisted by artillery and armor, linked up with the Y-Force, thereby connecting the Ledo Road directly to the Burma Road and opening a fully serviceable land route from India to China. Next day the first convoy from Ledo to use this route resumed its journey toward Kunming, crossing the border into China at Wanting. The convoy made a triumphal entry into Kunming on February 4.

Meanwhile Japanese forces in south China, instead of moving on Kweiyang and Kunming at the start of 1945, turned their attention to two other tasks. First, in an effort to reopen the Hengyang-to-Canton segment of the Hankow-Canton railroad, they moved south from the Hengyang area on January 10 and north from above Canton. Between January 19 and 22, they occupied key bridges and tunnels on the railway, and by the end of the month the last segment of the Hankow-Canton railroad was in their hands. In the course of the operation, Japanese forces from the Canton-Hong Kong area moved northward to take Swatow, located above Hong Kong.

The second Japanese move, begun on January 15, was to capture several east China airfields from which the Fourteenth Air Force was constantly hurting them. They advanced along the Chaling-Leinhua road and then swung down from the north, forming one arm of a pincers movement, on the Fourteenth's bases, occupying Siuchuan on January 29. On February 3 the southern arm of the pincers took the Fourteenth's field at Namyung. The two arms then met and took the base at Kanchow on February 7. Thus, by the middle of February 1945, Changting was the only east China airfield still held by the Fourteenth. Its units in the east had been pulled safely back to the west, and the East China Air Task Force had ceased to exist.

Across China the ground situation remained stable for over a month after Japanese took the east China airfields. On March 21, Japanese forces began a swift drive south from just below the Yellow River toward the Laohokow airfield. The enemy forces covered 125

miles in four days and on March 25 took their objective after personnel of the Fourteenth had destroyed the field's installations and evacuated the Laohokow base—the last base the Fourteenth would lose
to the enemy. Thereafter, Chinese resistance stiffened and subsequent Japanese threats toward Ankang and Sian were stopped short
by Chinese troops—supported by U.S. Air Force and Chinese-
American Composite Wing units and the P-40s of the Fourth and
Eleventh groups of the Chinese Air Force.

With the Japanese Army threatening Chinese lines and ready to
make further advances, it was decided in February to bring the B-24s
of the 308th Group north to the Chengtu area and employ them in
attacks on enemy transportation targets. While other squadrons
moved north in March and April, the 373rd Squadron remained at
Kunming, from which it continued to strike at enemy shipping and
pound away at enemy transportation facilities and supply depots
whenever gasoline was available.

On March 24, as indirect support to U.S. Navy operations off
Okinawa in preparation for the April 1 invasion of that island, six
P-51s of the 530th Squadron, flying from Ankang, swept the three
enemy airfields at Nanking, shooting down one Tojo and one Oscar
without loss. Returning to Nanking the next day, the Mustangs of the
squadron encountered twenty-two Tojos and an Oscar as one flight
strafed. In the mild melee which followed, Lt. Leonard R. Reeves
destroyed the Oscar and shot down a Tojo for his sixth victory. Six
more Tojos were damaged by the pilots of the 530th, who reported
that the Japanese pilots encountered in this engagement were definitely superior to those they had met in other parts of China. The
strafing flight was attacked by three Tojos, and one P-51 was hit and
crashed into the Yangtze River just south of Nanking. On return another P-51 had engine trouble, and the pilot bailed out over Chinese-
controlled territory.

As March turned into April in the spring of 1945, night-flying Japanese raiders almost ceased to exist in China and the 426th Night
Fighter Squadron found itself with almost nothing to do. As a result,
it began to operate more and more on night intruder missions. Staging
out of Liangshan, Sian, and Ankang, its P-51s concentrated on attacking enemy communication lines by night, hitting at road convoys
and railways.

On April 8 the Japanese started a full-scale drive toward Chihkiang, the site of one of the Twenty-third Fighter Group's best bases. It was to be their last offensive. The enemy advanced to within fifty miles of the field before Chinese ground forces, supported by the group's planes, turned the tide and began pushing the Japanese back. By the end of May, the enemy's forces began to beat a retreat northward. Until operations were concluded, the Twenty-third Fighter Group's pilots continued to harass the retreating Japanese by strafing and bombing their columns. They also flew surveillance missions over wide areas to report on the extent of the withdrawal.

As the Japanese moved on Chihkiang, air movement of the Chinese Twenty-second Division to that front was begun on April 21. By May 11, Chinese troops had halted the Japanese drive by outflanking maneuvers and had turned the enemy back. Thereafter, Chinese forces, numbering a hundred thousand, drove the retreating Japanese troops to Poaching, the point from which the Japanese had begun their offensive, retaking all the lost territory by June 7.

Air support for the Battle of Chihkiang was provided by the Fifth Group with P-40s and P-51s and the Fourth Squadron of the First Group with B-25s, both of the CACW, and by some American Air Force and Chinese Air Force planes. From April 10 through May 15, the Fifth Group and Fourth Squadron of the CACW engaged a brilliant battle against the advancing enemy which was principally responsible for the subsequent victory. With four enemy prongs aimed at Chihkiang, these units turned the full weight of their power against Japanese spearheads and strong points, lines of communications, and storage areas. In thirty-six days, they killed 6,024 enemy troops and slashed the enemy's supply lines so thoroughly and destroyed such quantities of supplies that the drive was completely paralyzed, allowing the Chinese ground forces to go over to the offensive and push the enemy back.

An event of great significance took place just before the Japanese drive on Chihkiang. On April 14, there came an order to move four divisions of Japanese troops to central and northern China. It was the first step of re-deploying Japanese troops to defend Japan. Meanwhile American forces in the Pacific, as they took the Philippines, Iwo Jima, and Okinawa, were forcing the Japanese in toward the home islands even more tightly. As a result of the order, the Japanese in China decided to withdraw from the Hunan-Kwangsi railroad, which linked Hengyang, Kweilin, and Liuchow—thus giving up what they had gained in the great campaign of 1944 which had ended so successfully only four months before. The pullback move began in May as the Japanese withdrew from Yungning and Chinese forces recaptured Nanning on May 26. The enemy's land route to Indochina was severed.

By May 15, the Chinese ground troops and the Fourteenth Air Force had the Japanese in full retreat along the Hsiang River Valley. By the end of July, the central and coastal areas of China were nearly free of Japanese.

Combat operations by the Fourteenth quickly petered out after May, and for this reason, the summary records for the Fourteenth and its units extend only down to the last day of May. Such is the case for the Twenty-third Fighter Group, its oldest unit, whose battle record from July 4, 1942, through May 31, 1945, reads: 621 enemy aircraft destroyed in the air and 320 destroyed on the ground; 13,738 tons of Japanese shipping sunk and approximately twenty thousand enemy troops killed—at a cost of 110 aircraft lost in air combat, ninety destroyed by antiaircraft fire, and twenty-eight destroyed on the ground by enemy attack.

By May 1945, the jungles of Burma and Indochina had begun the carnivorous reclamation of the dead and dying soldiers strewn about in the area that had marked the high tide of the ambitious Japanese military conquest. Remnants of their once invincible war machine lay spent and rusting in the tropical heat as starving survivors abandoned their heavy implements of war and hastily withdrew to the home islands to make their final stand.

Chennault's only task now lay in the harassment of the retreating Japanese armies fleeing eastern China. In their flight, deprived of vital supplies by the relentless attacks from the Fourteenth Air Force, soldiers stripped the country of all edible foods. They killed and devoured all livestock and poultry, leaving in their wake for stragglers only dogs and rats and seeds saved for the next year's planting. All that remained of the war for the Chinese was to reap the fruits of victory.

Lieutenant General Takahashi, commander of the Japanese forces in central China, would later say that 60 to 70 percent of the effective opposition his forces faced in China during World War II was due to the Fourteenth Air Force. "Without the air force we could have gone anywhere we wished." Yet in spite of the effectiveness of the Fourteenth Air Force, orders from Generals Marshall and Arnold in Washington were received by Wedemeyer, now commander of U.S. forces in the China Theater, for the "reorganization" of the China air forces. Many were to interpret this as being the final effort to ease out Claire Chennault on the eve of victory. Wedemeyer, a perceptive and truthful friend of both the Generalissimo and Chennault, was caught between his able personal evaluation of the situation and the subtle wishes of his superiors.

The plan consisted of creating a bloated Tenth Air Force commanded by Maj. Gen. George Stratemeyer to displace the existing Fourteenth Air Force in China commanded by General Chennault. The Tenth Air Force would move into China from defeated Burma for a dash to final victory with the Chinese armies while banishing the Fourteenth Air Force and its controversial commander to areas north of the Yangtze River, where significant targets and needed supplies were sparse. Yet the Tenth Air Force would extract from the Fourteenth, and wisely so, the crack veteran Twenty-third and Fifty-first fighter groups along with the two best B-25 squadrons before leaving the Fourteenth to die on the vine after whittling it down to the size of a normal wing. This was the fate of the Fourteenth Air Force—the air force which Chennault had nurtured from its meager beginning of 250 men and a hundred planes to twenty thousand men and a thousand planes and a record of air victories unsurpassed in the air annals of World War II.

Chennault had no intention of remaining in the service after Japan's defeat, but he was bitterly depressed at being deprived of participating in the final victory. He later wrote, "On V-J Day it was my fondest hope to be on board the battleship *Missouri* in Tokyo Bay and watch the Japanese formally acknowledge their defeat."

Instead, he felt compelled to request relief from active duty and retirement from the Army, giving reasons of ill health. When news of the tainted manipulation surrounding his retirement reached Stateside, there was a brief but energetic demand by friends, politicians, and members of the press to know the real reason for his untimely retirement. War Department spokesmen effectively smoothed the troubled waters and with the coming of final victory over Japan and the long-awaited conclusion of World War II, Claire Lee Chennault and his tide of personal troubles were swiftly forgotten by the American public. With the Japanese now leaving eastern China, Chennault had climbed his highest mountain, but like Moses, he was deprived of entry to his promised land. He was instead relegated into the valley of bitterness and despair during the moments of final victory. Thus at the age of fifty-five, the boy with boundless energy from the moss-draped cypress swamps of Louisiana, "different in character than his contemporaries and not wholly suited to the needs of modern society," began his sad farewells.

In Chungking, the capital of Free China, the automobile furnished him by the Generalissimo inched its way along the crowded city streets toward a public gathering place where thousands of grateful Chinese waited to present their respects to the man who had freed their lives of the terror in the sky. Along the way many Chinese and American flags flew in the breeze. Giant Flying Tiger posters and that famous Winston Churchill "V" for victory were proudly displayed. As far as he could see in all directions, Chennault was confronted with a view of a virtual sea of brown Chinese faces, bobbing and shouting and popping firecrackers, a sea which completely engulfed his car. Fearful that to drive any further might result in someone's injury, Chennault instructed the driver to kill the engine. And then it happened. . . . As with the great exodus out of eastern China after the fall of Shanghai, as in the perilous excavation of the Burma Road, the momentum of the event was now carried by the masses. Slowly, almost reverently, the mob began to push the Generalissimo's car containing their Number One Flying Tiger, "Chen-au-duh," toward the open square. Among cheers and jubilation, Chinese from all walks of life led Chennault to the place of honor on a wooden platform. There he received the heartfelt thanks of a nation which had survived. For the remainder of the day, countless numbers of Chinese crossed the wooden stage to shake his hand and to present him with gifts of appreciation. The scene was repeated in every city along his farewell tour. Finally, winding up back at Kunming he was told by his interpreter, "No foreigner since Marco Polo has so endeared himself to the Chinese."

On August 8, Chennault's C-47 rolled down the Kunming runway lined on both sides by hundreds of jubilant Chinese cheering and waving and popping firecrackers to ward off evil devils. As the plane lifted from the runway and circled the field before heading west, Chennault remembered his pledge to the Generalissimo—"I will return to China should my services ever again be needed." Thus the prophet returned home, though not without honor. His advice either ignored or unheeded, with him went hopes for a lasting peace and friendship with postwar China.

Gen. Douglas MacArthur was given command of all U.S. Army forces in the Pacific on April 6, 1945. He was directed with Adm. Chester W. Nimitz, the Navy Commander, to prepare for the war's final operations. This task was rendered far easier than the Joint Chiefs of Staff could foresee by the accomplishment of a scientific miracle—the atomic bomb.

At 8:15 A.M. on August 6, Col. Paul W. Tibbits, Jr., released a uranium bomb called "Little Boy" over Hiroshima. Three days later, a plutonium bomb was dropped on Nagasaki. Hiroshima was a well-chosen target—its normal population of 240,000 civilians was doubled by the presence of a large number of military and naval personnel. No one in Japan realized for some time what had caused the devastation.

Militarily, the denouement was swift. President Truman announced that the United States was prepared to obliterate rapidly and completely, every productive enterprise the Japanese had above the ground in any city. Then Russia announced that the Soviet Union was declaring war also. The very next day three Russian army groups rolled over Japan's Kwantung Army and within a few days had penetrated deep into Manchuria. On August 10, Tokyo sued for peace on the basis of the Allies' Potsdam Declaration but requested that Hirohito be retained as Emperor.

The actual surrender was decided at a final meeting of the Japanese Supreme War Council, in the presence of the Emperor, when Hirohito declared, "I cannot bear to see my innocent people suffer any longer."

On August 15, in a taped radio message, the Emperor informed his people that the war was over. But the Russians spurned the announcement as only a general statement of Japan's capitulation. They continued their brief but fierce offensive. The Kwangtang Army surrendered on August 22, but the Soviet airborne troops moved on to Manchuria. The Japanese fought sporadically until September 12.

China regained sovereignty over Inner Mongolia, Manchuria, Formosa, and Hainan, with the British reoccupying Hong Kong and accepting a formal Japanese surrender in Singapore on September 12.

But the crucial and historial act confirming Imperial Japan's defeat took place ten days earlier, on September 2, 1945, aboard the battleship *U.S.S. Missouri* in Tokyo Bay. It was staged with a high sense of drama. After MacArthur opened the ceremony with a brief and generous address, the Japanese Foreign Minister Mamoru Shigemitsu signed two copies of the surrender document in Japanese and English. Then MacArthur signed, followed by Nimitz and the Allied delegates.

And as the ink was drying, MacArthur surveyed the panorama of faces and asked his aide, "Where's Chennault?"

Appendix I

Fourteenth Air Force Aces

Name	Group	Air	Grd	Total
Lt. Col. John C. Herbst	23rd	15	2	17
Capt. John Hampshire	23rd	14	—	14
Lt. Col. Edward O. McComas	23rd	14	3	17
Col. Robert L. Scott, Jr.	23rd	13	1	14
Maj. James J. England	311th	10	1	11
Col. Bruce K. Holloway	23rd	10	—	10
Maj. John R. Alison	23rd	8	—	8
Maj. Arthur Cruikshank	23rd	8	—	8
Lt. Matthew M. Gordon, Jr.	23rd	8	—	8
Lt. Col. Charles Older	23rd	8	4	12
Capt. Elmer W. Richardson	23rd	8	3	11
Capt. John S. Stewart	23rd	8	2	10
Maj. William L. Turner	3rd CACW	7½	4	11½
Maj. Philip G. Chapman	23rd	7	16	23
Maj. William N. Reed	3rd CACW	7	1	8
Maj. Clyde R. Slocumb	23rd	7	6	13
Lt. Heyward A. Paxton	3rd CACW	6½	5	11½
Maj. Raymond L. Calloway	3rd CACW	6	—	6
Maj. Edmund R. Goss	23rd	6	—	6
Col. David L. "Tex" Hill	23rd	6	1	7
Capt. Robert L. Liles	23rd	6	—	6
Capt. John D. Lombard	23rd	6	—	6
Capt. Martin M. Lubner	23rd	6	—	6
Capt. Robert F. Mulhollen	311th	6	—	6
Maj. Leonard R. Reeves	311th	6	4	10
Capt. Wiltz Segura	23rd	6	—	6
Capt. Robert E. Smith	23rd	6	—	6
Col. Clinton D. Vincent	23rd	6	—	6
Capt. J. M. Williams	23rd	6	1	7
Maj. Charles W. Sawyer	23rd	5¾	—	5¾
Maj. Lester Arasmith	311th	5	1	6
Maj. Albert J. Baumler	23rd	5	—	5
Maj. John W. Bolyard	23rd	5	4	9

Name	Group	Air	Grd	Total
Capt. Stephen J. Bonner, Jr.	23rd	5	—	5
Lt. Jasper R. Brown	51st	5	—	5
Lt. Dallas A. Clinger	23rd	5	—	5
Lt. Philip E. Colman	5th CACW	5	—	5
Lt. Charles H. Dubois	23rd	5	—	5
Capt. William Grosvenor, Jr.	23rd	5	—	5
Capt. Lynn F. Jones	23rd	5	—	5
Lt. Melvin B. Kimball	23rd	5	—	5
Capt. S. P. Kinsey	23rd	5	—	5
Capt. James W. Little	23rd	5	—	5
Capt. Donald Lopez	23rd	5	—	5
Lt. Keith Mahon	51st	5	5	10
Capt. Edward M. Nollmeyer	51st	5	—	5
Capt. Forrest F. Parham	23rd	5	—	5
Maj. Roger C. Pryor	23rd	5	—	5
Maj. Donald L. Quigley	23rd	5	—	5
Capt. Robert B. Schultz	51st	5	—	5
Lt. Oran S. Watts	23rd	5	1	6
Lt. R. D. Williams	23rd	5	1	6
Lt. Col. Edward Rector	23rd	4	5	9
Capt. Robert C. Moss	23rd	3	—	3
Lt. Parker S. Dupouy	23rd	2½	—	2½
Capt. Robert J. Raines	23rd	2	—	2
Maj. John E. Petach	23rd	1½	—	1½
Lt. Col. John "Gil" Bright	23rd	1	—	1

Fourteenth Air Force Aces—Victories as AVGs

David Hill	12½
Charles Older	10½
William Reed	10½
Edward Rector	6½
John Bright	6
Robert Moss	4
John Petach	4
Parker Dupouy	2½
Charles Sawyer	2¼
Robert Raines	2

Appendix II

American Volunteer Group

Claire L. Chennault, Commander

Squadron Leaders

David Lee Hill
James H. Howard
Robert H. Neale
John V. Newkirk
Arvid E. Olson, Jr.
Robert J. Sandell

Vice Squad Commanders

Lewis S. Bishop
Charles Bond
Parker S. Dupouy
T. A. Jones
George McMillan
Edward F. Rector
Frank Schiel, Jr.

Flight Leaders

C. B. Adair
Frank W. Adkins
William E. Bartling
John G. Bright
Robert R. Brouk
Carl K. Brown
George T. Burgard
Herbert R. Cavanah
Allen B. Christman
Edwin S. Conant

John S. Croft
James D. Cross
John J. Dean
John W. Farrell
Henry M. Geselbracht, Jr.
Edgar T. Goyette
Paul J. Greene
Clifford G. Groh
Thomas Haywood
Robert P. Hedman
John J. Hennessy
Fred S. Hodges
Louis Hoffman
Kenneth O. Jernstedt
Robert Keeton
Matthew W. Kuykendall
C. H. Laughlin, Jr.
Frank E. Lawlor
Robert F. Layher
Edward J. Leibolt
Robert L. Little
Neil G. Martin
Einar I. Mickelson
Robert C. Moss
Charles D. Mott
Charles H. Older
Edmund F. Overend
George L. Paxton
John E. Petach, Jr.
Robert W. Prescott
Albert E. Probst

Robert J. Raines
William N. Reed
Freeman I. Ricketts
Camille J. Rosbert
John R. Rossi
Charles W. Sawyer
Eriksen Shilling
Curtis E. Smith
Robert H. Smith
Robert T. Smith
Fritz E. Wolf
Peter Wright

Wingmen

John D. Armstrong
Peter W. Atkinson
Marion F. Baugh
John E. Blackburn, III
Harry R. Bolster
Thomas I. Cole, Jr.
John T. Donovan
Ben C. Foshee
Henry G. Gilbert, Jr.
Lester J. Hall
Maax C. Hammer
E. W. Loane
William D. McGarry
Lacy F. Mangleburg
Kenneth T. Merritt
Arnold W. Shamblin

Van Shapard, Jr.
Frank W. Swartz
Allen M. Wright

Chief Surgeon

Thomas C. Gentry

Flight Surgeons

Joseph S. Lee
Samuel Prevo
Lewis J. Richards

Crew Chiefs

George R. Bailey
William J. Blackburn
Harold Blackwell
George Brice
Michael R. Callan
Charles Chaney
Jack Cornelius
Jesse R. Cruikshank
George F. Curran
Otto W. Daube
Walter J. Dolan
Charles R. Engle
John E. Fauth
Joseph Gasdick
Floyd L. Gorham
Irving P. Gove
Frank A. Jacobson
Daniel H. Keller
Merlin D. Kemph
Charles D. Kenner
George B. Kepka

Frank S. Losonsky
Gale E. McAllister
Edgar B. McClure
Charles V. Misenheimer
Willard L. Musgrove
Gerhard I. Neumann
Henry L. Olson
Harold L. Osborne
John L. Overley
Preston B. Paull
Joseph Peeden
Carl Quick
Robert P. Rasmussen
Stanley J. Regis
Robert W. Rogers
Wilfred E. Schaper
Leo J. Schramm
Wilfred R. Seiple
Robert A. Smith
Edward L. Stiles
Irving J. Stolet
Chester A. Tuley
George Tyrrell
John J. Uebele
Manning Wakefield, Jr.
Melvin H. Woodward

Armorers

Charles N. Baisden
Keith J. Christensen
Allen W. Fritzke
Stephen Kastay
Jack R. Linton
Eugene R. McKinney
James H. Musick

Robert J. Neale
Paul J. Perry
Herbert Pistole
Joseph A. Poshefko
Clarence W. Riffer
Donald L. Rodewald
John N. Rumen
Ralph F. Schiller
Earl Wagner
Harvey C. Wirta

Communications

Edmund G. Baughman
Ernest O. Bonham
Harvey G. Cross
John R. Engle
Richard J. Ernst
Charles H. Francisco
Robert J. King
Robert K. Linstedt
Elton V. Loomis
Joseph E. Lussier
Alex Mihalko
Arvold A. Miller
Roland L. Richardson
Garsen M. Roberts
Ralph W. Sasser
Loy F. Seamster
Roger Shreffler
Robert M. Smith
Joseph H. Sweeney
William A. Sykes
Morgan H. Vaux
Louis G. Wyatt

Appendix III

Japanese Aircraft Identification

During the middle thirties, Japan sought stature among the existing Great Powers—Russia, Britain, France, the Dutch, and the United States. It appeared to Japan that only nearby Russia, China, and the Western colonial outposts in Asia could offer any resistance to their becoming the strongest power in Asia. To assure their position, they felt the need for first-rate fighter aircraft to secure their borders and to protect their territorial expansion ambitions. During the late 1930s, there emerged from the rapidly growing Japanese industrial complex privately owned aviation companies (Kawasaki, Nakajima, and Mitsubishi) that were to vigorously pursue military fighter-development programs. In the best Western tradition, these young companies competed feverishly with one another for the lucrative army and navy contracts.

Contrary to popular belief among the Allies at the beginning of the Pacific war, Japan's aviation community had not merely copied Western aircraft designs but, in fact, had actually improved upon them. Consequently, at the beginning of hostilities in the Pacific, Japan's sleek little fighters represented the existing state of the art in aeronautical engineering—much to the surprise and chagrin of the western Allies.

At the time of the Japanese surprise attack on Pearl Harbor on December 7, 1941, the most numerous fighter in Japan's service, although growing obsolete, was the army's nimble little stiff-legged (non-retractable gear) fighter that had proven itself so admirably in aerial battles over Russia and China. The army gave its first monoplane fighter the official name Nakajima Ki. 27 Type 97 Fighter, but its pilots affectionately referred to it simply as the "97 Sen" (which the Allies first translated incorrectly as the "I-97"). However, at this time Mitsubishi had a first-line fighter entering into naval service and designed to replace its earlier and by then obsolete open cockpit A5M4. The navy called this new fighter the Mitsubishi A6M2 Zero-Sen. It would soon become the most sought-after mechanical prize of the early Pacific war, as word of its mythical performance vibrated throughout the Allied theaters—that is, until its vulnerability was demonstrated by Chennault's AVG in Burma. Although outnumbered in the service by the army's ubiquitous Ki. 27, Mitsubishi's new Zero-Sen was the fighter which participated in the Japanese naval engagement of Pearl Harbor. It, too, had successfully passed the acid test of aerial combat over war-torn China in 1940.

Not to be outdone by its competitor, Nakajima had already begun production on a genetic descendant of its successful 97 Sen fighter which bore the official army name Nakajima Ki. 43 Hayabusa Type 1 fighter. But only about forty were in service by late 1941, as opposed to over 300 Zero-Sens.

With the similarity in appearance between Japanese operational aircraft (the army Ki. 27 and the navy A5M4, as well as the Ki. 43 and the Zero-Sen), one can well appreciate the confusion on the part of the Allies who were suddenly confronted with the necessity of having to identify them—aircraft which were so diversely classified even by the Japanese army and navy. To rapidly solve this problem, the Air Technical Intelligence Unit of the Allied Air Forces, Southwest Pacific Area, in mid-1942 adopted and disseminated Allied code names which were quickly accepted by all units in the field. The codes were necessary because the name "Zero" was becoming synonymous with all Japanese single-seat aircraft.

The "code" consisted basically of assigning male names to fighters and float planes and female names to bombers and flying boats. Female names beginning with the letter "T" were also assigned to transports. For the same reason—simplicity and ease of recall—the Allied code names are used in this text for all Japanese aircraft, beginning with those which were operational at the opening of the Pacific war. In addition, the official Japanese army and navy names and identification markings are listed along with the Allied code names.

Allied Code Names	Imperial Service	Manufacture, Official Designation, Name, Type Numbers, Description
Ann	Army	MITSUBISHI Ki. 30 Type 97, a two-place, single-engine light bomber. This fixed-gear aircraft was a participant in the Sino-Japanese War, entering that service in late summer of 1938.
Betty	Navy	MITSUBISHI G4M, a twin-engine, land-based torpedo bomber. Flew its first combat mission in China in May, 1941. It was the navy's premier heavy bomber. It carried over 1,000 gallons of fuel and was so unprotected that it exploded easily under Allied attack. Pilots nicknamed it the "one-shot lighter" because it was so vulnerable.
Claud	Navy	MITSUBISHI A5M, Type 96, a single-seat carrier fighter. This was the primary navy fighter during the Sino-Japanese War, their first mono-

plane fighter. It entered combat on September 18, 1937, flying out of occupied Shanghai. On December 2, 1937, it destroyed ten Russian aircraft in one engagement over Nanking. Its maneuverability was unsurpassed. The open cockpits were later fitted with sliding canopies which the pilots did not like; they were later removed.

Dinah	Army	MITSUBISHI Ki. 46, a twin-engine, strategic reconnaissance and night fighter. One of the few Japanese aircraft that could penetrate Allied airspace with any assurance that it would be able to return. It was also one of the few aircraft that could intercept the high-flying American B-29s. It was Japan's most popular and trouble-free aircraft of the entire Pacific war.
Emily	Navy	KAWANISHI H8K, a four-engine reconnaissance and attack flying boat having a gross weight of 68,343 pounds. Through a technical agreement with the Short Brothers, Kawanishi added their refinements and thus produced the most advanced flying boat in the world, unexcelled until long after the conclusion of World War II.
Frank	Army	NAKAJIMA Ki. 84 Hayate (Hurricane) Type 4, a single-seat fighter-bomber. A beautiful fighter with a top speed of 388 m.p.h. and an initial rate of climb of 3,600 feet per minute. It could out-climb and out-maneuver the North American P-51 "Mustang," as well as the Republic P-47 "Thunderbolt." Its fuel-injected engine gave it the title of the best Japanese fighter of the war. War shortages at home prevented it from reaching its full potential; plagued by engine problems and poor materials, the Hayate was later built from wood (Ki. 106) and even later from steel (Ki. 113). It first entered combat in China in April, 1944. It was a formidable opponent for members of Chennault's 14th Air Force.

George   Navy   KAWANISHI N1K2-J Shiden (Violet Light-
                          ning), a single-seat fighter. Potentially one of
                          the best Japanese fighters because of such fea-
                          tures as its unique mercury U-tube manometer
                          that measured angle of attack for proper flap
                          position during combat maneuvers. They were
                          potent adversaries and encountered on all fronts
                          after May, 1944. Fortunately for the Allies, the
                          unreliable engine kept them mostly unservice-
                          able.

Grace   Navy   AICHI B7A Ryusei (Shooting Star), a two-
                          seat carrier torpedo and dive bomber. The
                          Tyusei was Japan's largest and most powerful
                          (1,825 horsepower) carrier aircraft, with per-
                          formance, speed and maneuverability on a par
                          with the nimble A6M Zero-Sen fighter. By the
                          time it entered service, most of the Japanese car-
                          riers had been sunk, relegating the Tyusei to
                          land-base operations.

Jack   Navy   MITSUBISHI J2M3 Raiden (Thunderbolt), a
                          single-seat, land-based interceptor. Design em-
                          phasis for the first time was on speed and fast
                          rate of climb, rather than on maneuverability
                          as in the past designs. It had tiny laminar-flow
                          wings with combat flaps to help boost maneu-
                          verability during combat. After being fitted with
                          a better engine, it became a formidable weapon
                          against the B-29.

Kate   Navy   NAKAJIMA B5N, a three-seat carrier bomber,
                          and later torpedo bomber. Designed around the
                          navy's 1935 requirements, the "Kate" was con-
                          sidered obsolete during most of the war. How-
                          ever, it was considered advanced when put into
                          production for the Sino-Japanese War. It was a
                          participant in the bombing of Pearl Harbor and
                          played the chief role in the sinking of the Ameri-
                          can carriers *Yorktown, Lexington, Wasp,* and
                          Hornet. The Japanese designers carefully copied
                          the new stressed-skin designs of Northrop, Doug-

las, and Clark, adding their own improvements. It entered service in various models in late 1937.

Lily	Army	KAWASAKI Ki. 48 Type 99, a four-seat, twin-engine light bomber. Cut its combat teeth (1944) over China, where it proved highly successful, and later became the most numerous light bomber in the Southwest Pacific. Yet, deficient performance and poor protection forced it later in the war to operate as a night bomber. It was next used as a test bed for the Ne-00 turbojet engine which was carried on a pylon under the bomb bay.
Nate	Army	NAKAJIMA Ki. 27 Type 97, a single-seat interceptor fighter and light attack bomber. This little fighter was the first Japanese low-wing monoplane fighter which closely resembled the appearance of the early navy Claud (A5M). It was also the first to have an enclosed cockpit. It outnumbered almost every Japanese warplane. Speed, fire-power, and armour received low priority, as everything was sacrificed for good visibility and maneuverability. The Allies found to their delight that the "Nate" could sustain little damage. They fought Chinese and Soviet aircraft with astounding success. It was the most maneuverable aircraft of its day and possibly in all of aviation history. It was replaced in service by the Ki. 43.
Nell	Navy	MITSUBISHI G3M, a twin-engine, long-range, land-based bomber. This was the first Japanese warplane found to be superior to Western contemporaries. On August 14, 1937, a large force of Nell bombers hit targets 1,250 miles away in China. This was an unprecedented accomplishment at the time. However, its most famous action was the sinking of the *HMS Prince of Wales* and *Repulse* on December 10, 1941, which the British thought were out of range.

Nick	Army	KAWASAKI Ki. 45 Toryu (Dragon Slayer) Type 2, a two-seat, long-range escort, later converted to a night fighter. The Dragon Slayer was the army's first twin-engine fighter, entering service in September, 1941. It was fast and maneuverable, claiming seven victories over the high-flying B-29s, and appeared on all Pacific fronts.
Oscar	Army	NAKAJIMA Ki. 43 Hayabusa (Peregrine Falcon) Type 1, a single-seat interceptor-fighter later modified to fighter-bomber service. Produced second in number (5,878) only to the Zero-Sen, with which it was frequently confused, the Oscar was smaller and lighter than its navy counterpart. Its first production flight was in January, 1937, when everything was sacrificed for maneuverability. After being fitted with a unique combat flap under the wings, the Oscar was turned into a dogfighter that had no equal, not even the "Zero." It was, however, deficient in firepower and disintegrated easily when struck by concentrated machine-gun fire from heavier-armed Allied fighters. It continued to be popular with most of Japan's army aces who gained their scores in this nimble aircraft.
Peggy	Both services	MITSUBISHI Ki. 67 Hiryu (Flying Dragon) Type 4, a twin-engine heavy bomber and torpedo bomber, later modified into a heavy escort fighter. A heavy bomber with a crew of six to eight, it had the maneuverability of a fighter, lacking nothing in armour and fuel-tank protection, and was the best all-round bomber produced in Japan during the war. It was looped and rolled with better control than some fighters. Service delivery was late, in April, 1944.
Sally	Army	MITSUBISHI Ki. 21, Type 97, a twin-engine, seven-seat heavy bomber. Also built by Nakajima with a total production of over two thousand aircraft, it began as the army's premier heavy bomber and served in China during the early

Sino-Japanese involvement. Having little protection, the Sally was fairly easy prey for the Allied fighters.

Tojo	Army	NAKAJIMA Ki. 44 Shoki (Demons) Type 2, a single-place interceptor-fighter and later fighter-bomber. Making a break with tradition, the Tojo was designed with greater speed and climb, rather than maneuverability. Various models first appeared in service in May, 1942 and in December, 1943. Pilots did not like this fighter, as it was difficult to handle. Snap-rolls and other violent maneuvers were forbidden. Many inexperienced pilots were accidentally killed in it. Later equipped with heavy cannons which were capable of firing 400 rounds per minute, the Ki. 44 became effective against Allied bombers. On one occasion (February 19, 1945), a small force of Ki. 44s so equipped climbed to intercept a formation of 120 B-29s and destroyed ten (including two by suicide collisions).
Tony	Army	KAWASAKI Ki. 61 Hien (Flying Swallow) Type 3, a single-seat fighter. Something new had been added, an inverted-vee-12 liquid-cooled engine, the only Japanese fighter so equipped. It performed well against a captured P-40E and a BF 109E which had been dispatched to Japan by submarine. Later, the unreliable liquid-cooled engine was replaced with a radial engine, and the Tony (Ki. 100) entered service February 1, 1945. In one of its first encounters in combat, a Ki. 100 unit destroyed 14 Hellcats without loss. Its pilots found this aircraft easy to fly and used it well against B-29s and Allied fighters to the end of the war.
Val	Navy	AICHI D3A Type 99, a two-seat carrier dive bomber. Entering the service in the late thirties, the "Val" was the dive bomber that attacked Pearl Harbor. After releasing their bombs, they became formidable dogfighters, thus having a

double sting in combat. As dive bombers they were highly accurate—80 to 82 percent effective. In April, 1942 they sank the British carrier *Hermes* and heavy cruisers *Cornwall* and *Dorsetshire*.

Zeke Navy MITSUBISHI A6M Reisen Zero-Sen Type 00, a single-seat carrier fighter, the famed Japanese navy "Zero." Designed for carrier-based operations, it was the first navy fighter that could outperform land-based aircraft. It had no equal during the early days of the Pacific war. It was the successor to the early A5M. Rushed to China while still considered a prototype, it quickly eliminated all enemy opposition. The first flight was on April 1, 1939, and it first saw combat over Chungking, China, in July, 1940. It was so effective in combat because of its unrivaled maneuverability and extreme operational range (with its small 780 horsepower engine) that it virtually swept Allied opposition from its path. The Zero pilot, and indeed the Japanese nation as a whole, felt invincible because of the Zero's rapid success over the Allies—that is, until they confronted Chennault's American Volunteer Group in Burma. Chennault's pilots were quick to discover the Zero's vulnerable spots and began to dispel the myth surrounding the A6M2.

Bibliography

BOOKS

Batchelor, John, and Bryan Cooper. *Fighter: A History of Fighter Aircraft.* New York: Scribner's, 1973.

Caidin, Martin. *Air Force: A Pictorial History of American Air Power.* New York: Rinehart, 1957.

Chennault, Claire L. *Way of a Fighter: The Memoirs of Claire Lee Chennault.* Edited by Robert Hotz. New York: Putnam's, 1949.

Collier, Basil. *The Second World War: A Military History.* New York: William Morrow, 1967.

Coye, Molly J., and Jon Livingston. *China: Yesterday and Today.* New York: Bantam Books, 1975.

Dollinger, Hans. *The Decline and Fall of Nazi Germany and Imperial Japan.* New York: Crown Publishers, 1968.

Dupuy, Trevor Nevitt. *Chronological Military History of World War II.* New York: Franklin Watts, 1965.

Fitzgerald, Charles P. *Communism Takes China: How the Revolution Went Red.* New York: American Heritage Press, 1971.

Freeman, Roger A. *The Mighty Eighth.* Garden City, New York: Doubleday, 1970.

———. *Mustang at War.* New York: Doubleday, 1974.

Greenlaw, Olga S. *The Lady and the Tigers.* New York: E. P. Dutton, 1943.

Gruenhagen, Robert W. *Mustang: The Story of the P-51 Fighter.* New York: Arco Publishing Co., 1969.

Gunston, Bill. *Combat Aircraft of World War II.* New York: Bookthrift, 1978.

Hahn, Emily. *The Soong Sisters.* Garden City, New York: Doubleday, Doran, 1943.

Hashimoto, Kikuo. *The World Aircraft in Colour: Volume II.* Warren, Michigan: Squadron/Signal Publications, 1973.

Heiferman, Ronald. *Flying Tigers: Chennault in China.* New York: Ballantine Books, 1971.

———. *World War II.* London: Octopus Books, 1978.

Kerrigan, Evans E. *American Badges and Insignia.* New York: Viking Press, 1967.

Langer, William L. (ed.). *The New Illustrated Encyclopedia of World History*. New York: H. N. Abrams, 1975.

Life Goes to War: A Picture History of World War II. Boston: Little, Brown, 1977.

Liu, Frederick F. *A Military History of Modern China: 1924–1949*. Princeton: Princeton University Press, 1956.

Loomis, Robert D. *Great American Fighter Pilots of World War II*. New York: Random House, 1961.

McClure, Glenn E. *Fire and Fall Back: The World War II "CBI" Story of "Casey" Vincent*. Universal City, Texas: Barnes Press, 1975.

Moser, Don. *China-Burma-India*. Alexandria, Virginia: Time-Life Books, 1978.

Oughton, Frederick. *The Aces*. New York: Putnam, 1960.

Parrish, Thomas (ed.). *The Simon and Schuster Encyclopedia of World War II*. New York: Simon and Schuster, 1978.

Rosholt, Malcolm. *Days of the Ching Pao*. Amherst, Wisconsin: Palmer Publications, 1978.

Rust, Kenn C., and Stephen Muth. *Fourteenth Air Force Story in World War II*. Temple City, California: Historical Aviation Album, 1977.

Sims, Edward H. *American Aces in Great Fighter Battles of World War II*. New York: Harper, 1958.

Sulzberger, Cyrus L. *The American Heritage Picture History of World War II*. New York: American Heritage Publishing Co., 1966.

Tan Pei-ying. *The Building of the Burma Road*. New York: McGraw-Hill, 1945.

Taylor, John W. R., and Kenneth Munson. *History of Aviation*. New York: Crown Publishers, 1972.

Time-Life Books. *This Fabulous Century: The Forties, 1940–1950*. New York: Time-Life Books, 1969.

USAF Historical Division, Research Studies Institute. *A Brief History of the Twenty-Third Fighter Group: 1941–1955*. Maxwell Air Force Base, Alabama: U. S. Air Force, 1956.

Wagner, Ray. *American Combat Planes*. Garden City, New York: Doubleday, 1960.

Wood, Tony, and Bill Gunston. *Hitler's Luftwaffe*. New York: Crown Publishers, n.d.

Zich, Arthur. *The Rising Sun*. Alexandria, Virginia: Time-Life Books, 1977.

BOOKLETS

Aero Publishers, Inc. *Curtiss P-40*. Aero Series No. 3, compiled by the aeronautical staff of Aero Publishers, Inc., 1965.

American Volunteer Group. *Flying Tigers American Volunteer Group—Chinese*

Air Force. A brief history with recollections and comments by General Claire Lee Chennault, compiled by the AVG.

Aviation Publications. *Pilots Manual for Curtiss P-40 Warhawk* (declassified). ISBN No. 0-87994-018-2, T.O. No. 01-25CF-1, 1943 (reprinted).

Bueschel, Richard M. *Mitsubishi A6M 1/2/-2N Zero-Sen in Imperial Japanese Naval Air Service; Nakajima Ki. 27A-B Manshu Ki. 79A-B in Japanese Army Air Force-Manchoukuo-IPSF-RACAF-PLAAF & CAF Service; Nakajima Ki. 43 Hayabusa I-III in Japanese Army Air Force-RTAF-CAF-IPSF Service*. Arco-Aircam Aviation Series Nos. 18, 20, and 15. Arco Publishing Company, Inc., 1970.

Shivers, Sydney P. *A Pictorial History of the American Volunteer Group, Flying Tigers*. Challenge Publications, Inc.

Index